CQ GUIDE TO

CURRENT AMERICAN GOVERNMENT

Fall 1986

Congressional Quarterly Inc.

Congressional Quarterly Inc.

Congressional Quarterly Inc., an editorial research service and publishing company, serves clients in the fields of news, education, business and government. It combines specific coverage of Congress, government and politics by Congressional Quarterly with the more general subject range of an affiliated service, Editorial Research Reports.

Congressional Quarterly publishes the *Congressional Quarterly Weekly Report* and a variety of books, including college political science textbooks under the CQ Press imprint and public affairs paperbacks designed as timely reports to keep journalists, scholars and the public abreast of developing issues and events. CQ also publishes information directories and reference books on the federal government, national elections and politics, including the *Guide to Congress,* the *Guide to the Supreme Court,* the *Guide to U.S. Elections* and *Politics in America.* The *CQ Almanac,* a compendium of legislation for one session of Congress, is published each year. *Congress and the Nation,* a record of government for a presidential term, is published every four years.

CQ publishes *The Congressional Monitor,* a daily report on current and future activities of congressional committees, and several newsletters including *Congressional Insight,* a weekly analysis of congressional action, and *Campaign Practices Reports,* a semimonthly update on campaign laws.

CQ's online Washington Alert Service provides government affairs specialists with details of congressional action on a continually updated basis.

Printed in the United States of America

Library of Congress Catalog No. 61-16893
International Standard Book No. 0-87187-395-8
International Standard Serial No. 0196-612X

1414 22nd Street, N.W., Washington, D.C. 20037

Editor: Susanna C. Spencer
Contributors: Robert Benenson, Mary Cohn, Nadine Cohodas, Rhodes Cook, John Cranford, Joseph A. Davis, Alan Ehrenhalt, John Felton, Diane Granat, Rob Gurwitt, Janet Hook, Steven Pressman, David Rapp, Eileen Shanahan, Tom Watson, Elder Witt
Graphics: Richard A. Pottern, Robert Redding, Kathleen A. Ossenfort
Index: Bernice Eisen
Production: I. D. Fuller, Maceo Mayo

Congressional Quarterly Inc.

Eugene Patterson *Chairman and Chief Executive Officer*
Andrew Barnes *Editor and President*
Wayne P. Kelley *Publisher*
Peter A. Harkness *Deputy Publisher and Executive Editor*
Robert E. Cuthriell *Director, Research and Development*
Robert C. Hur *Director, Book Division, and General Counsel*
Jonathan C. Angier *Business Manager*
Richard A. Shontz *Marketing Director*

Book Department

David R. Tarr *Director*
John L. Moore *Assistant Director*
Joanne D. Daniels *Director, CQ Press*
Kathryn C. Suárez *Book Marketing Manager*
Mary W. Cohn *Associate Editor*
Nola Healy Lynch *Developmental Editor, CQ Press*
Carolyn Goldinger *Project Editor*
Carolyn McGovern *Project Editor*
Colleen McGuiness *Project Editor*
Susanna C. Spencer *Project Editor*
Amy S. Meyers *Editorial Assistant*
Linda M. Pompa *Editorial Assistant*
Renée S. Reiner *Editorial Assistant*
Maria J. Sayers *Editorial Assistant*
Linda White *Secretary*

TABLE OF CONTENTS

POLITICS

LOBBIES

PRESIDENCY/EXECUTIVE

SUPREME COURT

CONGRESS

APPENDIX

THE CQ Guide to Current American Government is prepared twice yearly as an up-to-date handbook for the study of American government. It contains the most useful and instructional of recent Congressional Quarterly news research material, rearranged and edited for students of government and politics.

The Guide is designed to serve two main functions. First, it provides students with current illustrations of the continuing interplay of forces that constitute our political system. It shows not only how the president, Congress and judiciary act and react to one another but how this traditional interplay is tempered and influenced by other vital forces such as politics, changing social pressures, new administrations, current issues and lobbying. A study of the balance of power among the three branches of government, for example, at once raises questions about the current status of that balance — especially between the president and Congress — and likely changes in the balance to come. Illustrations of these forces at work will help the student see and learn from the important differences that exist between theory and operation, between format and function.

Second, the Guide is a starting point for discussion and individual research in the day-to-day operations of government. Such research may be as informal as the careful reading of good newspapers. With reliable news sources, a good library and ample amounts of curiosity and imagination, students can find in daily events — whether in Washington, D.C., their own state capital or hometown — a rich supply of case studies of government and politics in action. In the process, they stand to gain greater sophistication, not only as students, but as citizens.

To facilitate additional research on topical events, a new feature has been added to the Fall 1986 Guide. Citations to related and background articles in the Guide's basic sources of material, the CQ *Weekly Report* and the CQ *Almanac*, have been retained for the benefit of the Guide's users as well. CQ's *Weekly Report* and *Almanac* are available at most school and public libraries.

CQ GUIDE TO

CURRENT AMERICAN GOVERNMENT

Fall 1986

POLITICS

The Elections of 1986

The 1986 congressional elections are unlike any that have taken place in the past three decades.

For the first time since the mid-1950s, both parties are entering a campaign season fully aware that the political control of the Senate and the psychological domination of Congress are on the line.

Every election year finds someone willing to proclaim it a watershed, but this time the predictions seem to make sense. To most Democrats and some less-partisan observers, the past five years of Republican Senate control have had a temporary feel to them. Once the big GOP Class of 1980 came up for judgment, it has been argued, the "normal" Democratic majority would be restored.

In 1986 that prediction either will come true, or it will not. If Democrats — who are defending only 12 of the 34 seats up in 1986 — do not gain the four seats they need to take a majority, then it no longer will make much sense for anybody in the Democratic Party to bide his time waiting for the Restoration. Republicans will be able to assume they are in charge until further notice.

The legislative consequences of the 1986 elections are significant — for budgetary policy, for President Reagan's defense priorities, and especially for Reagan court appointees, who must win Senate confirmation.

But the elections will have an even more striking effect on the psychology of 1988. Democrats newly restored to Senate control in 1987 would carry with them the air of expectation their predecessors did in the last two years of Eisenhower's administration, when they took lopsided control of the Senate and House and began sounding like a party on the verge of winning the presidency, which they were. On the other hand, a Republican Party that survived the 1986 Senate ordeal would have every reason to behave as if its 20-year dominance of presidential politics still had a few years to run.

There have been decisive Senate campaigns in recent memory; 1980 obviously was one. What is hard to remember, though, is a campaign in which every move by a major candidate in a closely contested state was measured for its impact on the national result. In the 1980 campaign, the matter of ultimate Senate control simply was not considered. Neither party dreamed that Republicans could gain the nine seats they needed for a majority. Each state seemed to be conducting a discrete event.

Editor's note: Outlook for the 1986 congressional and gubernatorial elections was written in early 1986. Predictions of electoral outcomes are subject to change.

This year, the opposite is true. A leading Democratic Senate contender decides not to run, as did former Gov. James B. Hunt Jr. in North Carolina, and the national odds are recalculated. A Republican senator is arrested for drunken driving, as was Bob Kasten of Wisconsin, and they are recalculated again.

All these calculations reflect the common belief that the overall result is hanging right on the margin. If the elections had been held in February, the best guess was that Democrats would have emerged with 50 or 51 seats. Fifty-one is the magic number because a 50-50 split would allow Vice President George Bush to break the tie and keep the chamber in GOP control.

That Democrats have at least a respectable chance for control is more a function of sheer opportunity than of the quality of their campaigns or the national mood. Given the numbers, one might argue that it would be hard for them *not* to win control. Of the 34 Senate elections in 1986, Democrats need win only 16 to claim their majority. Republicans can win most of the contests and still lose the Senate.

Actually, had Democrats attracted top-rank challengers in all the states of highest opportunity, their chances of gaining control would have been even better. North Carolina, Wisconsin and Georgia all would have moved in a Democratic direction if the challengers were, respectively, Hunt, Rep. David R. Obey, and Rep. Ed Jenkins. All three considered a Senate campaign; all, for widely different reasons, turned it down. Partly as a result, the Democratic challenge became at least slightly uphill in all three of those places.

Republicans, by contrast, did not need to come up with many challengers, but in virtually every state where there was an obvious candidate, they got him. Former Gov. Christopher S. "Kit" Bond needed little coaxing to run for Missouri's open seat; former Gov. Richard A. Snelling needed a great deal of coaxing in Vermont but ultimately decided to challenge incumbent Patrick J. Leahy.

No Issue, No 'Itch'?

Plausible as the case for Democratic takeover might be, it lacks one obvious ingredient: an issue. Much has been made of the "six-year itch" factor in congressional elections. Throughout this century, the six-year point in presidential control has been a disaster for the party in power. In the entire record of popular Senate elections, no such party has lost fewer than four seats in its six-year election.

But in virtually all those six-year elections, something was happening in the country to turn voters against the

Congressional Departures

(as of February 17, 1986)

Retiring

Senate

	Date Announced	Began Service	Age
Thomas F. Eagleton (D-Mo.)	6/11/84	1969	56
Gary Hart (D-Colo.)	1/4/86	1975	49
Russell B. Long (D-La.)	2/25/85	1949	67
John P. East (R-N.C.)	9/17/85	1981	54
Barry Goldwater (R-Ariz.)	†	1953	77
Paul Laxalt (R-Nev.)	8/19/85	1975	63
Charles McC. Mathias Jr. (R-Md.)	9/27/85	1969	63

House

	Date Announced	Began Service	Age
Cathy (Mrs. Gillis) Long (D-La. 8)	10/18/85	1985	62
Parren J. Mitchell (D-Md. 7)	9/30/85	1971	63
Thomas P. O' Neill Jr. (D-Mass. 8)	3/1/84	1953	73
John F. Seiberling (D-Ohio 14)	12/31/85	1971	67
Charles Whitley (D-N.C. 3)	12/5/85	1977	59
Gene Chappie (R-Calif. 2)	12/30/85	1981	65
Cooper Evans (R-Iowa 3)	1/22/86	1981	61
Elwood Hillis (R-Ind. 5)	7/12/85	1971	59
Marjorie S. Holt (R-Md. 4)	8/1/85	1973	65
Eldon Rudd (R-Ariz. 4)	7/5/85	1977	65
Gene Snyder (R-Ky. 4)	4/5/85	1963	58
G. William Whitehurst (R-Va. 2)	2/18/85	1969	60

Seeking Other Office

House

	Began Service	Age	Office
John B. Breaux (D-La. 7)	1973	41	Senate
Michael D. Barnes (D-Md. 8)	1979	42	Senate
Thomas A. Daschle (D-S.D. AL) *	1979	38	Senate
Bob Edgar (D-Pa. 7)	1975	42	Senate
Wyche Fowler Jr. (D-Ga. 5)	1977	45	Senate
Cecil Heftel (D-Hawaii 1) *	1977	61	Governor
James R. Jones (D-Okla. 1) *	1973	46	Senate
Barbara A. Mikulski (D-Md. 3)	1977	49	Senate
Harry Reid (D-Nev. 1)	1983	46	Senate
Richard C. Shelby (D-Ala. 7)	1979	51	Senate
James Weaver (D-Ore. 4)	1975	58	Senate
Timothy E. Wirth (D-Colo. 2)	1975	46	Senate
James T. Broyhill (R-N.C. 10)	1963	58	Senate
Carroll A. Campbell Jr. (R-S.C. 4)	1979	45	Governor
Bobbi Fiedler (R-Calif. 21)	1981	48	Senate
Thomas F. Hartnett (R-S.C. 1)	1981	44	Lt. Gov.
Thomas N. Kindness (R-Ohio 8)	1975	56	Senate
Ken Kramer (R-Colo. 5)	1979	44	Senate
Tom Loeffler (R-Texas 21)	1979	39	Governor
John McCain (R-Ariz. 1)	1983	49	Senate
John R. McKernan Jr. (R-Maine 1)	1983	37	Governor
W. Henson Moore (R-La. 6)	1975	46	Senate
Ed Zschau (R-Calif. 12)	1983	46	Senate

† Plans to retire, but has not made a formal announcement.
* Expected to run, but has not formally announced.

party in power: recession and farm problems in 1958; the Vietnam War and social unrest in 1966; Watergate in 1974. There is no case of a party suffering disaster at the polls simply because voters looked at the calendar and saw that six years had passed.

A killer issue may yet emerge for Democrats at the Senate level in 1986. So far, though, there are few signs of one, even on a regional basis. James Abdnor is in trouble in South Dakota partly because of farm discontent, but elsewhere in the Midwest, Republican incumbents seem rather well insulated. Robert Dole in Kansas, Charles E. Grassley in Iowa and Dan Quayle in Indiana have escaped any major Democratic opposition at all.

Some Democratic strategists like to talk about the power of trade as an issue in some parts of the country, but in most of the campaigns so far, trade seems to be a motherhood issue. Regardless of Reagan's free-trade ideology, GOP incumbents are finding it relatively easy to stake out a position in favor of protecting local industries and use it to deflect criticism. There is no question that such Republicans as Mack Mattingly in Georgia and Arlen Specter in Pennsylvania could stir up serious trouble for themselves by appearing indifferent to the problems of textiles and steel, respectively, but they are unlikely to do that.

In the absence of an overriding national preoccupation such as Watergate or severe recession, a senator has to cooperate in order for the opposition to have a killer issue. Few of this year's incumbents seem inclined to do that.

There remains, of course, the specter of Gramm-Rudman. When this balanced-budget legislation was first offered in the fall of 1985, many Senate Democrats were concerned with finding a way to associate themselves with it. That appears slowly to be changing. Grassley's Democratic opponent, sacrificial lamb though he may be, launched his campaign by tying the senator to Gramm-Rudman, referring to it sarcastically as Gramm-Rudman-Grassley.

That may have been merely a lunge by a desperate challenger, or it may have been a sign of future attacks in other states by Democrats in real contention.

House: Settling In

As in 1984, the striking thing about the House contests is how few there are. In the two parties combined, there are no more than 40 to 50 serious challenges to incumbents, the largest number of those to Republicans elected in the 1984 Reagan landslide. The bulk of the House action in 1986 will be in the open seats — 35 by late February, probably a few more by Election Day Nov. 4.

There is no one explanation for this continuing slowdown in House competition. Some of it, though, clearly is related to the way district lines were drawn following the 1980 census. In most states, and particularly those where neither Democrats nor Republicans were in a position to impose a partisan remap, the two parties tended to join forces and draw a map guaranteeing maximum protection to incumbents regardless of party.

The result has been a sharp decline in the number of districts defined statistically as marginal. In 1984, for example, only six House Republicans were re-elected with less than 55 percent of the vote. It is not easy to find targets for Democrats to shoot at.

Republicans can find a considerable number of incumbent Democrats who were narrow winners in 1984 — 26 of them came in under 55 percent. But the Reagan presidential landslide is operating as a brake on GOP congressional

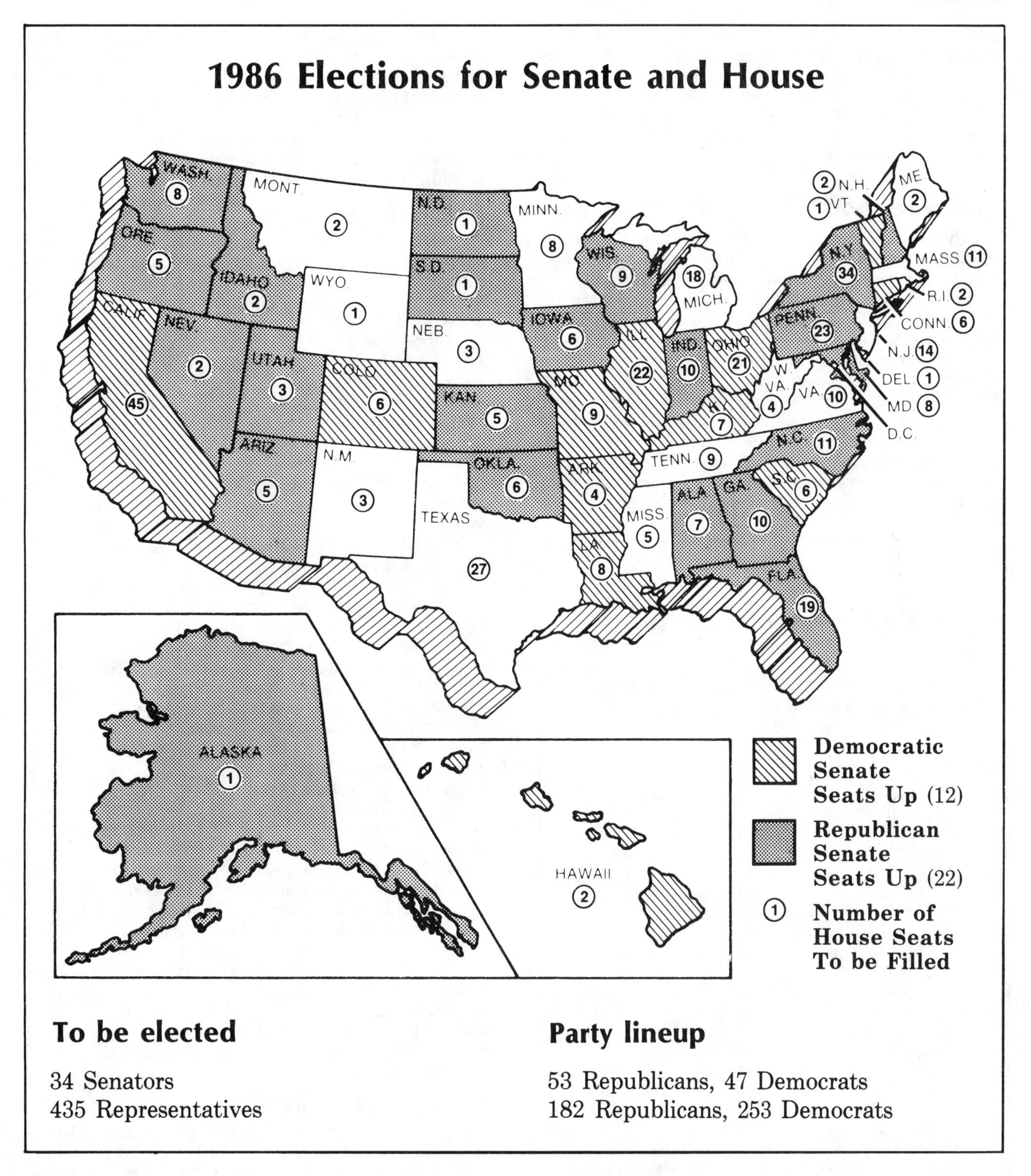

ambitions in 1986. Any Republican who is thinking about challenging a Democratic incumbent has to wonder whether his target, having survived the Reagan tide, is beatable in a year when presidential coattails are not a factor.

Democratic Rep. Philip R. Sharp, for example, managed to win 53 percent in 1984, even though Reagan carried his Indiana district by 2-to-1 and GOP nominee Ken MacKenzie campaigned for more than a year and raised more than $400,000. It is no surprise that MacKenzie is passing up a rematch in 1986, and that Republicans in Sharp's 2nd District have had to turn to a political novice.

The main effect of the decline in House competition is clear. Democrats benefit. To start with, they already hold 253 seats to the GOP's 182; they have no reason to complain about a quiet year in which turnover is small.

Also, a quiet year brings the parties closer to equality on the financial side of campaigns. The National Republican Congressional Committee, with its superior fund-raising ability, could offer the legal maximum of about $50,000 to candidates in nearly 200 districts. The Democratic Congressional Campaign Committee can afford to do that for perhaps 40 districts. But if the number of truly competitive districts is only 50 or 60, then the extra GOP money is relatively unimportant.

Governors: Will History Repeat?

The 1986 gubernatorial elections amount to a contest between history on one side and vulnerability on the other. History suggests big Republican losses — the party occupying the White House has not gained gubernatorial ground in any midterm election since World War II. But it is the Democrats who began 1986 with the most to lose.

Just as Republicans must defend a disproportionate number of the U.S. Senate seats up for election in 1986, Democrats have to defend a disproportionate number of governorships. They are the incumbent party in 27 of the 36 states that will choose governors in November.

The gubernatorial results are especially important to both sides as the next round of congressional and state legislative redistricting draws closer. Republicans hope to be in a stronger position after the 1990 elections than they were in the post-1980 period, when Democratic governors and legislative majorities were able to draw district lines in much of the country without having to consult Republicans at all. Many of the governors chosen in 1986 can expect to be starting second terms in 1991, so Republicans can help themselves in redistricting five years in advance by electing as many governors as possible in 1986.

Party Lineup of Governors

The number of governorships held by the parties after each election since 1950:

Year	D	R
1984	34	16
1982	34	16
1980	27	23
1978	32	18
1976 [1]	37	12
1974 [1]	36	13
1972	31	19
1970	29	21
1968	19	31
1966	25	25
1964	33	17
1962	34	16
1960 [2]	34	16
1958 [3]	35	14
1956	29	19
1954	27	21
1952	18	30
1950	23	25

Five states (Kentucky, Louisiana, Mississippi, New Jersey and Virginia) hold gubernatorial elections in odd-numbered years. In the chart, results of those contests are counted in the following year (e.g., the 1983 Ky., La. and Miss. results are counted under 1984, and the 1981 Va. and N.J. results under 1982).

[1] Independent James B. Longley of Maine was elected to a four-year term in 1974.

[2] Hawaii held its first gubernatorial election on July 28, 1959.

[3] Alaska held its first gubernatorial election on Nov. 25, 1958.

Midterm Slide Is Typical

To emerge from the 1986 elections with a majority of the nation's governorships, Republicans would have to post a net gain of 10. Such a turnover has taken place before — the Democrats gained 10 governorships in the 1970 midterm election — but it would be highly unusual.

Since World War II, the president's party has been able to pick up governorships only in presidential election years, with the largest gains almost always coming in the elections that put a new party in control of the White House. The Republicans, for instance, gained five governorships in 1980 when Ronald Reagan first won the presidency.

But the party holding the White House historically has not done well in midterm gubernatorial elections, losing an average of six governorships in contests over the past 40 years. That may not be coincidental, as political scientist John F. Bibby has pointed out. Bibby argues that in midterm years, without the president himself running for re-election, state executives become the most visible public figures on the ballot and serve as lightning rods for voter dissatisfaction.

The result is that every president from Harry S Truman to Jimmy Carter who has served at least one full term has had far more governors from his party at the beginning of his administration than at the finish. After Truman won a full term in the White House in 1948, for instance, there were 30 Democratic governors. When he left office four years later, there were only 18. The Republican gubernatorial total during the Eisenhower presidency fell from 30 at the outset to 16 at the end; the Democratic total under Lyndon B. Johnson collapsed from 34 when he assumed the office in November 1963 to 19 after the 1968 election. The 31 governorships that Republicans held at that point declined to 18 during Richard M. Nixon's five-year presidency. Under Jimmy Carter, the Democratic total fell from 37 to 27.

The same downward trend has continued under Reagan, even though he came into office with a smaller group of gubernatorial allies — 23 — than any other postwar president. Losses in 1982 dropped the GOP total to 16, where the figure remains in spite of Reagan's landslide re-election victory in 1984.

Democrats' Disadvantages

History aside, however, it seems improbable that the Republicans will lose any more governorships in 1986. Already near their postwar nadir of 12, the GOP has such vast opportunities in 1986 that at least a small gain seems inevitable. Not only are the Democrats defending three times as many seats as the Republicans, but at least 13 of the Democratic governorships will be open, compared with just four for the GOP.

A large number of popular Democratic incumbents are retiring — Arizona's Bruce Babbitt, Colorado's Richard D. Lamm, Florida's Bob Graham, Kansas' John Carlin, Maine's Joseph E. Brennan, Nebraska's Robert Kerrey,

Oklahoma's George Nigh, South Carolina's Richard W. Riley and Wyoming's Ed Herschler. Many of those seats will be difficult for the Democrats to hold. Eight Democratic governors who drew at least 60 percent their last time out will not be running for re-election in 1986. Only three will be running.

The number of retirements is nearly as large as the number of governors seeking another term. As of the beginning of 1986, 18 incumbents are expected to run for re-election — 13 Democrats and five Republicans. While none of the incumbents could be classified as underdogs, the casualty rate for governors seeking re-election has historically been fairly high. Nearly 30 percent of those who have sought re-election in the last quarter-century have lost.

To make major inroads in 1986, Republicans are relying heavily on comeback bids by popular ex-governors and on campaigns by converted Democrats.

Republican ex-governors either committed to or seriously considering a comeback include James A. Rhodes of Ohio, Henry L. Bellmon of Oklahoma, Winfield Dunn of Tennessee and William P. Clements of Texas. The Republican-convert group includes Tampa Mayor Bob Martinez and Wayne County (Mich.) Executive Bill Lucas.

A Mood for Change?

The large number of candidates willing to run under the Republican banner makes it obvious that the party sees 1986 as a year of opportunity. But along with opportunity comes problems. As the value of the GOP gubernatorial nomination has grown in a number of states, so has the potential for divisive primary contests that could undermine party harmony in the fall. Martinez and Lucas have drawn primary opposition from Republican candidates who claim they have better party credentials. And in some of the open Western states where Republicans have high hopes of winning, there is wide-open competition and no consensus.

As Republican candidates make their pitch in the 27 states currently governed by Democrats, they will be hoping that voters are more in a mood to transfer power than were voters in 1985's two gubernatorial contests, which saw the incumbent parties win impressive victories in low-turnout elections. In New Jersey, Republican Thomas H. Kean was re-elected with 70 percent of the vote, the largest share in the state's history. In Virginia, Democrat Gerald L. Baliles rode the coattails of the popular outgoing governor, Democrat Charles S. Robb, to win with a comfortable 55 percent of the vote.

In both of those states, voters indicated a preference for the status quo. If that mood of voter satisfaction extends to gubernatorial contests across the country in election year 1986, Republicans might find it difficult to capitalize on the opportunity that the year seems to guarantee them.

Technology, Strategy Bring New Campaign Era

Those who follow congressional campaigns are fond of comparing them to "races" — athletic events in which the contestants line up, set out gamely for the finish line, and hope they have the skill and stamina to get there ahead of the opposition.

Candidates across the country are learning that the race analogy is becoming obsolete. A well-financed congressional campaign in the mid-1980s is more like a complex and tortuous game of chess, based less on running than on attack and counterattack, on feinting and dodging, and on guessing where the other player is going to be several moves in advance.

Congressional campaigns have undergone a subtle but critical change since the elections in 1980, a shift fueled in part by technology and in part by trends in advertising and politics. Improved television production and advances in polling have made it possible for candidates to change course and redesign their campaigns literally overnight. The use and acceptance of negative commercials has made those moves, in many cases, all but essential.

The result is that a high-stakes House or Senate campaign is psychologically very different from what it was only a few years ago. This story traces those changes, largely in the words of the political consultants who have instituted most of them.

Bobbing and Weaving

It would be a mistake to isolate consultants or the media as the dominant force in congressional elections. Many — perhaps most — contests for the House and Senate still turn on the personal appeal of the candidates, as well as the demographics of the constituency and the feelings of the electorate on issues.

Increasingly, though, it is the consultants who design campaigns, share knowledge about techniques and strategy, and provide continuity from one election year to the next. And they spend considerable time thinking about the way their jobs are changing.

"In the 1970s," says Robert Squier, perhaps the most prominent Democratic media consultant, "you took a poll, analyzed yourself and your opponent, designed a strategy, and produced commercials. Three weeks before the election, you dropped everything on the voter. And your opponent did the same thing. Now, that whole process can take place in three days — and be repeated over and over during the campaign. What it means is that campaigns are more interesting. There are more decisions than in the past. The campaign is constantly growing and you're trying to stay ahead of it all the time."

Quick Response . . .

Illinois Senate: Shortly after Republican incumbent Charles H. Percy attacked Democratic challenger Paul Simon on the tax issue, Simon countered with ads portraying Percy as a one-time moderate who had shifted too far to the right.

In some of 1984's crucial Senate contests, the final campaign weeks took on the character of an electronic debate. One day's set of TV ads for one candidate was followed soon after by his opponent's set of counterads, and the process repeated several times in an intricate series of tactical moves.

Some who produce the ads see this as the latest positive step in the advancement of democracy. "You are seeing a dialogue," says Paul Wilson, a consultant who works with Republican candidates. "You are seeing the Lincoln-Douglas debates on TV."

A case in point is the 1984 Illinois U.S. Senate contest — waged, oddly enough, for the same seat that Abraham Lincoln and Stephen A. Douglas fought over in 1858.

Soon after Democratic presidential nominee Walter F. Mondale began warning of the need for higher taxes, GOP Sen. Charles H. Percy aired ads claiming that his Democratic challenger, Rep. Paul Simon, wanted even higher taxes than Mondale. "If you think you're not paying enough taxes," an announcer said, "Paul Simon's your man."

Simon immediately counterattacked with ads accusing Percy of distortion on the tax issue, and then followed with commercials aimed at portraying Percy as a conservative in moderate's clothing who had grown inattentive to the state's concerns.

At that point, Percy's advisers chose to shift their focus from the tax issue and offer commercials challenging Simon on water pollution and linking him to Iran's Ayatollah Khomeini. Some Democratic strategists believe that if Percy had kept up the pressure on taxes, he might have prevented Simon's victory in November.

That may or may not be correct. What is certain is that had the campaign been waged as recently as 1980, it would not have been waged in the same way.

At that time, the technology to produce commercials fast enough to simulate a debate was not yet employed in Senate campaigns. And even if it had been employed, candidates' pollsters could not have measured public response to a commercial fast enough to provide useful advice on what the response should be.

Tracking Is King

Basic to the ongoing change in campaign strategy is the development and perfection of the short-term tracking poll — a device that enables consultants to measure and describe the changes in voter sentiment about a campaign as often as every few hours. The quick response is possible because of the speed with which computers generate lists of randomly selected telephone numbers and process the data gleaned from phone polls.

Clever Negative . . .

Kentucky Senate: Trailing far behind Democratic Sen. Walter D. Huddleston, GOP challenger Mitch McConnell unleashed his "bloodhounds" negative advertisements; the dogs "tracked" Huddleston high and low but never found him, driving home McConnell's charge that Huddleston was shirking his Senate duties to give speeches for lucrative fees.

Presidential campaigns have been using tracking polls for at least a decade, but they were employed in Senate campaigns for the first time in 1980, when national GOP strategists polled in key states every night during October to determine which Senate challengers needed late infusions of money. In 1982, the GOP used the same technique to help its most vulnerable senators avoid defeat.

Once state-of-the-art campaign technology is used in high-visibility congressional races, it spreads fast. By 1984, almost every competitive Senate contest used tracking, and candidates demonstrated tactical moves that would have astonished the most adroit consultant only four years earlier.

"It's relatively simple and not very expensive now to sample public opinion," says Joseph Rothstein, who has been doing media work for Democrats since 1968. "In the last month of a campaign, both sides will poll nightly, test how that day's media and campaigning has played, and trace the results."

"Just having the media on is not enough," argues Harrison Hickman, a leading Democratic pollster. "You have to know if your media is working, and if your opponent's media is working. Information is now a much more important commodity."

Fastest Turnaround Wins

In the Percy-Simon contest, Simon's forces knew they had to respond to Percy's high-tax accusations because overnight tracking polls showed that statewide support for Simon dropped significantly after Percy's tax ads went on the air. "We took a poll and found out that commercial was devastating," says Squier, who was handling Simon's media. "We responded, we counterattacked, and they changed the subject."

In Texas' 1984 Senate race between GOP Rep. Phil Gramm and Democratic state Sen. Lloyd Doggett, Doggett usually hit the airwaves at 9:30 a.m. with any new commercials produced for that day. Gramm's staff and media consultant Roger Ailes held a conference call before noon on those days, sometimes wrote a responding ad by 2 p.m., recorded it by 4 p.m. and had it on TV at nine the next morning. In Kentucky, where Democratic Sen. Walter D. Huddleston offered his last set of radio advertisements on the Friday night before the election, strategists for Republican challenger Mitch McConnell listened and had their counterads on the air at noon Saturday.

Some consultants have become so comfortable with instant-response politics that they discuss it in terms that leave laymen several steps behind. "You have to remember," consultant Gary Nordlinger explained one day after showing an ad he produced, "that this was our response to his response to our response to his response to our original ad."

There is some reason to believe that consultants' tactical changes have started to influence candidates, producing a generation of office seekers less concerned about framing a message and presenting it than about being able to change the message on a moment's notice.

"When candidates come in here now," says Frank Greer, a Democratic consultant, "their first questions to me are: Can you respond quickly? Can you attack quickly? Can you do a fast turnaround?"

Going Negative

The advent of instant-response politics would not be so important had it not been for a parallel development: the rise of the negative campaign ad.

Negative advertising is not a new technique. Lyndon B. Johnson used it against Republican presidential nominee Barry Goldwater in 1964, and in 1970 the Nixon administration helped engineer negative ad campaigns against several Democratic senators facing re-election. But in the most recent congressional campaign cycles, there has been a dramatic surge in the number of commercials that criticize an opponent directly — sometimes brutally. That escalation has brought a growing demand that something be done to stop it.

In June 1985, Republican Sen. John C. Danforth of Missouri introduced a Clean Campaign Act (S 1310) that would grant an opponent free media time to answer a negative ad, unless the candidate making the charge had appeared on camera to deliver it in person. "Negative political campaigning is creating apathy and cynicism among the voting public," Danforth said, "and distorting our electoral process."

There is room for argument about whether negative ads will damage the political system in the long term; there is no argument about their short-term impact: They work, and they win elections. Voters pay attention to them.

That is a comparatively new piece of knowledge, even among campaign professionals. In the 1970s, House or Senate candidates who resorted to negative ads about their opposition were considered daring at best, and desperate at worst.

"Ten years ago," says consultant Wilson, "you had a few candidates experimenting with negative. They were the risk takers. The rule then was not to mention the opponent. Ignore the attack."

That attitude changed in the fall of 1980. Such Democratic congressional fixtures as Sens. Gaylord Nelson of Wisconsin and Herman E. Talmadge of Georgia, and Rep. Richardson Preyer of North Carolina, all fell victim to campaigns in which they declined to respond to challengers on the attack. Highly publicized in that election cycle was the National Conservative Political Action Committee (NCPAC), which ran independent negative advertising campaigns aimed at numerous candidates it deemed too liberal.

Since then, it has become conventional wisdom among consultants that incumbents ignore negative ads at their peril — and what is more, that the attacks pose remarkably little danger to the attacker.

"People say they hate negative advertising," says Jill Buckley, a Democratic consultant, "But it works. They hate it and remember it at the same time. The problem with positive is that you have to run it again and again and again to make it stick. With negative, the poll numbers will move in three or four days."

Consultants still find many candidates reluctant to "go negative," either because they consider it unseemly or because they are afraid it will boomerang. In fact, research does show that a wave of negative ads frequently reduces the attacker's poll standing a few points. But those numbers nearly always bounce back within a few days. Meanwhile, the target of the attack loses considerably more support — and that slippage lasts much longer.

"The message gets through," says Democratic consultant Karl Struble, "even though people don't know where they got it and can't identify it. . . . The ones that have the greatest effect are the subtle ones, the ones that seduce us. We are a society that likes to be seduced."

Idealism Gone to the Dogs

To measure the tactical change in campaigns over the past decade, one need only think back to some of the most creative and successful TV ads of the early 1970s — soft-sell commercials that featured candidates walking in shirt-sleeves along a beach, and announcers talking about idealism.

"That doesn't work any more," says Don Ringe, a GOP media consultant. "The notion of idealism as the reason for political involvement, that era is over." Like virtually all his colleagues, Ringe is convinced that it is far easier to impress voters with an opponent's weaknesses than to convince them of a client's strengths.

Just how easy that process can be was made clear in 1984 in Kentucky, where a single negative ad is widely believed to have turned the course of the Senate campaign and given Republican challenger McConnell his stunning victory over Democratic incumbent Huddleston. If there were any traditionalists among political strategists who still doubted the power of negative advertising, that campaign seemed to convert them.

McConnell, then the county executive of Jefferson County (Louisville), began 1984 trailing Huddleston by as many as 50 points in his own polls. In August, after months of positive TV ads aimed at introducing McConnell to Kentucky voters, Huddleston still held a 68 to 22 percent lead.

"We simply had to go negative," says Larry McCarthy, who handled McConnell's ads for the Ailes firm. "We had to take some points off Huddleston very quickly. We kept racking our brains looking for the home run. We brought 'Bloodhounds' out, and it was like lighting a match on a pool of gasoline. It simply exploded."

"Bloodhounds" was a television commercial in which a "detective" follows a pack of dogs through the U.S. Capitol grounds, past swimming pools and other scenic locations in search of Huddleston, who allegedly was impossible to find because he was always away giving speeches for his own personal gain. "We can't find Dee," the announcer finally says. "Maybe we ought to let him make speeches and switch to Mitch for senator."

Huddleston's strategists insist that the commercial was only one of many important factors in the campaign. But within a short time after the ad first appeared, McConnell surged into contention. He ended up defeating Huddleston by 5,269 votes.

Remarkably, most of the voters questioned after the ads appeared seemed not only unconcerned about their negative character, but also unaware of it. "People never held McConnell accountable for running a dirty campaign," says McCarthy. "They thought the bloodhounds were funny. But obviously it sank in."

The Year of Inoculation

Some have speculated that Huddleston might have negated McConnell's attacks had he hired his own set of bloodhounds, portrayed them in an ad searching the Capitol corridors and then shown them finding him at night in his Senate office, working late and virtually unnoticed "for the people of Kentucky."

But many campaign consultants believe that Huddleston's chief problem was not his failure to respond to the attack; it was his failure to secure himself against an attack before one ever was launched.

Partly because of Huddleston's loss, 1986 likely will be the year of inoculation in Senate elections. Consultants working for incumbents began early to design media campaigns to immunize their clients against McConnell-style attacks.

Republican Sen. James Abdnor

A New Breed of Consultant Joins the Fray

Most of what appears in the national media about campaign consultants still deals with the founding generation — people such as Robert Squier and David Garth on the Democratic side and Robert Goodman, Roger Ailes and John Deardourff on the Republican side. That is legitimate. All of these "elder statesmen" are relatively young and still important to the politics of any election year.

But the emphasis on big names can obscure the fact that political consulting is a growth industry, boosted in the past few years by the funds that flow from political action committees (PACs) to congressional campaigns. The checks written by PACs may or may not be "buying" members of Congress, but they unquestionably are subsidizing the services of media advisers and pollsters. As consultant Joseph Rothstein argues, "The route to political success now is money to media to votes."

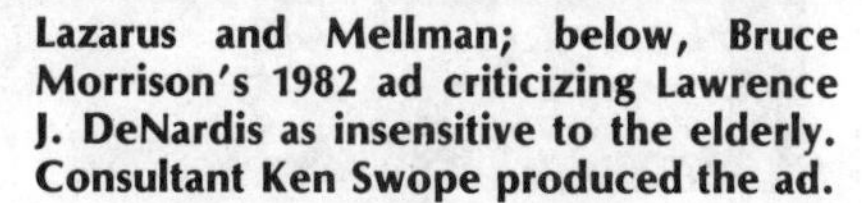

Lazarus and Mellman; below, Bruce Morrison's 1982 ad criticizing Lawrence J. DeNardis as insensitive to the elderly. Consultant Ken Swope produced the ad.

All this money in the political system has spawned a new generation of consultants who differ from the original generation in several interesting ways. Most of the early media people came into political campaigns from another field, usually advertising (Goodman and Ailes) or documentary films (Squier). Their work, even today, has the sophistication and visual appeal of consumer product ads or top-quality public TV. Many of the younger consultants are interested in politics first. They tend to master the technical aspects of the job as a way to further political goals.

One typical newcomer is Michael Murphy, 23, who along with partner Alex Castellanos, 31, leaped to attention among consultants with his commercials for the 1984 re-election campaign of Sen. Jesse Helms, R-N.C. It was Murphy and Castellanos who filmed the "Where Do You Stand, Jim?" ads that erased the formidable lead of Helms' Democratic challenger, Gov. James B. Hunt Jr. For 1986, their firm is involved in such diverse and high-stakes Senate campaigns as the one to re-elect GOP Sen. Mack Mattingly in Georgia, and the challenge by former Vermont GOP Gov. Richard A. Snelling to Democratic Sen. Patrick J. Leahy.

Although Murphy & Castellanos lists itself as an advertising firm, its partners do not come from a traditional advertising background. Murphy, who is a graduate of Georgetown University, worked for the National Conservative Political Action Committee (NCPAC), practicing TV production in NCPAC's efforts to unseat incumbent Democratic senators in 1980 and 1982. Castellanos learned his craft through the Congressional Club, Helms' political organization in North Carolina. Both men are protégés of Charlie Black, a NCPAC founder and chief strategist of Helms' campaigns.

A Murphy & Castellanos political ad does not have the visual slickness of one produced by a Squier or a Goodman. That is deliberate. "We don't spend incredible amounts of money on production values," Murphy says. "You can do art, or you can move numbers. We don't do art. We like to win."

Two rising stars at the other end of the political spectrum are Democratic pollsters Mark Mellman and Ed Lazarus, mavericks who are as suspicious of orthodoxy in their party and profession as Murphy and Castellanos.

Mellman, 30, and Lazarus, 26, were political science instructors at Yale University in 1982 when they agreed to provide polling help for an under-financed and largely ignored U.S. House challenger in Connecticut, Democrat Bruce A. Morrison. When Morrison won an upset victory over GOP Rep. Lawrence J. DeNardis, word of their abilities spread to Congress. By 1984, they were working with, among others, Sen. Carl Levin in Michigan and successful Senate candidate Albert Gore Jr. in Tennessee.

As far as Mellman and Lazarus are concerned, much of the advice provided by big-name pollsters is not worth the fee it commands. They believe that a good deal of it reflects the pollster's values and ideas, rather than the responses of the voters. They avoid coaxing voters into making yes-or-no responses early in a campaign, insisting that this common polling technique produces misleading data because it ignores differences in voters' intensity.

They also are willing to consider violating conventional wisdom. In the 1982 challenge to DeNardis, Morrison ran no positive ads at all, something aggressive challengers are supposed to do to "soften" their image; he also appeared in his negative ads, something nearly all campaign consultants tell candidates not to do. "Had we not violated the rules in that campaign, we'd have lost," says Mellman. "There are people who are always looking for a general rule. Context is everything."

of South Dakota, expecting Gov. William J. Janklow to challenge his renomination on grounds of ineffectiveness, began airing commercials in November 1985 that featured prominent Senate colleagues testifying as to how effective he is.

Testimonial ads are a time-honored device in congressional campaigns, but there is no previous comparable case of an incumbent deciding to use them so long before the voting. That choice was in some measure a legacy of McConnell and his bloodhounds — a point reinforced by the fact that Abdnor's ads were produced by Ailes, who was responsible for the bloodhounds in the first place.

"Inoculation and pre-emption are what win campaigns," says Jim Innocenzi, a Republican who works primarily for House candidates and who feels these techniques are now a staple of the modern tactical arsenal.

"If you know what your negatives are, and you know where you're vulnerable," agrees Charlie Black, "you can pre-empt it."

Some consultants believe there is also a tactical advantage in "negative inoculation" — using early advertising not only to create positive feelings about a candidate, but to plant doubts about his opponent before the opponent has launched his offensive. "If you want to attack your opponent's record," says Squier, "head him off at the pass. Don't wait until he's going through the gate."

Still, campaign strategists are far from unanimous on the power of inoculation to save potentially vulnerable incumbents. Media specialist Ed Blakely, a GOP veteran working for the Smith and Harroff firm, defends Huddleston's decision not to immunize himself against charges before they were made. "I would find it hard to sit down with an incumbent who has a 65-point lead," Blakely says, "and tell him to do inoculation ads."

Starting Early

The modern tactical campaign is a long-running affair. Abdnor was not the only incumbent senator who began running TV ads a year before the voting; virtually all major statewide candidates started early the series of moves and countermoves that lasted until Election Day. That situation was in large part the legacy of North Carolina's 1984 Senate contest.

Few congressional elections in American history have received the national attention lavished on the two-year struggle that culminated in Republican Sen. Jesse Helms' re-election over his Democratic challenger, Gov. James B. Hunt Jr.

The importance of Helms' victory for the conservative movement has been chronicled and debated at enormous length. Less has been written about its importance for future campaign strategy.

Helms challenged an informal rule of Senate campaigning — that there is a limit to how much advertising voters will tolerate before they turn against the candidate doing the advertising.

The Helms TV ads began running in June 1983, nearly 18 months before the balloting, and remained on the air, except for brief periods, until election week. Altogether, some 150 ads were produced for Helms' campaign.

When the commercials began running, Helms trailed Hunt substantially in all major polls, and his own polls showed him with a 45 percent negative rating among voters. In that situation, explains Charlie Black, Helms' chief strategist, "you might as well try to shoot your way out."

Although not all the Helms ads were negative, the most conspicuous ones featured the conservative incumbent staking out a position of his own on a controversial issue such as school prayer or the Panama Canal treaties, then challenging Hunt with the question, "Where do you stand, Jim?" These ads, produced by Michael Murphy and Alex Castellanos, have been widely identified as the vehicle for Helms' comeback and eventual 86,000-vote win. *(New Breed, p. 9)*

One clear lesson of the Helms-Hunt campaign is that voters will accept saturation-level political advertising for months, perhaps years. "The old adage that people get tired of campaigns if they go on too long is not true," says Black. "People were paying as much attention in North Carolina at the end as at the beginning. . . . McDonald's advertises 365 days a year. People never get tired of that. And they keep going to McDonald's."

Doomed by a Slow Counter

The Helms campaign taught another tactical lesson by discrediting Hunt early in the campaign cycle. Six months before the voting, the challenger had lost the offensive, and he never regained it.

Unlike Huddleston in Kentucky, Hunt was fully aware of the need to respond to attacks. The ads prepared for him by consultant David Sawyer were dramatic and aggressive, accusing Helms of pursuing an extremist course in the Senate and consorting with right-wing world figures such as El Salvador's Roberto d'Aubuisson.

But Hunt's campaign assumed it could answer Helms on its own well-prepared schedule. Rather than changing its plan to deal with the unprecedented volley of Helms' early attacks, Hunt did not begin countering with ads of his own until late spring of 1984. Many political consultants see that as Hunt's critical mistake. Its effect on the 1986 Senate campaigns was already being felt by late 1985.

"It was ridiculous to allow Helms on TV for six months, blasting away at the governor, and never answer him," says Squier. "An unanswered charge that is on that long is agreed to. By the

Too-Slow Response . . .

North Carolina Senate: In June 1983, GOP Sen. Jesse Helms began running ads attacking his challenger, Gov. James B. Hunt Jr., as vague on issues. Hunt waited several months before airing anti-Helms ads, including one linking the senator to various right-wing world figures. Hunt's slow counter enabled Helms to gain an advantage he never lost.

time Hunt got on, the war was over."

Florida: Another Epic Fight

As the 1986 campaigns began, many strategists assumed that the era of the rigid campaign plan was over. The chess game begins as soon as the first move is made, and every move thereafter is essentially a response.

The tactical changes were evident in Florida, where Democratic Gov. Bob Graham challenged GOP incumbent Paula Hawkins. Their battle had some surface similarities to Hunt-Helms — it pitted a popular and respected Southern governor and a controversial conservative incumbent, either of whom would probably be an easy winner against any other opponent. As in North Carolina two years ago, the governor started out ahead, and the senator had to figure out how to puncture his credibility.

Like Helms, Hawkins had Charlie Black designing campaign strategy. And like Helms, Hawkins chose to start early in an effort to gain a tactical advantage. In October 1985, she began airing four commercials touting her efforts to locate missing children and to combat illegal drugs.

After two weeks of exposure, Black decided to go another two weeks. "They tested out very well," he said of the commercials, produced by Baltimore consultant Robert Goodman. One year before the election, Hawkins already had spent some $750,000 on media alone. In 1980, her entire campaign cost less than $800,000. Graham did not respond with his own early ads, but the need for him to do so was less pressing than it was for Hunt because Hawkins' initial ads were not negative.

The 'Window' Peril

Black is the first to admit that Hawkins-Graham was no rerun of Hunt-Helms. Helms had an unlimited supply of money (he eventually spent nearly $17 million); neither Hawkins nor any other candidate who ran in 1986 was in that position.

"Helms-Hunt was a unique campaign," says Black. "We had total tactical flexibility. We could go on TV any time we wanted without having to worry that we'd have to go off later."

Candidates who follow Helms' early media strategy will be making a riskier decision than Helms made. They risk purchasing a modest improvement in polling numbers long before the election, then running out of money later and giving their opponents an opportunity consultants refer to as a "window" — a substantial bloc of time in which one candidate can afford TV ads and the other cannot.

"When you go off the air, and your opponent goes on, the whole picture changes," says Wilson. "Unless Paula Hawkins is able to raise millions, she runs the risk of wasting a tremendous amount of money and creating a tremendous window for Graham."

Still, even the less affluent 1986 candidates tested ways to seize an early edge. Democratic Rep. Thomas A. Daschle, even before he formally announced his Senate campaign, was on the air periodically in South Dakota, where TV time can be purchased relatively cheaply.

Early in 1985, Daschle bought time throughout the state to discuss his emergency farm credit bill; in the fall, he did the same thing to talk about the Gramm-Rudman deficit-reduction plan. Starting early has become an article of faith for Daschle's media consultant, Karl Struble. "It's smart to give people that kind of information in a non-election year," Struble says. "You freeze it in their memory."

Creeping Down

To an extent, any story about state-of-the-art technology in congressional campaigns is a story about the Senate. It is in Senate campaigns, with their multimillion-dollar budgets, that candidates and consultants have the luxury of trying the experiments that become standard practice in the next campaign cycle. House campaigns are not as quick to adapt.

"The technology creeps down slower than you'd think it would," says Murphy. "In House campaigns you still have arguments between media people and the door knockers who ask whether they really need TV. People win for sewer commissioner because they mailed out 25,000 potholders. They think the way to win for Congress is to mail out 50,000 potholders."

Still, the technology and the strategy do filter down, at least to competitive House districts where both parties are well funded. Several Republicans who unseated House Democrats in 1984 employed tactics developed earlier at the Senate level. *(Consultants and campaigns, 1984 CQ Weekly Report p. 3151)*

Starting Early . . .

Florida Senate, 1986: Freshman Republican Sen. Paula Hawkins, who is facing an uphill re-election battle against two-term Democratic Gov. Bob Graham, began running television advertisements in October touting her legislative efforts to locate missing children and to combat illegal drugs.

One was GOP challenger Beau Boulter, who defeated five-term Democratic Rep. Jack Hightower in Texas' 13th District. Boulter used some of the staples of lower-level contests — door-knocking, direct mail and precinct organization — but his campaign had a modern media flavor as well.

Boulter had the task of defeating a popular incumbent whose conservative record was not easy to attack. Boulter's media consultants, the firm of Sandler and Innocenzi, decided to start exceptionally early for a House campaign, running positive TV ads in May 1984 in the inexpensive Amarillo and Wichita Falls media markets.

"It was like a new product rollout," Innocenzi says. "It's nice before you go into the negative phase of your campaign to give your candidate some credibility so he doesn't sound like a wacko."

A few weeks later, Boulter's strategists decided on a pre-emption move. They felt they could seize the high ground on school prayer against Hightower, who had always supported school prayer measures. A series of Boulter ads accused Hightower of failing to take an activist role on the issue, and of cooperating with Democratic leadership efforts to keep school prayer initiatives off the House floor.

"We basically stole the issue from the guy," says Innocenzi. "Beau Boulter became the champion of school prayer, even though Jack Hightower had voted for it."

Slugfest-Shy Incumbents

Stories of successful challenges such as Boulter's quickly become part of campaign lore, told and retold to aspiring candidates at campaign schools run by both parties. The only real brake on negative campaigning by challengers is a shortage of funds.

For House incumbents, though, there is another limiting factor: Many of them believe that attacking a challenger demeans the office. "It's still difficult for incumbents who want to be above the fray to get down and slug it out with their opponents," says one longtime party strategist. "The older the incumbent, the more tenured the incumbent, the tougher it is."

One veteran House Democrat brought abruptly into the modern campaign era was Missouri's Harold L. Volkmer. Seeking a fifth term in 1984, Volkmer found himself facing a well-financed Republican more sophisticated than his previous opponents.

Republican Carrie Francke, using media consultant Wilson, aired ads accusing Volkmer of ineffectiveness. An actor on screen crumpled copies of Volkmer's legislative proposals and tossed them into a wastebasket.

Volkmer, although known as one of the House's most combative members, refused for weeks to respond with negative ads. Ultimately he sought help from the Democratic Congressional Campaign Committee. Media consultant Jill Buckley designed a set of ads that stressed Volkmer's accomplishments and also questioned Francke's educational credentials. Volkmer won by about 13,000 votes.

A Chilling Effect

Many thoughtful observers wince at the trend toward negative, hyper-responsive campaigns and worry that clever consultants are manipulating the system to elect candidates less deserving than their opponents.

It is not so certain that this is the main problem. At the highest level of expertise, negative advertising is its own deterrent. A blast from one side is vulnerable to retaliation that will be equally effective. A negative ad that goes too far is even more vulnerable to being discredited by the opposition.

"The big lie works when it's used in a vacuum," Democrat Squier insists. "The only time it's dangerous is when you have one side firing and the other side isn't firing back." Republican Black agrees. "If you get two people of equal capability to oppose each others' negatives," he says, "the better one will win. That's how it should be."

If the new techniques are not changing the results of campaigns, though, they are changing their nature. And they are influencing legislators' behavior between elections as well as Congress' overall performance.

In 1984, Iowa Democratic Senate hopeful Tom Harkin gained considerable mileage with a TV ad in which he boasted that during a 10-year House career, he never had voted to increase the national debt. "I don't believe in it," he flatly told the audience.

Harkin's avoidance of debt-increase voting in the House made it easier for him as a Senate candidate to fend off accusations from GOP Sen. Roger W. Jepsen, who tried to portray Harkin as a "liberal big spender."

But by repeatedly refusing to go along with obligatory debt-ceiling increases so the government could pay bills it already had incurred, Harkin and other politically sensitive legislators had periodically stalled House proceedings and distracted members from pressing legislative duties.

Some incumbents discovered in 1984 that obscure and seemingly inconsequential votes on the House floor could prove damaging to them when made the basis of oversimplified 30-second commercials by their opponents. Such negative ads can have a chilling effect on the legislative process, as members ponder whether stands they regard as reasonable could prove embarrassing in a negative campaign ad in the next election.

"Roughly half the senators on each side," says pollster Hickman, "think much more about how any individual vote can be used against them than they ever have before."

Pressure to Simplify

Even consultants who insist they are not tampering with the results of elections seem concerned that they are cheapening the process. "At times, what we do as consultants is abuse the system," a prominent Democratic consultant concedes. "Any consultant who says he doesn't do that can't have much of a conscience. But we're employed to help a candidate win. I'd be taking money under false pretenses if I didn't do everything I could to help the candidate win. Sometimes that means simplifying an argument or fuzzing up a position."

A prominent Republican says much the same: "Most Americans don't understand the complicated web of compromise that makes up the legislative process. They respond to absolutes. What we do is make a simple argument that creates black-and-white choices. A 30-second dog food commercial. That's something our profession is guilty of. Trivializing the process. Nobody hired a consultant for moral judgments. Moralist political consultants don't last long."

Finally, there is room for concern that hyper-responsive campaigns are creating hyper-responsive congressmen — people who bring from their campaigns a penchant for attack and counterattack and a casual approach to long-term planning and fixed values.

But it is far from clear that this is a problem confined to the political system. Many would argue that it is a problem in the society at large. "Our whole society has become very reactive," says consultant Struble. "The changes and the decisions you have to make are much quicker. It's getting to be a microwave society. That's the way life is now." ▮

Poll Fever Infects 1986 Campaign Coverage

On Dec. 5, 1985, just as South Dakota's U.S. Senate campaign was beginning in earnest, readers in Sioux Falls picked up the morning *Argus-Leader* and learned something interesting.

A new poll said that James Abdnor, the GOP incumbent who earlier in the year had been trailing his rivals for both renomination and re-election, had recovered and now was ahead. The headline read, "Abdnor Leads, Poll Says."

The senator's campaign director was delighted. "A lot of Abdnor's supporters," he said, "are becoming more visible and vocal for him." At the national level, some analysts who had seen Abdnor as a sure primary loser to GOP Gov. William J. Janklow began to backtrack.

There was nothing deceptive about either the poll or the story. The reporter did his job. The story made clear that the survey was financed by Abdnor, and a leading Democrat was quoted prominently in response to it.

Still, that story was a symbol of an outbreak of poll fever that has infected news coverage of Senate campaigns all over the country this year. Polls have been part of campaign news for a generation, of course, but not in quite the same way they were in 1986.

Contests in some states never seem to move much beyond a volley of conflicting public opinion data. Every poll anybody chooses to take gets printed or broadcast, and while it is usually clear where a particular set of numbers came from, polls bought and paid for by candidates show up in the same news columns as those done by a presumably neutral source. As far as most readers are concerned, they are all news.

That doesn't make much sense. If anything, the media should be paying less attention to candidates' polls than ever. More than in the past, these polls are simply adjuncts to a campaign's public relations apparatus.

As recently as four years ago, a poll taken 12 months before Election Day might have been a fair measure of political opinion at a relatively stable time.

Now, however, embattled Senate incumbents are on the air with television commercials a year in advance. A poll taken just after a wave of commercials — such as the survey Abdnor conducted last fall — is bound to make the incumbent look good. A poll taken after the challenger's media wave can make the same officeholder look terrible.

All of it is artificial. It has very little relation to the ultimate result. Leaking a favorable poll can generate some contributions and cause the national media to stop writing off a candidate as a sure loser. And that is a worthy goal for many candidates. But that doesn't make it news.

A leading Democratic candidate, talking anonymously, is candid about polls and the media:

"There's incredible naiveté in the press about how to interpret data," he says. "You see these numbers bouncing around like crazy because people are measuring things that aren't really there.... Campaigns can interpret data in any way they choose. The tidbits you leak are designed to get your point across."

Completely within the bounds of accepted survey techniques, a pollster can make lots of decisions that affect the numbers he eventually is going to leak to a newspaper about his candidate. Some of them sound trivial but turn out to be crucial.

For example, there is the question of whom to telephone. A pollster can either pick numbers out of the phone book or forget about the book and start dialing a random series of seven-digit combinations.

Using a phone book means the survey will leave out the unlisted subscribers who comprise about 20 percent of households nationwide. Those 20 percent are not typical of the country as a whole: A few are very wealthy, but most tend to be young, single, transient and weighted toward minority groups.

A pollster whose candidate is weak among the young and minorities can buy himself a few points by calling listed numbers rather than random digits. No reader is going to find out about that.

It also matters whether the voter is asked to choose between two candidates at the beginning of the interview, or later. Many polls do both — after making a choice, the voter gets to hear some subjective information or some new questions about the two candidates, then chooses again.

One would hope that any candidate's poll appearing in the paper or on TV would be based only on questions asked right at the beginning. But nobody knows for sure. While it is hard to find a pollster who says that he leaks data about candidate match-ups from questions at the end of a survey, nearly all of them say other people do it.

The point is that candidates' polls, leaked to the press, do not constitute information. They constitute propaganda.

That does not make them insidious; any hard-working candidate or pollster has a right to try to sell the media anything he thinks they will buy.

And it is unrealistic to think the media will ever stop publicizing polls that purport to say something new about the election.

But journalists could help political consumers by exercising a little more skepticism than they do now. Reporters don't believe everything government officials tell them; in fact, they sometimes make a fetish out of disbelieving it. Campaigns and polls deserve the same treatment.

PAC Pilgrimage Becomes Candidates' Ritual

D.C. Is Mecca In Quest for Cash

Though congressional candidates talk passionately about someday coming to Washington, many of them spend a lot of time here prior to election stalking one of the capital's corridors of power — political action committees (PACs).

For months before an election, congressional contenders from across the country troop to Washington in search of PAC contributions they hope will help pave the way to victory.

This pilgrimage has become an integral part of running for Congress in recent years, as challengers and open-seat contenders have come to view PACs as vital to their political welfare.

Consultants and professional fund-raisers have helped promote the pilgrimage by peddling opportunities for access to the PAC community. They are finding an increasing number of candidates eager for their services.

Candidates make their journeys in the face of intimidating odds. According to a Federal Election Commission study released in May of 1985, incumbents sopped up 72 percent of all PAC contributions made during the 1983-84 election cycle. Challengers to incumbents attracted only 16 percent of all PAC money, while candidates for open seats netted 11 percent. Most PACs have been showing decidedly pro-incumbent tendencies for many years. *(Graph, p. 16)*

What little money political action committees do invest in non-incumbents often is funneled to a small coterie of top-flight contenders who are strongly favored to win. PAC managers who amass a poor won-lost record know that they will be required to account for their defeats by the board of directors of their organization. As a result, they are extremely wary of taking risks.

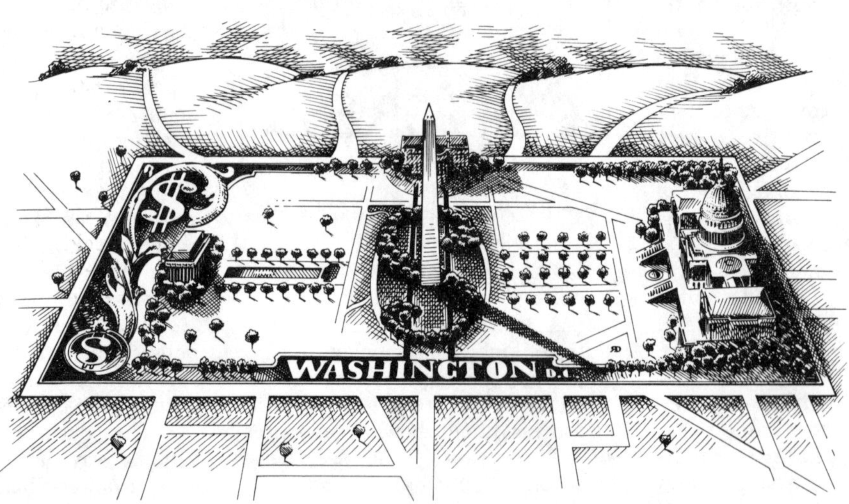

Beating Down the Doors

But if candidates realize the problems they face in trying to tap the Washington PAC community, one would not know it from the way they behave. The number of candidates making the Washington pilgrimage seems to be growing with each election cycle, as they eagerly compete for a slice of the PAC pie.

"Nearly everybody comes through here," says Bernadette Budde, political strategist for the Business-Industry Political Action Committee (BIPAC), one of the country's most influential corporate PACs. "Sometimes even after I've told them that we have consistently supported the incumbent, they still want to come by."

Tom Baker, vice president for political affairs for the National Association of Home Builders (NAHB), concurs. "Frankly," Baker says, "it's hard to keep most of them out of town."

Candidates not only are showing up in Washington in increasing numbers; they are showing up earlier and earlier with each passing campaign. Far from being a biennial event, the Washington pilgrimage often begins immediately after Election Day for a contest two years down the road.

"We started seeing 1986 candidates in 1984," said one analyst for a health association PAC. "We view it as a two-year process.... It's a full-time job."

"There's a parade that starts in September of the off-year," echoes Al Jackson, political director of the liberal-minded National Committee for an Effective Congress (NCEC). "It can be a revolving door some days."

Washington is not the only place to which candidates travel in search of PAC money. Houston and Los Angeles are prominent among the other cities that are emerging as important PAC centers. But Washington still is regarded as the symbolic and financial capital of the PAC world.

"There are PACs in other places," said Baker of the NAHB, whose Build PAC gave more money to federal candidates than all but two other political action committees during the 1983-84 cycle. "But Washington ... is the mecca. This is the mother lode."

"I recognize that I'm going to have to have financial help from Washington," says Indiana state Sen. Jim Jontz, a Democratic candidate who ran for retiring GOP Rep. Elwood Hillis' House seat. "I'm committed to spending time seeking it.... It's a part of the process I have to pursue."

Value of Visits

While it is clear that a desire to collect campaign cash is the major reason candidates come to Washington to visit PACs, there are other potential

"A lot of people in this business are like me. . . . They like to look and see and evaluate candidates from firsthand. The guy may have great numbers, but he may be a nerd."

—David Michael Staton, manager of political action programs, U.S. Chamber of Commerce

"An amazing number of candidates walk into their first PAC meeting without having their act down."

—Denis Calabrese, vice president, Southern Political Consulting

benefits from such journeys that may not be as apparent. The PAC pilgrimage affords candidates an opportunity to test their political appeal before a critical, seasoned audience. It also gives them valuable practice at trying to raise funds — practice that could pay off when they return home.

Some candidates feel that a trip to Washington can help them convince PAC managers they are serious about their race.

"I think making the trip shows that you're really . . . committed to your campaign," says Minnesota state Sen. Collin C. Peterson, a Democrat who decided to challenge Republican Rep. Arland Stangeland again in 1986 after losing his initial bid in 1984. "If you don't go to Washington . . . it sends a negative signal. They expect you to make the trip."

Candidates also may gain an intangible sense of purpose and excitement from visiting the capital that fires their imaginations — and their campaigns.

"There may be some deep psychological reasons why a candidate has to come to Washington to feel that he is a real candidate," says BIPAC's Budde. "They may have been told by people who have been elected . . . 'Once you come and see the Capitol at night, and see your party heroes in action on the floor, you may never feel the same again.' They may need the charge that they get out of being here. The search for dollars may be secondary."

Weeding Out the Dogs

PAC managers, too, can benefit from the pilgrimage. It often provides the only chance they get to develop a firsthand feel for contenders they have known only through press clippings, poll numbers and other analysts' remarks.

"I think a lot of people in this business are like me," said David Michael Staton, a former House Republican from West Virginia (1981-83) who now heads the political action programs for the U.S. Chamber of Commerce. "They like to look and see and evaluate candidates from firsthand. The guy may have great numbers, but he may be a nerd."

By meeting personally with a particular candidate, PAC managers say, they stand a better chance of keeping track of that contender's campaign. With a field of hundreds of candidates for federal office, that is no easy task.

"If you're a challenger, you've got to come — and more than once," says the NCEC's Jackson. "You've got to come and make sure that everyone sees your name and your face a lot . . . so that we remember who you are. There are too many races, too many candidates for us to keep track of it unless you keep your name in front of us."

"They get the challengers mixed up," echoes GOP consultant Terry Cooper, who also has worked as director of a corporate PAC. "They're going to forget whether that neat story they heard was about you in Oregon or about somebody who is running against somebody with a similar name in Missouri."

Secrets to Success

A variety of factors determine whether candidates succeed when they solicit funds from the Washington PAC community, but a surprising number of those factors are already decided before candidates arrive in town.

At a fundamental level, candidates strengthen their case if they are committed to waging a campaign before they come looking for money. A potentially strong contender arguably should face no penalty for visiting a PAC director in the course of deciding whether to run. But in practice, it often does not work out that way.

"We see some candidates who aren't even candidates," laments Budde, expressing irritation at being used as a sounding board for a prospective campaign. "I don't understand why they come to me to get my opinion about whether they should run. At the very least, they should have decided and announced. We don't like making decisions based on shadows and phantoms."

Many challengers also misuse time and resources trying to get money from PACs that have a strong record of support for the incumbents the contenders hope to unseat.

"There's no point in bringing a guy up here against an incumbent with a 90 percent voting record on our issues, the kind of guy we've maxed with," warns the NAHB's Baker. "Those records are all available. . . . That's something someone could find out in advance and save the guy a trip.

"It's not only a bad use of time," Baker continues, "it's also not good for a candidate's morale. . . . I've had guys who go through the drill with me and then ask how to get to the next association . . . where I know they're going to get exactly the same thing. My God, by the end of the day this guy is going to be totally depressed."

Primaries: Peril or Promise?

Many PAC managers also have a tendency to avoid candidates who are involved in crowded or difficult primaries. Most PACs are leery of being on the losing side of an intraparty battle, so they steer clear of primaries until one candidate emerges as the likely nominee.

Freshman Republican Rep. John G. Rowland of Connecticut learned that lesson in a painful way during his 1984 challenge to Democratic Rep. William R. Ratchford.

"When I went down to Washington, I didn't have the nomination yet," Rowland recalls. "I had 25 appointments, a poll under my arm, but no nomination. I got zero out of those visits. It was a total waste of time and money."

There is, however, an important exception to that rule. Directors of ideologically oriented PACs are much more likely than their corporate or labor colleagues to enter a primary if they find a candidate who is a clear philosophical ally.

"We use two criteria," says Jackson of the liberal NCEC. "One is that there is a clear philosophical difference between the two candidates involved. That involves both primaries and generals. The second criteria is that the race is marginal and winnable."

That policy also applies to ideological PACs on the conservative side. Jim Ellis, who until late 1985 worked as assistant director of the Free Congress PAC (affiliated with the Committee for the Survival of a Free Congress), said his organization also was willing to foray into a primary for an ideologically compatible candidate because "philosophical commitment for us is No. 1."

Naive Need Not Apply

Perhaps the most decisive event in a candidate's PAC pilgrimage takes place behind the PAC manager's door. There, a congressional hopeful faces the same kind of pressure to make a favorable impression that is felt by an anxious applicant interviewing with a potential employer.

"You've got to know what you're talking about, and you've got to come across well ... the simplest things you'd think a candidate would know to have," says Denis Calabrese, vice president of Southern Political Consulting, a Texas-based Republican firm. "But an amazing number of candidates walk into their first PAC meeting without having their act down."

A good performance at that meeting can help a candidate establish credibility and spread interest in his campaign throughout the PAC community. A bad showing can effectively shut a candidate out of PAC money.

"They have to convince the PAC that they are viable," says Gary Nordlinger, head of a consulting firm that caters to a Democratic clientele. "Most of them lose it right there."

Adds Calabrese, "You've got to say, 'I'm politically sophisticated and I'm not charging at windmills here.' You've got to be able to go in there and talk about streets and counties. You can buy yourself so many points if you're not naive."

'Just the Facts, Mister'

PAC managers also agree that political naiveté on the part of the candidates is a recurrent problem that damages their chances of establishing credibility. Too often, contenders cite broad partisan trends and offer shallow political complaints in lieu of a developed case for their candidacy.

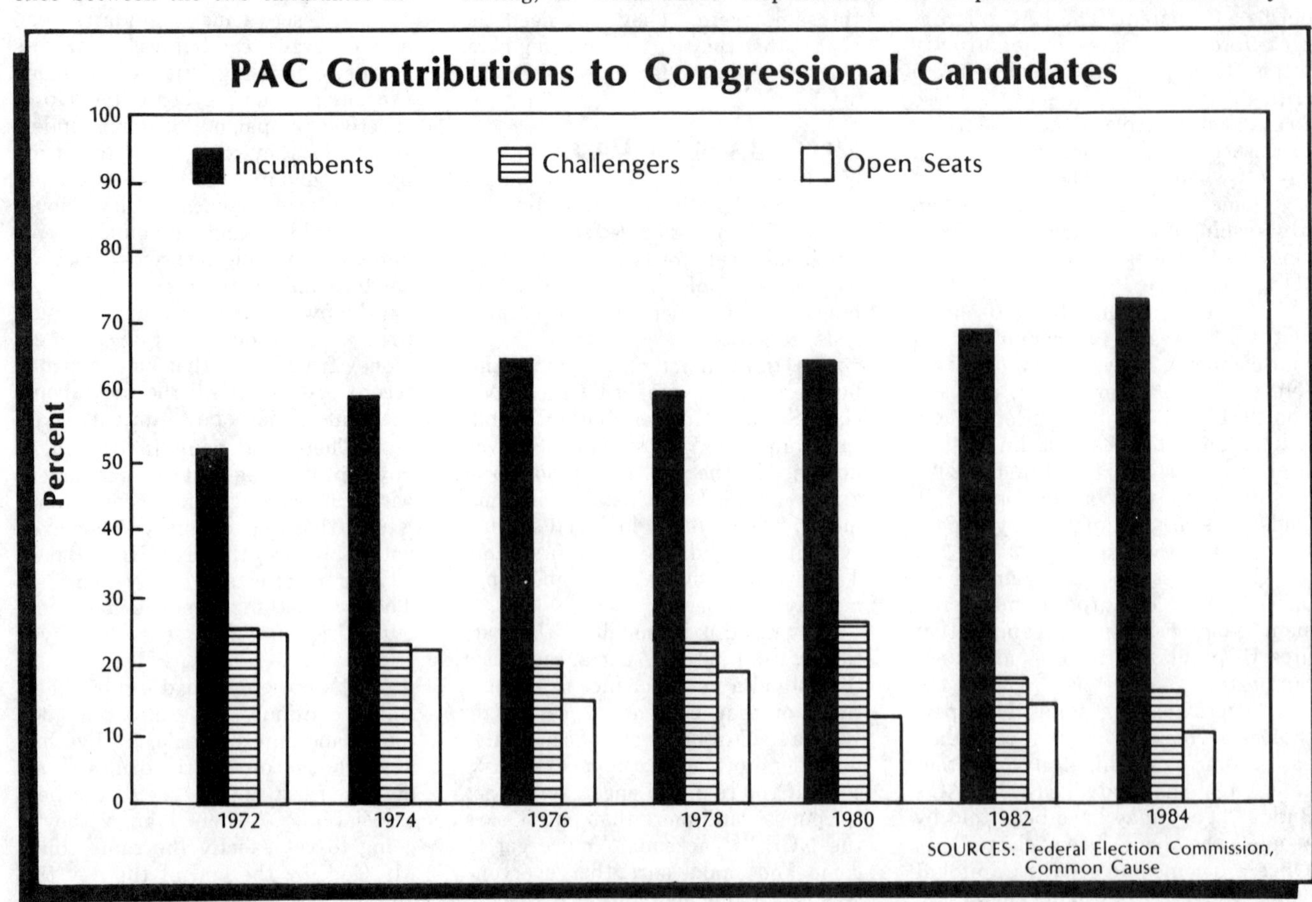

SOURCES: Federal Election Commission, Common Cause

"If you come in and say, 'I could beat Teddy Kennedy, because he has not voted the way the people of Massachusetts think,' ... I'm going to say I'm interested in seeing this happen, but how will it take place?" says the Chamber's Staton. "You're going to have to come up with some pretty concrete evidence to back up what you've got to say, or no one is going to pay much attention to your campaign."

"But if you come in with the right information ...," Staton continues, "about how you're going to win this race, how you're going to take the resources, what you're going to do in fund raising, what's your campaign plan.... If you spell out what you're going to do, then you're going to impress a lot of people."

PAC managers say a candidate can build credibility by presenting poll results, a realistic budget, an assessment of an opponent's vulnerabilities and names of prominent political and financial supporters back home.

Keep Cards and Letters Coming

A successful PAC pilgrimage seldom ends with a single visit. By supplying a steady barrage of updated poll results, press releases and newspaper clippings, a candidate can keep the PAC community abreast of his progress and reinforce PAC interest in the campaign. PAC fund raising has become, as one consultant put it, "almost a constant public relations job."

Michigan Republican Rep. Bill Schuette demonstrated his understanding of that law of PAC politics in his successful 1984 challenge to three-term Democrat Donald J. Albosta.

"The key thing is follow-up," Schuette reflects. "I would do a personal follow-up: letters, notes, newsletters and press clips to let them know that you have something ongoing. In that respect, it's no different than when you're going after votes. I would go back to individuals time and time again, saying, 'I need your support.' Sometimes, approaching the PAC community is a similar process."

GOP consultant Cooper also sees similarities between the campaign a candidate undertakes for PAC money and the one he wages for votes back home. "You've got to keep hitting the PACs with material that establishes an identity. Nobody thinks of [the need to establish] name identification in the PAC community. But there is such a thing as name ID in the PAC community. You've really got to get it."

"They are running to be 1/435th of one-half of one-third of the U.S. government. Yet somehow they think ... the coffers will open and millions will roll into their war chest."

—Consultant Gary Nordlinger

Great Expectations

Those who counsel candidates about PAC fund raising often urge them to temper their expectations about what their PAC pilgrimage will bring. Challengers and open-seat contenders who think a PAC visit pays big monetary dividends up front are in for a big shock.

"Candidates arrive here thinking that they're going to get $1 million just because they're wonderful and special and running," says Nordlinger, who advises Democratic campaigns. "They are running to be 1/435th of one-half of one-third of the U.S. government. Yet somehow they think that they're a man of destiny at the moment of destiny and that the coffers will open and millions will roll into their war chest.... There's kind of a rude awakening."

Some candidates apparently are unaware of the pro-incumbent bias most PACs maintain; others misunderstand the limits governing the legal amount a PAC can contribute. Under the Federal Election Campaign Act, PACs can give $5,000 to a candidate in any primary, runoff or general election.

Still others fail to make a distinction between the different kinds of aid offered a candidate by different kinds of political committees. Most corporate and labor PACs make financial contributions as well as so-called "in-kind" contributions — assistance of an organizational or technical nature.

For the ideological PACs, however, in-kind contributions usually are the rule. "We very rarely do any financial contributing," said Ellis of the conservative Free Congress PAC. "We might pay for a staff member on a candidate's staff to run the organization.... If they have a specific action, we might give cash for that. But the field man would make sure it goes for a specific project — manning phone banks, paying to install phones, that type of thing."

Jackson of the liberal NCEC buttresses that point. "NCEC doesn't just give cash," he says. "In fact, we'd rather not give money away. We do services better than we do money."

Heard It Through the Grapevine

If candidates often overestimate the amount of money they will receive from their Washington forays, they often underestimate how much their requests for money are influenced by communication within the PAC community. The conversation between one PAC director and another about a candidate may be crucial to that candidate's chances of receiving PAC support.

Pennsylvania Democrat Joe Hoeffel, seeking to avenge his 1984 loss to GOP Rep. Lawrence Coughlin, learned that the Washington PAC community acts as a network. "I was advised," Hoeffel says, "that the PACs in Washington are ... somewhat inbred. They talk to themselves."

By landing a PAC's endorsement, a candidate assures himself access to that PAC grapevine. Through regular meetings, "meet-and-greet" sessions with candidates and other informal contact, members of the Washington PAC community share their lists of contenders who are strong and incumbents who are in trouble.

"These lists are the key to all of this," says Jackson. "Nobody gives away without looking at somebody's list."

Some PAC directors urge candidates to use their endorsement as a way of courting other PAC support. "We ask you to carry [our endorsement] with you as entree," says Staton of the Chamber of Commerce. "Because if people have confidence in us as an organization and feel that we've done good work in analyzing your race, then you won't have to work as hard to convince them to ... help you."

Support for a candidate also can

spread through the PAC community via the national parties, which have become an increasingly vital link between PACs and campaigns. PAC managers of all stripes say both national party organizations generally provide good intelligence about challengers and open-seat candidates — as well as coaching contenders about how to win support from PACs.

The national parties' attitude toward a challenger often helps PAC managers decide whether or not to recommend committing support.

"You need to get the NRCC [National Republican Congressional Committee] to run around saying, 'This is a great race; this is a targeted race; we need this race,'" said Calabrese. "PACs don't say, 'OK, the NRCC has targeted this race, so we should support.' What they say is, 'That guy got the NRCC to target; therefore that guy convinced the NRCC of the same thing he convinced me of — that he's got his act together, that he's got a plan, that he's a viable contender."

Fund Raising in Reverse

Candidates who do not find themselves on PAC support lists should not abandon hope. An increasing number of contenders are taking advantage of a defensive strategy toward PACs.

Courting PACs that are unlikely to give to a challenger's campaign can prove profitable — if the challenger can convince the PAC to remain neutral or scale back support for the incumbent. Consultant Cooper calls this process "negative fund raising."

"In negative fund raising ... you don't expect a nickel from anybody you send a communication to," says Cooper. "You're just trying to shut the opposition down."

"What you have to do is go out and be the salesman for the other side," Cooper continues. "Point out that, really, the incumbent is not a good bet — based on issues, winnability or otherwise."

GOP Rep. Pat Swindall of Georgia, who won his suburban Atlanta House seat by ousting veteran Democrat Elliott H. Levitas in 1984, is quite familiar with negative fund raising.

"Much of my objective in coming to Washington," Swindall said of his 1984 PAC trips, "was not so much to raise money, but to minimize the contributions PACs gave to my opponent. If you can't get their PAC dollars, at least minimize their impact on your race."

"You'd certainly rather have the cash," echoed Missouri Republican Carrie Francke, who hoped to reverse the outcome of her unsuccessful 1984 challenge to Democratic Rep. Harold L. Volkmer. "But if you can make a presentation to a PAC and influence them so they think it's questionable who will win — and so stay out of it — you've benefited your campaign."

Democrats also play the negative fund-raising game. "You've still got to go around to the Republican-oriented PACs, if for no other reason than to neutralize them or to keep their contributions lower," said Nordlinger, whose firm advised Jontz' bid for the open 5th District in Indiana.

No Place Like Home?

While there is little argument that the Washington pilgrimage has become an institution in congressional campaigns, not everyone agrees that this is a positive development. A significant number of PAC directors feel that many candidates place too much emphasis on Washington — when they should be tending to PACs' local constituencies back home.

BIPAC's Budde is a prominent member of that camp. "I firmly believe that a good candidate with the right support from the local business community never has to leave the district in order to raise PAC money."

"They all have it backwards.... A good candidate with the right support from the local business community never has to leave the district to raise PAC money."

—Bernadette Budde, BIPAC vice president of education

She places special emphasis on local support. Budde says that BIPAC's decision to back a challenger is influenced heavily by the level of support that candidate enjoys among members of his district's corporate community. The trip to Washington, she says, takes a back seat.

"They all have it backwards," Budde says. "They think that they come to Washington first ... then they go back home and do all the rest of the stuff. But the real action is back home.... We're a lot more interested in how it plays in Peoria than how does it play in Washington."

Budde cites Connecticut's Rowland as one 1984 challenger who played the PAC game correctly. Following a rocky first trip to Washington in early spring of the election year, Rowland decided to steer clear of the PAC community and concentrate on cultivating elements closer to home.

"In essence ... I didn't go back down to Washington," says Rowland. "I just realized that all I needed was some good people. I didn't need a bunch of fancy consultants and fancy polls. What I needed to do was go to supermarkets and win votes."

Rowland's analysis may sound like wishful thinking to challengers facing the rigors of raising money against an entrenched incumbent. But his strategy of courting local business backing did help him attract BIPAC's attention.

Impressed with Rowland's support in the local business community, Budde says that BIPAC gave him a better-than-average campaign contribution in 1984 — even though she did not meet him until roughly a year after the election.

Not all of Budde's PAC colleagues share her militant attitude toward the Washington pilgrimage. But there is widespread agreement that by sowing seeds at home, candidates vastly enhance their chances of reaping benefits from Washington PACs.

"You always have to struggle to convince candidates that they must raise ... most of their money in their districts," said a political analyst working with a labor PAC. "They look at you like you're crazy. PACs are everything to them."

"I cannot envision a House race in which any of my clients — and they are all non-incumbents — is ever going to get more than 30 percent of his budget from PACs," said Cooper. "It would be folly for me to say, 'Focus on 30 percent and ignore the 70 percent.'" ∎

1986 Elections Generate GOP Power Struggle

Preoccupied by the ideological rift they expect will strike their party in 1988, many Republicans are missing a set of fractures that already are changing the GOP landscape. Crucial battles for the party's soul were fought in 1986 — in Republican congressional primaries across the country.

On one side of this clash are the traditional local Republican establishments. On the other is an increasingly organized and politically sophisticated network of conservative evangelical Christians.

Most national GOP leaders have eagerly encouraged evangelical Christians to get involved in politics. The reasons are obvious: They tend to side with Republican candidates, and they are a potentially huge voting bloc. Estimates of the number of born-again Christians in this country range from 40 million to 60 million.

At the national level, the GOP has gone out of its way to make these new voters feel at home. Republican officials estimate that as many as a fifth of the delegates to the 1988 national convention will be drawn from the conservative evangelical movement. Presidential candidates such as Vice President George Bush and Rep. Jack F. Kemp of New York have for months been dueling for Christian support.

But down at the grass roots level, within the precinct caucuses and county organizations that drive the party forward, the glances exchanged by party establishments and

Christian Right vs. Party Establishment

conservative Christians are looks not of affection, but of mutual mistrust.

That is because evangelicals are no longer content simply to vote. Spurred by a politically militant leadership that includes television evangelists, local ministers and national political organizers, they have begun moving from the ranks of mere voters into launching active campaigns for office or for positions of influence within party organizations.

As they do, some are meeting resistance. In some cases, establishment party leaders are more moderate politically than the evangelicals; in other instances, the GOP establishment is suspicious of evangelicals because it sees them as a group that values ideological purity more than Republican victory.

"What really is causing the problem," contends New Right architect Paul Weyrich, who has had a good deal to do with the political training and mobilization of the Christian Right, "is the fact that this elitist group that has controlled the Republican Party is now actually threatened in terms of control. [Evangelicals] in the long term are not going to keep the same kinds of leaders. The character of the party is going to change."

Weyrich and others maintain that the Christian Right forces are drawn from a different part of society than the "country club" Republicans they are targeting.

"The mainline Republican has elitist tendencies, and the religious impulse has a more populist constituency," says Christian Right activist Carl Horn, who lost a congressional primary in 1984 in North Carolina.

"In many cases there's a cultural, sociological, denominational and doctrinal gap between these people," adds Christian Right consultant Gary Jarmin. "Let's face it — your three-martini Episcopalians just don't have a lot in common with a teetotalling Baptist. They don't move and live and work in the same circles."

There are differences within the evangelical community as well, but they tend to be doctrinal rather than political. The evangelical label

takes in a wide range of Christians who believe the Bible is the infallible word of God but vary in their interpretations of it. Fundamentalists believe the Bible is literally true, and while they are not averse to cooperating with evangelicals in the political sphere, they tend to hold themselves apart in religious matters. 'Charismatics' can belong to any denomination, but they are brought together by a belief in God-given "gifts" such as speaking in tongues and faith-healing.

Battle Line: The Primaries

Although intraparty tensions between evangelicals and the establishment have been quietly at play since the mid-1970s, in 1986 they surfaced publicly in GOP primaries. In no modern election year have there been so many primaries in which the split between evangelicals and the GOP establishment has been a central — if often unspoken — issue.

House contests in Arizona, North and South Carolina, Tennessee, Indiana and Michigan, and Senate and gubernatorial primaries in states such as North Carolina, Oregon, Nebraska and Minnesota all pitted evangelical candidates (or conservatives with strong evangelical support) against mainstream Republicans with establishment ties.

The conflicts in some districts threatened to create tensions that could persist long after the nominee has been chosen. In Indiana's open 5th District, for example, state Sen. James Butcher, an evangelical Christian from Kokomo, bumped up against the local Republican hierarchy in his bid to replace veteran Republican Rep. Elwood Hillis.

His opponent in the contest for the GOP nomination was state Treasurer Julian Ridlen, a longtime party loyalist who had the support of district GOP Chairman Don Heckard and most of the 5th's county chairmen. That forced Butcher to build his organization by relying heavily on his connections within the district's large evangelical community.

Hard Feelings Ahead?

The party structure's willingness to choose sides in the contest annoyed Butcher. "Until now," he said, "I've never had a primary fight. I'm in a swing [Senate] district, and they've been perfectly happy that I've been able to hold onto it.... But now I'm running against one of the good ol' boys, and when the going gets tough, the good ol' boy — who is a moderate and whom they can pretty much control — gets their support."

"I'm running against one of the good ol' boys, and when the going gets tough, the good ol' boy — who is a moderate and whom [the party establishment] can pretty much control — gets their support."

—State Sen. James Butcher, R-Ind.

Because the Democratic nominee, state Sen. Jim Jontz, was widely considered a strong contender for the seat, mainstream Republicans worried about appealing to as broad an audience as possible in the general election. Butcher's evangelical background, with its emphasis on moral issues, made him seem too one-sided, they contended. "I think Julian's a much broader candidate," said Heckard.

Heckard and other Republican regulars also worried that Butcher might not work closely with the party if he won the office. "There is some concern that people from that group have a tendency not to work with organizational people," Heckard said. "I would think if Butcher should be elected to Congress, he probably wouldn't work through the organization much, and that just weakens the party structure."

Butcher had little time for that kind of talk. "I've been a Republican most of my life," he argued. "People know I've paid my dues to the party. I am not trying to skirt it."

But there is a chance that Heckard's concern may become a self-fulfilling prophecy. The experience of being shut out by party regulars in the primary has not made it easy for Butcher and his allies to consider patching over their differences with the establishment later on. "It would be a little difficult to be enthusiastic in future efforts if the party calls on me, after they've been trying to defeat me," Butcher said.

Family Feud

If hard feelings remain after the primary there, Indiana's 5th could begin to look something like Michigan's 4th District, a staunchly Republican constituency that is home to probably the longest-running feud between conservative evangelicals and a local party establishment. In 1981, voters there stunned the local party structure by giving the GOP House nomination — and hence the election — to Mark D. Siljander, an enthusiastically evangelical Christian who made moral issues a centerpiece of his campaign.

Siljander won in large part by mobilizing conservative evangelicals who had never been organized as an electoral force. Dwelling on what he called "moral-type issues" — abortion, sexual promiscuity, homosexuality, the "secular humanist" threat to the country's moral values — Siljander made himself the logical candidate for evangelicals who were concerned about those issues but had never found a candidate who stressed them.

Wooing pastors, speaking in their churches, relying on conservative Christian organizations to help put him in touch with local religious leaders and get out the word on his behalf, Siljander galvanized Christian voters.

Since then, he has retained their loyalty by serving as a steadfast spokesman for their concerns in the House. He also has broadened his agenda — working on foreign affairs and pushing a proposal to impose a single, flat income tax rate — and he has tried hard to expand his electoral base.

Unpardonable Sin

Even Siljander's detractors admit there is not much difference between his voting record and the votes that his predecessor, David A. Stockman, likely would have cast. But there is still a distance between Siljander and the old guard. Local business leaders, for example, complain that he has pursued his own agenda without paying much attention to their needs. "Businessmen feel that Mark Siljan-

Believing 'Fields Are Ripe,' Workers Respond

The flood of conservative Christians into the GOP and into political work in general is part of a striking shift in philosophy that began in the early 1970s and is still going on. For decades, many evangelicals and fundamentalists felt their emphasis ought to be on saving individual souls; politics, their ministers argued, was a worldly pursuit that good Christians should eschew.

By the early 1970s, however, that thinking was changing. Faced with the Supreme Court's *Roe v. Wade* abortion decision, the social turmoil of the 1960s, the growing visibility of the homosexual-rights movement and of pornography and drug abuse, some conservative evangelicals who had counseled separation from politics began to urge that Christians get involved. For those not stirred by the social trends, impetus was provided by a suggested change in Internal Revenue Service regulations that would have affected the tax-exempt status and admission policies of some church schools.

"We have moved many people across America from believing it's sinful to be involved to thinking it's sinful not to be involved."

—Curtis Maynard

To a multitude of conservative Christians, political involvement has begun to take on a biblical dimension. "More and more of us are beginning to realize that God doesn't just need workers in Heaven," says Paul French, an evangelical who is the GOP newsletter chairman in Michigan's 4th District. "If in fact God is the God of all, if He is the true Creator and if Jesus is His son, He doesn't need workers in Heaven. He needs workers right now. He says, 'The fields are ripe.' He said, 'Pray to the Lord of the harvest,' and He'd send workers. Well, we're workers. We're workers."

Sentiments like those, although rooted in individual moral concerns, are not springing up spontaneously. Beginning with the Rev. Jerry Falwell's Moral Majority, which was founded in 1979, a mini-industry of religious groups has arisen with the mission of convincing conservative Christians that political involvement is both a practical and a moral duty.

"It's biblical to be involved," says Curtis Maynard, chairman of the board of governors of the American Coalition for Traditional Values (ACTV), an umbrella group of religious right organizations. "We have moved many people across America from believing it's sinful to be involved to thinking it's sinful not to be involved."

Religious right leaders have advanced from simple exhortations urging their followers to register and vote to learning how to mobilize them. Groups like Christian Voice, ACTV and the Freedom Council all are working not only to convince Christians of the need for involvement, but to train them for it. Contacts in the late 1970s between religious leaders like Falwell and organizers of the burgeoning New Right have led to close working relationships in which New Right leaders with practical political organizing experience pass on their tactical skills to a cadre of interested Christians.

In California, state Sen. H. L. Richardson, one of the most prominent New Right politicians in the state, is trying to set up a network of lay church leaders that would aim to mobilize their congregations for election campaigns, letter-writing efforts aimed at legislators and other political purposes. He plans to call it the "Salt Network," after the biblical injunction that Christians should be "the salt of the earth." The religious right interprets that concept to mean that Christians have a responsibility to act as a "preservative" in society, protecting "traditional values."

The goal of all this activity is to give the troops mobilized by the Christian Right experience in the nuts and bolts of politics and a level of sophistication many of them have lacked.

Conservative evangelical leaders have learned through experience that enthusiastic discussion by their rank and file of such concepts as a "Christian America" and controversial statements that turn off mainstream voters can harm their cause.

In California's 27th District, for example, Republican candidate Rob Scribner in 1985 sent out a fund-raising letter telling area ministers, "I hope you will agree to link arms with us as we literally 'take territory' for our Lord Jesus Christ." Scribner, a lay minister in the Church of the Four-Square Gospel, angered not only Democratic incumbent Mel Levine, who is Jewish, but Republicans who felt the letter could be interpreted as anti-Semitic.

Christian Right leaders now urge members of their movement to be careful in what they say. "We've learned some lessons from the early days when Jerry Falwell and others helped get things going," says Michael Carrington, an aide to Richardson. "We got into trouble when we tried to too narrowly define morality to other people, because people turn you off then. We need to always go forward under the banner of traditional Judeo-Christian values — that's an unassailable commodity with the public. As opposed to 'Christian' things or morality issues. The enemy hits us terribly there."

"We need to always go forward under the banner of traditional Judeo-Christian values — that's an unassailable commodity with the public."

—Michael Carrington

Christian Right strategists say that developing better public relations skills is an important part of learning how to use the political system to push their agenda. "Takeover is fine," Christian activist Gary Jarmin comments, "but what good is it to take over [Republican] party county committees with a lot of people in charge who don't know what to do with it once they've got it?"

der ignores them," says one local corporate leader.

And the Republican hierarchy, concentrated in the Benton Harbor and St. Joseph business communities, feels even more neglected by Siljander and his allies. "They don't work within the party," laments Carol Stockman, David Stockman's mother and one of the leaders of the old-line establishment. "Even his staff does not really function within the party. They occasionally come to a meeting, but they're not workers." To people who have given their adult lives to working for the Republican Party, that is unforgivable.

The continuing tension between the two branches of the GOP has brought former Stockman aide Fred Upton into the 1986 primary against Siljander. Upton comes from the heart of the district's establishment. He is the grandson of one of the founders of the Whirlpool Corporation, which is headquartered in Benton Harbor and is the 4th's major employer. Upton's family is well known in the local business community and is consummately well connected to Republican Party insiders.

But all those connections may not be sufficient for Upton to topple Siljander, because the incumbent has built such a strong personal following that he does not need to pay attention to the party hierarchy to win. The hierarchy, as a result, may be in danger of becoming irrelevant.

"The moderate Republicans who are wringing their hands about Mark Siljander have done very little to organize themselves to win a primary, or to articulate their issues," says one moderate GOP politician in the district. "The old Stockman group doesn't have the horses anymore."

Unspoken, but Understood

Even in districts where the evangelical-establishment conflict is less openly talked about, it is central to the contest.

In North Carolina's 5th District, broadcast executive Stu Epperson is trying for a rematch against Democratic Rep. Stephen L. Neal, who prevailed by only 3,232 votes in 1984. Epperson, with a strong base in the evangelical community, ran an amicable primary campaign against his former finance chairman, Lyons Gray, who has close ties to Winston-Salem's business community. "The fact that I'm an evangelical Christian is just not an issue that's mentioned," says Epperson.

But then, it does not need to be; Epperson's 1984 campaign won him enough publicity that his base is well known in the district. A graduate of fundamentalist Bob Jones University and owner of several Christian-oriented radio stations, Epperson built a strong grass-roots organization in 1984 that capitalized on his enthusiastic support from evangelicals. In that election, Epperson had some support from the GOP hierarchy; this year, Gray was the favorite of most in the city Republican establishment.

In Tennessee's 3rd District, the GOP primary pits John Davis, who held Democratic Rep. Marilyn Lloyd to 52 percent in 1984, against Chattanooga lawyer Jim Golden, who has broad support among evangelicals.

Davis, a political consultant who returned to the district not long before the 1984 campaign and was generally seen as an outsider by the Chattanooga business establishment, is now its favorite. Golden, who has a track record of work within the local party, has several prominent mainstream Republicans on his side, but his base is mostly in the Christian community.

The division between the two candidates is understood in activist GOP circles, but it has not become widely publicized. That is partly because Golden, concerned about losing mainstream votes, has worked hard to prevent his evangelical background from becoming the center of campaign debate. When a newspaper reported that the Religious Roundtable listed Golden as a member of its board, Golden assured local GOP leaders he was not on the board. A Roundtable spokesman said Golden agreed to serve on the board, but changed his mind after the group's stationery was printed.

Divide and Be Conquered

In South Carolina's 4th District, there is an unusual byplay in the Republican primary involving three candidates who claim backing in the conservative Christian community. A fourth hopeful, Greenville Mayor William Workman, is running with strong support in the city's business and mainstream Republican circles. All want to replace GOP Rep. Carroll A. Campbell Jr., a candidate for governor.

Of the three who are vying for evangelical support, the strongest may be state Rep. Thomas M. Marchant, an Episcopalian who is a tennis partner of the Rev. Bob Jones III, the fervently fundamentalist head of Bob Jones University in Greenville. Though Jones' followers in the area have gone their separate ways in past elections, his backing is likely to give Marchant a strong boost in Greenville's fundamentalist Baptist community.

The other two who are competing for the evangelical vote — state Rep. Richard L. Rigdon and airline pilot

Ted Adams — both claim a following in the charismatic branch of the evangelical community. Not surprisingly, the split within conservative Christian ranks is expected to help Workman.

Reverse circumstances prevail in Arizona's 4th District GOP primary, where several candidates probably will split the vote of the business and party establishments, thereby benefiting evangelical candidate John B. Conlan. GOP Rep. Eldon Rudd is retiring from the 4th.

Conlan is trying to regain the congressional seat he gave up in 1976. He first won the 4th in 1972 and for four years used his position to preach a fervent brand of conservatism informed by his deeply held Christian beliefs. Conlan left the House for an unsuccessful Senate primary bid.

Tolerance Varies

As Epperson's case in North Carolina suggests, evangelicals in the South have rarely provoked the kind of hard feelings that their brethren have encountered in the North and Midwest.

In many parts of the South, the Republican Party is still in its childhood; party structures are less settled, and GOP leaders still think of themselves as electoral underdogs. Their tolerance for new sources of strength is high — especially when many of the party's new supporters are former Democrats, as are many of the Southern evangelicals and fundamentalists who are now voting Republican.

"When you're as much in a minority as we are, you welcome whatever help you can get," says Jack Hawke, an adviser to Republican Gov. James G. Martin of North Carolina, a leader in the moderate wing of North Carolina's GOP.

In the North and Midwest, however, conservative evangelicals' efforts to have a say in running the GOP have often been interpreted as threats. In large part, that is because local Republican Party structures in those regions have a far longer history than they do in the South. The people who have been active in the party for years have a proprietary attitude toward it.

Just north of Siljander's district, in Michigan's 9th District, for example, former GOP Chairman Field Reichardt went public in 1985 with his fears about evangelical organizing on his turf. The group that sparked his concern was the Freedom Council, a Virginia-based organization set up in 1981 by television evangelist and prospective GOP presidential candidate Pat Robertson.

An Agenda, or Just 'Concerns'?

The group, which has pilot political organizing projects in Michigan, North Carolina and Florida, describes itself as a "Christian, non-profit organization that was formed to help maintain the great gift of religious freedom which we have enjoyed in this land." It aims to get "moral citizens deeply involved in the political process"; its handsomely produced literature includes articles such as, "Do Christians Have a Responsibility to be Involved in Government?" and "The Struggle for America's Soul."

In Michigan, the Freedom Council has been recruiting Christians to run as precinct delegates in the state's 1986 primary. That work, Reichardt argues, is "a precinct delegate recruitment effort designed to advance the candidacy of Pat Robertson."

GOP precinct delegates elected this year will meet in early 1988 caucuses to begin the state's presidential delegate selection process. They also will become key players in the grassroots foundation of the party, a fact that leads Reichardt to worry about evangelicals' impact on the party.

"They have an agenda which they wish to impose on our party," he says. "It would of course mean that some of our Republican candidates and some of our existing Republican elected officials would not meet their agenda and eventually these people would wish to replace them."

Freedom Council activists respond that Reichardt's fears are groundless. "We just let Christians know if there is a concern that they may want to take issue with," says Jerry David, the Council's coordinator in Michigan's 4th and 5th districts. "We don't organize them — if they want to organize, they do. We're just fighting the feeling of apathy within the Christian community."

"Where high-profile [evangelical] participation hurts a candidate . . . we have to work under cover and accomplish our goals without putting baggage on the person we want to support."

—The Rev. Jerry Falwell

Right Turn for Minnesota GOP

Reichardt and others who are worried about growing evangelical involvement in party affairs look warily at Minnesota, where the evangelical right has taken over the Independent Republican organization in several congressional districts.

Riding on the back of Minnesota's strong anti-abortion movement, conservative Christians began in the early 1980s to become involved in GOP affairs. In 1984, they flooded precinct caucuses, putting their own representatives in official positions and driving the once-moderate party to the right.

The party platform has been stripped of its plank supporting the Equal Rights Amendment and now includes one calling for the teaching of the biblical account of creation in addition to the theory of evolution. At some precinct caucuses in 1984, Catholics reportedly were denied delegate positions because, doctrinally, they could not be "born again."

Many of Minnesota's GOP moderates complain they have been locked out. "You have to be white, male and an absolute born-again person to begin to have the tickets necessary to make your way through the structure," said one who asked not to be identified.

The Minnesota insurgency spread to neighboring Iowa, where evangelicals won voting control of the Republican Party convention in Polk County (Des Moines). Polk is the most populous and politically dominant county in the state.

That development guarantees a strong evangelical influence at the state GOP convention May 3, and a significant role in the 1988 Iowa presidential skirmishing now under way.

Social Stigma

For many moderates, the issue is the survival of the party. They argue that conservative evangelicals' overriding concern with social issues will drive away mainstream voters — especially young people who have been drawn to the GOP by its laissez-faire economic policies.

"The evangelicals' limited vision, it seems to me, will destroy the Republican Party, because it will narrow its focus so much," says Sally Howard, a former Republican member of the Minneapolis City Council.

Minnesota moderates point as an example to the 1984 congressional contests in the 1st and 6th districts, in which candidates with strong ties to the evangelical movement were nominated, then devastated by Democratic incumbents in November.

Conservative Christian leaders themselves admit that a candidate tagged with a Religious Right label can be at a disadvantage in an election, though they tend to see the media as the cause of any negative public response to them. "The media has done all it can to blemish religious conservatives, to tar them as persons who want to take over the government and create a theocracy," says the Rev. Jerry Falwell, one of the Christian Right's most visible leaders.

Observers of the Christian Right agree that its growing ties to the Republican Party can be a problem. "The trick for the Republicans," argues political scientist A. James Reichley of the Brookings Institution, "is to get the support of the evangelicals and the Religious Right without being identified with it."

Falwell argues that conservative Christians have developed the sophistication to deal with the problem. "Where high-profile participation hurts a candidate, we're foolish to do it," he says. "Where low-profile is best, we do it that way.... We have to work under cover and accomplish our goals without putting baggage on the person we want to support. We've learned to do that."

The Winning Edge?

In buttressing their claim that they help the GOP, evangelicals can cite some compelling success stories. In North Carolina and Texas, for example, Republicans' resounding victories in 1984 were significantly aided by the mobilization of conservative Christian voters.

In Texas, Christian activists got involved in numerous House campaigns, helping conservative Republicans capture four Democratic seats and two Republican-held open seats.

To highlight the records of Democratic incumbents, the evangelicals independently distributed voting "scorecards" issued by the Christian Voice organization. As "moral" issues, the cards listed opposition to the nuclear freeze and support for a balanced-budget amendment as well as opposition to abortion and homosexual rights and support for school prayer.

Evangelicals also worked — often quietly — in Republican campaigns. "They didn't come in and say, 'We're the Christians, the born-agains,'" comments Texas political consultant Denis Calabrese, who helped run several of the winning GOP efforts. "You just found out that five or six of your best volunteers were born-agains, sort of Christian foot-soldiers."

The evangelical effort "was responsible for 5 percent, maybe 10 percent maximum, in the voting totals," claims Abilene-born preacher Ray Allen, a former Christian Voice president who coordinated the effort. "By our directed, energetic efforts, we made that difference." Three of the four Democratic-held House seats went Republican by 6-point margins or less.

> ***"The evangelicals' limited vision . . . will destroy the Republican Party, because it will narrow its focus so much."***
>
> **—Sally Howard, former member, Minneapolis City Council**

In North Carolina, GOP Sen. Jesse Helms actively wooed evangelicals in his battle with former Democratic Gov. James B. Hunt, campaigning with Falwell and working closely with local ministers to turn out Christian voters. The conservative Christian vote helped not only Helms, but also gubernatorial candidate Martin.

However, North Carolina is not seeing that sort of evangelical-moderate alliance. In the GOP Senate primary, Helms' Congressional Club tried to get evangelicals to help conservative David Funderburk against Rep. James T. Broyhill, an establishment Republican prominent in the state party's moderate wing.

Third-Party Rumblings

Conservative evangelicals believe that efforts like those they made in Texas and North Carolina in 1984 have earned them the right to receive more attention from the GOP establishment. But some evangelicals are unsure they will ever get it.

"My prediction is, the Republican Party is going to blow it," says Jarmin. "Even some of the people that are opening the door are doing it with, 'Here, why don't you sit out in the parlor while the rest of us have dinner; if we want your opinion, we'll invite you in for a few minutes.'"

Anger at being kept at arm's length by the establishment has led Jarmin and some other Christian activists to begin talking about forming a third party.

"Even though I've worked pretty much for getting Republican candidates elected, it's not unqualified that I would back any Republican," says Bruce Townsend, pastor of the Conquering Faith Fellowship in Kalamazoo, Mich. "I've not sold out to the Republican Party. My loyalty would be toward a conservative evangelical ideology, rather than to the party."

But most evangelicals recognize that their movement lacks the political structure it would need to compete with the GOP. Even Jarmin admits most people think the Christian Right's future is within the GOP.

"There are some people who feel very strongly that we ought to organize our people and take over county committees and so on," he says. "There are others who feel it's more important to urge people to get involved but do it in a gradual, evolutionary process — pardon the expression — working our way up the ladder and moving into positions of leadership."

Seeing the process through, evangelical leaders hope, will eventually lead to wide-scale acceptance both within the party and beyond its bounds. "I remember when the black church in the '50s was the base of support for black political activists; churches were blown up because of it," says Falwell, who in the 1950s and 1960s spoke out forcefully against churches' involvement in politics. "But nobody thinks anything of it these days. My guess is in 10 years, the conservative religious movement will be just as accepted a part of the political fabric of this country as the black church activists." ■

Jackson, Democrats: Marriage on the Rocks?

Though the Rev. Jesse Jackson and the Democratic Party may not be a political match made in heaven, they did not seem headed for divorce. Yet a split is a growing possibility as Jackson steps up efforts to unify the Democratic left while most of the party leadership edges toward the political center.

Under the banner of his Rainbow Coalition, Jackson is trying to draw together a disparate array of "have nots" — elements of the Hispanic, farm, labor, anti-nuclear and environmental communities as well as the black constituency that was the base of his 1984 campaign for the Democratic presidential nomination. It is an effort that will test Jackson's political ability as well as the forbearance of the Democratic Party.

Jackson says his Rainbow Coalition is composed of "enlightened Democrats" rather than "anti-Democrats." But at the Coalition's national organizing convention, held during the week of April 17-19, 1986, in Washington, D.C., there was enough angry rhetoric to indicate that while the Coalition has one foot inside the party, the other is outside.

Coalition leaders say they may endorse independent candidates in races where Democratic nominees are unacceptable. "We will not sit idly by," declares Jackson, "and watch the party shift to the right of center."

A confrontation in 1986 between Jackson and Democratic leaders may come in Vermont; the state's Rainbow Coalition indicated its support for the independent gubernatorial bid of Burlington Mayor Bernard Sanders against Democratic Gov. Madeleine M. Kunin.

Whether or not Jackson and the Coalition's national board of directors decided to veto an endorsement of Sanders, it was unlikely to do so merely out of loyalty to the Democratic Party. "We will select candidates on their merits," says Ronald Walters, a Howard University political scientist and leading Jackson adviser.

Gripes Aplenty

Loyalty to the Democratic Party does not appear to be a major concern of the Coalition. Its leadership consists of single-issue devotees and political novices — many of them clergy, academics and community activists attracted to politics by Jackson — as well as veteran black Democratic politicians. While many of those black leaders hold elective office and party positions, they feel they are ill-treated by the white Democratic leadership.

Speaker after speaker at the Rainbow convention criticized either the direction or the openness of the Democratic Party. U.S. Rep. John Conyers Jr. of Michigan complained that minorities and liberal allies in the Coalition are the faithful core of the party but are made to ride "in the back of the bus." Washington Mayor Marion Barry described the Coalition as "the locked out and the shut out."

Jackson has his own gripes with the party, focused mainly on its presidential nominating process. He complains that party rules were unfair in 1984 because they did not distribute delegates to candidates in strict proportion to the number of votes each candidate received. Jackson received 18 percent of the vote in the 1984 Democratic primaries but won only 12 percent of the delegates. For 1988, the Democratic National Committee approved limited rules changes, rebuffing Jackson's calls for an overhaul. *(Rules, 1986 CQ Weekly Report p. 627)*

Some in the Rainbow Coalition are encouraging Jackson to run for president as an independent in 1988. A number of delegates to the Rainbow convention wore yellow-and-black buttons that read, "Run Jesse Run: Independent in '88." While such a candidacy would have virtually no hope of victory, it almost surely would draw enough black Democratic votes to undercut the chances of the Democratic nominee in the 1988 election.

But it is much more likely Jackson will remain in the Democratic Party — at least through spring 1988. The early Southern "mega-primary" shaping up on "Super Tuesday" (March 8, 1988) seems to offer the promise of a strong Jackson showing.

In 1984, only three Southern states — Alabama, Florida and

"We will not sit idly by and watch the party shift to the right of center."

—The Rev. Jesse Jackson

Georgia — held primaries on "Super Tuesday." Close to a dozen could vote on that early date in 1988, presenting such a large prize of delegates that few in the Democratic field of candidates would drop out beforehand.

As a result, Jackson might be competing against six or seven white candidates across the South in 1988, compared with the three others that were in the field on "Super Tuesday" in March 1984. With a large black vote in virtually every Southern state, Jackson could win several Dixie primaries without having to increase markedly his share of the vote from 1984.

Jackson has skirted discussion about his 1988 presidential plans, saying that early 1987 would be soon enough to discuss them. But there is reason to believe he could be a more formidable contender in 1988 than he was in 1984. When he launched that bid in November 1983, he was an unproven fund-raiser with an untested organization, and much of the black political leadership already was signed up with former Vice President Walter F. Mondale. In 1988, Jackson would have a long list of supporters, access to money and a larger proportion of the black leadership behind him.

Blending in Farmers

A key for Jackson is to expand his constituency beyond the black community. According to a *New York Times* study of the 1984 Democratic primary results, Jackson won the support of more than three out of every four blacks who voted, but only one out of every 20 whites.

The recent Rainbow convention also was heavily black. Coalition leaders boasted that 771 delegates from 43 states attended. But roughly half were from the states of the industrial Northeast and California. There was a large bloc of delegates from Missouri but only a handful from other Farm Belt states.

Jackson, though, has worked hard to expand his coalition of "have nots." Before the convention, he appeared in Austin, Minn., offering to mediate the bitter dispute between Geo. A. Hormel & Co. and the striking local chapter of United Food and Commercial Workers International Union. He also addressed a Chillicothe, Mo., rally of farmers protesting foreclosure policies.

Farmers and agricultural issues drew center stage at the Rainbow convention. A well-publicized "Solidarity With Family Farmers" breakfast drew several busloads of Midwestern farmers. "The farm question is a social justice thing. We're a part of this team," said Merle Hansen, president of the North American Farm Alliance and a Jackson farm adviser.

But it is not a natural alliance. At one point during the convention, Jackson implored delegates to intermingle. "I have to ask black males to make room for women," he said, "and urban aggressive types to make room for farmers."

Organizing and Electing

The focus of the Rainbow Coalition in 1986 was on grass-roots organization, establishing chapters at the state and congressional district level and enlisting voters who will pay the $25 annual dues.

The Coalition also planned to be involved in voter registration, in efforts to enforce the Voting Rights Act and in promoting candidates for office.

Coalition officials expressed an early interest in about 30 congressional contests. Nearly two-thirds of those involved black incumbents, the vast majority of them solidly entrenched. The Coalition's influence may be more decisive in the other dozen or so districts, where typically there is a large minority population but no black incumbent on the ballot.

Coalition leaders identified at least a half dozen black congressional candidates who were of interest to the Coalition in their Democratic primaries: Sam Taylor, a farmer running in the open Alabama 7th District; former U.S. Rep. Katie Hall, in the Democratic-held Indiana 1st; Faye Williams, a former staff member of the House District of Columbia Committee, in the open Louisiana 8th; veteran black activist Mel King in the open Massachusetts 8th; former state Assistant Attorney General Mike Espy in the Republican-held Mississippi 2nd; and state Sen. Robert C. Scott in the GOP-held Virginia 1st.

There also were black challengers to veteran white Democratic incumbents in the New Jersey 10th (Peter W. Rodino Jr.) and the Ohio 3rd (Tony P. Hall). In each case, the Coalition had to mull a range of options — endorsing the incumbent, backing a challenger or not getting involved.

The Coalition also was interested in the outcome in two open, predominantly black districts — Georgia's 5th and Maryland's 7th. But it is likely to stay neutral in each because a number of Coalition backers are competing for the Democratic nominations. The Coalition also is watching developments in another black-majority district, the late Joseph P. Addabbo's New York 6th.

Long Struggle Ahead

Jackson sees the Coalition's base as the five dozen or so congressional districts he claims to have won in 1984. They are a collection of urban minority districts in the industrial Frost Belt and California and heavily black districts in the South.

Robert Farrell, Los Angeles councilman and president of the National Black Coalition of Local Elected Officials, added that the Coalition's initial victories probably will occur in the cities — for offices such as mayor, city council and city attorney. Not only are a high proportion of black elected officials already in cities, but Jackson carried a number of urban centers in 1984 — including Philadelphia, Baltimore, Washington, D.C., Hartford, Conn., and Fulton County (Atlanta), Ga.

It might take quite a while to gauge whether the Rainbow Coalition is a success or a failure. Jackson seems aware of the difficulties ahead; though he talks of his "have not" Coalition comprising a new majority in American politics, he also warns members not to expect a lot of early successes.

"We have been a movement trying to become an organization," he says. "We're in formation. We don't even know each other and we must. Once we get to know each other, this will be a powerful movement." ■

New Generation Poised to Tip Voting Scales

Is GOP Era Dawning? Democrats Say 'No'

In the fall of 1985, when University of Michigan Professor Greg Markus asked his undergraduate political science class how many of them had voted for President Reagan in the 1984 election, more than two-thirds of the students in the class raised their hands.

But when Markus asked the same class several weeks later who they would prefer for president in 1988 if the choice was between Vice President George Bush and Democratic Sen. Gary Hart of Colorado, about twice as many students preferred Hart.

Markus' informal findings underscore two features of the youth vote nationally — its Republican proclivity in 1984, but also its potential volatility for 1986 and beyond.

Youth support for Reagan was one of the biggest stories of the 1984 campaign, in part because it was largely unexpected until late in the election cycle. Although young voters never had been as faithful a part of the Democratic coalition as had black, Hispanic and Jewish voters, they consistently had given the Democratic ticket a higher percentage of their vote than the rest of the electorate in every presidential election from 1952 through 1980.

That pattern was broken last year. The nation's youngest voters (18- to 24-year-olds) supported the oldest president in American history by a 3-to-2 margin that matched Reagan's showing nationally. *(Youth vote, 1984 CQ Weekly Report p. 2696)*

Democratic Party leaders were shocked by Reagan's sweep of the youth vote, and they have been busy trying to understand why it happened. The House Democratic Caucus on Oct. 17, 1985, launched a series of campus outreach sessions — dubbed "Forums for the Future" — aimed at sounding out students' complaints and erasing the negative image of the party left over from Walter F. Mondale's decisive 1984 loss.

"We want to at least let the college-aged Americans know that there are younger people in the Democratic Party who believe the party has a future and [who] would like to get them involved in ... developing that future," says Illinois Democratic Rep. Richard J. Durbin, chief architect of the program. "We are trying to figure out ... what went wrong."

That mission puts the Democrats in direct competition with the Republicans, who are plumbing ways to sustain the success they enjoyed among students in the 1984 election. As the parties seek a better understanding of the values of the current college generation, they are finding that today's students differ dramatically from those who were on campus even as recently as a decade ago.

Rebelling Against Uncertainty

The rightward turn in many students' attitudes stems partly from the fact that youth today are reacting against the unsettled conditions that prevailed when they were growing up.

"The students of the '60s were reacting to the values of the 1950s," argues Kent Moors, an assistant professor of political science at Duquesne University in Pittsburgh, site of one of the Democrats' forums. "The current students like the image of the nice smiling authority figure. It appeals to them because of the instability of their own families. Maybe we got too loose in the '60s and '70s and it frightened them."

Republican Rep. Joe L. Barton of Texas voices a similar sentiment. "In the '60s and '70s, we tried to love everybody to death and we tried to give everybody all the money," says Bar-

Non-Student Youth: Quiet Majority

Perhaps no element of the youth vote is more quiet and more overlooked than its largest segment, the non-students. According to the Census Bureau, nearly three-fourths of the nation's 28 million 18- to 24-year-olds do not attend college.

A major reason the voting behavior of young non-students receives little attention is that they are not a concentrated voting bloc. Most young students are congregated on college campuses, where they are easily accessible to vote-seeking politicians and can have a large impact on specific state and local races if they are registered to vote in their college towns. In contrast, non-student youth are dispersed through the community at large. Many live with their parents or are married and have set up households.

The turnout proclivity of non-students also limits their influence. Barely one-third of all non-student youth reported to the Census Bureau that they voted in 1984, while the reported turnout rate for 18- to 24-year-old college students was 54 percent.

Non-student youth have more in common with their families and their colleagues in the work force than with college students their age. This affinity has meant that non-students, like the majority of the electorate, have been more likely to vote Republican than students have. According to pollster Daniel Yankelovich, 1972 Democratic presidential nominee George McGovern won 57 percent of the student vote, but non-student youth split evenly between McGovern and President Nixon. That same pattern was evident in 1984, according to *The New York Times*-CBS News Election Day exit poll: 56 percent of full-time students aged 18 to 24 voted for Reagan, compared with 62 percent of other voters in that age group.

ton, whose 1984 House election owed much to help from students at Texas A&M University, the only large university in his 6th District. "It didn't work. What you see now among students is a going-back the other way."

Another determinant of students' political values is the economic climate in which they grew up. The students of the '60s came of age in an era of relatively few economic worries. Confident that employment was available to virtually anyone with a college degree, many students of that era spent little time fretting about their future economic security.

That is no longer the case. The recessionary environment of the '70s and early '80s and a glut of college-educated job-seekers intensified competition for employment. As a result, many of today's students adopted the mind-set that personal economic security should be their first priority.

Polling data highlight this contrast. In 1970, 39 percent of college freshmen viewed "being well-off financially" as an important goal, according to an annual survey of U.S. college freshmen conducted by Alexander Astin at UCLA. In 1984, 71 percent of freshmen felt that way.

Concern over their economic security has led many students to take a more pragmatic, vocational approach to their education and to conform their attitudes so as not to jeopardize their ability to get a job.

"In Michigan, we have come through a rough recession," says Beth Zinman, an undergraduate adviser in the political science department at Michigan State University (MSU). "We're seeing the product of that now. These kids were in their formative stage in high school when that was going on. . . . It has made them much more conservative politically, much less willing to take risks."

Joseph J. Serwach, a junior at MSU, feels that his classmates' preoccupation with their future economic well-being eclipses their interest in other, more global issues.

"If you want to talk about a real issue that comes up among your typical Joe Students, it's 'How high is tuition going to be?' and 'Am I going to get a job when I graduate?'" says Serwach, editor in chief of the *State News*, MSU's daily campus newspaper. "There aren't many students who really are just dying over a cause."

Todd Shelton, president of the University Democrats at the University of Virginia, agrees. "In the '60s it was easy to be idealistic and for social change and all these things. I think students today are scared to death about their futures."

Vietnam Is History, Iran Is Real

The economic realm is not the only one in which student attitudes have been changing in recent years. To a great extent, the assumptions that today's students make about foreign policy differ significantly from those made by students a decade ago.

The Vietnam War helped shape the world view of the generation that came of age in the '60s and early '70s. The prudence of U.S. involvement in Southeast Asia was the primary topic of debate on many campuses; the prospect of being drafted into the military gave many students a personal stake in the controversy.

"There wasn't a decision made by a male on college campuses in the '60s that wasn't colored to some extent by Vietnam," says Durbin, who was attending Georgetown University during the late '60s.

But on campus today, the Vietnam War has lost its status as the seminal foreign policy event; in the minds of many students, it has been eclipsed by the Iranian hostage crisis and other acts of anti-American terrorism that have been played and replayed on the nightly news.

"I had one conversation about foreign policy with a student," Durbin noted upon returning from a trip to the University of Wisconsin, "in which

I found myself referring frequently to the Vietnam War.... The student said to me, 'I'm aware of Vietnam, I've read about it. But the most important foreign policy event of my generation is the hostage crisis in Iran.' Can you imagine the different conclusions you would draw if the hostage crisis was more influential to you than Vietnam? That was good for me to hear."

The hostage crisis is a searing memory for Mary Beth Neitznick, a political science major at Duquesne. "I was devastated by the way the Iranian students saw America, tearing down the American flag and stomping on it and spitting on it," says Neitznick, founder of a new conservative newspaper at Duquesne.

Like many students active in the conservative movement on campus, Neitznick finds that her political and religious views are intertwined. President of the Student Christian Fellowship at Duquesne, she feels that her religious beliefs compel her to take a strong anti-communist stance, and she disdains those who argue that Christian doctrine can be used only in service of liberal social action goals. "Jesus was not a Sandinista.... Christ died for the rich as well as the poor."

Carter's Party Gets Blamed

For many of those currently on campus, attitudes on economic and foreign policy have been relatively easy to translate into partisan terms. Coming of age during Jimmy Carter's presidency, many of them found the Democratic Party wanting for leadership on both the domestic and foreign policy fronts.

"I do think that Jimmy Carter had a lot to do with the conservative trend among students," says James Maines Jr., an economics major at Texas A&M who has worked in several Texas GOP congressional campaigns. "We were laughing at him. To use harsh terms, he seemed like a bumbling fool.

"There's not really a recollection of Ford's policy, Nixon's policy," Maines says. "What Carter was and what Reagan has been is a lot of what people use as a measuring stick."

To many young voters, Reagan stands for optimism, national strength and economic growth, while Carter led the party of pessimism and malaise.

The 1984 presidential contest did not help Democrats change that paradigm. In the minds of many students, Mondale was an extension of a Carter presidency they regard as a failure.

"Many students were embarrassed to say they were Mondale supporters," says Jim Lofgren, director of the University of California Student Lobby. "It used to be if you were a student Republican, you were a closet Republican. But that changed in 1984."

Is Politics Dead?

While some believe that the strong anti-Democratic bias on many campuses is the crucial influence on student political attitudes, others argue that it is a *lack* of politics on campus that most shapes the attitudes of the current college generation.

Seymour Martin Lipset, professor of political science at Stanford University, contends that students today are not exposed to the kind of active political environment experienced by the students of the '60s. Thus, he says, today's students retain the relatively conservative views that they grew up with in their middle- to upper-middle-class homes.

Most students of the '60s grew up in the same type of conservative environment, Lipset says, but when they attended college, there were forces at work that challenged their views. "Once they arrived on campus, they were exposed to different values, to political discussion," Lipset says. Such discussion was responsible for altering many students' political opinions.

"Today, the dormitories don't talk politics like they used to. If you come with certain views, they're not challenged as much ... and they're not as likely to change.

"It's not so much what kind of politics, but how *much* politics there is on campus that makes the difference. Today, there's less politics on campus than, say, in the late '60s. People don't see politics as having as much impact," Lipset says.

Republican activists would dispute Lipset's claim that politics on campus is moribund. Part of the reason today's students have taken a rightward turn is that the GOP aggressively has courted the student vote in recent years, while Democrats basically have neglected it.

In 1984, Republicans mounted an extensive drive for support on college campuses. By Election Day, they claimed to have registered nearly 300,000 new student voters and to have distributed thousands of absentee ballots to students registered to vote back in their hometowns. "We had an outstanding product and we had a good market strategy," says David Miner, chairman of the College Republican National Committee.

Possibly the most significant aspect of GOP strategy was the molding of student opinion through the cultivation of campus leaders. In a report analyzing student voting behavior in 1972 — the first election after the voting age was lowered to 18 — the California Student Lobby emphasized the importance of a "numerous and attitudinally dominant peer group" in affecting the votes of other students.

Prior to a Democratic outreach forum with students, Rep. Steny H. Hoyer of Maryland and Rep. Martin Olav Sabo of Minnesota tour with Rep. Bob Carr at Michigan State University, which is in Carr's 6th District.

Divided Academia: No Republican Monolith

Although droves of college students abandoned the Democratic Party and voted for President Reagan in 1984, the rightward shift was not monolithic. While Reagan was a big winner at many of the large state universities and at private colleges with religious connections or military tradition, Democratic nominee Walter F. Mondale swept the student vote at colleges with a history of liberal politics — namely, elite private colleges, predominantly black colleges and a handful of large state universities like the University of California at Berkeley. An election-eve survey by the University of California Student Lobby found that 76 percent of Berkeley students preferred Mondale.

The percentages for the colleges featured below are based on actual 1984 vote totals. In most cases, results from only on-campus precincts are used, since by definition they are comprised entirely of student voters. But in cases where no precincts neatly cover the campus student community or where there are large, identifiable concentrations of students off campus, other precincts are included. Results from community colleges are not included in the sample because many students attending those schools are commuters rather than residents at an identifiable campus community.

Percentages in the chart are based on the major-party vote for Reagan and Mondale in 1984; no third-party or write-in votes are included. The winner's percentage is highlighted in boldface type.

	Reagan	Mondale
"Elite" Private Colleges		
Amherst College (Amherst, Mass.)	25%	**75%**
Colby College (Waterville, Maine)	46	**54**
Oberlin College (Oberlin, Ohio)	17	**83**
University of Pennsylvania (Philadelphia)	34	**66**
Vanderbilt University (Nashville, Tenn.)	41	**59**
Predominantly Black Universities		
Florida A&M University (Tallahassee)	3	**97**
Tennessee State University (Nashville)	4	**96**
"Liberal" State Universities		
University of Iowa (Iowa City)	**50**	50
University of Michigan (Ann Arbor)	38	**62**
University of Oregon (Eugene)	34	**66**
University of Wisconsin (Madison)	38	**62**

	Reagan	Mondale
Other State Universities		
University of Florida (Gainesville)	**59**	41
University of Nebraska (Lincoln)	**72**	28
Oregon State University (Corvallis)	**59**	41
Pennsylvania State University (University Park)	**64**	36
University of Tennessee (Knoxville)	**70**	30
Private Colleges With Religious Connection		
Baylor University (Southern Baptist) (Waco, Texas)	**89**	11
Brigham Young University (Mormon) (Provo, Utah)	**95**	5
Notre Dame University (Roman Catholic) (South Bend, Ind.)	**59**	41
Oral Roberts University (Evangelical) (Tulsa, Okla.)	**92**	8
Colleges With Military Tradition		
Air Force Academy (Colorado Springs, Colo.)	**85**	15
Texas A&M University (College Station)	**92**	8

For years, the dominant peer group at many colleges was liberal and Democratic.

But that has not been the case in recent years. "Conservative politicians are more acceptable on campus than they were," observes Duke University political scientist David Price. "They are seen as a live and respectable option."

In part, that is because Democrats have offered little competition. "Republicans in recent years have done a more extensive job than we have," says Price, a former executive director of the North Carolina Democratic Party. "They have more money and they have put organizers on campus. What we have done on the Democratic side was more informal and inexpensive."

Price's comments were echoed by a young Mississippi Democrat named Ron Krotoszynski in testimony before the Democratic National Committee's rules review panel earlier this year. He outlined the GOP's effort to recruit student leaders with "page positions, internships, trips to Washington and paid trips to Dallas" for the 1984 national convention.

"The whole thing," Krotoszynski said, "takes on a fun, communal effort-type atmosphere that is encouraged by Republican operatives. The need to fit in, the need to belong, is a powerful weapon, and one which is particularly effective when the Republicans are the only game in town."

Looking for Vision and a Leader

In its effort to reach out to students, the Democratic Party is plagued by some of the same image problems that have hurt it among other segments of the electorate. To many young people, the party seems to be an amalgam of special-interest groups that lacks a charismatic leader and is bereft of an overall vision for governing the country.

"I don't think the Democratic Party has any kind of unified vision of the world," says Maines. "They seem to be lost in trying to get re-elected. They're seeing if they can get the women's vote, and, 'OK, we've got that, then let's get the black vote, then the gay vote.' The party is wooing groups too much. People can see that."

Even some young Democrats acknowledge that their party has had difficulty communicating the core principles it represents.

"The problem is we don't let people know where we stand," says Kate Spears, an MSU senior who serves as secretary of the Ingham County (Lansing) Democratic Party. "The Republicans are saying Democrats were the New Deal, were this, were that. Democrats haven't stood up and said that's not true."

When the Democrats do communicate their policies, students say, their views often appear worn and outdated. In the minds of many young people, the GOP has better positioned itself as the party of the future.

"I think they're grasping onto the old ways that may have worked at one time," says Jennifer Bennett, head of the MSU chapter of the College Republicans. "But we're in a new century, a new era, and we have new ideas about things.... Sometimes you've got to let go of that old comfortable blanket and try something new."

'Dusty Relics' Don't Sell

Judging from its efforts to reach out to college students, that is a lesson Democrats are still learning.

After sifting through the responses from some 20 campus forums conducted by numerous House Democrats across the country, Durbin concluded that what students dislike most about Democrats is their tendency to play up past successes.

"The one overall criticism we got [from students] is that the Democratic Party is not specific in terms of our agenda for the future," Durbin says. "I agree with them.... It is clear to me that students are interested in the contests of today — instead of standing in front of the Democratic trophy case of the past."

During the forums, that "trophy case" tendency was most evident in the frequent fond recollections of former President John F. Kennedy voiced by House Democrats. Many of them were inspired to get involved in politics during Kennedy's presidency.

As Democratic Rep. Steny H. Hoyer of Maryland told students at the forum at MSU, "I was a sophomore at the University of Maryland when John Kennedy was running for president. He came to a campus forum and spoke about the need to get young people involved in politics. He said their energy and enthusiasm could make a difference. Because of that, I began thinking about politics and switched my major from public relations to pre-law."

But if Kennedy holds a special place for people of Hoyer's generation, his name is more like a dusty relic to many students today.

"At Georgetown, I think four of the six speakers mentioned JFK," Durbin said, recalling a forum held at Georgetown University that kicked off the campus outreach program. "I thought about this afterward. But for a handful of people, there wasn't a single student now on campus even alive at the time of Kennedy's assassination. That reminded me that we can't dwell on the past."

Virginia's Shelton concurs with Durbin. "There's nobody in college even born then [at the time of Kennedy's death], much less anybody who remembers it happening," he says. References to Kennedy are thus of limited use in making political appeals to youth, Shelton thinks.

Barking Up Some Wrong Trees

Some Democrats who participated in the outreach program found favor among students by playing up the party's positions on such topics as arms control, waste and fraud in the defense budget, federal funding for education and South Africa's apartheid policy.

But other Democrats clearly had trouble finding engaging themes. At the Duquesne forum, New York Rep. Stan Lundine sought to rally students behind his party by reminding them, "It's no accident that the Democratic Party passed mortgage insurance." His observation drew only a limited audience response.

At another point, Rep. Doug Walgren, the local congressman, tried to appeal to students by casting the Democrats as the party of the "downwardly mobile."

"We're going to do very well among young urban types because statistics show that for every young person who's upwardly mobile, there's two who are downwardly mobile," Walgren said. "Any party that exhibits a sympathy for the downwardly mobile will come out with the majority because the majority are downwardly mobile."

Walgren also tried another unorthodox pitch: He urged the young crowd to support the Democrats because the party lacks a firm identity — just as college students often do.

"One of the great virtues of the Democratic Party is that it is in fact undefinable," Walgren said. "We're like the 90-year-old fellow who said, 'I'm alive today, and considering the alternative, that's pretty damned good.' "

Democrats Still Have a Foothold

Despite the problems that Democrats are having in courting students, any impression that the student vote today is monolithically Republican is just as inaccurate as the impression that the student vote of the '60s and '70s was monolithically Democratic.

It is easy to get a one-sided picture of student political attitudes because so much attention focuses on the most vocal campus elements. Today, conservatives are the most vocal political group on many campuses; the liberals, while still a sizable contingent, are searching for a voice. "In the student protest days of the 1960s, it worked in the other direction," says Florida State University political scientist Paul Beck.

Beck says that liberal Democratic sympathizers on campus today are engulfed in a "spiral of silence" that causes their minority status to be exaggerated by many observers.

While Reagan's 1984 margin over Mondale among young voters was sizable, the Democratic nominee did run well in some segments of the student vote. There was a particularly striking disparity between the preference of younger and older students.

A *New York Times*-CBS News Election Day exit poll that found Reagan drawing 56 percent of the vote from full-time students age 18 to 24 found Mondale the favorite of 63 percent of full-time students age 25 to 29. Older students tend to have political memories that extend back to the Vietnam War and Watergate, a point of reference that younger, Republican-leaning students lack.

This dramatic split in the student vote was borne out by 1984 precinct returns. In college after college, Reagan ran better in on-campus precincts filled with undergraduate dormitories and fraternity houses than he did in off-campus precincts where married students or faculty are dominant.

Typical was the vote from the University of Wisconsin in Madison. The largest undergraduate student precinct gave nearly 60 percent of its vote to Reagan. But in two other precincts dominated by members of the academic community — one by older students, the other by faculty members — Mondale won by margins of more than 2-to-1.

In addition to the split between younger and older students, the 1984 returns also showed that certain types of colleges remain loyally Democratic despite the general upswing in GOP support. Mondale usually fared well at colleges with a legacy of student activism — such as the prestigious Eastern private schools and certain large state universities. He also ran strongly among students at black colleges. Public schools with little history of student activism generally went for Reagan, as did religious- and military-affiliated institutions. *(Divided academia, p. 30)*

Shunning the Straight Slate

Another encouraging fact for the Democrats is that even in college communities where Reagan ran well, Republicans had trouble transferring his popularity to GOP ticket mates. In a number of places across the country, the students split their ballots — voting Republican for president, but Democratic for the Senate or House.

For example, three student precincts that Reagan carried at the University of Colorado also voted overwhelmingly for Democratic Rep. Timothy E. Wirth. And two student-dominated precincts won by Reagan at the University of Iowa also voted decisively for Democratic Senate challenger Tom Harkin over GOP incumbent Roger W. Jepsen. The only on-campus precinct at the University of Tennessee voted for Democratic Senate candidate Albert Gore Jr. after handing Reagan a majority of more than 2-to-1. And five on-campus precincts at Pennsylvania State University that Reagan carried easily supported unsuccessful Democratic House challenger Bill Wachob against GOP Rep. William F. Clinger Jr.

There were some liberal academic communities that split their ballots the other way. The Waterville, Maine, ward dominated by Colby College voted in 1984 for both Mondale and Republican Rep. John R. McKernan Jr. The Eugene, Ore., precinct located in the heart of the University of Oregon campus backed both Mondale and GOP Sen. Mark O. Hatfield.

Social 'Stuff' and Other Perils

Democrats regard all of these examples of ticket-splitting as evidence for their contention that the student vote is volatile and independent — hardly a firm part of the GOP constituency. Indeed, there are numerous stumbling blocks ahead that could trip up Republican efforts to secure the long-term support of today's youth.

> ***"... For every young person who's upwardly mobile, there's two who are downwardly mobile. Any party that exhibits a sympathy for the downwardly mobile will come out with the majority because the majority are downwardly mobile."***
>
> **—Rep. Doug Walgren, D-Pa.**

One is the obvious fact that the GOP will never again enjoy the advantage of Reagan at the top of its ticket. A number of Democrats explain away the youth vote for the GOP in 1984 as a short-term flirtation based strictly on Reagan's personal popularity.

It certainly is true that Reagan's popularity attracted a number of young voters to the GOP who did not agree with all elements of GOP policy. Many students happy with Reagan's stands on defense and economic matters are considerably less comfortable with the social issue agenda of the

New Right. If that wing of the GOP becomes more prevalent in the post-Reagan years, many students could sever their ties with the party.

"Myself, I don't believe that stuff about abortion and school prayer," says MSU's Serwach. "Those are just issues I think Reagan campaigns on to get a few votes. As long as nothing happens with school prayer and abortion, I don't think we're going to complain."

Young Democrats are elated with the prospect of an increased conservative presence within the GOP. "I think [the New Right social agenda] is more or less repugnant to most people," says Virginia's Shelton. "When [evangelist] Pat Robertson starts talking about running for president, I think that's great."

Another potential threat to continued Republican success among young people is economic turbulence. Many students have joined the GOP because they believe the party has a better blueprint for the economy than the Democrats. An economic downturn during a Republican administration could well send those security-conscious youth scurrying to the Democrats.

Republicans are confident the GOP will maintain its image as the party of economic growth, but party Chairman Frank J. Fahrenkopf Jr. acknowledges that students will undergo changes after leaving campus that could affect their political views. "While students are in college, certain factors affect them," he says. "Those are different from the factors that affect people who've been out in the job force for a few years."

Professor Beck agrees with the Democrats' claim that today's young people may shift voting allegiances in the future. "The movement of the youth vote in the Republican direction is often exaggerated," he says. "Young people are most often moved by short-run patterns. Long-term voting behavior is not yet developed."

A Republican Generation?

Republicans believe the youth vote for the GOP in 1984 was not a fluke but a departure point — one that will set today's students on a path of lifelong commitment to the party.

"Our review indicates that 75 to 85 percent of the American people historically have remained in the party that they first registered in throughout their whole life," says Fahrenkopf. "That doesn't mean straight ticket. But they do tend to remain in that party. As [former Democrat] Ronald Reagan has said, it is traumatic to switch."

"I don't believe that stuff about abortion and school prayer. Those are just issues I think Reagan campaigns on to get a few votes. As long as nothing happens with school prayer and abortion, I don't think we're going to complain."

—Reagan supporter Joseph J. Serwach, editor in chief, MSU *State News*

Others lend credence to Fahrenkopf's view. "There is a generational theory," explains Professor Lipset. "People come of political consciousness when they are 18 to 20, and that's when they form their attitudes. People who came of consciousness in the 1930s were more liberal and Democratic ... throughout their lifetimes than those in the '50s. People who came of consciousness in the late '70s and the '80s are conservative."

Poll data show a growing identification with the GOP among the nation's youngest voters. A Gallup Poll released in April 1985 showed that a 35 to 28 percent Democratic preference among 18- to 29-year-old voters in 1984 had become a 38 to 31 percent Republican preference.

"We have a Republican generation," declares College Republican Chairman Miner. "It's not cool to be a Democrat on campus anymore. A lot of students identify with the business community." Certainly students today are more interested in fields such as business and engineering than were students a decade or so ago. And they are less likely to classify themselves as liberal. According to the annual survey of college freshmen directed by UCLA's Astin, the number of students labeling themselves as liberal declined from 37 percent in 1970 to 22 percent in 1984.

But there has not been a corresponding gain in the conservative category, which grew from only 18 percent of the nation's college freshmen in 1970 to just 21 percent last year. The clear majority of young students see themselves as middle-of-the-road, mixing economic pragmatism with an interest in issues such as environmental and consumer protection.

Still, Republicans have gained an acceptance among the young that they did not have before, and some Democrats are concerned about what that could mean in the years ahead. "Realignment often results from generational replacement," warns Professor Price. "If the young are moving Republican even to a slight extent, it could affect the political balance." ∎

LOBBIES

The Washington Lobby: A Continuing Effort To Influence Government Policy

Of all the pressures on Congress, none has received such widespread publicity and yet is so dimly understood as the role of Washington-based lobbyists and the groups they represent. The popular image of a rotund agent for special interests buying up members' votes is a vast oversimplification. The role of today's lobbyist is far more subtle, his or her techniques more refined.

Lobbyists and lobby groups have played an increasingly active part in the modern legislative process. The corps of Washington lobbyists has grown steadily since the New Deal, but especially since the early 1970s. The growth in the number of lobbyists has paralleled the growth in federal spending and the expansion of federal authority into new areas. The federal government has become a tremendous force in the life of the nation, and the number of fields in which changes in federal policy may spell success or failure for special interest groups has been greatly enlarged.

With the drive to reduce federal spending that gained impetus during the Reagan administration, the competition for the dwindling supply of federal dollars has become more intense. Lobbyists have to compete with one another to safeguard traditional spending in their area of interest or to gain some portion of the smaller federal pool of funds. Thus commercial and industrial interests, labor unions, ethnic and racial groups, professional organizations, citizen groups and representatives of foreign interests — all from time to time and some continuously — have sought by one method or another to exert pressure on Congress to attain their legislative goals.

The pressure usually has selfish aims — to assert rights or to win a special privilege or financial benefit for the group exerting it. But in other cases the objective may be disinterested — to achieve an ideological goal or to further a group's particular conception of the national interest.

Lobbying: Pros and Cons

It is widely recognized that pressure groups, whether operating through general campaigns designed to sway public opinion or through direct contacts with members of Congress, perform some important and indispensable functions. Such functions include helping to inform both Congress and the public about problems and issues, stimulating public debate, opening a path to Congress for the wronged and needy, and making known to Congress the practical aspects of proposed legislation — whom it would help, whom it would hurt, who is for it and who against it. The spinoff from this process is considerable technical information produced by research on legislative proposals.

Against benefits to the public that result from pressure activities, critics point to certain serious liabilities. The most important is that in pursuing their own objectives, the pressure groups are apt to lead Congress into decisions that benefit the pressure group but do not necessarily serve other parts of the public or the national interest. A group's power to influence legislation often is based less on its arguments than on the size of its membership, the amount of financial and manpower resources it can commit to a legislative pressure campaign and the astuteness of its representatives.

Origins of Lobbying

Representatives of special interests haunted the environs of the First Continental Congress, but the word "lobby" was not recorded until 1808 when it appeared in the annals of the 10th Congress. By 1829 the term "lobby-agents" was applied to favor-seekers at the state capitol in Albany, N.Y. By 1832 it had been shortened to "lobbyist" and was in wide use at the U.S. Capitol.

Although the term had not yet been coined, the right to "lobby" was made implicit by the First Amendment to the Constitution, which provided that "Congress shall make no law ... abridging the freedom of speech or of the press; or the right of the people peaceably to assemble and to petition the Government for redress of grievances." Among the Founding Fathers, only James Madison expressed concern over the dangers posed by pressure groups. In *The Federalist* (No. 10), Madison warned against the self-serving activities of the "factions." "Among the numerous advantages promised by a well-constructed union," he wrote, "none deserves to be more accurately developed than its tendency to break and control the violence of faction.... By a faction, I understand a number of citizens, whether amounting to a majority or minority of the whole, who are united and actuated by some common impulse of passion, or of interest, adverse to the rights of other citizens, or to the permanent and aggregate interests of the community." A strong federal government, Madison concluded, was the only effective counterbalance to the influence of such "factions."

Sources of Pressure

Traditionally, pressure groups in the United States have been composed of similar economic or social interests. Classic examples of such traditional lobbies are those representing farmers, business executives and labor union members. Each of these groups has specific interests that usually draw the support of a large majority of its members.

As the federal government broadened its activities, a new type of pressure group developed — the coalition of diverse economic and social interests brought together by concern for a certain issue. Most major legislation is backed by alliances of interest groups on one side and opposed by alliances on the other. Such lobby coalitions, while having the advantages of bigger memberships and more financial resources for lobbying, may be difficult to control because of the differences of opinion that are likely to arise within any coalition. Despite these inner tensions, lobby coalitions nonetheless have been instrumental in obtaining passage of much major legislation, such as the civil rights and Alaska lands bills.

A notable effort that did not succeed was the coalition for ratification of the Equal Rights Amendment (ERA), which failed to win ratification by the deadline of June 30, 1982. Only 35 states approved it, three short of the necessary 38. Also traditional secular and religious advocates for the underprivileged that have formed a coalition for the poor — such as the National Conference of Catholic Bishops, the National Low Income Housing Coalition and the Food Research and Action Center — have been challenged by the budget cutbacks of the conservative administration of Ronald Reagan.

Executive Branch. Equally prominent among forces exerting pressures on Congress is the executive branch. Executive lobbying activities have been described as the most pervasive, influential and costly of any of the pressures converging on Capitol Hill.

Although every president since George Washington has sought to influence the content of legislation, it was not until the administration of Dwight D. Eisenhower that a formal congressional liaison office in the White House was created. In addition, each executive department has a congressional liaison office charged with selling the department's legislative program to Congress.

While senators and representatives sometimes criticize what they regard as excessive executive pressures, they tend on the other hand to complain of lack of leadership when executive influence is missing. The inter-branch pressure process also works in reverse. Members of Congress exert pressure on executive agencies, if only through inquiries that demonstrate an interest on the part of the body that must pass agency appropriations.

Foreign Interests. Since World War II, lobbying by foreign interests and by American groups with foreign members or interests has become an increasingly important factor in Washington legislative and executive decision making. Foreign-oriented lobbying is based on international politics, world trade and many American domestic issues, for any action by the U.S. government may have foreign or global implications.

Approximately 800 active registered agents representing the interests of foreign principals (governments, political parties, corporations and individuals) were listed with the Justice Department under the Foreign Agents Registration Act in mid-1985, despite Congress' narrowing of the act's coverage in 1966. Counting partners and associates who may participate in representing overseas clients, the number of individuals listed as being in the service of foreign "principals" swelled to over 7,000.

Public Interest Lobbies. Finally there is a collection of groups with no single special interest to promote or protect. These self-styled citizens' or public interest lobbies are concerned with a vast array of issues, and usually have large numbers of individual members. Two of the oldest public interest lobbies are the League of Women Voters and Americans for Democratic Action. Their activities set the pattern for the public interest groups that followed in this relatively new lobbying development.

Two groups, Common Cause and Public Citizen, have attracted wide attention over the last decade and have come almost to characterize liberal public interest lobbies. Developed by Ralph Nader, Public Citizen groups pursue a broad agenda of substantive economic, consumer, environmental, legal and social policy issues. Common Cause has focused on issues of political structure and procedure.

Conservative public interest groups have gained in prominence in recent years as well. Evangelical lobby groups, including the Moral Majority and Christian Voice, have joined other more traditional conservative groups, including the Conservative Caucus, in legislative fights against abortion, homosexual rights, and the Equal Rights Amendment, and in favor of budget-balancing, an anti-communist foreign policy and heavier defense spending. This loose coalition of conservative groups has come to be called The New Right.

Pressure Methods

A Washington lobby group is out to get results. It pursues them wherever they are likely to be found in the governmental process. Many organizations, directed by professionals in the art of government, focus major efforts at key points where decisions are made and policy interpreted into action. If a group loses a round in Congress, it may continue the fight in the agency charged with implementation of the legislation or in the courts. A year or two later, it may resume the struggle in Congress. This process can continue indefinitely.

Whether they focus on Congress or the executive branch, lobbyists use the methods they deem appropriate for the circumstances within the limits of their resources, group policies and ethical outlook.

Bribery

Bribery of members of Congress was a well-documented occurrence in the 19th and early 20th centuries.

When Congress in the 1830s became embroiled in President Andrew Jackson's battle with the Bank of the United States, it was disclosed that Daniel Webster, then a senator from Massachusetts, enjoyed a retainer from the bank. On Dec. 21, 1833, Webster complained to bank President Nicholas Biddle: "My retainer has not been renewed or refreshed as usual. If it is wished that my relation to the Bank should be continued, it may be well to send me the usual retainers."

Col. Martin M. Mulhall, a lobbyist for the National Association of Manufacturers (NAM), stated publicly in 1913 that he had bribed members of Congress for legislative favors, had paid the chief House page $50 a month for inside information from the cloakrooms, and had influenced House leaders to place members friendly to the NAM on House committees and subcommittees. In a subsequent congressional probe, six members were exonerated but one was censured and resigned.

After World War II, direct vote-buying by lobbyists

Ex-Members as Lobbyists

Among the most influential and active lobbyists in Washington are former members of Congress, who, after leaving office, are hired as lobbyists for private organizations.

In some cases, former members become permanently associated with a single organization whose views they share. On the other hand, some former members work for many different organizations as lobbyists, frequently changing or adding employers from year to year.

Because of their service in Congress, former members of the House or Senate enjoy several advantages in lobbying activities. They have an excellent knowledge of the legislative process and frequently a good "feel" for the operations of the House or Senate, which help them decide precisely when and what kind of pressure to exert on behalf of their clients. They often enjoy easy access to congressional staff members and members who are friends and former colleagues. This enables them to see and speak with key legislative personnel, perhaps the chairman of a committee or subcommittee, at the proper time. The ordinary lobbyist might spend weeks trying to obtain an appointment. Former members also frequently have an expert knowledge of the subject matter of legislation through having dealt with it while in Congress.

The privileges of being admitted to the floor and adjacent halls of the House and Senate, which is granted in each chamber to former members of that chamber, is used relatively little by former members directly for lobbying purposes, although it is useful for maintaining contacts and acquaintances. In the House, use of the floor by former members for lobbying purposes has been circumscribed by House Rule 32 and a chair ruling in 1945 by Speaker Sam Rayburn, D-Texas. Under the "Rayburn rule," a former member is forbidden the privilege of the floor at any time the House is debating or voting on legislation in which he is interested, either personally or as an employee of some other person or organization.

No similar formal rule exists in the Senate. But as a matter of custom it is considered improper for a former senator, or any other non-member granted the privilege of the floor, to use that privilege to lobby for legislation.

was replaced, for the most part, by more sophisticated techniques. Indirect, grass-roots pressures and political support became more powerful tools of persuasion. But bribery did not disappear altogether and the Abscam scandal that surfaced in 1980 demonstrated its persistence. The government undercover investigation of political corruption — known as "Abscam" — in which agents of the Federal Bureau of Investigation, posing as businessmen or wealthy Arabs, attempted to bribe members of Congress and other elected officials to help Arabs obtain U.S. residency, get federal grants and arrange real estate deals, resulted in the convictions of seven members of Congress — six representatives and one senator. The charges ranged from bribery to conspiracy.

Campaign Support

Campaign contributions to members of Congress serve two important functions for lobbying organizations. Political support may not only induce a congressman to back the pressure group's legislative interests in Congress but also helps assure that members friendly to the group's goals will remain in office.

While corporations have been barred since 1907, and labor unions since 1943, from making direct contributions to campaigns for federal office, contributors have found numerous ways to get around the restrictions. Although unions are prohibited from using dues money to assist political candidates in federal elections, it is legal for them to set up separate political arms, such as the AFL-CIO's Committee on Political Education (COPE), which collect voluntary contributions from union members and their families and use the funds for political expenditures calculated to benefit senators and representatives friendly to labor. It is also legal for unions to endorse political candidates.

Similarly, while corporations are prohibited from making direct campaign contributions, they can set up corporate political action committees (PACs) to seek contributions from stockholders and executive and administrative personnel and their families. Corporate PACs have proliferated in recent years and their influences rival, if not surpass, those of labor.

Twice a year union and corporate political action committees may seek anonymous contributions by mail from all employees, not just those to which they are initially restricted.

The same general resources for political support and opposition are available to members of citizens' groups and, indeed, to a wide range of organizations seeking to exert political pressure on members of Congress.

In approaching the typical member, a pressure group has no need to tell the member outright that future political support or opposition, and perhaps future political expenditures and the voluntary campaign efforts of its members, depend on how the member votes on a particular bill or whether, over a long period, the member acts favorably toward the group. The member understands this without being told. He or she knows that when the vital interests of some group are at stake in legislation, a vote supporting those interests would normally win the group's friendship and future support, and a vote against them would mean the group's enmity and future opposition.

Lobbyists themselves frequently deny that this is the intention of their campaign support. But lobbyists do admit that political support gives them access — that they otherwise might not have — to the legislator to present their case.

Grass-Roots Pressures

Except on obscure or highly specialized legislation, most lobby campaigns now are accompanied by massive propaganda or "educational" drives in which pressure groups seek to mobilize public opinion to support their aims. In most cases, citizens are urged to respond by contacting members of Congress in support of or opposition to a particular bill.

The most outstanding example of a successful grass-roots lobbying group is the National Rifle Association (NRA). Despite polls showing a majority of Americans favoring some strengthening of gun controls, and despite periodic waves of revulsion brought on by the shooting of public figures, efforts aimed at stricter gun control legislation have been consistently subdued by the NRA, and other similar groups.

NRA has all the advantages of a successful grass-roots lobby organization going for it: a large, well-organized, passionately concerned constituency, concentrated on a single issue.

"In politics you learn to identify the issues of the highest intensity," said Rep. Dan Glickman, a Democrat from Kansas. "This issue [gun control] is of the highest intensity. Those people who care about guns, care very strongly, almost to the exclusion of other issues."

Even in the aftermath of the assassinations of President John F. Kennedy, the Rev. Martin Luther King Jr. and Sen. Robert F. Kennedy, D-N.Y. (1965-68), the gun lobby, through an outpouring of mail opposing tighter gun controls, was able to bottle up proposals for tough controls. All that was passed in 1968 was watered-down legislation not vigorously opposed by the NRA. And it was widely perceived that the only real legislative impact of the shootings of John Lennon in December 1980 and President Reagan in March 1981 would be to diminish NRA's chances of rolling back the 1968 law.

Disadvantages. Despite the frequent success of grass-roots lobbying, such an approach has several inherent limitations that make its use questionable unless it is carefully and cleverly managed. If a member's mail on an issue appears artificially generated, by a professional public relations firm for instance, the member may feel that the response is not representative of the member's constituency. Such pressure mail is easily recognized because the letters all arrive at about the same time, are mimeographed or printed, or are identically or similarly worded.

G. Colburn Aker, a Washington lobbyist, said: "Anybody who believes you can use advertising or public relations techniques to create a groundswell that doesn't have a good basis to begin with is misconceiving the power of those techniques."

But others say a sense of insecurity has pervaded Congress recently, especially among the large number of relative newcomers. Skittish members are more eager to avoid controversy. Norman J. Ornstein, a politics professor associated with the American Enterprise Institute, agreed that the dramatic turnovers in the past few elections have taught many politicians to practice "damage limitation" — never taking a chance of making someone angry.

But Ornstein said that as lawmakers gather experience they likely will learn when it is safe to trust their own judgment.

Direct Lobbying

Much lobbying still is conducted on a face-to-face basis. In a study of pressures on the Senate, Donald R. Matthews, a political scientist, observed that the vast majority of such lobbying was directed at members "who are already convinced." He added: "The services a lobby can provide a friendly senator are substantial. Few senators could survive without them. First, they can perform much of the research and speech-writing chores of the senator's office. This service is especially attractive to the more publicity-oriented senators. Members of the party that does not control the White House also find this service especially valuable, since they cannot draw upon the research services of the departments as much as can the other members. But most senators find this service at first a convenience and soon a necessity."

Once established, Matthews has said, "Senator-lobbyist friendships also tend to reinforce the senator's commitment to a particular group and line of policy.... Relatively few senators are actually changed by lobbyists from a hostile or neutral position to a friendly one. Perhaps a few on every major issue are converted and this handful of votes may carry the day. But quantitatively, the conversion effect is relatively small."

Ensuring continued access to members of Congress requires considerable tact on the part of the lobbyist. Lobbyists must be particularly wary of overstaying their welcome and appearing overly aggressive. Rep. Emanuel Celler, D-N.Y. (1923-73), wrote: "The man who keeps his appointment, presents his problem or proposal and lets the congressman get on with his other work comes to be liked and respected. His message has an excellent chance of being effective. The man who feels that it somehow adds to his usefulness and prestige to be seen constantly in the company of one legislator or another, or who seeks to ingratiate himself with congressional staffs, gets under foot and becomes a nuisance. He does his principal and cause no good."

Above all, the lobbyist must be certain that the information he gives the member is accurate and complete. In their book, *Interest Groups, Lobbying and Policymaking*, Norman J. Ornstein and Shirley Elder quoted a member of Congress: "It doesn't take very long to figure which lobbyists are straightforward, and which ones are trying to snow you. The good ones will give you the weak points as well as the strong points of their case. If anyone ever gives me false or misleading information, that's it — I'll never see him again."

Strategic Contacts. In fights over a specific bill, most direct approaches by lobbyists are likely to center on a few strategic members instead of a large part of the membership of the House or Senate. Generally the key members sit on the committees that have jurisdiction over the legislation in question. As one former member of the House said in 1970, "The committee system is still the crux of the legislative process and is still the basis for congressional action. Laws are not really made here on the floor of the House or on the floor of the other body. They are only revised here. Ninety percent of all legislation that has been passed was passed in the form reported by the committee to the floor."

The committee's power to prevent legislation or to determine its nature narrows down the number of targets for the great majority of specialized interests. Their Washington representatives become experts not only in their field but also on the House and Senate committees that deal with that specialty. This focus in some cases narrows still further to certain subcommittees.

Pressure groups pay their Washington staffs to keep them abreast of developments in government that could affect their constituents. These agents make it their business to watch the work of committees in which they have an interest, to establish and maintain working relationships with key members and staff members and to stay informed on potential and actual legislative developments.

Testimony at Hearings

Another useful technique for lobbyists is testimony at congressional hearings. The hearing provides the lobbyist with a propaganda forum that has few parallels in Washington. It also provides access to key members whom the lobbyist may not have been able to contact in any other way. On important legislation, lobbyists normally rehearse their statements before the hearing, seek to ensure a large turnout from their constituency on the hearing day, and may even hand friendly committee members leading questions for the group's witness to answer.

The degree of propaganda success for the hearing, however, is likely to depend on how well the committee's controlling factions are disposed to the group's position. In his book, *House Out of Order,* Rep. Richard Bolling, D-Mo. (1949-1983), says that within congressional committees "proponents and opponents of legislation jockey for position — each complementing the activities of their alter egos in lobbies outside." He points out: "Adverse witnesses can be kept to a minimum, for example, or they can be sandwiched among friendly witnesses in scheduled appearances so that their testimony does not receive as much attention from the press as it deserves. Scant attention will be given, for example, to a knowledgeable opponent of the federal fallout shelter program if he is scheduled to testify on such legislation on the same day as are Dr. Edward Teller, an assistant secretary of Defense and a three-star general. The opponent is neatly boxed in."

Regulation of Lobbying

In the 19th and 20th centuries, abundant evidence accumulated that venal, selfish or misguided methods used by pressure groups could often result in legislation designed to enrich the pressure group at the expense of the public or to impose the group's own standards on the nation.

The first regulation of lobbyists occurred in 1876 when the House passed a resolution requiring lobbyists to register during the 44th Congress with the clerk of the House. Since the advent of the 62nd Congress in 1911, federal legislation to regulate lobbyists and lobbying activities has continued to be proposed in practically every Congress. Yet only one comprehensive lobbying regulation law and only a handful of more specialized measures have been enacted.

The principal method of regulating lobbying has been disclosure rather than control. In four laws, lobbyists have been required to identify themselves, whom they represent and their legislative interests. In one law, lobbyists also have been required to report how much they and their employers spend on lobbying. But definitions have been unclear, and enforcement has been minimal. As a result, the few existing disclosure laws have produced only limited information, and its effects have been questionable.

One reason for the relative lack of restrictions on lobbies has been the difficulty of imposing meaningful restrictions without infringing on the constitutional rights of free speech, press, assembly and petition. Other reasons include a fear that restrictions would hamper legitimate lobbies without reaching more serious lobby abuses; the consolidated and highly effective opposition of lobbies to restrictions; and the desire of some members to keep open avenues to a possible lobbying career they may wish to pursue later.

The two major lobbying laws that Congress has succeeded in enacting have dealt with lobbyists in general who meet certain definitions of lobbying. The Foreign Agents Registration Act was first enacted in 1938 amid reports of fascist and Nazi propaganda circulating in the United States in the period before World War II. It has been amended frequently since then, and its history is as much a part of this country's struggle with internal security as it is a part of efforts to regulate lobbying.

The one existing omnibus lobbying law, the Federal Regulation of Lobbying Act, was enacted in 1946 as part of the Legislative Reorganization Act. It requires paid lobbyists to register with the House and the Senate and to file quarterly reports with the House. However, large loopholes in the law exempt many interests from registering. The 1954 U.S. Supreme Court decision in *United States v. Harriss* further limited the scope of the law.

Since then congressional committees have investigated the situation and proposed replacements for the 1946 act. Both the House and Senate passed versions of a new bill in 1976 but conferees were not able to resolve differences between the two versions before Congress adjourned. Although various versions of a lobby disclosure bill have been introduced each year since then, including one passed by the House in 1978, no bill has been enacted.

New 'Revolving Door' Restrictions Proposed

As questions mounted in the spring of 1986 about the special influence of White House aide-turned-lobbyist Michael K. Deaver, the Senate's senior Republican was preparing legislation to place sweeping new restrictions on federal employees who take jobs as lobbyists upon leaving the government.

Strom Thurmond, R-S.C., chairman of the Senate Judiciary Committee, announced April 9, 1986, that he was drafting a bill to prohibit departing federal employees from lobbying anyone in the government for one year, or working for a foreign government or business for two years.

The bill also would prevent certain Cabinet-level officials from ever representing or advising foreign entities, his aides said.

The 1978 Ethics in Government Act (PL 95-521) bars mid- to high-level officials from representing anyone before their former agency for one year after leaving government. The law permanently bars officials from representing anyone in connection with an issue they had direct involvement with while in government.

Efforts since then to tighten the restrictions have focused on Defense Department procurement officials. The House Judiciary Committee approved a bill (HR 2554) March 11 that would bar some Pentagon officials from accepting employment with defense firms for two years after leaving government. *(1978 CQ Almanac p. 840; 1985 CQ Weekly Report p. 551; 1986 CQ Weekly Report p. 608)*

While details of Thurmond's bill were yet to be worked out, Thurmond said he wants to restrict lobbying by members of Congress and the Judiciary, as well as by executive branch officials.

"I think he wants this interpreted in the broadest possible sense," a spokesman said.

Thrumond introduced his bill (S 2334) on April 17 and held a Judiciary Committee hearing April 29.

Textile Threat

Thurmond said his plans for the bill were not connected to the controversy surrounding Deaver, who resigned in May 1985 as White House deputy chief of staff and has since become a highly successful lobbyist and public relations consultant for corporations and foreign governments.

Thurmond appeared more concerned about lobbyists representing foreign governments on trade issues. South Carolina is a major producer of textiles, and U.S. textile firms see a threat from cheap foreign imports.

Thurmond was told that some foreign governments were privy to U.S. strategy for the negotiations to renew the Multifiber Arrangement (MFA), which governs textile trade agreements between countries. Thurmond was concerned that competing foreign countries may have obtained confidential information by hiring lobbyists who used to work for trade agencies, such as the U.S. Trade Representative and the State Department.

> ***"I'm trying to protect the American people."***
>
> **—Sen. Strom Thurmond, R-S.C.**

"That made him about as mad as I've ever seen him," said Mark Goodin, Thurmond's press secretary.

Thurmond declined to discuss the textile trade issue specifically.

"I have always believed it was improper for people to hold high positions in the government and then turn right around and use that position for profit," Thurmond said. "I'm trying to protect the American people."

Both Republican and Democratic Judiciary Committee members said they would favor tougher laws on lobbying by former officials, though they were quick to disassociate Thurmond's initiative from the Deaver controversy.

"I wouldn't say it's a result of Michael Deaver or anyone else in particular," said Arlen Specter, R-Pa. "But as a matter of principle, it's a good idea."

Charles E. Grassley, R-Iowa, said the "revolving door" between the Defense Department and defense-related industries is a more serious problem. "Deaver doesn't necessarily provide a better case [for tougher laws]," Grassley said. "If you look below the obvious cases, they're peanuts compared to the abuse in the Defense Department."

But Orrin G. Hatch, R-Utah, complained that Thurmond's bill would be nothing more than an attempt to "legislate morality." Yet he conceded that it had a good chance of passage because most legislators would be embarrassed to argue against it.

"It's the type of thing people would vote for even if they think it's ridiculous," he said. "It's probably one of those things that would just sluice through here on that basis."

Debate Over Deaver

Deaver's activities are so controversial because, in addition to his professional connection to the administration, he also is a longtime personal friend of President and Nancy Reagan.

The General Accounting Office is investigating his lobbying activities for the Canadian government, which won reversal of the president's policy on acid rain.

Deaver also met with James C. Miller III, director of the Office of Management and Budget, on behalf of Rockwell International Corp., which wants to continue production of the B-1 bomber after the first 100 are completed in 1988. The administration is considering dropping the B-1 in favor of the Stealth bomber, manufactured by Northrop Corp.

Deaver has said he was never involved with acid rain policy while working for the president. He said he abides by the laws restricting improper contacts and was advised that meeting with OMB officials, for instance, was "not illegal" because it is an agency separate from the White House.

"I wonder what people thought I was going to do when I left the White House. Be a brain surgeon?" Deaver said April 4 on the MacNeil/Lehrer NewsHour.

Lobbying was his business before he joined the administration, he said, and "that was the business I went back to." ∎

Oilmen Struggle to Keep High Political Profile

Less Cash Available For Campaign Giving

For Texas oilman H. E. "Eddie" Chiles, the current economic crisis in the energy industry has been more than just bad for business. It also has hampered his ability to engage in one of his favorite pastimes — contributing to congressional campaigns.

In good business years, Chiles has invested thousands of dollars in campaigns, seeking to bolster candidates who hew closely to his anti-big-government, pro-free-market philosphy.

It has not been unusual for him to bump up against the $25,000 limit federal law sets as the amount an individual can give to federal candidates, national parties and political action committees in a year. Chiles also contributes in numerous state and local races.

But 1986 was not a good business year for Chiles. Chairman and chief executive officer of the Western Co. of North America, an oil field supply company, he was fighting just to keep his 2,600-employee firm afloat in the face of plummeting petroleum prices. The capital available for investing in campaigns was substantially less than it has been in recent years.

"Certainly, I won't be able to put anywhere near as much money into politics in general this year as I have in past years," Chiles said. "I just don't have it to give."

He is not alone. Throughout the industry, many petroleum company executives and independent oilmen who grew accustomed to generous political giving during the boom of the late 1970s and early 1980s are finding they cannot afford to play politics the way they did in the past.

Some Democrats, mindful of the energy industry's history of giving disproportionately to the GOP, think Republican candidates are bound to suffer from the drop-off in giving. Republicans say their candidates will compensate by finding other sources of campaign contributions.

One thing is certain. The slump in energy industry giving did not take long to affect candidates' behavior. During the boom years, it was customary for a large number of congressional hopefuls to tour Texas, Oklahoma and Louisiana in search of a share of the region's abundant wealth. But in the industry's current recessionary climate, many candidates skipped that trip in 1986.

Industrywide Pinch

With less revenue coming in, energy industry leaders say they have less income to invest in any cause — charitable, political or otherwise.

"I expect that there will be less [industry] money [contributed to campaigns] in 1986," said William C. Anderson, vice president for political and legislative relations for the Independent Petroleum Association of America (IPAA), an organization that claims 7,000 members. *(Anderson profile, p. 42)*

"The amount of non-committed cash out there in my community — cash that's available to go to everything from the church to the United Fund to the university alumni fund to political giving to IPAA dues — has just got to be less than it has been at any time in the last 10 years," Anderson said.

"When you're sitting there fighting to try to keep the doors open," echoed an Oklahoma independent oilman, "you've got to make a choice."

Campaign cash has not been so scarce among major oil companies, whose strong capital bases and diversified business profiles have shielded them from the industry's worst economic woes. But even some major company representatives admit they face hard decisions about the amount of cash they earmark for campaigns.

At Phillips Petroleum Co., for instance, personnel cutbacks are trimming the support base of the company's employee-funded political action committee (PAC). "We have had two

Anderson's Wildcatting Political Strategy . . .

A gruff, gravel-voiced man who peppers his speech with profanities and chews on an ever-present thin cigar, William C. Anderson does not fit the refined profile that marks much of Washington's political elite.

But Anderson's manner melds perfectly with the rough-and-tumble culture of the independent oil community, and that is what matters most to him. Vice president for political and legislative relations for the Independent Petroleum Association of America (IPAA), Anderson advises independent oilmen on how to invest their money in congressional campaigns across the country.

It is a job that has earned him considerable power and prestige.

"Anderson's influence is quite extensive as far as the independent oilman is concerned," said Jack M. Webb, who is executive director of HOUPAC, a political action committee whose board of directors is made up of Houston-based businessmen involved in energy exploration and other industrial pursuits.

"His publication [*The Political Wildcatter*, a political "tip sheet" issued periodically by Anderson] is the only publication they get."

Others say that Anderson's clout extends far beyond the boundaries of the independent oil community.

"I have had a variety of PACs tell me, 'Don't waste your time with me on behalf of any candidate that doesn't have Bill Anderson's endorsement,'" said Terry Cooper, a fund-raising consultant who caters to a Republican clientele.

"In tough times . . . you've got to spend more on political action than you do in good times."

—William C. Anderson

IPAA Nod Opens Doors, Wallets

Cooper regards Anderson's endorsement "as one leg of the Triple Crown," along with the endorsements of the Business-Industry Political Action Committee (BIPAC) and the Chamber of Commerce of the United States.

The vehicle for Anderson's influence is a political education program, dubbed "Political Wildcatting," that was launched by IPAA leaders in the mid-1970s in an effort to help elect a Congress that would be more sympathetic to the goals of the independent petroleum industry.

Instead of forming a political action committee (PAC) to give money directly, IPAA's leaders established an endorsing program. They decided to lend their support only to non-incumbent candidates, a strategy that seemed consistent with the nature of their business enterprise.

"The idea evolved . . . out of the fact that we were wildcatters," Anderson explained. "That meant that our business was such that we went out to new areas where oil hadn't been found before. That's the definition of a wildcat well — one where nobody else has been.

---

early retirement programs . . . that cost us as much as 40 percent of our PAC contributors and 50 percent of our money," said Martin Garber, Phillips' director of political affairs and chairman of the company's PAC.

"The question is, how aggressive do you want to be in soliciting contributions during a third early retirement program and potential layoffs?" Garber asked.

Region's 'Eagles' Grounded

Members of the industry say that they expect the economic downturn to force some oilmen out of the political market altogether. Others are likely to be reduced to writing smaller checks, or to focusing exclusively on congressional candidates and ignoring contests for local offices.

"I would guess by and large it will be smaller checks to their PACs and fewer individual contributions," said the IPAA's Anderson.

One oilman uniquely qualified to compare recent industry political giving patterns is Houston's Rob Mosbacher. In 1984, he was an unsuccessful candidate for the GOP Senate nomination; this year, he was a fundraiser for losing GOP gubernatorial candidate Kent Hance.

In Mosbacher's view, "The level of giving has gone way down. At one time, a disproportionate share of the Republican Eagles were from Texas and Oklahoma," he said, referring to the elite club of Republican contributors who give $10,000 or more to the party. "That has evaporated, by and large."

A Democratic Advantage?

Many Democrats see a silver lining in the cloud hanging over the oil and gas industry. For years, they argue, they have faced GOP candidates whose treasuries were brimming with contributions from the energy community. They regard the current situation as a reprieve.

"It's great news for the Democrats, because the oil companies can't afford to finance Republican candidates to the extent that they would normally," said Democratic Rep. Mike Synar of Oklahoma, whose stance on petroleum-related issues in the House is often at odds with that of the major oil companies.

Even some Republicans concede Synar's point. "I'm afraid that there will be a significant decrease in the amount of money going to Republican members of the House and Senate," said Mosbacher.

But Mosbacher also maintained that Reagan-era Republican gains in Texas will help minimize damage to GOP candidates that a shortage of oil money might cause.

"The good news is that we're in a defensive mode this year," he said. "We've got 10 incumbents in the House from Texas [compared with six before the 1984 elections]. So while it's less likely that we'll be able to

. . . Makes Him Part of D.C.'s 'Triple Crown'

"The decision was made that we should be political wildcatters," he continued. "Let's go with challengers and candidates for open seats. Let's not run with the pack and try to buy access with members of Congress. Hell, we can see anybody we need to see if we've got a story to tell."

Instead of supporting incumbents, Anderson offers endorsements to the challengers and open-seat contenders he deems philosophically compatible and politically competitive. His endorsement can help attract thousands of dollars in contributions from independent oilmen — and from other sectors of the business community as well.

Anderson shies from endorsing candidates running for office in major producing areas, preferring to focus on contests outside the oil patch instead.

"Our members know who's their friend and who isn't in the 13th District of Texas," Anderson said. "We're not going to sit up here and make a judgment on that. But the guy in Abilene, Texas, doesn't really have a feeling as to whether some son of a bitch in the 13th District of New Jersey has a chance."

Seeking More Wells and More Freshmen

Anderson acknowledges that the current economic crunch in the energy industry has taken its toll on political giving by IPAA's members. But he maintains that the drop in contributions has been most noticeable among oilmen who joined the organization during the boom years. Long-time dues-payers have not been as hard-hit, he argues — and those are the members who have traditionally been most active in campaigns.

As he seeks to encourage his membership to continue contributing despite the oil recession, Anderson argues that political contributions are more important in a bad business climate than they are in boom years.

"I have had a variety of PACs tell me, 'Don't waste your time with me on behalf of any candidate that doesn't have Bill Anderson's endorsement.' "

—Political consultant Terry Cooper

"In tough times, to the extent that you can, you've got to spend more on political action than you do in good times," he argued. "Because even the smallest of political gains on Capitol Hill can mean the difference between success and failure in a tough time. In good times, it doesn't make a hell of a lot of difference what happens.... When political decisions on the smallest of things can be that crucial, you sure don't want to go backwards politically."

To buttress his argument, Anderson applies business philosophy in the independent petroleum industry to the political realm.

"If you quit drilling wells, and you're satisfied with your current production, eventually you'll go out of business, because it's declining all the time," Anderson continued. "Well, if we quit wildcatting in the political field, and are satisfied with what we've got, eventually we'll get worse because there's folks retiring and dying all the time.

"So just as you've got to continually be putting new wells in all the time, you've got to continually be putting new freshman classes in all the time . . . to avoid eroding your political base through attrition."

defeat Democratic incumbents this year . . . it's also less likely that a Democratic challenger will be able to raise the kind of money it would take to defeat a Republican incumbent.... I don't think we stand to lose as much."

Some Republicans go further, professing little alarm at the prospect of a decline in giving from the energy industry. "What we lack in funding from that traditional source . . . I think we can more than make up for in other areas," said Randy Moorhead, business and labor liaison for the National Republican Congressional Committee. "I don't think that any of our candidates who are in good position politically will lose because of a lack of money."

Hard Road for Challengers

Democrats and Republicans alike speculate that a downturn in energy contributions is likely to do less damage to incumbents than to challengers, who typically have difficulty raising money even in the best of business years. The current oil slump makes their task harder than ever.

Challengers have sometimes found it difficult to raise money among the major oil companies, whose PACs often display the same pro-incumbent bias exhibited by the corporate establishment in general. *(PAC contributions to congressional candidates, 1986 CQ Weekly Report p. 657)*

But in past years, challengers have enjoyed a somewhat higher rate of success in getting contributions from independent oilmen, whose sheer numbers (roughly 12,000) enable them to overshadow the influence of three dozen or so major companies in the realm of campaign finance.

One reason independents traditionally have been friendlier to challengers lies in the organizational difference between independent and major companies. The people who make political decisions for the major firms must answer to a corporate hierarchy. The executive who runs an independent company typically answers to no one but himself.

At Phillips Petroleum, Garber said, "we have to make our decisions based on what we think is right for the company, what is right for the employees.... And we have to be considerate of what we think the employees who make contributions can live with.... That's a lot of options that go into a decision to contribute.

"The independent oilman doesn't have to worry about all those options. He can do it more based upon a gut feeling."

'Wildcatting' Cash Scarce

Another reason that challengers usually make more headway with independent oilmen lies in the independent's personality. The typical independent oilman makes his living by prospecting for oil and natural gas in unexplored territory. He is a risk-taker, and that trait extends to his involvement in politics.

"You can incite the emotion of the independent oilman," said Denis Calabrese, a political consultant for a Houston-based, Republican firm. "He's gone out and done something on his own. An independent will say to a challenger, 'I admire your spirit. I don't know if you're going to do it or not, but good luck to you.' It's almost as though they want to see spirit."

In contrast, said Calabrese, "an accountant looks at your spreadsheets and precinct numbers, looks down his glasses and analytically tells you you don't have a prayer."

Despite the independent's predilection for taking chances, the energy industry's current economic situation is so tough that even the most risk-oriented independent oilmen are taking a harder look before putting their money into politics.

"They may have to be more selective," said Bernadette Budde, political strategist for the Business-Industry Political Action Committee. "They likely will do less of the prospecting, less wildcatting."

Southwest: Mecca No More

The shortage of campaign cash in the energy industry may reduce the political reach and clout of the Southwest. Members of the industry accustomed to giving to candidates from around the country seem likely to slight those from far-flung states in times of economic trouble — and focus instead on congressional races closer to home.

"The Southwest will be able to take care of its own," contended James R. Whittinghill, an aide to Republican Rep. Tom Loeffler of Texas. "But people from other regions of the country may find it much harder to raise money in Texas."

Doyce Boesch, an aide to Oklahoma GOP Sen. Don Nickles, voiced a similar theme when discussing the senator's fund raising for his re-election bid this year.

"We had our fund-raiser in Texas some time ago, early in 1985. Our function was pretty successful. But I understand through the grapevine that . . . those senators who are touring through Texas at this time aren't doing very well," Boesch said.

There are signs of a downturn in the number of candidates from around the country who are making fund-raising forays into the Southwest's oil patch.

"Over the last six to eight years, I've received call after call after call," said Anderson. "Candidates saying, 'I'm going to be going to Dallas and Houston and Midland and who should I see and will it be worth stopping in Oklahoma City?' I think I've had one such call so far this year."

"Those have been the places every candidate in the country ran to," Anderson continued. "The idea was that money was lying in the streets. . . . But the political mecca now is going to be somewhere else."

Money Isn't Everything

For Anderson and other politically active members of the energy community, the most pressing challenge at hand is to find ways to retain a level of influence in congressional campaigns despite the economic problems wracking their industry.

Many in the industry are likely to adjust to the new economic realities by substituting in-kind services for the financial contributions they would make in a better business year.

"If I can't give them money, I may try to help them in other ways," said one Texas independent oilman. "Maybe I'll go to a meeting with them, or introduce them to organizations . . . help get the people out, and do registration work. There are ways you can help a candidate other than just giving them money."

Democratic Rep. W. J. "Billy" Tauzin of Louisiana agreed. "My gut tells me people who want to help you politically who can't make a contribution to you because they're having a hard time with their bank — meeting their mortgage — will be more likely this year to give you empty office space," he said. "There's a lot of it. Or loan you the use of some vehicle that may be unused. Or some other office equipment."

Political strategists for some oil companies say they hope to combat any reluctance to contribute by waging more aggressive solicitation campaigns.

"We'll just do a lot more personal solicitations, group meetings rather than direct mail . . . trying to explain why it's really important not to abandon the effort and encouraging people as best we can to continue to be involved," said Don Cogman, vice president for governmental affairs for MAPCO, a Tulsa, Okla.-based firm that mines coal and refines and markets petroleum.

Those who are trying to wrest contributions from the energy industry can rest assured that some members of the community are likely to keep on giving no matter how bad business gets.

"Take Eddie Chiles," said consultant Calabrese. "His business is about to go under. It's very, very bad. But even though the guy's hurting financially, he's still in campaigns. He's so committed ideologically, you can still count on him for contributions."

"To the extent that I can afford it," Chiles said, "I still try to give a little bit to good conservatives." ∎

Rep. W. J. "Billy" Tauzin, D-La., left, says, "My gut tells me" that cash-poor oilmen will find other ways to help candidates they admire.

Though he is financially strapped, oilman H. E. "Eddie" Chiles says, "I still try to give a little bit to good conservatives."

House Votes to Weaken U.S. Gun Control Law

In a decisive reversal of long-standing federal policy, the House April 10, 1986, approved legislation to weaken the landmark 1968 Gun Control Act.

The bill (HR 4332) would make it easier to buy and sell rifles and shotguns and to transport them interstate. However, the House refused to lift the restriction in current law that bars interstate sales of handguns.

The bill, approved 292-130, is very similar to a measure (S 49) passed by the Senate in July 1985. The Senate's version permitted interstate handgun sales. However, on May 6 the Senate voted to accept the House version. President Reagan signed the bill May 19. *(Vote 69, 1986 CQ Weekly Report, p. 828)*

The vote was an impressive victory for the National Rifle Association (NRA), which has complained about federal gun law ever since the 1968 measure was enacted. On two key votes April 9, the NRA demonstrated its political power by crushing a highly visible and determined effort by national law enforcement groups to keep the 1968 law basically intact.

The police groups and their ally, Handgun Control, prevailed only on the handgun sale issue, and while police spokesmen said that was an important victory, it was far less than they had hoped for.

"We are extremely disappointed that Congress is not listening to us," said Jerald Vaughn, executive director of the International Association of Chiefs of Police, one of 12 groups that make up the Law Enforcement Steering Committee. *(1986 CQ Weekly Report p. 680)*

However, Sarah Brady, a Handgun Control board member, said she was "delighted we beat the NRA on the big one." Brady's husband, presidential press secretary James S. Brady, suffered a serious brain injury when he was shot during the 1981 assassination attempt on President Reagan.

NRA officials said they were satisfied despite the handgun loss. "We're real happy," said Wayne LaPierre, the NRA's legislative director.

Triumph for Volkmer

For sponsor Harold L. Volkmer, D-Mo., passage of HR 4332 was a personal triumph. He began to push in 1979 to amend the 1968 law, and on April 10 he pronounced himself "very pleased." The bill, he said, "protects many of our citizens" from abuses by federal agents. *(Volkmer profile, p. 47)*

That argument — that law-abiding citizens had suffered under the 1968 law — was at the heart of the NRA's effort. The organization has contended for more than a decade that the law, passed in the wake of the assassinations of the Rev. Dr. Martin Luther King Jr. and Robert F. Kennedy, was too broad and subjected innocent gun owners to harassment by federal agents.

Volkmer, his congressional allies and the NRA sought to frame the House debate in terms of civil and constitutional rights. Their arguments centered on the Second Amendment to the Constitution, which says "the right of the people to keep and bear arms shall not be infringed."

During debate April 9, Volkmer called consideration of his bill the "second most important step in the history of American gun owners. The first was the Second Amendment to the U.S. Constitution."

But William J. Hughes, D-N.J., sponsor of a competing bill, tried to portray the issue as one of law enforcement and safety. He claimed Volkmer's legislation "would elevate gun dealers to a special level of privilege never before seen in the law." By contrast, he said, his bill sought a balance between the interests of sportsmen and hunters and the interests of police and citizens.

However, the Hughes alternative, reported by the Judiciary Committee March 14 (H Rept 99-495) and supported by the police groups, was never directly considered by the House. Instead, members voted 286-136 April 10 to adopt the Volkmer substitute. *(Vote 68, 1986 CQ Weekly Report, p. 828)*

Pressured to the Floor

Even before House debate began, Hughes and Judiciary Chairman Peter W. Rodino Jr., D-N.J., knew the committee bill was in trouble. While it was approved 35-0 by the panel, it was immediately blasted by the NRA and its supporters as unworkable.

Angry that Rodino had stymied

Policemen from around the country massed on the Capitol steps to lobby against legislation weakening the 1968 Gun Control Act. The House rejected their pleas.

gun legislation for nearly seven years, Volkmer had circulated a "discharge petition" to get the legislation to the floor without a committee vote. When 218 members sign a petition, the House must act.

The committee approved HR 4332 on March 11, and Volkmer secured his 218 signatures on March 13. His petition did not directly affect HR 4332, but it played an important political role. With the backing of half the members of the House, Volkmer could virtually dictate the terms under which his substitute and HR 4332 would be considered by the full House.

On March 19 the Rules Committee approved a rule that foreclosed a clear yes-or-no vote on HR 4332. Instead, Volkmer was given the chance to offer his bill as a replacement for the Judiciary bill. In addition, Rules allowed only five hours of debate on the legislation, including the time required for roll-call votes. This had the effect of limiting the number of amendments that could be offered.

Hughes and his allies decided then that their best hope was to try to amend Volkmer's bill to meet police concerns.

Floor Amendments

On April 9 Hughes offered a package of law enforcement amendments to the Volkmer bill. Chief among them was the ban on interstate sales of handguns, a ban on interstate transportation of handguns and tighter record-keeping requirements.

The interstate transportation provision prompted the most debate, particularly from Westerners and longtime NRA members such as John D. Dingell, D-Mich., who contended that hunters should be able to travel interstate with their guns without fear of prosecution by local authorities. They pointed out that 37 states allow hunting with handguns.

Hughes and Dan Lungren, R-Calif., another Judiciary member, said they had no objection to interstate transportation of rifles and shotguns for sporting purposes. But they said they could see no reason for taking handguns interstate.

Dingell retorted that if a sportsman from Maryland or Virginia wants to go bear hunting in Maine, he risks prosecution on his way through New Jersey because it is "presumably illegal for him to have a firearm or handgun" in that state. Volkmer's bill would correct that problem, Dingell said, but Hughes' proposal would make "criminals every day out of law-abiding sportsmen and citizens."

Hughes' package was rejected by a 176-248 vote — a margin that was a sobering disappointment to the law enforcement groups. *(Vote 64, 1986 CQ Weekly Report, p. 828)*

They had hoped their aggressive lobbying in the previous weeks as well as their presence April 9 around the House chamber would make a difference. During the voting, groups of state and local police officers stood at parade rest in full dress uniform at the doors of the chamber, staring silently at members as they filed in to vote.

After Hughes' package was defeated, he offered the interstate transportation provision separately. It also was handily rejected, 177-242. *(Vote 65, 1986 CQ Weekly Report, p. 828)*

Hughes then tried to offer another amendment, which would have banned the interstate sale of handguns. But he was interrupted by Speaker Thomas P. O'Neill Jr., D-Mass., who said he wanted to end work for the evening to keep the House from having to pay overtime to Capitol workers.

> ***"Sixty to 70 million people own a firearm — 40 percent of American households. They see it every day. It becomes like a set of golf clubs, and they say, 'Why does everybody want to take it away from me?' "***
>
> **—Wayne LaPierre, National Rifle Association**

When the House reconvened April 10, members took up the amendment that retained the ban on interstate handgun sales. It was adopted 233-184. *(Vote 66, 1986 CQ Weekly Report, p. 828)*

The short debate on the proposal suggested that it would pass. Three Southern members — Florida Republicans Bill McCollum and E. Clay Shaw Jr. and Louisiana Democrat Buddy Roemer, who had voted against Hughes' earlier amendments, said they supported him on the handgun proposal. Shaw even passed out a leaflet at the House doors urging members to back the amendment.

Shaw said there was a difference between interstate sale of handguns and transporting them interstate. Preventing transportation, Shaw said, was just "an inconvenience" for sportsmen. But banning interstate sale of handguns served a legitimate law enforcement purpose.

The House position was a clear shift from Senate sentiment. When Edward M. Kennedy, D-Mass., offered a similar amendment during debate on S 49, it garnered only 26 votes. *(1985 CQ Weekly Report p. 1391)*

The NRA's LaPierre said his organization could live with the handgun ban because it simply maintained the status quo.

The NRA was less pleased with a fourth amendment offered by Hughes in the closing minutes of debate. Adopted by voice vote, it would bar all future sales and possession of machine guns by private citizens. It would not affect existing machine guns.

Lobbying Battle

For six weeks, the looming fight on the gun bill was billed as a showdown between the police and the NRA. It turned out to be a rather mismatched affair. While the police groups were able to get more than 100 uniformed officers to Washington, they were, in the words of some members, too little too late.

"The police misunderstood the force of lobbying," Roemer said. "Lobbying is not standing in long lines at the door. Lobbying is good information early; it is a presence when minds are being made up. Minds were already made up yesterday," he said, referring to the April 9 vote.

Butler Derrick, D-S.C., said he thought the police leaders did not accurately represent rank-and-file police officers, who were NRA supporters.

Hughes and other members have attributed the NRA's success to the millions of dollars it has poured into congressional campaigns. But an equally important factor is the organization's ability to generate broad grass-roots support.

"Sixty to 70 million people own a firearm — 40 percent of American households," LaPierre said. "They see it every day. It becomes like a set of golf clubs, and they say, 'Why does everybody want to take it away from me?' "

Some members from the South and Midwest said privately that while they supported Hughes, they could not afford to vote against the NRA. "This is one vote where I have to be

For Volkmer, Persistence Pays on Gun Issue

In the age of telegenic media politicians, Missouri Democrat Harold L. Volkmer is not a promoter's dream. With his gruff voice, brusque manner and lined face, he is no match — on a TV screen, at least — for many of the smooth, glib members cropping up in Congress.

But the 55-year-old Volkmer is a seasoned pro, and what he lacks in flash he more than makes up for in perseverance. His dedication paid off April 10 when the House finally approved legislation to weaken the 1968 Gun Control Act. *(Story, p. 45)*

A hunter since childhood, Volkmer has been the leading advocate of changing the law since he came to Congress in 1977. He opposed the 1968 law when it was first enacted, but as a Missouri state legislator, he was in no position to do anything about it. When he came to Washington, however, he already was armed with "horror stories" from gun dealers who claimed they had been victimized by federal agents.

In 1978, Volkmer and his staff began drafting legislation to curb the federal government's authority to regulate guns. At the same time, he contacted the National Rifle Association (NRA), the aggressive firearms lobby, for its suggestions. At that point, a long and mutually beneficial relationship was born.

Volkmer has been the NRA's point man on Capitol Hill ever since. A former aide, Kenneth Schloman, now works for the NRA, and Schloman's wife, Cherry, is Volkmer's legislative assistant. While Mr. Schloman kept his eye on the House debate from the Gallery April 9-10, Mrs. Schloman sat at Volkmer's side on the floor.

Like many NRA supporters in Congress, Volkmer brings to the issue a lifelong reverence for guns. It is born of his background in rural Missouri and cemented by his training as a lawyer. The pivotal factor, he says, is the Second Amendment to the Constitution, which protects the right of people to bear arms.

Volkmer himself owns only rifles and shotguns. But he resists the notion that handguns should be treated any differently. "People have legitimate uses for handguns," he says.

Volkmer served on the House Judiciary Committee from 1977 through 1980 but was never in the mainstream of the generally liberal Democratic majority. While he tangled with House Judiciary Chairman Peter W. Rodino Jr., D-N.J., over strengthening fair housing laws, that clash was brief compared with the fight over firearms legislation.

In Volkmer's view, Rodino has been the person most responsible for blocking gun legislation. The last straw, Volkmer said April 9, was when Rodino declared a Senate-passed gun bill "dead on arrival" in the House.

Rep. Harold L. Volkmer

When he heard that, Volkmer decided he would petition the House to consider firearms legislation without Judiciary's participation. The committee finally reported out a bill when the petition had attracted nearly enough signatures to force action, but by the time the panel acted, it was almost irrelevant. The Judiciary measure was never considered by the full House, which opted instead for the Volkmer proposal. The Senate voted to accept the House measure.

Although Volkmer has been identified principally with the firearms debate, he is deeply involved in farm issues as well. He does not anticipate any lull in his activities now that the gun fight is over. "I've got lots of other issues," he said.

representational," said one Southerner, calling his district a "frontier" area where guns are a fact of life.

A Congressional Quarterly analysis of the key vote on Hughes' law enforcement package showed that Southerners voted overwhelmingly — 83 percent — against it. In the West, 59 percent of members were opposed. Midwestern members split 50-50, while in the East, Hughes got backing from 62 percent of the members.

Provisions

As passed by the House and accepted by the Senate HR 4332 is similar in key respects to S 49, but there are three important differences: The Senate bill would have lifted the current ban on interstate sales of handguns, did not include the ban on machine guns, and would have barred unannounced federal inspections of gun dealers.

The House bill allows one unannounced inspection per year. Current law allows unannounced inspections at any reasonable time.

It also will allow interstate sales of rifles and shotguns and will ease record-keeping requirements for transactions involving firearms. It will make clear that only persons who buy and sell guns to obtain a "livelihood and pecuniary gain" must get a federal gun dealer's license and keep records of firearms transactions.

This differs from current law, which does not include a precise definition of who must get a dealer's license. The NRA contends that the lack of a clear definition has allowed the Bureau of Alcohol, Tobacco and Firearms, which administers the 1968 law, to harass innocent gun owners.

The House bill also will allow licensed dealers to transfer guns from their business collection to their personal collections and then sell them from their private stock without keeping records. However, dealers could be punished if such transfers were made "willfully" in order to evade record-keeping requirements.

Finally, the bill makes it legal to transport an unloaded, "inaccessible" firearm interstate, thus barring prosecutions under state laws that prohibit the carrying of handguns in vehicles.

After adopting the Volkmer substitute, the House substituted the House language for the text of S 49. ∎

Guns in America: The Debate

When you think of guns, do you visualize them in the hands of the pioneer, the Western lawman, the sportsman, the soldier whose markmanship helped preserve American liberty? Or do you view guns as the tools of outlaws, urban hoodlums, gangsters and political assassins? The answer probably determines your position on gun control. But the questions also illustrate the American gun dilemma: how to balance the rights of legitimate gun owners against the demands of citizens to be protected from illegitimate uses.

There may be as many as 200 million guns — rifles, shotguns, pistols — in private hands in the United States, nearly enough for every man, woman and child to have one. The majority of these weapons are owned by law-abiding citizens who use them responsibly for legitimate purposes like hunting and target shooting. But many are held by criminals; firearms were used in more than half of all murders in 1984, not to mention those used in holdups, burglaries, rapes and other crimes. About 1,800 people die each year in firearms accidents, and approximately 12,000 people use guns to kill themselves.

Gun control is one of the few issues on which the opposing camps are so far apart, with so little apparent willingness to compromise. Pro-gun activists, led by the well-financed and aggressive National Rifle Association, accuse the gun controllers of disarming law-abiding citizens, leaving them vulnerable to armed marauders. Anti-gun advocates, represented by Handgun Control Inc. and the National Coalition to Ban Handguns among others, assail the gun lobby for sacrificing thousands of Americans to their Second Amendment principles. Each side has its list of statistics and examples, convincing when viewed in isolation but contradictory when compared with the other side's evidence.

It is thought that hunters own over half of all firearms — primarily rifles and shotguns. Hunters have objected so loudly to attempts to restrict ownership of hunting weapons that anti-gun groups are now focusing their efforts almost exclusively on handguns. "We don't deal with rifles and shotguns; we have nothing against hunting," said Josh Sugarmann, public affairs director for the National Coalition to Ban Handguns (NCBH).

NRA statistics indicate that most of the estimated 50 million-60 million handguns in the United States are owned for the purpose of self-protection. "It may well prove to be the most immediate means of thwarting criminal activity," an NRA pamphlet reads. "In that sense, it serves to provide security in a manner similar to health or life insurance."

Gun control advocates counter with statistics showing that it is far more likely for a "self-defense" handgun to be used to commit murder or suicide, be involved in a fatal accident, or be stolen by burglars than to prevent a criminal act. Anti-gun groups are also concerned about the proliferation of machine guns and semiautomatic military-type weapons in private ownership — and their use in several recent mass-shootings *(see p. 52)*.

Applying their famous slogan "Guns Don't Kill People — People Do," the gun lobby is adamant that any restriction on gun ownership by law-abiding citizens is an abridgment of the Second Amendment of the U.S. Constitution, which guarantees the right to keep and bear arms.

Primary Uses: Hunting, Shooting Sports

The earliest American settlers depended on their guns to hunt game, which was a vital part of the colonial diet. Today most hunting is for sport. "Nationally very few people hunt for food," said Jack Berryman, the executive director of the International Association of Fish and Wildlife Agencies (IAFWA). Berryman added that most states prohibit wastage of game meat. Hunters have "got to eat it or give it to somebody to eat," he said.

Like most issues involving the use of firearms, it is hard to determine how many Americans actually use guns to hunt. Over 16 million people hold hunting licenses; the NRA says there are 28.8 million hunters. Whatever their numbers, hunters as a group are most protective of their right to own guns. Calling gun control advocates "gun-grabbers," many hunters subscribe to the "domino theory" of gun control — that the banning of any kind of firearm or ammunition is the first step on the road to confiscation of all weapons.

Periodically hunters have faced serious image problems. The massive and unsportsmanlike slaughters that wiped out or endangered such species as the passenger pigeon and buffalo in the late 19th and early 20th centuries fueled an anti-hunting movement and spurred the conservation efforts of President Theodore Roosevelt, himself an avid hunter. More recently, the number of fatal hunting accidents and what Berryman called "hunting vandalism, bad manners and poor ethics ... threatened the sport." In September 1981 the IAFWA recommended that the states adopt a mandatory certification process for hunters that would include education on wildlife and their habits, the safe handling of firearms and other elements of hunter safety. In October 1985, Wisconsin became the 34th state to require some form of hunter training.

Yet many hunters complain that anti-gun forces and urban elitists continue to stereotype them as machismo-motivated primitives. Hunters say they hunt not because of bloodlust but because they appreciate the sport as a form of outdoor recreation. "Someone has to defend hunting as being worthwhile, as important to our growth and development," Berryman said. "There is something good and worthwhile in people going outdoors and pursuing game, as long as they do it with respect. It is part of what we are.... Something of the American personality is lost when people don't go out-of-doors."

The Friends of Animals, the Humane Society of America, the Fund for Animals and other animal rights' organizations strongly disagree. They believe hunting is cruel to animals. Wild animals must be released "from the bondage of the arms manufacturers and the gun and ammo magazines," wrote Cleveland Amory, president of Fund for Animals. The fund joined in a successful effort to block this year's bear hunt in Wisconsin. Anti-hunting activists have gone so far as to walk through woods playing music to scare animals away from hunting areas.

Hunters counter that they are the real conservationists. In 1984 the $292 million paid for state hunting licenses, $89.2 million in excise taxes on sporting arms and ammunition and $13.8 million for duck stamps went to state wildlife management agencies, wildlife restoration projects and wetlands acquisition. The National Wildlife Federation, Izaak Walton League and Wildlife Management Institute are among the conservation-oriented groups that support hunting. "The conservation movement and in fact the environmental movement really had its beginnings with hunters," Berryman said. "It was hunter and fisherman's dollars that supported the only conservation program a state had, the state fish and game department.... They were the only ones who showed an interest in pesticides and wetland drainage and other environmental issues."

Most hunters use long guns, but the National Shooting Sports Foundation (NSSF) says 1.5 million hunters use handguns, 49 states permit handgun hunting for small game and 37 states allow big-game handgun hunting. "Because of the limitations of the equipment used, handgun hunting demands a high level of marksmanship as well as excellent hunting and stalking skills to bring the shooter within effective range," an NSSF pamphlet entitled "Handgun Hunting" reads.

However, the anti-gun lobby has long insisted that any inconvenience to the relatively small numbers of handgun hunters caused by handgun controls is minor compared with the benefits that would be gained from restricting or banning handgun use. "Because the vast majority of hunters use a rifle or a shotgun, there is no reason why their pursuit of game (and sport) should be affected by handgun control," wrote Pete Shields, chairman of Handgun Control Inc. Sugarmann said the effort of NSSF and other groups to promote handgun hunting was really a political strategy "to make the handgun control issue a hunting issue, saying, 'Look at this, they're going to take away your handgun to hunt with.' And basically, yeah, we are. We look at hunting and you use long guns, there's a readily replaceable method for using a handgun."

Dispute on Link Between Crime, Handguns

Guns are lethal whether they are fired at animals or humans. Hardly a day goes by without a report of some senseless gun slaying. On a single day in October 1985, two high school students in the Washington, D.C., area died of gunshot wounds, including one who was shot while resisting a robbery in the school building. In Baltimore the same day, a high school football star died after a friend playing with a handgun accidentally shot him. In suburban Philadelphia the next day, Sylvia Seegrist, a former mental patient with known violent tendencies walked into a shopping mall and allegedly shot 10 people, three fatally, with a semiautomatic rifle. In the 1980s alone, tens of thousands of Americans have shared a grim distinction with President Reagan and John Lennon: they have found themselves on the wrong end of a gun.

Of the 16,689 reported homicides in 1984, 9,819 were killed with guns. Of those, 7,277 murders were committed with handguns. The number of murders has declined steadily since 1980. However, the percentage committed with handguns has remained fairly constant, just above or below 50 percent *(see below)*. Handgun murders are double the number of stabbing murders, the second most common method *(see box, p. 50)*. In addition, handgun-wielding assailants rob, rape or threaten countless thousands of people each year. Shotguns and rifles are used in about 10 percent of all homicides each year.

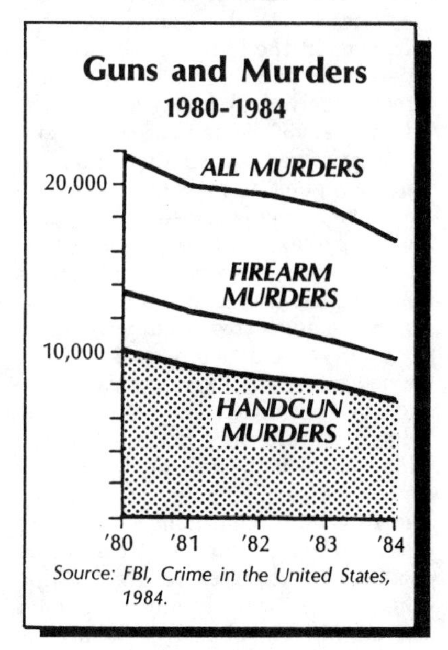

Source: FBI, Crime in the United States, 1984.

Gun control groups contend that murder and suicide rates would fall if it were harder for criminals to obtain handguns. Handgun Control Inc. notes that handguns account for 90 percent of firearms misuse, although they comprise only 30 percent of firearms in private possession. The organization refers to the current situation as The Great American Handgun War, pointing out that during the peak years of the Vietnam War, 40,000 American soldiers were killed in action, while 50,000 civilians were killed by handguns on the streets of America.

A recently issued National Institute of Justice (NIJ) study found that 50 percent of the state prisoners surveyed had used guns in crimes, and 22 percent said they had used them frequently. Criminals prefer handguns because they are concealable, easy to use and relatively cheap. Guns with barrel lengths of three inches or under, known as snub-nosed guns, "snubbies" or "Saturday night specials," can often be purchased for less than $100. Although it is widely believed that criminals rely on these guns, the prisoners surveyed in the NIJ study said they preferred larger caliber, more powerful handguns and often stole them or bought them "off the street."

Gun control advocates also observe that hardened criminals do not commit all the murders. FBI statistics show that 57 percent of all murders in 1984 were committed by relatives or persons acquainted with the victim. "Millions of the handguns now in America were acquired for self-protection . . .," Jervis Anderson wrote. "Yet a terrible irony of this justifiable precaution is that guns bought for family and self-protection end up doing far more harm to the owners, their loved ones, and their personal acquaintances than they do to intruders."

Gun control advocates contend that a family argument is more likely to end in murder if a gun is available. "If you have a handgun around, it lends itself well to spontaneity, unfortunately," Sugarmann said. This spontaneity is also blamed for the large number of suicides by handgun. In an average year, between 11,000 and 12,000 Americans kill themselves with handguns. "While pills, gas, or razor blades allow time for a change of heart, there are no second chances

Crime by Weapon, 1984

Crime	Firearms	Knife	Personal*	Other
Murder	58.8%	21.2%	5.5%	13.4%[1]
Robbery	35.8	13.4	41.5[2]	9.4
Aggravated assault	21.1	23.2	25.0	30.7

* *Hands, feet, etc.*
[1] *Includes murders where weapon was unknown*
[2] *Strong-arm tactics*

Source: FBI, Crime in the United States, 1984

with a bullet," an NCBH suicide fact sheet reads. In addition, handguns are blamed for approximately 800 accidental deaths each year. Overall, between 1,800 and 1,900 people die each year in firearms accidents.

The NRA and its supporters say the high crime rate is not caused by widespread handgun ownership but by failures in the justice system. "To the extent that government's sole effective mode of deterring crime is criminal law enforcement, the crime rate is itself a barometer of the success of the criminal justice system....," sociologists Randall R. Rader and Patrick B. McGuigan wrote. "In that sense, the statistics and accounts of growing lawlessness are both a stern indictment of current criminal law enforcement standards and a verification that those standards have become more lax over the past decades."

According to sociologists James D. Wright, Peter H. Rossi and Kathleen Daly, "There is little or no conclusive evidence to show that gun ownership among the larger population is, per se, an important cause of criminal violence. It is true by definition that gun crimes require guns, and it is true that guns, mainly handguns, are involved in a very large share of criminally violent incidents.... But it does not follow from any of this that reducing the private ownership of weapons would be accompanied by similar reductions in the rates of violent crime, or (what amounts to the same thing) that private weapons ownership is itself a cause of violent crime."

Gun advocates also deny that the presence of handguns contributes to the frequency of "crimes of passion." According to John Aquilino, NRA director of public education, gun control supporters "take the FBI statistics on the homicides by acquaintances and try to make people think those are just normal, wonderful, loving people who become unloving and murderous because of the presence of a gun." Aquilino said many of these murders occur in families with histories of domestic violence or are committed by criminals who choose their neighbors or partners in crime for victims.

Gun Lobby Stresses Right to Self-Defense

The NRA and other pro-gun organizations also contend that bans or restrictions on handguns would deprive law-abiding citizens of an effective means of self-defense. The NRA claims that 300,000 to 350,000 Americans use handguns each year to scare off would-be burglars, rapists, muggers and murderers, a figure hotly disputed by gun control groups. "Literally tens of millions of Americans disagree with the prohibitionist position," an NRA self-defense pamphlet reads. "They see their handguns as critical tools that might spell the difference between becoming the victim of a crime or the victor in a confrontation with a criminal predator."

The NRA also maintains that "firearms in the hands of law-abiding citizens can and do produce a chilling effect on criminal behavior." In the NIJ survey, 56 percent of the prisoners interviewed agreed that "a criminal is not going to mess around with a victim he knows is armed with a gun," and 74 percent said "one reason burglars avoid houses when people are at home is that they fear being shot."

Some advocates of gun ownership say that law-abiding citizens should be trained as an auxiliary to local police and be permitted to carry guns. "Hoodlums are only brave when the odds are all in their favor, when they can predict what's going to happen," said Roy Innis, chairman of the Congress of Racial Equality. "If he hears of this plan, that there are growing numbers of citizens legally armed and trained, when he plans to victimize his next prey he has to think, 'Is this prey really a prey?' "

Many applauded Bernhard Goetz, New York's "subway vigilante," after he shot four youths he claimed were threatening him last December. But gun control advocates reject the idea that even more guns in private hands will prevent crime. "We have 50 to 60 million handguns," Sugarmann said. "Why is all this crime going on? It's because there is no relationship between stopping crime and ownership of handguns."

The Constitutional Issue

The gun debate goes beyond the question of whether the easy availability of guns contributes to increased crime and accidental deaths. Gun owners regard ownership as a constitutional right guaranteed by the Second Amendment. Their opponents contend that the amendment does not apply to ownership restrictions on private citizens.

Both the tradition of gun ownership in the United States and the Second Amendment have their roots deep in English history. When the Anglo-Saxons ruled England 1,000 years ago, all able-bodied men were required to own weapons so that they were prepared for military service and to respond to the "hue and cry" sounded when a criminal was being pursued. By the time English settlers arrived in the New World, a militia composed of the entire male population was deemed preferable to a standing army in Britain. In 1765 Sir William Blackstone, the English jurist, wrote that the possession of arms was a "natural right of resistance and self-preservation, when the sanctions of society and laws are found insufficient to restrain the violence of oppression."

Universal arms ownership carried over to the American colonies out of necessity — hunting was not only a vital source of food, but weapons were needed to defend against attacks from hostile Indians and wild animals. But as the colonies moved toward independence, state militias comprised of all adult males assumed new importance. It was members of the local militias, calling themselves the Minutemen, who confronted British soldiers at Lexington and Concord in the opening battles of the American Revolution.

Several of the original 13 states also required all adult men to serve in the state militia and guaranteed the right of private citizens to keep and bear arms. When addition of the Bill of Rights to the Constitution was being considered in 1789, those guarantees were a priority of legislators who feared that a strong central government with a standing army could usurp the power of the states.

As ratified, the Second Amendment of the Constitution reads "A well-regulated militia being necessary to the security of a free state, the right of the people to keep and bear arms shall not be infringed." Had it simply guaranteed the right to keep and bear arms, there likely would be little debate today. However, the link between the right to own arms and the need for a trained militia has created confusion for almost two centuries and remains at the core of the debate over gun control.

To those favoring private possession of firearms, the Second Amendment implies an *individual* right to keep and bear arms. This belief is based in part on the theory, widely held in the early days of the Republic, that a militia was to be composed of "the body of the people." Don B. Kates Jr., a lawyer active in the pro-gun movement, wrote in the *Michigan Law Review* that the authors of the Second Amendment understood the individual right to own arms as a given. "They must necessarily have known that their undefined phrase 'right of the people to keep and bear arms' would be understood by their contemporaries in light of common law formulations like Blackstone's 'absolute rights of individuals,'" Kates wrote.

Gun control theorists emphasize the militia aspect of the amendment's wording. "Alone among the provisions of the Bill of Rights, the Second Amendment contains a statement of its rationale: 'a well-regulated militia being necessary to the security of a free state . . .,'" wrote Martin C. Ashman, attorney for Morton Grove, Ill., one of the few communities in the United States to ban handguns. "The circumstances surrounding the adoption and ratification of the United States Constitution and its Second Amendment, however, reflect debate over the proper balance of power between state and federal governments with respect to armed forces — and not over a right to arms for any individual purpose."

Viewed this way, the right to keep and bear arms is a *collective* right, applying to the people as a militia in defense of the state and not the people as individuals. Many say even this collective right is now an anachronism. Once feared as a threat to civil liberty, a standing army is now accepted as a necessity of national security. Gun control advocates say the states' National Guards, funded and armed by the federal government since 1903, have become the militias to which the Constitution referred.

Court Finds 'Special' Inherently Dangerous

On Oct. 3, 1985, the Maryland Court of Appeals set a precedent when it upheld a new strategy in the gun control effort. The case involved Olen Kelley who in 1981 was shot in the shoulder during a holdup of the Maryland grocery store that he managed. Kelley sued the manufacturer of the handgun used in the robbery, R. G. Industries, charging that because a handgun is an inherently dangerous product, its manufacturer is liable under the state's product liability laws. Although the appeals court denied that such laws applied to all handguns, it accepted Kelley's claim concerning small, cheap handguns — "Saturday night specials" — like the one Kelley was shot with.

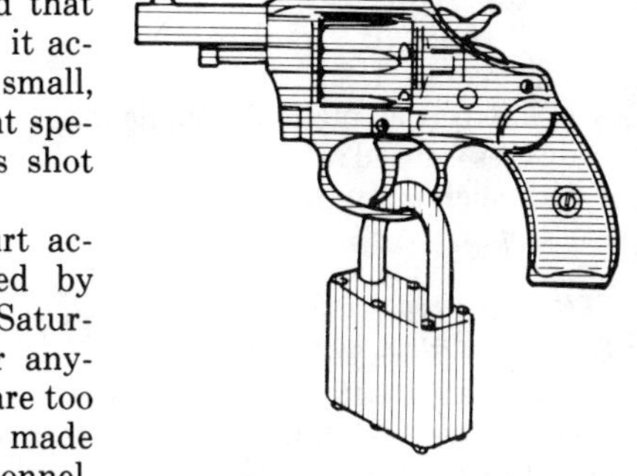

In making its ruling, the court accepted a theory long propounded by handgun control advocates — that Saturday night specials are useless for anything but criminal activity. "They are too inaccurate, unreliable and poorly made for use by law enforcement personnel, sportsmen, homeowners, or businessmen," the court ruled. "The chief 'value' a Saturday Night Special handgun has is in criminal activity, because of its easy concealability and low price." Injuries caused by such guns are actionable under product liability laws, the court said, because "the manufacturer or marketer of a Saturday Night Special knows or ought to know that he is making or selling a product principally to be used in criminal activity."

Gun advocates say that handguns are no more inherently dangerous than cars, which accounted for more than twice as many deaths in 1984 as handguns, or even common objects like kitchen knives or baseball bats. National Rifle Association spokesman David Warner, quoted in *USA Today* Oct. 22, 1985, said cheap handguns "are a useful tool to the people that need them most — the people who are poor, people that are black, people that are usually affected by crime."

Court Interpretations of Second Amendment

The Supreme Court of the United States has never ruled on the meaning of the militia clause. However, it has affirmed the authority of the state and federal governments to restrict the use or ownership of firearms in several cases. In *United States v. Cruikshank* (1876), the court ruled that private ownership of arms, even for a lawful purpose, was not "a right granted by the Constitution." In *Presser v. Illinois* (1886), the court upheld an Illinois law barring parades by armed paramilitary organizations, stating not only that the paraders had abused their right to keep and bear arms, but that the Second Amendment applied only to acts of Congress, and not to restrictions imposed by the states.

While not defining the term "militia," the court ruled on its scope in *United States v. Miller* (1939). The defendant had been convicted of interstate transportation of an unregistered sawed-off shotgun under the first federal gun control law, the National Firearms Act of 1934, which required registration of "gangster-style" weapons. The court ruled that the Second Amendment protected only those weapons necessary for the preservation or efficiency of a well-regulated militia and that the defendant had failed to prove that a shotgun with a barrel length of less than 18 inches fulfilled such a purpose.

On numerous occasions, state courts have upheld state and local gun control laws, some basing their decisions on the collective right theory of gun ownership. In October 1983, the Supreme Court declined to hear an appeal of a ruling by the Seventh Circuit Court of Appeals in Chicago that upheld the Morton Grove (Ill.) handgun ban. The appeals court said that "the Second Amendment is not applicable to Morton Grove and ... possession of handguns by individuals is not part of the right to keep and bear arms...." And in October 1985 a Maryland court held the manufacturer of a Saturday night special liable for damages caused when a man was shot with such a gun during a holdup *(see box, p. 51)*.

Police Opposition to Moves to Relax Laws

Taking an unusually strong advocacy position, nearly all major police organizations joined with the gun control forces to oppose changes to the Gun Control Act of 1968. In the past the police groups had often supported and rarely vocally opposed the positions of gun lobby groups like the NRA. However, they came out strongly against the McClure-Volkmer bill and sent representatives to testify at field hearings.

The police groups and the gun lobby are at odds on other gun issues as well. The police organizations favored bills that were proposed by Sen. Strom Thurmond, R-S.C., and Rep. Jack Brooks, D-Texas, that would have banned the sale of armor-piercing bullets, also known as "cop-killers" because they can penetrate most bullet-proof vests. "Any legislation that would restrict the availability of this ammunition ... will help to ensure the safety of those who have dedicated their lives to protecting the public against crime," said David Konstantin, research associate at the Police Executive Research Forum. The gun lobby denies that armor-piercing bullets are a danger to police officers and claims that the wording of the bill would have barred the sale of large-caliber hunting ammunition that is also capable of penetrating armor.

Law enforcement officials also expressed concern about the growing number of machine guns and semiautomatic military-type rifles, some of which are convertible to automatic use, in circulation.

Most of these guns are used by target shooters. But they are also being used by criminals to devastating effect; semiautomatics were used in a July 1984 shooting rampage in a California McDonald's and the 1985 shootings in a suburban Philadelphia shopping mall *(see p. 52)*. Drug dealers and racketeers are said to favor these weapons. And in April 1985, federal agents raided the rural Arkansas compound of the Covenant, Sword and Arm of the Lord, a fanatical anti-Semitic and racist group associated with the "Christian Identity" and neo-Nazi movement. They confiscated dozens of automatic and semiautomatic weapons, and reported that the Covenant was the likely arsenal for several violent right-wing hate groups.

Many police officials support federal legislative measures like those Rodino and Rep. William J. Hughes, D-N.J., proposed in the "Racketeer Weapons and Violent Crime Control Bill of 1985." That bill would have banned future sales of machine guns and silencers to private citizens and established a 15-day national waiting period prior to the purchase of a handgun. Gun control advocates believed police support for such legislation indicated that the tide was turning against the well-financed gun lobby. "The police were really taken aback when the NRA came out and fought them [on the armor-piercing bullet].... They were stunned again by the NRA defending the right of people to own machine guns....," said Charles Orasin, executive director of Handgun Control Inc. "When 'law-and-order' starts saying they're wrong, we think it's going to turn this thing."

The NRA's Aquilino denied that there is a schism between police and the pro-gun forces. "It's a perceived split," Aquilino said, fueled by "some rather selfish individuals [from] gun control groups." He added that while "too many of the national [police] leadership groups are buying it," the police rank-and-file does not go along with everything their national leadership says. "I really feel that the other side is losing badly, losing a tremendous amount of support," Aquilino said. "One reason is that academics over the past decade are starting to delve into givens, and they're finding that their givens hold no weight."

Congress and President Reagan apparently agree with Aquilino. In the spring of 1986 a new law (HR 4332) that weakens the 1968 Gun Control Act was passed by both houses and signed by Reagan. *(See Gun Control Law, p. 45.)*

PRESIDENCY/EXECUTIVE

Powers of the President

The place of the executive branch in the new plan of government greatly troubled the framers of the Constitution. A longstanding fear of authority, arising from experience with England's monarchy, led them to consider first a plan in which the executive deferred to the national legislature. The final draft of the Constitution, however, provided for a more balanced system in which some powers were to be shared between the president and Congress. Explicit congressional powers were enumerated at length, but Article II on the presidency was short and somewhat vague.

The looseness of the constitutional grant of power to the president allowed strong 19th century chief executives such as Thomas Jefferson, Andrew Jackson and Abraham Lincoln to establish precedents that steadily enhanced the position. Laws that provided them special powers in emergencies further strengthened presidents' authority.

Presidential power grew rapidly in the 20th century, spurred by a major economic depression and two world wars, until it posed a threat to the viability of Congress as a coequal branch of government. As the volume and complexity of federal business increased, legislative initiative shifted from the Capitol to the White House. Congress with its antiquated procedures found that it often was no match for the tremendous resources of the executive branch.

The result was repeated clashes between Congress and the president, particularly over the spending, war and treaty powers, as legislators resisted executive usurpation of the powers assigned to them by the Constitution.

Authorities for Powers

Constitutional Grant of Power

In sharp contrast to the explicit power granted the legislative branch (almost half the words of the Constitution are devoted to the functions of Congress), Article II of the Constitution describes only briefly the powers of the president. It begins with the ambiguous sentence: "The executive Power shall be vested in a President of the United States of America." But the nature of the president's authority has evolved only through practice.

The only authority for what has become presidential dominance in foreign affairs is contained in Section 2. In addition to appointing ambassadors and making treaties, the Constitution provides that "The President shall be Commander in Chief of the Army and Navy of the United States and of the Militia of the several states." Even those powers, however, were to be shared with the legislative branch; the Constitution gave Congress power to "provide for the common Defence," declare war, raise and support armies, ratify presidential treaties and confirm presidential nominations. Conversely, the Constitution requires Congress to share its legislative function by authorizing the president to provide Congress with certain information and to propose legislation.

The president's legislative role always has been important, but the complexity of running today's government has put the chief executive at the center of the legislative process. Political scientist Lawrence H. Chamberlain has observed that "When so much of the life of the individual is influenced by federal legislation, the attitude of the President toward this legislation and his skill in gaining legislative approval of his proposals are matters of practical interest to millions of people. . . ."

While the Constitution vests "all legislative powers" in Congress, it also directs the president to "give to the Congress Information of the State of the Union and recommend to their Consideration such Measures as he shall judge necessary and expedient." Congress has broadened this function to direct the president to present to Congress each year, in addition to the State of the Union message, two other general statements of presidential aims — an economic report including proposals directed to the maintenance of maximum employment, and a budget message outlining spending and revenue proposals. During a typical session, the president transmits to Congress scores of other legislative proposals, some initiated by the White House and others in conformity with various statutes. The president's responsibility for proposing legislation has become so important that one measure of his effectiveness is how successful he is in persuading Congress to adopt those proposals.

Article I of the Constitution gives the president an additional legislative power, that of the veto. Congress must submit every bill and joint resolution (except those joint resolutions proposing constitutional amendments) to the president, who may approve the measure, let it become law without his signature, or veto it and return it to Congress within 10 days. If a president disapproves a bill, Congress can override the veto only by a two-thirds vote of both houses. Because presidents usually find it relatively easy to muster the support of at least one-third plus one member of either the House or Senate, the veto has been used with deadly effect; fewer than 6 percent of all vetoes have been overridden.

In addition to the regular veto, the Constitution gives the president the special power of the pocket veto, which he may use at the end of a congressional session. Under this procedure the president, presented with a bill 10 days or less (Sundays excepted) prior to the adjournment of Congress, can merely ignore or "pocket" it, depriving Congress of an opportunity to override the veto.

Court decisions in 1974 and 1976 specified that a president's power to use the pocket veto was restricted to final adjournments of Congress and not to holiday recesses. This provision was reaffirmed in 1984 when a federal appeals court ruled that President Ronald Reagan had acted unconstitutionally when he pocket vetoed a bill between two sessions of the same Congress in November 1983.

The first American presidents conceived of the veto as a device to be used rarely and then only against legislative encroachment on the prerogatives of another branch of government. Presidents increased use of the veto in the 19th century, often to prevent Congress from passing private bills benefiting specific individuals. In the 20th century presidents began to use the threat of a veto as a powerful tool of persuasion.

Another major power the Constitution granted to the president is the power to make appointments. Article II, Section 2 empowers the president to appoint, besides ambassadors, "other public Ministers and Consuls, Judges of the Supreme Court, and all other Officers of the United States," subject to Senate confirmation. In the case of high offices such as Supreme Court justices and Cabinet officers, the president is able to pick persons of his own philosophy who presumably will aid his program.

The president's patronage power — gained through making appointments to increase political strength — derives from the constitutional authority to appoint lower court judges and other federal officials.

Despite the chance to reward a friend or political ally, many members of Congress bemoan their task of recommending patronage recipients to the president. The late Sen. Patrick McCarran, D-Nev. (1933-54) once said of judicial appointments, "It's the lousiest duty in the world because what you end up with is 100 enemies and one ingrate."

Powers Authorized by Congress

A number of the president's powers have been conferred by Congress. It was common at one time for Congress to grant special powers during emergencies. During World War I, for example, President Woodrow Wilson acquired sweeping control of the economy in what political scientist Rexford G. Tugwell has called "the most fantastic expansion of the executive known to the American experience." The numerous powers granted to him by Congress included prohibition of exports, takeover of the railroads and requisition of food and fuel for public use.

Statutes passed during World War I were still in effect as the United States prepared to enter World War II. In 1941 there were approximately 250 different laws delegating discretionary authority to the president and other executive officials. Congress also had given the executive emergency powers to deal with economic crises, most notably in the case of Franklin Delano Roosevelt and the Great Depression. Scholars theorized that an activist president probably could find some legislative grant for any action he deemed appropriate in an emergency.

In 1976 Congress moved to reassert its authority in this area by subjecting to congressional review all states of national emergency declared by the president. The measure also terminated, as of Sept. 14, 1978, all existing powers of the president and federal employees that were based on national emergency declarations in effect in 1976. Four such states of emergency, dating back to 1933, were in effect when the legislation was approved.

Modern laws authorizing the president to assign federal contract awards and to choose the location of government installations have given the president the powerful weapon of preferment. Preferment makes it possible for the president to reward or punish members of Congress quite spectacularly. It became particularly important after World War II as federal budgets skyrocketed. Members of the powerful committees and subcommittees dealing with defense, for example, frequently received defense installations in their districts in return for their support for military requests.

Powers From Precedent

Certain presidential powers are considered part of the office today simply because they were assumed by strong presidents and then carried on by their successors. Executive orders, by which the president can alter legislation, fall into this category. There is no legislative or constitutional basis for such orders. An example of an executive order with far-reaching effect was President Ronald Reagan's decontrol of crude oil, gasoline and propane prices issued on Jan. 28, 1981, for which no concurring act of Congress was necessary.

The president also holds certain powers simply because of the prestige of his office and the respect with which it is generally approached. This gives the president the ability to shape public opinion through his command of television, radio and the press. Such techniques as live televised news conferences, introduced by John F. Kennedy, and televised addresses before Congress have enabled presidents to gain public support for their legislative programs. President Reagan used television to his advantage in gathering support for his Economic Recovery Program in 1981.

The prestige of the president's office also helps him in persuading members of Congress to go along with his programs. Breakfast at the White House, a walk in the Rose Garden or a publicity picture taken with the president all are flattering to members of Congress and useful in their re-election campaigns.

War Powers

Probably the most fateful of the president's powers is the authority to act as commander in chief in times of war. The president's war powers are ambiguously stated in the Constitution but, in presenting the new charter to the nation, the authors of *The Federalist Papers* — James Madison, Alexander Hamilton and John Jay — made it clear that they construed the president's war powers narrowly.

Richard B. Morris, professor emeritus of history at Columbia University, told the Senate Foreign Relations Committee in 1971 that the Constitution's authors intended the presidential war powers to be "little more than the power to defend against imminent invasion when Congress was not in session."

Historically, however, the president has exercised much more than a defensive war-making power. Successive presidents — following the precedent of Lincoln's administration perhaps — have interpreted their authority in this realm broadly and dynamically. The list of specific actions taken by the White House under the authority of this constitutional provision is almost endless.

Throughout its history, the United States has been involved in more than 125 instances in which American troops have been sent into areas of conflict under presidential authority and without specific congressional approval. For example, in 1846 President James K. Polk unquestionably provoked Mexico into war when he ordered the army to occupy disputed territory along the Rio Grande River.

Recent years have seen increasingly frequent examples of presidential moves that involved the country in armed conflicts without the prior authorization of Congress. In 1950 President Harry S Truman ordered American armed forces in the Pacific to resist North Korea's aggressive drives into South Korea, thereby involving the United States in one of the most prolonged and expensive undeclared wars in its history. Beginning with President Dwight D. Eisenhower, a succession of chief executives expanded America's military commitments to the government of South Vietnam, thereby in time virtually guaranteeing massive American involvement in the conflict between North and South Vietnam.

Until it became clear that the war in Vietnam would not be easily or quickly won, most members of Congress thought that modern diplomatic and military conditions required that the president be free to conduct foreign policy and defend the nation. But as opposition to the war grew both among the public and on Capitol Hill, a number of members of Congress began to question the authority of the Lyndon B. Johnson administration to involve the United States so heavily in Vietnam. Many Americans came to equate White House reliance upon the armed forces to achieve diplomatic objectives — often with little or no consultation with Congress — as a symbol of the "imperial presidency."

In response, Congress sought to assume some of the responsibility for determining whether the United States should engage in armed conflict. On Nov. 7, 1973, Congress enacted, over President Richard Nixon's veto, the War Powers Resolution (PL 93-148). Intended to restrict the president's war-making powers, the measure set a 60-day limit on the president's authority to wage undeclared war and required him to report within 48 hours to House and Senate officers on any commitment of U.S. combat forces abroad. It also required the president to consult with Congress "in every possible instance" in advance of a troop commitment overseas.

Presidents Gerald R. Ford, Jimmy Carter and Reagan submitted reports to Congress under the War Powers Resolution in sending troops to Southeast Asia and the Middle East, but Congress never has tried to use its veto power to force a withdrawal of troops.

Moreover, that power was called into question by the Supreme Court's June 23, 1983, decision nullifying so-called "legislative veto" provisions in legislation.

The possibility of a confrontation between the White House and Congress loomed over the American presence in Lebanon. As U.S. Marines were drawn into the hostilities in 1983, some members of Congress began questioning their presence in the country and the president's power to keep U.S. forces in hostile situations without congressional approval. Shortly after Congress reluctantly approved a resolution in September authorizing the Marines to remain for another 18 months, 241 servicemen were killed in an explosion at their headquarters. Faced with the likelihood of a congressional resolution calling for removal of the troops, President Ronald Reagan withdrew the Marines in February 1984 to offshore ships, and ended all U.S. participation within a few weeks.

Spending Power

For the first 134 years of the republic, Congress held undisputed sway over the government's purse strings, except for scattered incidents of executive impoundment, where the president refuses to spend money Congress has appropriated. But the increasing complexity of both the economy and government led to fragmentation of congressional control over the budget and an expanded role for the executive. In 1921 Congress itself ceded coordination over government spending and revenue estimates to the executive branch, and the next half-century was marked by further erosion of the congressional budget-making power. Nonetheless, Congress clung jealously to its taxing and appropriating powers specifically granted by the Constitution.

Then in the late 1960s and 1970s an intense dispute between Congress and the Nixon administration over impoundment prompted Congress to try to reclaim some of its control over fiscal policy and spending priorities.

Although the Constitution gave Congress complete authority to appropriate federal funds, it left vague whether a president was required to spend the appropriated money or whether he could make independent judgment on the timing and need for outlays. The issue had been a nettlesome one throughout the nation's history; precedent for such impoundments apparently went back to the administration of Thomas Jefferson. But impoundments became a major dispute only when President Nixon refused to spend appropriated funds running into the billions of dollars.

Nixon argued that he was withholding funds to combat inflation, but opposition Democrats contended that Nixon was using impoundment primarily to assert his own spending priorities.

This conflict prompted Congress to enact the Congressional Budget and Impoundment Control Act of 1974 (PL 93-344) to reassert control over the federal budget. In full operation for the first time in 1976, the measure streamlined congressional procedures for handling spending and tax legislation and created a mechanism for congressional disapproval of presidential impoundments. The legislation called for the president, when deciding to withhold funds, to submit a report to Congress. If the withholding was intended to be temporary (a deferral), either chamber could disapprove it at any time. The funds then would have to be released for obligation by the agencies. If the withholding was intended to be permanent (a rescission), the president would have to obtain the support of both houses within 45 days of continuous session. Otherwise, the funds would have to be released.

Congress lost some of this control over spending with the Supreme Court's 1983 decision striking down the legislative veto. The ruling nullified Congress' power to halt deferrals without the president's consent. It did not affect rescissions.

As part of the budget process, Congress could direct its authorizing and appropriating committees to enact a single omnibus bill reconciling the spending and revenue requirements with the levels set out in the budget resolutions. It was the reconciliation tool that the White House and Republican strategists seized upon in 1981 to achieve the Reagan administration's desired budget cuts.

Record Number of Advisory Briefs:

Reagan Crusade Before Court Unprecedented in Intensity

Despite its stated opposition to judicial activism, the Reagan administration has engaged in an unprecedented degree of legal activism before the Supreme Court.

Since President Reagan took office in 1981, the solicitor general — who speaks for the government before the high court — has volunteered the administration's views to the justices more often than any of his predecessors.

The federal government is always the leading litigant before the court, simply because so many of the cases accepted for review by the justices involve federal laws or regulations.

But the Reagan administration, more than any earlier administration, also has been bombarding the court with *amicus curiae* (friend of the court) briefs. These are arguments designed to influence the court in cases that do not directly involve the federal government. Occasionally, the court has invited the government to submit an *amicus* brief on a particular issue; more often, the administration's arguments have been unsolicited.

In nearly every instance in which it has gone before the court, Reagan administration *amicus* briefs have urged the court to narrow its view of individual rights or to restrict the scope of government regulation.

In fact, the Justice Department has been pressing the court to make sweeping policy changes it has been unable to persuade Congress to adopt on issues such as abortion, school prayer, affirmative action and busing. So far, it has fared no better with the court than with Congress.

Comparison With Others

The solicitor general began to file friend-of-the-court briefs with the court as early as 1909, but not until the late 1950s was this vehicle used with any frequency.

Since 1957, the use of *amicus* briefs by the government has increased steadily. In 1966-70, according to the solicitor general's office, such briefs accounted for just under 20 percent of all government briefs filed at the court. In 1971-74, this figure rose to about 25 percent, and by the last half of the 1970s, to almost 33 percent.

In the October 1981 term, the first of Reagan's presidency, there was a notable leap in the government's use of *amicus* briefs. That year, 45 percent of the government's arguments to the court were friend-of-the-court briefs.

In the October 1982, 1983 and 1984 terms, *amicus* filings by the Justice Department dropped some, to 33 percent for two years and then 38 percent in the October 1984 term that ended in the summer of 1985.

But in the 1985-86 term, 45 percent of the briefs the government filed fell into this category.

This level of frequency of *amicus* filings is "substantially higher than the previous pattern of government briefs," said Steven Puro, an associate professor of political science at St. Louis University who has studied the government's use of *amicus* briefs.

The Kennedy and Johnson administrations were aggressive in using these briefs, Puro noted, but they also were selective, submitting a total of 77 *amicus* briefs during the five-year period from 1961 until 1966.

As of March 13, 1986, the Reagan administration, by contrast, had filed *amicus* briefs in 206 cases over the previous five years.

In an interview, Solicitor General Charles Fried said that what matters is not the number of *amicus* briefs filed, but how the court rules on issues addressed by the administration. "The really important part of the story," he said, "is whether we got it right."

Puro noted that from 1920 through the Johnson presidency, the government's *amicus* briefs were generally quite liberal in tone, arguing for an expansion of individual and civil rights. The Reagan administration, in its filings, has sought a more restrictive interpretation of those rights.

Why Briefs Are Filed

In an interview March 13, 1986, Lee, who served as solicitor general from 1981 until June 1985, described two categories of cases in which the government files *amicus* briefs.

The first, he said, includes "cases in which there is an identifiable federal interest in the sense that the federal government's law enforcement responsibility is implicated by someone else's case." Examples include an employee's civil-rights damage suit against his company, which could lead to changes in federal enforcement of Title VII of the 1964 Civil Rights Act, or private antitrust suits brought by one company against another, which could result in a court ruling that reshapes federal antitrust enforcement practices.

The second category, Lee said, includes cases that "do not involve any direct responsibility of the United States to enforce the law but concern some issue that is part of the president's program." He pointed to several church-state cases in which he filed such briefs, including a 1984 case in which the administration successfully urged the court to permit a Nativity scene on public property in Pawtucket, R.I.

Lee said that in general, he personally considered it "more appropriate to file an *amicus* brief in the first category rather than the second."

However, he said, "on occasion, it is appropriate to file an *amicus* brief whose only purpose is to further the president's program."

Fried agreed. "There are cases where what is at stake is not some particular government program but an important and pervasive view of the law or the Constitution. Here we must be particularly infrequent and rare in making a contribution, but historically this office has always spoken on such matters. We have never confined ourselves to filing only in cases where some distinct government program was affected."

Lee said, "It is certainly proper for the solicitor general to try to achieve broader objectives than law enforcement, but ... he must remember that his only audience is the Supreme Court.

"To try to use *amicus* filings to reach a larger audience can be counterproductive," Lee added, recalling that his 1983 *amicus* brief urging the court to give states and cities more discretion in regulating abortions resulted in the court's reaffirmation of its landmark 1973 decision in *Roe v. Wade* that struck down state laws banning abortion.

The administration seems undaunted by such setbacks. In a new pair of abortion cases this term, Fried filed an *amicus* brief urging the court to overturn *Roe v. Wade* entirely.

"Most of the time," Puro said, "solicitors general have taken the hint [from a rebuff by the court] and backed off. But there seems to be a very conscious strategy on the part of this administration to press issues despite the court's displeasure."

The Reagan administration, he said, seems "now to be filing briefs in order to stand up and be counted on a particular issue."

This impression is underscored, Puro said, by the fact that numerous details of the administration's briefs sometimes appear in the newspapers before the papers arrive at the Supreme Court.

Things are changing, he observed, "when you can find out about the government's *amicus* briefs by reading *The New York Times* as fast as you can by reading *U.S. Law Week*," a weekly publication of the Bureau of National Affairs that reports the Supreme Court's actions.

Although the court has not yet ruled on the pending abortion cases, it denied the administration's request to participate in the oral arguments on them — an indication that the justices have little interest in reconsidering *Roe v. Wade*.

Earlier in 1985, the solicitor general used an *amicus* brief to make sure the justices knew that Reagan wanted them to uphold an Alabama law permitting silent prayer in public schools. The court ruled the other way, just as it did on the 1983 abortion cases.

Recent Cases

When the court reassembled March 24, 1986, it heard two dozen cases argued that week and the week of March 31. The administration filed briefs in 19 of those cases. The government was a party to 10 of the cases and had to file its views in those. But in the others, the government volunteered its views.

It is primarily in those *amicus* briefs that the administration urged change in the court's treatment of certain issues in criminal law, civil liberties, business matters and discrimination.

There were exceptions, however. In one case directly involving the government, *U.S. Department of Transportation v. Paralyzed Veterans of America*, the administration sought to capitalize on the court's 1984 *Grove City College v. Bell* decision limiting the reach of the federal anti-discrimination laws.

The *Grove City* decision involved sex discrimination; the new case centered on discrimination against the handicapped. But the basic issue is the same: the sweep of a legal prohibition against discrimination in any "program or activity" receiving federal funds.

The solicitor general urged the justices to hold that a ban on discrimination against the handicapped applies only within airports that receive federal funds, not aboard a commercial airplane.

In another case, *International Union, United Auto Workers of America v. Brock*, the government contended that a union had no right to sue in federal court on behalf of members who claimed they were denied trade readjustment benefits provided under federal law. This position is in line with the Reagan administration's continuing effort to persuade the Supreme Court to limit access to the federal courts in general.

The Institutional View

In most of the cases in which the government is a party, the administration is arguing the same institutional point of view that any administration would, defending the interests and prerogatives of the executive branch.

In *Secretary of Agriculture v. Payne*, for example, the administration asked the justices to reverse a lower court order requiring it to reopen a multimillion-dollar program of emergency loans for farmers hard hit by natural disasters in the early 1970s.

The lower court held that because the program was inadequately publicized at the time it was operational, the government denied eligible farmers their "property" — emergency loans — without due process of law.

"There are cases where what is at stake is not some particular government program but an important and pervasive view of the law or the Constitution.... We have never confined ourselves to filing only in cases where some distinct government program was affected."

—Solicitor General Charles Fried

In *Federal Trade Commission v. Indiana Federation of Dentists*, the government urged the court to uphold a 1973 FTC ruling that Indiana dentists engaged in anti-competitive conduct and violated federal antitrust laws by refusing to submit X-rays to insurance companies seeking to use the films to validate benefit claims.

A federal court of appeals overturned the FTC ruling, finding that the dentists had legal, moral and ethical reasons for their refusal that shielded their conduct from challenge under the antitrust laws. The court's decision in this case could have wide significance in indicating whether professionals such as dentists, doctors and lawyers are subject to the same standards of antitrust law enforcement as businessmen in general.

In *U.S. Department of Treasury v. Galioto*, the government argued that the justices should reinstate a provision of the 1968 Gun Control Act that denies permission to own a gun to anyone once committed to a mental institution. A lower court struck that provision down because the law provides a way for convicted felons to regain their rights to gun ownership under certain circumstances, but not for former mental patients to do so.

In *United States v. Dion,* the Justice Department argued that the federal laws protecting bald and golden eagles prevent Sioux Indians in South Dakota from hunting those eagles, even on their own reservations.

And in *Brock v. Pierce County,* the government sought reversal of a ruling that an administrative agency forfeits its right to recover federal funds that were misspent under the Comprehensive Employment and Training Act if it does not move to do so within a period fixed by law.

The Advisory Arguments

When the administration can choose with whom to side in a case, it tends to side with property owners, businessmen or prosecutors — not with regulators, employees or defendants.

For example, in the *amicus* briefs filed in the cases the court heard late in March and early in April 1986, the administration took the following positions.

In *Meritor Savings Bank v. Vinson,* a case of alleged sexual harassment, the government argued that "an employer ... should generally be able to insulate itself from liability by publicizing a policy against sexual harassment and implementing a procedure designed to resolve sexual harassment complaints."

This "novel suggestion" is strongly opposed by the Women's Legal Defense Fund and others who filed briefs on the side of the employee in this case. Just because a procedure for resolving such complaints exists, they argue, there is no guarantee that it will be useful or effective.

In *Baker v. General Motors Corporation,* the government argued that a state court was correct in disqualifying workers who sought unemployment compensation if they had helped finance the labor dispute causing their unemployment by contributing to an emergency strike fund.

A significant policy shift is apparent in another administration *amicus* brief, this time in a case involving land-use regulation. Traditionally, the federal government has staunchly defended its own authority, and that of state and local governments, to regulate the use of land, free of any responsibility to compensate landowners for any adverse effects.

In *MacDonald, Sommer & Frates v. Yolo County,* the government for the first time agreed with landowners that in some instances, land-use regulation may be so drastic in its effects on property rights that it may constitute the sort of "taking" of property for which the Constitution requires just compensation.

In a case that ended inconclusively in 1985, the administration sounded quite another tune, contending that a damage award against a government agency in such cases was "a wholly unwarranted and peremptory intrusion by the federal courts into the orderly administration of the zoning and land-use laws of the states and their local governments."

If the court agrees with the administration's new view of this matter, state and local government officials warn that it could cost government at all levels billions of dollars in damages — and would certainly chill efforts to enforce land-use restrictions of every type.

In *Memphis Community Schools v. Stachura,* the administration urged the court to limit damage awards compensating people whose civil rights have been violated by government action.

Edward Stachura was suspended from his junior high school teaching job in Memphis, Mich., in 1979 because of community criticism of his method of teaching children about human sexuality. Stachura challenged his suspension as a violation of his First Amendment right of free speech and as depriving him of his job without due process of law.

A jury awarded him $321,000 in damages, an amount that the administration termed "extravagant" and criticized as awarded "merely on the basis of the jury's unguided assessment of the intrinsic value of the constitutional rights that were claimed to have been violated."

It is time to limit such awards, the government's *amicus* brief contended, to prevent future windfalls to plaintiffs and unjust and unforeseeable liability for government agencies.

In another case in the same vein, *City of Riverside v. Rivera,* the government said that courts should not approve awards of attorneys' fees in civil rights cases that exceed the damages awarded to the clients those lawyers represent.

In this case, a group of individuals who sued the city of Riverside after being wrongly arrested by city police won $33,000 in damages. Their attorneys were awarded $245,000 in fees. The government argued that a fee that exceeds or approximates the damages awarded in such a case should be presumed to be unreasonable.

The government sided with the prosecution in two criminal cases to be argued in this round.

In *Rose v. Clark,* the solicitor general argued that even if jury instructions challenged by a man convicted of murder were improper, they constituted only a "harmless error" that should not be used as the basis for overturning his conviction.

And in *Smalis v. Pennsylvania,* the administration agreed with a lower court ruling that the constitutional guarantee against double jeopardy does not prevent the retrial of a person whose first trial was erroneously terminated halfway through by a judge who found the evidence insufficient to proceed.

But at least one of this group of *amicus* briefs reflects an institutional interest rather than a policy preference. In *Wardair Canada Inc. v. Florida Department of Revenue,* the administration sided with the airline, which challenged as unconstitutional a state tax on the aviation fuel used by foreign airlines in foreign commerce.

This, the solicitor general argued, will impair and undermine the federal government's power to engage in international negotiations and so should be struck down by the court. ∎

Background:

Reagan activism: 1985 CQ Almanac p. 3-A; 1984 Almanac p. 3-A; 1985 CQ Weekly Report pp. 1340, 1463, 1934.

Rebuffs to Reagan: abortion, 1983 Almanac p. 306; school prayer, 1984 Almanac pp. 245, 247; busing, 1983 Weekly Report p. 224.

Affirmative action: 1984 Almanac p. 8-A; 1985 Weekly Report p. 2104; Weekly Report p. 315.

Crèche case: 1984 Almanac p. 11-A.

Pending abortion cases: 1985 Weekly Report p. 2153.

Silent prayer: 1985 Weekly Report p. 1111.

Discrimination cases: 1984 Almanac p. 239; 1985 Weekly Report p. 2185.

Land-use regulation: 1985 Weekly Report p. 307.

In Wake of Libya, Skirmishing Over War Powers

President Reagan's military actions against Libya have renewed debate about the role of Congress in initiating armed conflict.

By declaring that he has the exclusive power to act in "self-defense" against terrorism, Reagan has prompted two contradictory responses in Congress: Some members want him to consult more extensively with them before sending U.S. troops into combat, while others want to give him even more flexibility to act against terrorism without interference from Capitol Hill.

Much of the attention has been focused on the 1973 War Powers Resolution, which requires the president to "consult" with Congress before sending troops into hostilities and to report to Congress immediately after military engagements.

Enacted in the aftermath of the Vietnam War, the law also requires the withdrawal of troops from hostile action after 60 days unless Congress authorizes their presence.

Reagan employed military power against Libya twice in less than a month, and in neither case did he seek extensive advice or approval from Congress.

In late March 1986, the president sent massive air and naval forces to challenge Libya's claim to sovereignty over the Gulf of Sidra, provoking a shooting match during which U.S. planes destroyed several Libyan missile sites and ships.

On April 14, Reagan launched a bombardment of Libyan military targets in retaliation for that country's alleged backing of terrorism. Announcing the April 14 raid, Reagan said he would "do it again" if necessary.

Both military actions generated strong support in Congress. But some members, especially Democrats, said Reagan failed to meet the War Powers act requirements for consulting with Congress in advance.

By saying he was acting in self-defense against terrorism, Reagan was developing "a new way of going to war which totally bypasses the Constitution" and its requirement that only Congress can declare war, said Dante B. Fascell, D-Fla., chairman of the House Foreign Affairs Committee.

Although Reagan sent reports to Congress after both incidents, in neither report did he say he was acting in accordance with the War Powers Resolution.

The president did not consult with Congress before the Gulf of Sidra operation, and he called in top congressional leaders only three hours before the April 14 bombing got under way.

To remedy the lack of consultation, senior Democrats in the Senate have proposed creation of a "leadership committee" to which the president would turn when he contemplates military action. As outlined by Minority Leader Robert C. Byrd, D-W.Va., the proposal calls for an official committee with 18 members.

Establishment of an informal leadership group, proposed by Senate Foreign Relations Committee Chairman Richard G. Lugar, R-Ind., has gained the blessing of Secretary of State George P. Shultz.

Others, led by Senate Majority Leader Robert Dole, R-Kan., drew the opposite conclusion: that the Libyan actions showed the need to give the president more freedom from congressional oversight. They introduced legislation (S 2335, HR 4611) to exempt military strikes against terrorists from the War Powers act and to give the president broad powers to carry out such actions.

The Reagan administration has called the bill unnecessary, but sponsors said they will press for its enactment, possibly by offering it as an amendment to the upcoming Defense Department authorizations legislation.

Debating War Powers

The Libyan incidents gave "new impetus" to the War Powers debate, Fascell said, with most of the discussion centering on how to improve the consultation process.

The Reagan administration has fueled questions about its actions by telling Congress that some forms of military response to terrorism are exempt from the consultations require-

The Reagan administration has been "waltzing around the act," complying with it "only when it suits them," complains Rep. Dante B. Fascell, D-Fla., left.

"Let us not try to cope with our terrorist adversaries hobbled by restrictions," says Sen. Robert Dole, R-Kan.

Sounding Off Over Who Isn't Keeping Quiet

Can Congress keep a secret?

Administration officials ask that question — and quickly answer "no" — whenever members of Congress complain about being excluded from a decision to send U.S. armed forces into combat.

In an unusually direct challenge to Congress, State Department legal adviser Abraham D. Sofaer on April 29 cited the danger of leaks as one reason President Reagan has been reluctant to consult with Capitol Hill leaders before launching military actions, such as attacks on Libya.

Testifying before a House Foreign Affairs Subcommittee, Sofaer recalled an incident on April 14, 1986, the day Reagan ordered U.S. warplanes to bomb Libya.

Key congressional leaders were called to the White House three hours before the bombers reached their targets. The arrival of the legislators alerted reporters that something was up, Sofaer said, and when the meeting was over some members confirmed that Reagan would make a televised address to the nation that evening.

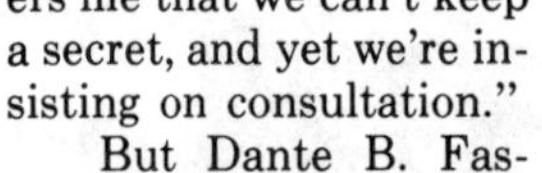

Rep. Henry J. Hyde

Those events "led to rumors of imminent military action that could have jeopardized the success of the operation and the lives of our men," Sofaer said.

Rep. Henry J. Hyde, R-Ill., echoed Sofaer's charge, saying: "It bothers me that we can't keep a secret, and yet we're insisting on consultation."

But Dante B. Fascell, D-Fla., chairman of the Foreign Affairs Committee, scoffed at such accusations. Administration officials for days had hinted at military action and had leaked information to the news media about U.S. maneuvering in the Mediterranean Sea, he said. The White House itself raised speculation shortly before the raid by asking television networks for time for Reagan's speech, Fascell noted.

And Rep. Stephen J. Solarz, D-N.Y., turned the administration's question on its head. Citing the repeated use by the White House of classified information to bolster official policy, Solarz said that "the executive branch is responsible for many more leaks than the Congress."

The two leaders of the Senate Intelligence Committee — Chairman Dave Durenberger, R-Minn., and Vice Chairman Patrick J. Leahy, D-Vt. — in recent months have drawn attention to leaks by the administration. In an April 4 speech, Durenberger said that "every administration has faced the problem of leaks, but none so much as this one."

Sen. Dave Durenberger

Officials who attack the congressional Intelligence committees for leaking sensitive information, Durenberger added, "are more often than not trying to destroy the credibility of the oversight process, rather than to improve security."

The two senators on May 2 released a statement accusing administration officials of revealing top-secret information about CIA attempts to oust Libyan leader Muammar el-Qaddafi. "These aren't leaks; this is a flood of information coming from the administration," they said.

In a speech Oct. 21, 1985, Durenberger predicted that the administration, bypassing Congress because of secrecy concerns, would use "covert" means to battle terrorists, and that "one of these daring deals will blow up in their face. In the aftermath of failure, a predictable Congress will enact a new War Powers act or [intelligence] oversight act."

As a result, he added, Congress will, "in effect, continue to write the parameters of administration policy."

ments of the War Powers Resolution (PL 93-148). *(1973 CQ Almanac p. 95)*

Congressional leaders and administration officials are approaching the matter with some hesitation, apparently fearing the consequences of reopening sensitive political and legal issues that Congress carefully skirted when it wrote the law in 1973 and enacted it over President Ford's veto.

For that reason, it is still not clear whether Congress will pass legislation making changes in the act. Even Dole's bill — which he said "supersedes" the act — was drafted as free-standing legislation that would not directly amend the law.

Although widely supported across the full political spectrum in Congress, the War Powers act is most staunchly defended by Democrats who fear another Vietnam-type war and who are intensely suspicious of Reagan's readiness to use military might.

Byrd, Fascell and other Democrats also had complained that President Carter failed to consult with Congress, but they have had more occasion to criticize Reagan because he has sent troops into hostilities more often than Carter did.

Fascell said the Reagan administration has been "waltzing around the act" and complying with it "only when it suits them." But he told administration officials they must recognize that the War Powers act "is still the law, whether you like it or not."

Some congressional leaders long have considered amending the law to toughen it — for example by eliminating loopholes in the consultation requirement. Sen. Alan Cranston, D-Calif., and liberals in the House repeatedly have introduced legislation

(S 937, HR 1304) to require the president to get approval from Congress before sending troops to war, with limited exceptions for emergencies.

Faced with the prospect of a presidential veto and resulting political furor, no one has ever pressed the issue, and bills such as Cranston's have languished in committee.

Some conservatives in Congress, most prominently Sen. Barry Goldwater, R-Ariz., never have accepted the War Powers act and have demanded its repeal. Goldwater's bill (S 305) to banish the law from the books also has never gotten anywhere.

The Reagan administration has called portions of the act unconstitutional and has avoided taking actions that could be seen as accepting the validity of its provisions.

Nevertheless, the administration insists it has complied with the law, and Reagan was the first president to invoke officially the law's key section requiring congressional approval for a long-term military action; in 1983 he signed into law a resolution (PL 98-119) authorizing the presence of Marines in a Beirut "peacekeeping" force.

Justifying Reagan's use of force against Libya, the administration contended that the War Powers act does not apply to some military steps directed against terrorists. Under that view, the president also is not required to keep Congress informed about military exercises, even ones such as the recent challenge to Libya's territorial claim in the Gulf of Sidra.

Testifying on April 29 before the House Foreign Affairs Subcommittee on Arms Control, International Security and Science, State Department legal adviser Abraham D. Sofaer drew distinctions among three types of military actions. Other experts called by the subcommittee disagreed with some of Sofaer's statements.

The three types of force cited by Sofaer are:

- A conventional military action against a sovereign country, such as the April 14 attack on Libya. Such an action comes under the War Powers act, Sofaer said, and the president should consult ahead of time with Congress. But, he added, "the need for swiftness and secrecy" might reduce the amount of advance notice.

Some members of Congress challenged Sofaer's insistence that Reagan consulted properly with Congress before the Libya attack. Fascell noted that congressional leaders were called to the White House as U.S. bombers were approaching Libya — just three hours before the actual attack took place.

"We were informed that a decision had been made," Fascell said. "We were not consulted."

In a letter to Reagan, Byrd and other Senate Democratic leaders noted that the raid had been the subject of intense press speculation for days before April 14, fueled by leaks and public statements from administration officials. In that context, they said, calling members of Congress to the White House shortly before the raid "amounts to a notification of your actions rather than the consultation required by law. . . ."

Sofaer cited the advance press reports as evidence that Congress was kept informed of Reagan's plans.

- The use of special anti-terrorist units for limited missions, such as securing the release of hostages held overseas or capturing terrorists.

Some on Capitol Hill dispute the administration's view that President Reagan consulted properly with Congress before an April 14 attack on Libya, in which Muammar el-Qaddafi's headquarters was hit.

Such actions generally would not come under the War Powers act requirements, Sofaer said, because a commando unit most likely would attack a limited number of terrorists, rather than the military forces of a sovereign country. That "is more analogous to law enforcement activity by police" than to the acts of war governed by the War Powers act, he said.

Even if such actions do come under the law, Sofaer added, advance notice likely will be curtailed because of the need for speed and secrecy.

Archibald Cox, chairman of Common Cause and former Watergate special prosecutor, told the Foreign Affairs subcommittee on May 1 that Sofaer appeared justified in exempting small-scale, anti-terrorist actions from the War Powers requirements.

The law's descriptions of hostilities "left considerable room" for the president to use small units to combat terrorism when a government is not the target and probably will not respond, Cox said.

- Military exercises, such as training missions, even when there is a chance of meeting or provoking hostilities. Routine exercises never have been considered as coming under the

War Powers act, Sofaer said.

J. Brian Atwood, assistant secretary of state for legislative affairs in the Carter administration, told the Foreign Affairs subcommittee that the Pentagon has devised a "probability-of-conflict" formula to determine when Congress should be notified about exercises. Congress is informed only if the Pentagon determines that the chance of encountering conflict in an exercise is greater than 50 percent, Atwood said. In recent cases, he added, the Pentagon skewed the formula to avoid notifying Congress.

In the Gulf of Sidra case, Reagan did not consult with Congress even through Libyan leader Muammar el-Qaddafi had threatened to attack any forces entering the gulf and thereby crossing what he called a "line of death."

Sofaer said the administration decided that U.S. forces were not likely to encounter hostilities. Fascell sharply rejected that contention, saying "any reasonable person would have concluded that there might be hostilities," especially since U.S. and Libyan forces had clashed under similar circumstances in 1981.

A Leadership Panel

Byrd's suggestion for an 18-member leadership committee to consult with the president before he takes military actions has attracted wide support from advocates of the War Powers act. Byrd first proposed the committee in his letter to Reagan cosigned by ranking Democrats on the Senate Armed Services, Foreign Relations and Intelligence committees: Sam Nunn of Georgia, Claiborne Pell of Rhode Island and Patrick J. Leahy of Vermont, respectively.

Fascell and leading House Democrats generally support the proposal, but are expected to introduce some changes of their own.

As outlined in the letter to Reagan, the committee would include: the Speaker of the House, the president pro tempore of the Senate, the majority and minority leaders of both chambers, and the chairmen and ranking minority members of the House and Senate Armed Services, Foreign Affairs and Foreign Relations, and Intelligence committees.

Byrd, Pell, Nunn and Leahy all would qualify for membership by virtue of their committee posts.

The Democrats told Reagan that the committee would be one "to which you could look with more predictability" in consulting with Congress.

Taylor Reveley, a private attorney who helped develop the proposal, told the Foreign Affairs subcommittee that the leadership panel should have several attributes: It should be a joint committee of the two houses; the number of members should be kept as small as possible; all members should be senior leaders and should be expert in foreign, military or intelligence matters; and it should be able to meet quickly and secretly.

Rep. Stephen J. Solarz, D-N.Y., a senior Foreign Affairs member and frequent Reagan critic, said the president should "seize the opportunity" offered by the Byrd proposal. Consulting with such a committee, Solarz said, would give the president the chance to "bring the congressional leaders on board" for any military action, thus reducing the prospect of criticism from Capitol Hill.

Some versions of the proposal being discussed on Capitol Hill, such as Byrd's bill, would establish the group as a formal committee, complete with a small staff.

Lugar, chairman of the Foreign Relations Committee, and Secretary of State Shultz have discussed creating an informal panel, similar to the group of senators who have been monitoring U.S.-Soviet arms control negotiations in Geneva. Lugar wants a small committee — possibly as few as two members from each chamber — appointed by the leadership.

Similar suggestions have circulated for years on Capitol Hill — primarily as a way of allowing congressional involvement in any president's decision to use nuclear weapons.

While reluctant to criticize senior Democratic leaders, some advocates of the War Powers act privately expressed two concerns about the Byrd proposal.

First, they noted that the leadership committee would be composed of senior members who, by virtue of age or experience, probably are more conservative than Congress as a whole and therefore might be reluctant to challenge any action proposed by the president.

Second, creating such a committee with fixed membership might exclude members of Congress who are experts in certain fields and who could offer valuable advice. For example, Rep. Lee H. Hamilton, D-Ind., widely viewed as Congress' ranking authority on the Middle East, would be a member of the leadership panel because he is chairman of the House Intelligence Committee. But under House rules Hamilton must relinquish the Intelligence seat at the end of 1986, and so he no longer would qualify for the leadership committee.

Needed Power, or Blank Check?

Dole's bill would go in the opposite direction of the Democratic proposal by deliberately excluding Congress from advance involvement with any military steps the president says are needed to combat terrorism.

Such an action is necessary, according to the bill's preamble, because terrorism is "a form of aggression" and a threat "to the national security and national interests of the United States."

The key provision of the bill would authorize the president "to undertake actions to protect United States persons against terrorists and terrorist activity through the use of all such anti-terrorism and counter-terrorism measures as he deems necessary."

The bill would apply only to military actions overseas.

The main effect of that provision, Dole said, would be to exempt military actions against terrorism from the consultation and other requirements of the 1973 War Powers act.

"We don't fight our military adversaries with 1973 weapons," Dole said in a statement on April 30. "Let us not try to cope with our terrorist adversaries hobbled by restrictions built into 1973 laws."

Archibald Cox called the bill a "rash and highly dangerous overreaction" because it would allow the president to use military force "at any time and on any scale that the president may say is useful to deter terrorism."

Cox noted, for example, that Reagan has charged Nicaragua with supporting terrorism, and so the Dole bill would authorize him to send troops there "to punish or topple that regime and to keep them there indefinitely."

The Reagan administration has been cool to the proposal, with Sofaer calling it unnecessary.

Other officials said they fear such a bill might bring the War Powers debate full circle by causing needless controversy and imposing further restrictions on the president rather than giving him more flexibility.

"The last thing we need right now is Congress mucking around with the War Powers act," said one State Department official. ∎

Hill Backing for Reagan Continues to Decline

Although President Reagan tried to brush off the "lame duck" label in the first year of his second term, congressional support for the president's positions dropped in 1985 to the lowest level since he took office.

Congress agreed with Reagan on 59.9 percent of the roll-call votes on which he staked out a position, according to Congressional Quarterly's annual study of legislators' backing for presidential positions.

Reagan's legislative success rate was down almost 6 percentage points from 1984. The drop accelerates the decline in support that has occurred since 1981, when Reagan won a stunning series of legislative victories on key parts of his economic program. Until 1985, the decline in congressional backing had been slowing to the point that 1984 presidential support dropped only 1 percentage point.

At year's end in 1985, Reagan dismissed charges of "lame-duckery" after the House passed legislation (HR 3838) overhauling the tax code, a top Reagan priority for his second term.

But in analysis of votes taken throughout the year, Congressional Quarterly found that Reagan lost more votes than he won in the House. The president prevailed in 45 percent of the House roll-call votes where he had declared a clear, well-known stand. That is down from a 52 percent success rate in the House in 1984.

In the Senate, Reagan's roll-call victories dropped to 72 percent, as the GOP-dominated chamber parted ways with the president on a variety of issues, among them trade and farm policy. In 1984, the Senate supported Reagan on 86 percent of the roll calls considered by the CQ study.

The drop in Reagan's congressional support is in keeping with the experience of recent past presidents. Every president since Dwight D. Eisenhower who remained in office more than four years saw a drop in congressional support in his fifth year in the White House.

Reagan's score marked the sixth time in the 33 years since CQ began the vote study that congressional support for a president has dipped below 60 percent. *(Charts, this page, p. 64)*

Success Rate

Following are the annual percentages of presidential victories since 1953 on congressional votes where the presidents took a clear-cut position:

Eisenhower	
1953	89.0%
1954	82.8
1955	75.0
1956	70.0
1957	68.0
1958	76.0
1959	52.0
1960	65.0
Kennedy	
1961	81.0%
1962	85.4
1963	87.1
Johnson	
1964	88.0%
1965	93.0
1966	79.0
1967	79.0
1968	75.0
Nixon	
1969	74.0%
1970	77.0
1971	75.0
1972	66.0
1973	50.6
1974	59.6
Ford	
1974	58.2%
1975	61.0
1976	53.8
Carter	
1977	75.4%
1978	78.3
1979	76.8
1980	75.1
Reagan	
1981	82.4%
1982	72.4
1983	67.1
1984	65.8
1985	59.9

Words of Caution

The CQ study is based on the results of 182 roll-call votes for which the president had a clearly stated position. Of those, 102 of the roll calls were in the Senate and 80 were in the House. *(Ground rules, box, p. 65)*

The analysis is a good indication of the White House's increasing political problems in Congress, but it does not measure how much of the president's program was enacted. As an indicator of a member's loyalty to the president, the study should be used with caution, and readers should keep several caveats in mind.

First, the study included only issues that were brought to a roll-call vote on the House or Senate floor. Not taken into account are elements of the White House agenda that were shelved before they got to the floor, extensively revised or compromised in private or whisked through by voice vote.

For example, because the House approved its tax-overhaul bill by voice vote, Reagan's 1985 support score is unaffected by the final vote on the most important item on the president's domestic agenda.

Second, the study takes account only of votes in which the president's support or opposition was clear and known to members.

Third, all votes are given equal weight, regardless of whether they involve momentous or trivial issues, narrow or resounding margins, administration proposals or congressional initiatives.

So, for example, the unanimous Senate vote to confirm James A. Baker III to be secretary of the Treasury was given the same weight as a cliffhanger Senate vote to approve a sweeping fiscal 1986 budget plan (S Con Res 32), when Vice President George Bush was called in to break a 49-49 tie.

Finally, issues that are the subject of many roll-call votes may have influenced the study more than questions that are the subject of a single vote. One of the most

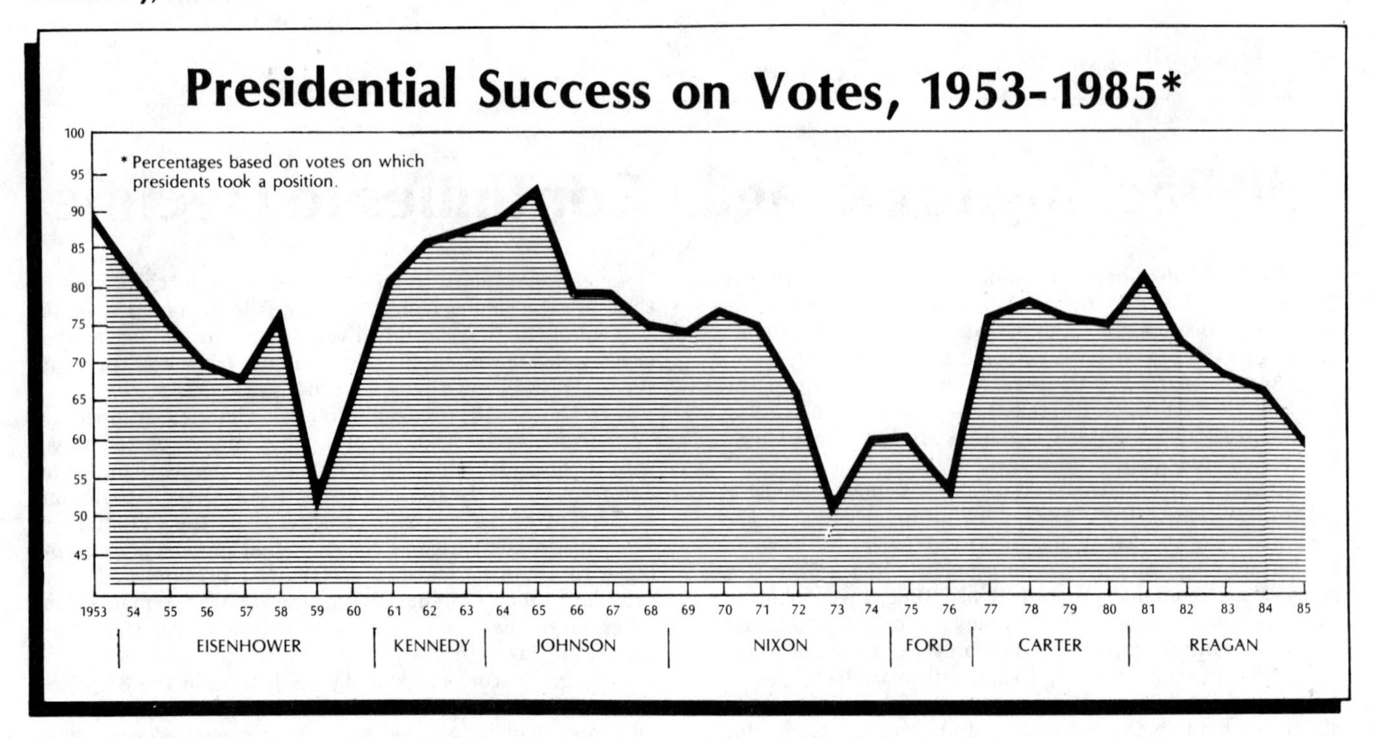

striking examples was in 1978, when President Carter's congressional support rating was bolstered dramatically by 55 winning roll-call votes, mostly procedural, on ratification of the Panama Canal treaties.

In 1985, the House took 20 roll-call votes during debate on legislation rewriting federal farm policy, and 11 of those tallies were considered in the CQ study. But in debate over an extraordinary budget-process overhaul designed to eliminate federal deficits by fiscal 1991, there was only one House roll-call vote where the president's position was clear enough to be considered in the study.

A reporter or researcher interested in how an individual lawmaker voted on the various parts of the Reagan program is advised to look at the specifics of the member's legislative actions, including his or her record on CQ's selection of key votes.

Within those limitations, the presidential support rating is a rough gauge of the relationship between the president and Congress. Over time, the score reflects the rises and drops in those relations, and individuals' ratings show how particular members fit the trends.

The study was begun in 1953, President Eisenhower's first year in office, and has long been considered a yardstick of presidential success on Capitol Hill. A careful reading of the study's ground rules shows its limitations as a measure of executive clout, but not all readers have used the figures with care.

During the 1980 presidential campaign, President Carter's supporters cited his 77 percent support score in 1979 as evidence that Congress had passed four-fifths of the president's program. A Carter aide later conceded that CQ's statistics had been "mistranslated or misused."

Patterns Within Parties, Regions

As might be expected of a Republican president, Reagan was supported more often by GOP lawmakers than by Democrats.

Among Democrats in the Senate, support for the president dipped to 35 percent. That is down from 41 percent in 1984, an election year when more Democrats may have been wary of opposing a president as popular as Reagan.

House Democrats backed Reagan 30 percent of the time, down 4 points from 1984.

Senate Republicans supported the president 75 percent of the time, about the same as in 1984.

The only quarter from which Reagan drew increased support was among House Republicans. Although tensions between the House GOP and Reagan reached a breaking point over the 1985 tax overhaul bill, which Republicans helped sidetrack temporarily, they increasingly backed his positions on earlier votes.

The support score for House Republicans climbed 7 points to 67 percent, almost reversing the 10-point decline in support these members registered in 1984.

An analysis of voting patterns by party and region (East, West, South, Midwest) shows that support for Reagan waned among Democrats from all regions. The largest drop was registered among senators from the South, who in 1984 had been more likely than not to support the president's positions. Southern senators' support score dropped to 44 percent in 1985, from 52 percent.

Among Republicans, Reagan lost support among Western and Southern senators, but gained ground in other regions. Nonetheless, Southern Republicans remained among Reagan's most reliable backers in the Senate, supporting his position 78 percent of the time.

Top Senate Friends, Foes

The president's two most reliable supporters in the Senate came from the top of the new leadership team: Majority Leader Robert Dole of Kansas headed the list, backing the president 92 percent of the time, followed by Assistant Majority Leader Alan K. Simpson, R-Wyo., who racked up a 90 percent support score.

A key player in the year's ongoing debate about deficit reduction, Budget Committee Chairman Pete V. Domenici, R-N.M., was no longer among the president's top 10 Senate supporters as he was in 1984. Domenici, who helped draft a

Ground Rules for CQ Presidential Support-Opposition

Presidential Issues — CQ tries to determine what the president personally, as distinct from other administration officials, does and does not want in the way of legislative action by analyzing his messages to Congress, press conference remarks and other public statements and documents. Members must be aware of the position when the vote is taken.

Borderline Cases — By the time an issue reaches a vote, it may differ from the original form in which the president expressed himself. In such cases, CQ analyzes the measure to determine whether, on balance, the features favored by the president outweigh those he opposed or vice versa. Only then is the vote classified.

Some Votes Excluded — Occasionally, important measures are so extensively amended on the floor that it is impossible to characterize final passage as a victory or defeat for the president.

Procedural Votes — Votes on motions to recommit, to reconsider or to table often are key tests that govern the legislative outcome. Such votes are necessarily included in the presidential support tabulations.

Appropriations — Generally, votes on passage of appropriations bills are not included in the tabulations, since it is rarely possible to determine the president's position on the revisions Congress almost invariably makes in the sums allowed. However, votes on amendments to cut or increase specific amounts requested in the president's budget are included.

Failure to Vote — In tabulating the support or opposition scores of members on the selected presidential-issue votes, CQ counts only "yea" and "nay" votes on the ground that only these affect the outcome. Most failures to vote reflect absences because of illness or official business. Failures to vote lower both support and opposition scores equally.

Weighting — All presidential-issue votes have equal statistical weight in the analysis.

Changed Positions — Presidential support is determined by the position of the president at the time of a vote, even though that position may be different from an earlier position, or may have been reversed after the vote was taken.

budget that reordered Reagan's spending priorities, supported the president 82 percent of the time, down from 88 percent in 1984.

The Republican who was most likely to oppose Reagan was, for the second year in a row, Lowell P. Weicker Jr. of Connecticut. He parted ways with the president on 53 percent of the roll-call votes considered.

The president's top Democratic supporters continued to come largely from the South. But they registered lower levels of support than in 1984.

In 1985, Sam Nunn of Georgia voted with the president 58 percent of the time — more often than any other Senate Democrat. But that was down from his 1984 support score of 69 percent.

The support score of Howell Heflin of Alabama fell sharply to 54 percent, down from 75 percent in 1984 when he was the Democrat most likely to back the president.

Gary Hart of Colorado, the former presidential candidate who is expected to make a second run for the White House in 1988, was among the three Democrats who opposed Reagan most often. Hart posted a 77 percent opposition score, as did Spark M. Matsunaga of Hawaii and freshman Tom Harkin of Iowa.

House Support, Opposition Ratings

The member of Congress who voted most often with the president in 1985 was freshman Fred J. Eckert, R-N.Y., who supported Reagan 94 percent of the time.

Texas sent to Congress some of Reagan's most reliable backers. Half of Reagan's top 10 supporters in the House are Republicans from the Lone Star State. Also among the 10 top House backers is Minority Leader Robert H. Michel, R-Ill., who had an 85 percent support rating.

Majority Leader Jim Wright, D-Texas, the leading contender to be the next House Speaker, put himself increasingly at odds with the president. Wright opposed Reagan 68 percent of the time in 1985, up from 47 percent in 1984.

As in past years, the Republicans most likely to part ways with the president were generally from the Northeast. The Republican most likely to oppose Reagan, Frank Horton of New York, was at odds with the president 68 percent of the time — up from 45 percent in 1984.

Horton was more prone to oppose the president than many senior Democrats — including Ways and Means Chairman Dan Rostenkowski of Illinois and Armed Services Chairman Les Aspin of Wisconsin, who had opposition ratings of 61 percent and 60 percent, respectively.

Average Scores

Following are composites of Democratic and Republican scores for 1985 and 1984:

	1985		1984	
	Dem.	Rep.	Dem.	Rep.
SUPPORT				
Senate	35%	75%	41%	76%
House	30	67	34	60
OPPOSITION				
Senate	61%	19%	49%	18%
House	66	30	58	33

Regional Averages

SUPPORT

Regional presidential support scores for 1985; scores for 1984 are in parentheses:

	East		West		South		Midwest	
DEMOCRATS								
Senate	31%	(35)	27%	(32)	44%	(52)	34%	(40)
House	26	(31)	23	(28)	41	(43)	25	(30)
REPUBLICANS								
Senate	67%	(63)	77%	(79)	78%	(84)	78%	(76)
House	58	(54)	72	(65)	72	(62)	66	(60)

OPPOSITION

Regional presidential opposition scores for 1985; scores for 1984 are in parentheses:

	East		West		South		Midwest	
DEMOCRATS								
Senate	66%	(57)	69%	(52)	52%	(37)	62%	(53)
House	70	(61)	72	(64)	55	(48)	72	(63)
REPUBLICANS								
Senate	29%	(30)	16%	(14)	16%	(10)	20%	(19)
House	39	(40)	24	(28)	26	(30)	31	(33)

(CQ defines regions of the United States as follows: ***East:*** *Conn., Del., Maine, Md., Mass., N.H., N.J., N.Y., Pa., R.I., Vt., W.Va.* ***West:*** *Alaska, Ariz., Calif., Colo., Hawaii, Idaho, Mont., Nev., N.M., Ore., Utah, Wash., Wyo.* ***South:*** *Ala., Ark., Fla., Ga., Ky., La., Miss., N.C., Okla., S.C., Tenn., Texas, Va.* ***Midwest:*** *Ill., Ind., Iowa, Kan., Mich., Minn., Mo., Neb., N.D., Ohio, S.D., Wis.)*

Highest Scorers — Support

Highest individual scorers in presidential support — those who voted most often for Reagan's position in 1985:

SENATE

Democrats		Republicans	
Nunn, Ga.	58%	Dole, Kan.	92%
Heflin, Ala.	54	Simpson, Wyo.	90
Zorinsky, Neb.	53	Lugar, Ind.	89
Long, La.	52	Hecht, Nev.	89
Hollings, S.C.	52	Quayle, Ind.	88
Bentsen, Texas	50	Thurmond, S.C.	87
Proxmire, Wis.	48	Gramm, Texas	87
Boren, Okla.	47	Boschwitz, Minn.	87

HOUSE

Democrats [1]		Republicans	
Daniel, Va.	66%	Eckert, N.Y.	94%
Stenholm, Texas	66	Bartlett, Texas	89
Roemer, La.	66	Archer, Texas	88
Montgomery, Miss.	66	Armey, Texas	88
Nichols, Ala.	61	Cheney, Wyo.	86
Stratton, N.Y.	59	DeLay, Texas	85
Hubbard, Ky.	59	Mack, Fla.	85
Hall, Ralph M., Texas	58	Fawell, Ill.	85
English, Okla.	58	Michel, Ill.	85
Ray, Ga.	56	Barton, Texas	85
Hutto, Fla.	56	Latta, Ohio	85

1. Rep. Sam B. Hall Jr., D-Texas, who was sworn in as a federal judge May 28, 1985, had the highest House Democratic presidential support score with 69 percent.

1985 Presidential Position Votes

Following is a list of all Senate and House recorded votes in 1985 on which President Reagan took a position. The votes, listed by CQ vote number, appear in the vote charts in the 1985 CQ Weekly Reports.

Senate Votes (102)

Presidential Victories (73) — 1, 2, 3, 4, 9, 11, 19, 20, 26, 27, 30, 31, 34, 51, 52, 61, 62, 63, 64, 68, 71, 72, 73, 74, 76, 80, 85, 89, 90, 93, 95, 107, 108, 109, 110, 111, 112, 113, 114, 117, 123, 124, 127, 130, 139, 140, 141, 142, 150, 151, 152, 153, 155, 171, 173, 191, 193, 202, 204, 213, 222, 249, 283, 288, 315, 334, 337, 352, 354, 359, 371, 373, 377.

Presidential Defeats (29) — 13, 14, 16, 17, 28, 35, 36, 37, 115, 126, 156, 157, 158, 180, 229, 231, 244, 253, 266, 296, 305, 308, 310, 314, 317, 321, 325, 356, 379.

House Votes (80)

Presidential Victories (36) — 21, 32, 34, 36, 89, 122, 140, 141, 142, 143, 147, 151, 155, 156, 157, 159, 160, 162, 196, 197, 198, 199, 251, 291, 293, 301, 311, 312, 329, 330, 335, 342, 365, 415, 425, 428.

Presidential Defeats (44) — 17, 25, 31, 40, 58, 60, 61, 120, 130, 145, 152, 153, 161, 170, 178, 185, 192, 205, 211, 225, 226, 266, 269, 289, 290, 294, 302, 303, 307, 309, 318, 320, 336, 341, 347, 358, 359, 364, 370, 379, 386, 389, 391, 411.

High Scorers — Opposition

Highest individual scorers in presidential opposition — those who voted most often against Reagan's position in 1985:

SENATE

Democrats		Republicans	
Matsunaga, Hawaii	77%	Weicker, Conn.	53%
Hart, Colo.	77	Mathias, Md.	44
Harkin, Iowa	77	Hatfield, Ore.	40
Riegle, Mich.	74	Andrews, N.D.	39
Sarbanes, Md.	74	Grassley, Iowa	34
Melcher, Mont.	74	Specter, Pa.	34
Kerry, Mass.	73	Heinz, Pa.	31
Burdick, N.D.	73		
Levin, Mich.	73		
Cranston, Calif.	73		

HOUSE

Democrats		Republicans	
Evans, Ill.	86%	Horton, N.Y.	68%
Boxer, Calif.	86	Leach, Iowa	64
Traficant, Ohio	85	Schneider, R.I.	61
Oberstar, Minn.	84	Green, N.Y.	61
Wheat, Mo.	84	Conte, Mass.	60
Hayes, Ill.	84	Boehlert, N.Y.	59
Sabo, Minn.	84	McKinney, Conn.	56
Obey, Wis.	84	Jeffords, Vt.	56
Kastenmeier, Wis.	84	Gilman, N.Y.	55
Savage, Ill.	84	Smith, N.J.	55
		Evans, Iowa	55

SUPREME COURT

Power to Rule Legislation Unconstitutional Exerts Deterrent Effect

Under the United States' system of checks and balances, the Supreme Court stands at the pinnacle of the federal judicial structure as the final reviewing authority of congressional legislation and executive action.

However, as is implicit in a checks-and-balance system of government, the high court and the lower federal judiciary do not function with complete independence. On the one hand, the size, salaries and jurisdiction of the judicial branch are determined by the legislative branch. On the other hand, the membership of the judicial branch is selected by the executive branch.

Federal and State Courts

Two types of judicial systems, state and federal, provide forums for the resolution of disputes. The state judicial systems are composed of the state supreme court, or state court of appeals, intermediate appellate courts and trial courts with general jurisdiction over disputes where most cases of a serious nature begin. In addition, states usually have a group of lower courts, such as municipal, police and justice-of-the-peace courts, which are the lowest courts in the judicial hierarchy and have limited jurisdiction in both civil and criminal cases. The federal system forms a tri-level pyramid, comprised of district courts at the bottom, circuit courts of appeals in the middle, and the Supreme Court at the top. *(Chart, p. 73)*

Provision for a federal judiciary was made by Article III, Section 1, of the Constitution, which stated: "The judicial power of the United States shall be vested in one supreme court, and in such inferior courts as the Congress may from time to time ordain and establish." Thus, aside from the required "supreme court," the structure of the lower federal judicial system was left entirely to the discretion of Congress.

Congress and Federal Courts

The Judiciary Act of 1789 established the Supreme Court; 13 district courts, each with a single judge; and, above the district courts, three circuit courts, each presided over by one district and two Supreme Court judges. Thereafter, as the nation grew and the federal judiciary's workload increased, Congress established additional circuit and district courts. In 1985 there were 12 circuit courts of appeals, 89 district courts and three territorial courts. Supreme Court justices no longer presided over federal circuit courts; each level of courts had its own judges.

The influence of Congress over the federal judiciary goes beyond the creation of courts. Although the power to appoint federal judges resides with the president, by and with the Senate's advice and consent, the power to create judgeships to which appointments can be made resides with Congress. It is in this area that politics historically plays its most critical role in the federal judicial system. For example, in 1801 the Federalist Congress created additional circuit court judgeships to be filled by a Federalist president. However, in 1802, when the Jeffersonian Republicans came into power, the new posts were abolished.

As federal judges are appointed to serve during good behavior, the power of Congress to abolish judgeships is limited to providing that when one becomes vacant, it cannot be filled. The history of the Supreme Court's size provides the best illustration of the earlier habit of creating and abolishing judgeships. Originally, the Supreme Court was composed of six justices. Subsequently, however, its membership varied: seven justices, 1807-37; nine justices, 1837-63; 10 justices, 1863-66; seven justices, 1866-69; and nine justices since 1869.

Jurisdiction of Federal Courts

Article III, Section 2, of the Constitution vests in the Supreme Court original jurisdiction — the power to hear a case argued for the first time — over only a few kinds of cases. The most important of these are suits between two states, which might concern such issues as water rights or offshore lands. Article III, Section 2, also extends to the court "judicial power" over all cases arising under the Constitution, federal laws and treaties. This jurisdiction, however, is appellate (i.e., limited to review of decisions from lower courts) and is subject to "such exceptions and ... regulations as Congress shall make."

Most of the high court's present jurisdiction is defined by the Judiciary Act of 1925, largely drafted by the court itself under Chief Justice William Howard Taft.

The Judiciary Act of 1925 made exercise of the court's appellate jurisdiction largely discretionary, giving the justices more leeway to refuse to review cases.

Except for certain limited types of cases in which the court is still "obligated" to take appeals, the court is allowed to decide whether the decisions from the lower courts present questions or conflicts important enough or of such a constitutional nature as to warrant the court's consideration on review.

But only in this way is the court able to control the

issues with which it deals. Its power is limited by the fact that it cannot reach out to bring issues before it, but must wait until they are properly presented in a case which has made its way through the lower courts.

In the relationship between federal and state judicial systems, federal courts have jurisdiction over cases relating to federal rights or actions in which the parties are citizens of different states. The state courts, on the other hand, are concerned with cases generally involving citizens of that state and their own state laws. There is some overlap of jurisdiction. The state courts are empowered to hear litigation concerning some federal rights, and federal constitutional rights often form the basis of decisions in state court cases. In the federal courts, where jurisdiction is based on a "diversity of citizenship" (i.e., the litigants are from different states), the court is obliged to find and apply the pertinent law of the state in which the court is sitting. In state court cases, similarly, in those few instances where a "federal question" might be resolved, the court is obliged to disregard its own precedents and apply appropriate federal law.

The Power of Judicial Review

The Supreme Court exerts a strong restraining influence upon Congress through its power to declare that certain of its legislative acts are unconstitutional and invalid. Although the Constitution does not expressly authorize the court to strike down acts it deems unconstitutional, the court assumed that important authority in 1803 through its own broad interpretation of its vested powers. Without this process, known as judicial review, there would be no assurance (not even in the president's veto) against domination of the entire government by runaway congressional majorities.

The court has been restrained in its exercise of this power; only a few more than 100 acts of Congress have been declared unconstitutional. Of those invalidated, many were relatively unimportant and others, such as the measures prohibiting the spread of slavery and those carrying out parts of Franklin D. Roosevelt's New Deal program, were replaced by legislation revised so as to pass muster with the Supreme Court.

Most constitutional scholars find the real significance of the Supreme Court's power of judicial review in the awareness of Congress that all of its acts are subject to a final veto by the Supreme Court.

With a few exceptions, the court has interpreted the legislature's power to enact specific laws as broadly as it has viewed its own authority to sit in review of the statutes.

The court's traditional approach to its duty of judicial review was outlined in 1827 by one of its first members — Justice Bushrod Washington. Justice Washington observed that "it is but a decent respect due to the wisdom, the integrity and the patriotism of the legislative body, by which any law is passed, to presume in favor of its validity until its violation of the Constitution is proved beyond all reasonable doubt." Justices on almost every court since Justice Washington's day have reaffirmed that attitude.

Changes in Court's Philosophy

Because Supreme Court justices are appointed for life terms, changes in the court's philosophy occur less frequently than in the other two branches of the federal government.

For its first 150 years, the court served primarily as a bulwark against encroachment on property rights. Even in the 1930s, with the passage of precedent-shattering legislation aimed at the nation's economic crisis, the court struck down 11 New Deal statutes — the heart of the recovery program. After his reelection in 1936, President Roosevelt threatened to "pack" the court with six additional justices who presumably would favor his program. However, before Congress had turned to his proposal, a judicial about-face was under way. On March 29, 1937, the court upheld Washington State's minimum wage law. Implicit in *West Coast Hotel v. Parrish* was the willingness of a majority of the justices to accept government authority to protect the general welfare and to discard the court's role as censor of economic legislation. On the same day, the court also upheld two New Deal statutes.

This shift of doctrine was completed during the term of Chief Justice Earl Warren (1954-1969), when the court promulgated a series of sweeping decisions in support of individual rights.

But with Warren's retirement, the pendulum began to swing back. The membership of the court changed. By 1985 only three Warren court justices remained. The court's rulings in the 1970s were less protective of individual rights, making clear that they were rarely absolute.

Moreover, in 1976 the court for the first time in 40 years held that Congress exceeded its authority to regulate commerce when it extended the coverage of federal wages and hours legislation to state and local government employees. The action was reminiscent of the court's actions overturning New Deal legislation applying to the private sector of the economy and raised questions about whether the justices in future years would place additional limits on the power of Congress to control the actions of state and local governments.

Whatever the court's philosophy, it has always had its share of congressional critics quick to accuse it of usurping undue powers. The early Anti-Federalists (later known as Democratic-Republicans and finally as Democrats) thought the court nullified the Constitution by a series of rulings strengthening federal power at the expense of individuals and the states. New Deal Democrats thought the court was attempting to seize the pre-eminent role in government by voiding much of their legislative program. In the 1950s and 1960s, Republicans and Southern Democrats were driven virtually to despair by the Warren court's decisions on school desegregation, criminal law, and voter representation. In the 1970s, as the court became more conservative, criticism came again from liberal observers who worried that the court unduly favored the state at the expense of the individual.

Such criticism of the court has led to a number of proposals to curb the tribunal's powers. Among the proposals have been a requirement of more than a majority vote to render a statute unconstitutional, removal of justices upon concurrence of the president and both houses of Congress, and restriction of the court's appellate jurisdiction to exclude certain types of cases in which the court has made decisions not to the liking of some members of Congress. Although certain of these proposals have attracted wide support, only one — in 1868 — has ever been enacted into law. The only sanctions effectively wielded by Congress have been the Senate's refusal to confirm court nominees and the reversal or modification of court rulings through legislation. The court's critics have blocked 27 of 139 court nominations submitted by successive presidents. Eleven of the 27 nominations were rejected outright, and the others were withdrawn or allowed to lapse in the face of Senate opposition.

Sources of Court's Power

Unlike the rebels who framed the Declaration of Independence, the men who met at Philadelphia in 1787 to shape the U.S. Constitution represented conservative financial interests. These interests had suffered heavily during the period of national confederation following the Revolution, when state legislatures, controlled mostly by agrarian interests, made repeated assaults on vested rights.

While the framers of the Constitution deprecated the excesses of the legislatures, they held a high respect for the courts, which gave judgments in favor of creditors and sent delinquent debtors to jail. As political scientist Charles A. Beard, a leading constitutional scholar, once put it in his book *The Supreme Court and the Constitution:* "The conservative interests, made desperate by the imbecilities of the Confederation and harried by the state legislatures, roused themselves from their lethargy, drew together in a mighty effort to establish a government that would be strong enough to pay the national debt, regulate interstate and foreign commerce, provide for national defense, prevent fluctuations in the currency created by paper emissions, and control the propensities of legislative majorities to attack private rights."

At the time the framers met, judicial review had not yet been instituted in any country in the world. And despite considerable discussion of some means to check the excesses of Congress, the matter of a judicial veto never came up for a direct vote. The closest the convention got to considering such a scheme was when it rejected the Virginia Plan of government. That plan contained a section establishing a Council of Revision, consisting of Supreme Court justices and the president, to consider the constitutionality of proposed acts prior to final congressional passage. As submitted to the state conventions for ratification, the Constitution did not designate a final arbiter of constitutional disputes. Wilfred E. Binkley and Malcolm C. Moos have pointed out in their book *A Grammar of American Politics* that there were matters the delegates "dared not baldly assert in the Constitution without imperiling its ratification, but they doubtless hoped that implications would eventually be interpreted to supply the thing desired." Judicial review appeared to be one of those things. Most other constitutional scholars have supported this view.

In *The Federalist,* a series of essays written to promote adoption of the Constitution, Alexander Hamilton made clear that the framers expected the judiciary to rule on constitutional issues. In Number 78 of *The Federalist,* Hamilton wrote: "The complete independence of the courts of justice is peculiarly essential in a limited constitution. By a limited constitution, I understand one which contains certain specified exceptions to the legislative authority, such for instance, as that it shall pass no bills of attainder, no ex post facto laws, and the like. Limitations of this kind can be preserved in practice no other way than through the courts of justice, whose duty it must be to declare all acts contrary to the manifest tenor of the Constitution void. Without this, all the reservations of particular rights or privileges would amount to nothing."

The court itself set out the doctrine of judicial review in the famous case of *Marbury v. Madison* (5 U.S. (1 Cranch) 137) in 1803.

The Judiciary Act of 1789, among other provisions, empowered the court to issue writs of mandamus compelling federal officials to perform their duties. Citing this authority, William Marbury, named by outgoing President John Adams as justice of the peace for the District of Columbia, asked the court to order James Madison, secretary of state to the new president, Thomas Jefferson, to deliver to Marbury his commission. Upon taking office, Jefferson had ordered all such commissions withheld.

Chief Justice John Marshall wrote that Marbury was entitled to his commission, but that the Supreme Court did not have the power to issue the requested writ, because Congress in attempting to give the court this power had acted unconstitutionally to expand its original jurisdiction. Therefore, held the court, that portion of the Judiciary Act was unconstitutional and invalid.

Judicial review thus became firmly established as part of the American system of government. Binkley and Moos asserted: "Whether or not the Supreme Court 'usurped' the practice of judicial review is now purely an academic question. So completely has the practice been woven into the warp and woof of our constitutional fabric that the garment could now scarcely endure its elimination."

Court-Curbing Proposals

Intermittently throughout American history, congressional critics of judicial power have sought to impose restrictions on the Supreme Court. The methods have ranged from proposed curbs on the court's authority to the Senate's rejection of court nominees.

Early Proposals

Charles Warren details the circumstances of the first move against the court in his study *The Supreme Court.* In 1802 the newly elected Congress dominated by Jeffersonian Republicans abolished the additional federal circuit courts set up the year before by the old Congress and staffed with 16 Federalist judges (the "midnight judges") appointed by President Adams on the eve of his departure from office. To delay a decision in the *Marbury* and other controversial cases, Congress also enacted legislation postponing the Supreme Court's term for 14 months, until February 1803. In 1805 Rep. John Randolph, a Virginia Republican, proposed a constitutional amendment providing for removal of Supreme Court justices by the president upon the approval of both houses of Congress. However, Randolph's proposal attracted little support and was dropped.

Alarmed by a series of Supreme Court decisions strengthening federal power at the expense of the states, states' rights advocates in Congress introduced a variety of other court-curbing proposals. In 1807 Republicans proposed a constitutional amendment providing for a limited tenure of office for federal judges and for their removal by the president upon a two-thirds vote of each house.

Warren also points out other attempts in the early years of the Republic to limit the court. In 1831 congressional Democrats (the old Jeffersonian Republican Party) launched a determined effort to repeal Section 25 of the Judiciary Act of 1789, which authorized writs of error to the Supreme Court to review state court judgments. (A writ of error is a process under which an appellate court may bring up a case from a lower court to examine the trial record as to questions of law but not of fact.) On Jan. 29, 1831, the House rejected this proposal by a wide margin. Later that year, Democrats introduced another proposal directing the House Judiciary Committee to study the feasibility of amending the Constitution to limit the tenure of federal judges. That proposal was also overwhelmingly rejected.

In a later study, *Congress, The Constitution and Supreme Court,* Warren discusses another series of attacks on the court launched in the early 1900s by critics of the court's decisions protecting property rights. In 1923 Sen. William E. Borah, R-Idaho, introduced a bill to require concurrence by seven of the nine justices to invalidate an act of Congress. The following year Sen. Robert M. La Follette, R-Wis., proposed a constitutional amendment providing that a statute once struck down by the Supreme Court could be declared constitutional and immune from further court consideration by a two-thirds majority of both houses of Congress. Neither the Borah nor the La Follette proposal received serious consideration.

After Congress rejected the Roosevelt court-packing plan in 1937, the Supreme Court experienced a period of relatively placid relations with Congress until the Warren court launched on its course of judicial activism in the mid-1950s. The only proposed curb on the court that attracted much support from the mid-1930s to the early 1950s was a 1953 proposal to amend the Constitution to make retirement mandatory for all federal judges at age 75. The resolution proposing the amendment, suggested by the American Bar Association, was adopted by the Senate in 1954 but was shelved by the House.

Attacks on the Warren Court

Congressional attacks on the Warren court began in 1954, the year of the court's famous school desegregation decision. On May 17, 1954, the court had declared in the case of *Brown v. Board of Education of Topeka, Kansas* that racial segregation in public schools was inherently discriminatory and therefore in contravention of the equal protection clause of the Fourteenth Amendment. The period of the next four years was a time of unusual anti-court activity in Congress, spurred at first by Southern members. Some 19 senators and 74 representatives from the South signed a "Declaration of Constitutional Principles" — the so-called Southern Manifesto — on March 12, 1956, protesting the "decision of the Supreme Court in the school cases as a clear abuse of judicial power." The Southerners were joined in time by colleagues from other sections who were dismayed by the court's decisions in such matters as federal-state relations, communist activities, and contempt of Congress.

From 1955 through 1962 proposals were introduced in Congress to curb the Supreme Court's power to strike down state laws as pre-empted by federal laws. Under Article VI, Section 2, of the Constitution, making federal law the "supreme law of the land," the courts had invalidated state laws in cases where: (1) Congress had stated an intention to take over ("pre-empt") a given field of legislation; (2) there was a direct conflict between a federal law and a state law; or (3) congressional intention to pre-empt a field of legislation could be inferred, even though it had not been specified by Congress (the doctrine of "pre-emption by implication"). In 1958 a broad anti-pre-emption bill was passed overwhelmingly by the House and was defeated in the Senate by only one vote.

The other major threat to the court's jurisdiction during this period was the Jenner-Butler bill (for Republican Sens. William E. Jenner of Indiana and John Marshall Butler of Maryland). It would have deprived the Supreme Court of authority to review several types of cases, including those concerning contempt of Congress, the federal loyalty-security program, state anti-subversive statutes and admission to the practice of law in any state. After lengthy committee hearings and bitter floor debate, the Senate tabled the bill by a vote of 49 to 41 on Aug. 20, 1958.

Attacks on the Supreme Court came not only from Congress but also from the judiciary itself. Three days after the Jenner-Butler bill was shelved by the Senate, the Conference of State Chief Justices approved a statement asserting that the court "too often has tended to adopt the role of policy-maker without proper judicial restraint." The statement added: "We are not alone in our view that the Court, in many cases . . . has assumed what seems to us primarily legislative powers."

Senate Republican Leader Everett McKinley Dirksen, Ill., was the leader of congressional efforts to modify the Supreme Court's "one man, one vote" doctrine on legislative apportionment set out in a series of decisions during the early 1960s. The House passed a bill in 1964 to deny federal courts jurisdiction over apportionment of state legislatures, but it was blocked in the Senate. At this juncture, court foes proposed a constitutional amendment to permit states to apportion one house of their legislatures on some basis other than population. The proposal came to a vote in the Senate in 1965 and again in 1966 — each time failing by seven votes to achieve a two-thirds majority.

A new move to restrict the jurisdiction of the Supreme Court emerged in the early 1980s. Angered by years of decisions by a "liberal" Supreme Court establishing a woman's right to an abortion, affirming the need to continue the effort to desegregate public schools, and refusing to condone official prayer in schools, Congress proposed to strip the court of jurisdiction to hear cases involving these issues. Republican Senator Jesse Helms of North Carolina proposed one such amendment in 1982 that would have barred federal courts, including the Supreme Court, from hearing "voluntary" school prayer cases. After a prolonged filibuster, the amendment was dropped.

Several measures designed to relieve the increased workload of the court were introduced during the 97th Congress. One proposed to eliminate the court's "mandatory" jurisdiction, that is, certain types of cases that the court must hear. Among the cases now guaranteed review are those involving the invalidation of an act of Congress or the unconstitutionality of a state law.

Congressional Reversals of Rulings

Of all its methods of influencing the Supreme Court, Congress has had the most success in reversing individual rulings either through adoption of a constitutional amendment or passage of legislation.

Four of the 26 amendments to the Constitution were adopted specifically to overrule the Supreme Court's interpretation of that document. The amendments reversed the court's rulings on the ability of citizens of one state to bring suit against another state, the application of the Bill of Rights to the states, the income tax and the 18-year-old vote.

But it is difficult and time-consuming to amend the Constitution. Each chamber of Congress must approve the proposed amendment by a two-thirds vote and it must then be ratified by three-fourths of all the states. Moreover, there is longstanding and deeply held sentiment that amendments to the Constitution should not be adopted every time there is a significant disagreement with a Supreme Court ruling. As a result, most proposals for such constitutional amendments never emerge from Congress.

Despite these acknowledged difficulties three issues — school prayer, abortion and busing — have provoked determined efforts in Congress during the last two decades to curb or undo Supreme Court rulings through constitutional amendments.

The court in 1962 ruled unconstitutional the use of a 22-word prayer in New York state public schools. Justice Hugo L. Black, speaking for the court in the case of *Engel v. Vitale*, said the prayer requirement violated the First Amendment's clause forbidding laws "respecting the establishment of religion." Soon afterward, Senate Republican leader Dirksen championed a proposed constitutional amendment to legalize voluntary student participation in prayers in public schools. Four years later, the proposal came to a vote in the Senate and fell nine votes short of receiving the necessary two-thirds majority. In 1971 and 1984 Congress defeated similar constitutional amendments permitting prayer in public schools.

Early in 1973 the court limited the power of states to ban abortions in the case of *Roe v. Wade*, allowing such prohibitions only in the last months of pregnancy. In 1975 a Senate subcommittee rejected several amendments intended to reverse that ruling and in 1976 the Senate refused to debate such an amendment. Renewed efforts in 1982 to pass anti-abortion legislation again came to a halt in the Senate after members voted to lay aside a proposal to ban virtually all abortions.

In a 1983 case, *Akron v. Akron Center for Reproductive Health*, the court reaffirmed its 1973 ruling. The decision reversed many local restrictions on access to abortions that had been established in the aftermath of the 1973 ruling.

In several rulings, the Supreme Court upheld the use of court-ordered busing to desegregate public school systems. The proposed anti-busing constitutional amendments before Congress would have denied lower federal courts the power to issue such orders. In mid-1979 the House soundly rejected an anti-busing amendment.

The more frequent — and successful — way of reversing the Supreme Court is for Congress to repass the offending statute after modifying it to meet the court's objections. This kind of reversal through simple legislation is easily accomplished if the court has interpreted a statute contrary to the construction intended by Congress. The House and Senate may then pass new legislation explicitly setting forth their intention. In many cases of this type, the court in its opinion will suggest the course the legislation should take to achieve its original purpose.

Reversal is not so easily accomplished when the court and Congress are at political or philosophical odds. Twice in the early 1900s Congress passed legislation to end child labor, for example, and twice the Supreme Court ruled that such legislation was not within Congress' power to enact. That its interpretation was based on philosophical differences rather than constitutional considerations was evident when the court reversed these two decisions several years later. In the mid-1930s it appeared that a similar confrontation would develop over New Deal legislation, but the court's re-examination of its position on congressional authority to regulate economic matters eased the crisis.

Three recent congressional reversals of Supreme Court decisions concerned pregnant women, news organizations and bankruptcy. Congress in 1978 required employers to include benefits for pregnancy, childbirth and related medical conditions in their health insurance and temporary disability plans. This measure overturned a 1976 court ruling that pregnancy did not have to be covered by such plans.

In 1980 Congress required law enforcement officers to subpoena news organizations and newsmen for information they sought, instead of obtaining a search warrant and searching a news organization's office. This law overturned a 1978 decision upholding police power to conduct such searches.

In February 1984, the court ruled that federal law allowed companies attempting to organize their affairs under the bankruptcy code to unilaterally repudiate their labor contracts. Four months later Congress overturned the decision by requiring companies in financial straits to seek court approval to break their labor contracts. Prior to filing the application the company would have to make a proposal to the union to alter the contract and seek to negotiate changes.

Not all attempts at congressional reversal are successful. In June 1984, the House approved legislation to overturn a court ruling on Title IX of the 1972 Education Amendments. On Feb. 28, 1984, the court stated that Title IX's general ban on sex discrimination does not apply to all school activities, but only to the particular program receiving funds. The legislation, however, failed to be approved by the Senate before adjournment of the 98th Congress.

Court Nominees

Congress exerts influence over the judiciary in another major way — through the Senate's prerogative to "advise and consent" in the president's selection of candidates for judicial offices, including not only Supreme Court justices but also other federal court judges.

Patronage

The power to name members of the federal judiciary — to well-paid, prestigious, lifetime posts — is perhaps the strongest patronage lever possessed by an incumbent president. As a result federal judgeships traditionally go to persons of the president's political party, despite the stated intention of almost every chief executive to make nonpartisan judicial appointments.

In apparent contradiction of the American ideal of an independent non-partisan judiciary, the process of selecting federal judges is pure politics. No constitutional guidelines exist beyond the provision that the president "shall nominate, and by and with the advice and consent of the Senate, shall appoint . . . judges of the Supreme Court, and all other officers of the United States. . . ."

Only custom dictates that the president nominate and the Senate confirm federal judges below the Supreme Court level.

Only tradition requires that federal judges reside in their districts or that they be attorneys.

The president has complete independence in selecting his Supreme Court nominees, but since 1840 tradition has awarded to senators of the president's party the prerogative of selecting persons for vacant or newly-created federal judgeships within their states. If there are no senators of the appropriate party from that state, the White House usually looks to its party organization in the state for suggested nominess.

Senatorial recommendations carry less weight in the

choice of persons for seats on the courts of appeals, each of which has jurisdiction over cases from a number of states. On most circuit courts of appeals, however, it is traditional that each state have a certain representation on the court at all times.

Once the nomination is made, it is sent from the White House to the Senate, where it is referred to the Senate Judiciary Committee. Hearings are held on virtually every nomination, but they are rarely more than perfunctory proceedings of brief length. The Senate committee then routinely recommends that the Senate confirm the nominees, which usually occurs by voice vote and without debate.

Senatorial Courtesy

Prior to confirmation, a senator can object to a nominee for specific reasons or using the stock, but rare, objection that the nominee is "personally obnoxious" to him. In this case, the other senators usually join in blocking confirmation out of courtesy to their colleague.

This practice of "senatorial courtesy" began as early as 1789 when the Senate refused to confirm Benjamin Fishbourn, nominated naval officer for the port of Savannah, Ga., by George Washington. More recently, in 1976, the Senate Judiciary Committee tabled, and thereby killed, President Ford's nomination of William B. Poff to a federal judgeship in Virginia, a selection objected to by Sen. William Lloyd Scott, R-Va.

Recess Appointments

Aside from the regular appointment route outlined above, a president can make a "recess" appointment to the Supreme Court or any other federal court vacancy. The Constitution states that "The President shall have the power to fill up all vacancies that may happen during the recess of the Senate, by granting commissions which shall expire at the end of their next session."

The president can fill a vacant post while Congress is not in session and the new judge can take his seat without confirmation. When Congress reconvenes, the president has 40 days within which to submit the recess appointee's name for confirmation. If he does not do so, the judge's pay is terminated. If the name is submitted, but Congress fails to confirm or reject the nomination during the session, the appointment is good until Congress adjourns.

Chief Justice Earl Warren and Justices William J. Brennan Jr. and Potter Stewart were the last three men to accept recess appointments to the Supreme Court.

Rejection of Nominees

Starting with George Washington, 15 presidents have seen 26 of their nominees for the Supreme Court fail to win Senate confirmation — among a total of 139 appointments. One nominee, Edward King, failed to be confirmed despite two attempts in 1844, for a total of 27 unsuccessful nominations. In contrast, only eight Cabinet nominees have been rejected by the Senate. The last time a Cabinet nomination was rejected was in 1959, when Senate Democrats refused to approve President Eisenhower's selection of Lewis L. Strauss as secretary of commerce.

Although Congress also has authority to remove federal judges by impeachment, only one such attempt with respect to a Supreme Court justice has moved past the preliminary stage, and that attempt failed. In 1804 the House impeached Justice Samuel Chase, a staunch Federalist who had rankled Republicans with his partisan political statements and his vigorous prosecution of the Sedition Act, which had finally been repealed in 1802. But Chase was not convicted by the Senate even though his opponents obtained a majority on three of the eight articles of impeachment. (A total of 23 senators — two-thirds of the Senate — was necessary for conviction. The greatest number of votes for conviction on any of the articles was 19.) After the trial, President Jefferson, a strong foe of the Federalist-dominated court, criticized impeachment as "a bungling way of removing judges" and "a farce which will not be tried again" in a letter of Sept. 6, 1819, cited in Warren's book *The Supreme Court in United States History.*

Senate rejection of court nominations was common in the 19th century, when political ideology often colored the confirmation process. But from 1900 to 1968 the Senate refused a seat on the Supreme Court to only one man, John J. Parker in 1930. Then, in a 19-month period from late 1968 to early 1970, the Senate refused to approve four Supreme Court nominees — Abe Fortas and Homer Thornberry, nominated by President Johnson, and Clement F. Haynsworth Jr. and G. Harrold Carswell, nominated by President Nixon. (Fortas, already an associate justice, had been nominated for chief justice. Thornberry was to take his place as an associate justice. Both nominations were withdrawn when Senate supporters of the nominees were unable to break a Republican-Southern Democratic filibuster on the Fortas nomination.)

President Hoover thought Parker would be a noncontroversial nominee. He was a federal judge and a Republican from North Carolina. Hoover later wrote in his memoirs that "No member of the Court at that time was from the southern states, and the regional distribution of justices had always been regarded as of some importance." But Hoover misjudged the temper of the times. Social and economic issues were more important than geography. A bipartisan group in Congress charged that Parker had made anti-Negro statements as a political candidate and an anti-Negro ruling from the bench. His nomination was rejected, 39 to 41.

The Senate's refusal to take up the Fortas and Thornberry nominations resulted largely from Fortas' affirmative votes in some of the most controversial decisions of the Warren court and from the desire of Senate Republicans to have a Republican president name the new chief justice. The GOP strategy paid off when Republican presidential candidate Richard M. Nixon won the 1968 election. But after Nixon's nominee for Chief Justice, Warren E. Burger, had been confirmed, Senate Democrats retaliated for the Fortas affair by successfully opposing confirmation of the president's next two court nominees — Haynsworth and Carswell. Critics of the nominations based their opposition primarily on allegations that Haynsworth had failed to observe high standards of professional ethics while serving as an appellate judge, and that Carswell was not qualified for such a high judicial post. Republicans contended, however, that the avowedly conservative views of both men were responsible for their rejection.

Despite the low incidence of rejection for most of the 20th century, at least four other court nominations faced stiff opposition — those of Louis D. Brandeis in 1916, Harlan F. Stone in 1925, Charles Evans Hughes in 1930, and Thurgood Marshall, the only black ever named to the court. The Senate Judiciary Committee, under the chairmanship of Sen. James O. Eastland, D-Miss., held up Mar-

Federal Judicial System

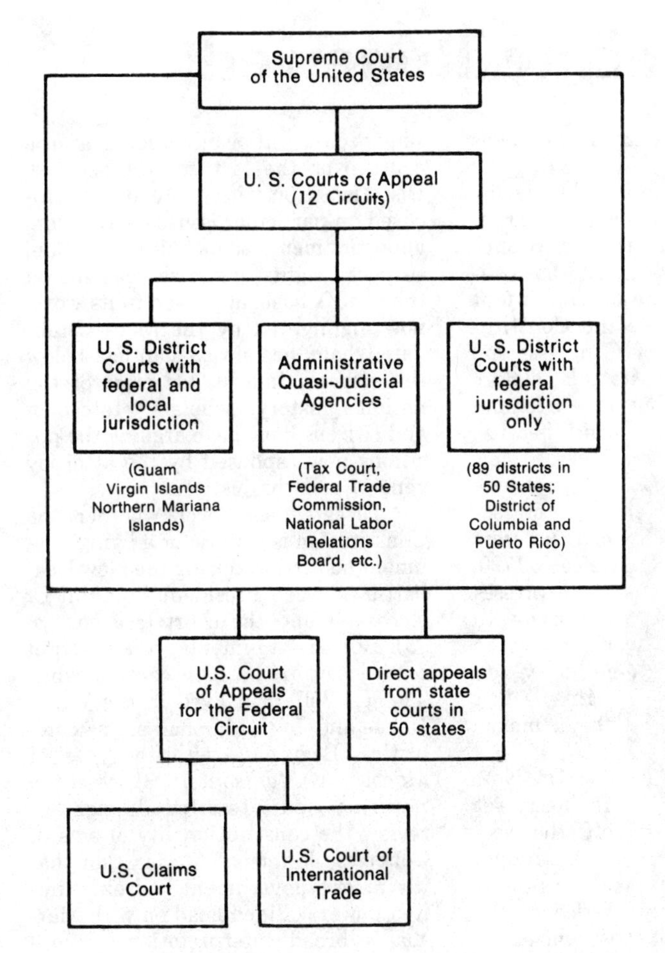

State Judicial System

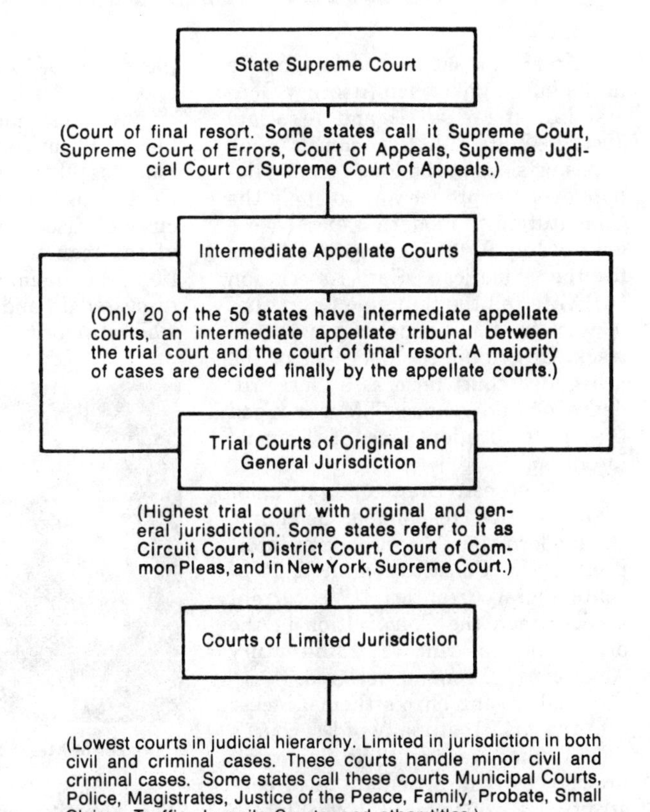

shall's confirmation as a judge of the Second Circuit Court of Appeals for a year before approving it. But in 1965 the same committee approved Marshall's nomination as solicitor general in less than a month, and in 1967 Marshall's nomination to the Supreme Court was confirmed by a comfortable 69-11 vote.

Action on the Brandeis nomination a half-century earlier was delayed for months by the same committee while it pondered the nominee's "radical views." While opposition to the nomination focused on Brandeis' liberal economic, political and social posture, there is evidence that much of it was motivated by anti-Semitic prejudice.

The nomination of Hughes as chief justice was made in 1930 when the country was entering the Great Depression and the nominee's views were attacked as too conservative.

Stone, at the time of his nomination, was U.S. attorney general and was in the midst of prosecuting Burton K. Wheeler, a recently elected Democratic senator from Montana. Wheeler was accused, but later acquitted of charges of participating in an oil-land fraud.

Wheeler's home state Democratic colleague, Sen. Thomas J. Walsh, used the committee hearings on the Stone nomination to criticize the Justice Department's handling of the Wheeler case.

To these four might be added the name of Hugo L. Black, who encountered difficulties after his confirmation when it was learned that he had once been a member of the Ku Klux Klan.

Black repudiated his Klan involvement in a dramatic radio broadcast and criticism waned.

Original Intent vs. Contemporary Content:

Constitutional Debate Renewed

Americans sat up and took notice in the fall of 1985 when Attorney General Edwin Meese III and Associate Justice William J. Brennan Jr. took opposing sides in the long-running debate over the proper way to apply the Constitution to modern issues. Meese led off July 9, 1985, using an address to the American Bar Association (ABA) to tell the Supreme Court that it was on the wrong constitutional track. Describing the decisions of the just-ended court term as a "jurisprudence of idiosyncrasy," Meese urged the court to adopt one of "original intention."

In October, Brennan, the senior sitting justice, responded, defending the modern court's approach of interpreting the Constitution in light of contemporary realities. "We current justices read the Constitution in the only way we can: as 20th-century Americans," Brennan declared.

Elaborating on his theme, Meese told the ABA that many of the court's recent rulings seemed to be "more policy choices than articulations of constitutional principle ... reveal[ing] a greater allegiance to what the court thinks constitutes sound public policy than a deference to what the Constitution — its text and intention — may demand." It is the Reagan administration's belief, he continued, "that only 'the sense in which the Constitution was accepted and ratified by the nation,' and only the sense in which laws were drafted and passed provide a solid foundation for adjudication. Any other standard suffers the defect of pouring new meaning into old words, thus creating new powers and new rights totally at odds with the logic of our Constitution and its commitment to the rule of law."

Rejecting Meese's views out of hand, Brennan said, "The ultimate question must be, what do the words of the text mean in our time. For the genius of the Constitution rests not in any static meaning it might have had in a world that is dead and gone, but in the adaptability of its great principles to cope with current problems and current needs."

Without mentioning Meese by name, Brennan described his argument as "little more than arrogance cloaked as humility" given the difficulty of discerning the original intent of the men who wrote the Constitution, the members of Congress who discussed it and the state legislators who ratified it. Furthermore, Brennan said, because Meese's view does not take note of social progress since 1790, "it expresses antipathy to claims of the minority to rights against the majority."

Edwin Meese III

On Nov. 15 Meese set off the second round. The Constitution, he said, is not "a mirror that simply reflects the thoughts and ideas of those who stand before it." While a jurisprudence of original intention "seeks to de-politicize the law," emphasizing process, not results, "an activist jurisprudence, one which anchors the Constitution only in the consciences of jurists, is a chameleon jurisprudence, changing color and form in each era," the attorney general warned.

Meese and Brennan have provided a constitutional yardstick by which to measure the decisions of the Supreme Court over the next several terms. The rulings and their rationale will be closely analyzed for clues that the court is espousing the more literal view, argued by Meese, or reaffirming the liberal view, advocated by Brennan.

Modern Arguments

The sweep of these arguments is quite different from the vigorous issue-specific criticism directed at the court over the last several decades. Dissatisfaction with the court has focused on particular issues — abortion, apportionment, school desegregation, suspects' rights. Yet disagreement on the court's basic approach to its work, now highlighted by the Meese-Brennan debate, has always lain just below the surface. Indeed, for most of the nation's history, scholars, statesmen and citizens have been arguing the positions now espoused by the attorney general and the justice.

Disagreement over whether the Constitution is a static or a living document last flared during the New Deal battle between President Franklin D. Roosevelt and the court *(see box, p. 75)*. But the arguments were first put forth early in the 19th century when Thomas Jefferson lived in the White House and John Marshall sat as chief justice. Beginning with the case of *Marbury v. Madison* (1803) when the Supreme Court asserted its right to review the constitutionality of acts of Congress, Jefferson's declaration that the federal government had only limited power collided head on with Marshall's broad interpretation of constitutional provisions. "The Constitution ... is a mere thing of wax in the hands of the judiciary, which they may twist and shape into any form they please," Jefferson wrote, using words that are strikingly similar to Meese's.

Abraham Lincoln also found himself quite at odds with the court's reading of the Constitution. He rode to the White House on the shock waves resounding from the court's 1857 decision in the Dred Scott case, which held that blacks could not become citizens and Congress could not stop the spread of slavery into the territories. In his first inaugural address, Lincoln continued his push to have that decision overridden, stating that "if the policy of the government upon vital questions ... is to be irrevocably fixed by decisions of the Supreme Court, the instant they are made ...

the people will have ceased to be their own rulers. . . ."

Ever since Ronald Reagan moved into the White House it has been clear that he intended to use all the powers at his disposal to persuade the Supreme Court to turn away from the approach to justice it adopted during the tenure of Chief Justice Earl Warren (1953-1969). The landmark rulings of the Warren court gave new meaning to the guarantees of individual rights and liberties spelled out in the Bill of Rights. Moving into areas where politicians refused to act, the court declared state-imposed school segregation unconstitutional, imposed new rules on police treatment of suspects, opened the door for federal judges to enter the political thicket of reapportionment and denied state officials the power to dictate prayers for use in public schools. With those decisions, the Warren court gave federal judges across the country a new role in shaping American life.

William J. Brennan Jr.

Reagan and Meese began to try to curtail this activist tradition immediately. Their single most successful move was the selection of Sandra Day O'Connor to replace Justice Potter Stewart in mid-1981. Reagan won political points for placing the first woman on the court, but even more important, he won policy points by selecting a jurist whose votes and views during her first four terms on the court so precisely fit with his.

No other vacancies on the court have occurred during Reagan's presidency, forcing him to channel his campaign to change the course of justice through the arguments that the solicitor general has made to the court during those years. With varying degrees of success, the administration argued that the court should curtail the use of affirmative action, relax the rule denying prosecutors the use of illegally obtained evidence, permit a moment of silence for prayer in public schools, restrict access to federal courts, give states more leeway to regulate abortions and lower the wall of separation between church and state.

Meese was the moving force behind a number of these arguments from his position as White House counselor. But only after he became attorney general in February 1985 did the administration articulate a philosophy in which these various policy positions could be grounded. Whether the philosophy was the product or the source of the various policy shifts, it provided a coherence to those positions that had earlier been lacking.

Call for Counterrevolutionary Approach

Embedded within Meese's call for a jurisprudence of original intention was a proposal for a constitutional counterrevolution. "The Bill of Rights, as debated, created and ratified was designed to apply *only* to the national government," Meese declared in his July speech. Few would argue that point. In 1833 the court held that the Bill of Rights did not apply to the states. That was the prevailing view until 1925, when the Supreme Court ruled that the due process guarantee of the 14th Amendment, ratified in 1868, extended the First Amendment guarantee of free speech to the states. With that decision, the Supreme Court began "incorporating" each of the major provisions of the Bill of Rights into the 14th Amendment, thereby protecting an individual's rights against state, as well as federal, action.

Had this process of incorporation not applied the First Amendment's ban on establishment of religion to the states as well as Congress, the Supreme Court in 1962 could not have ruled state-dictated prayer out of place in public schools. Nor, without incorporation, could the court in 1966 have required police to precede any questioning of criminal suspects in custody with an explicit statement advising them of their rights to remain silent and to have the assistance of a lawyer. Without earlier decisions in which the court found that the 14th Amendment incorporated the Fifth Amendment right to be free from

FDR and the Court

"The [Supreme] Court has been acting not as a judicial body, but as a policy-making body. . . . The court . . . has improperly set itself up as a third House of the Congress — a super-legislature, as one of the justices has called it — reading into the Constitution words and implications which are not there, and which were never intended to be there."

Attorney General Edwin Meese III? No. Those are the words of President Franklin D. Roosevelt, frustrated by the Supreme Court's wholesale rejection of the New Deal program that he and Congress had enacted.

Roosevelt's threat to add enough new seats and justices to get his way from the court is the most direct attack a president has ever launched at the third branch of government.

The changes in the law that Roosevelt proposed were not approved — due to popular and congressional distaste for the idea — but Roosevelt did end up packing the court after all. During his long presidency, he appointed eight men to the court and promoted another to chief justice.

Although some of the rhetoric sounds the same in 1986, today's situation differs in at least one very significant respect. Roosevelt was upset because the court was striking down new policies and programs upon which he and Congress agreed. In large part, Reagan and Meese are looking to the court in 1986 to approve changes in social and economic policy that Congress has refused to make. Because Congress has refused to approve a constitutional amendment outlawing abortion, for example, the administration is arguing that the court should permit states to outlaw it.

The American government, Roosevelt said during the court-packing fight, was like a "three-horse team provided by the Constitution to the American people so that their field might be plowed. The three horses are, of course, the three branches of government — the Congress, the Executive and the Courts. Two of the horses are pulling in unison today; the third is not."

In 1986 the three horses seem to be going in different directions, and it appears that more than the rhetoric of the current constitutional debate is needed to get them pulling together again.

compelled self-incrimination and the Sixth Amendment right to legal counsel, those rights applied only to suspects apprehended by federal authorities — a very small percentage of those arrested in the United States where law enforcement has always been primarily a local responsibility.

Meese described as "intellectually shaky" the foundation of this incorporation process, raising the possibility that the administration was preparing to challenge the application of these guarantees to state action. In October this argument drew a sharp and pointed response from another member of the Supreme Court, Justice John Paul Stevens. Meese "overlooks the profound importance of the Civil War and the postwar amendments on the structure of our government, and particularly upon the relationship between the federal government and the separate states," Stevens said.

"Moreover," Stevens continued, "the attorney general fails to mention the fact that no justice who has sat on the Supreme Court during the past 60 years has questioned the proposition that the prohibitions against state action that are incorporated in the 14th Amendment include the prohibitions against federal action that are found in the First Amendment."

Comment, Criticism Generated by Debate

After their October rejoinders, both Brennan and Stevens resumed the traditional judicial stance of public silence. The court's response to Meese would come now in its opinions. But the shock waves from this exchange of views generated considerable diverse commentary in the nation's magazines and newspapers in the last months of 1985 and early 1986.

Brennan "is an angry man ... filled to the brim with righteous liberal indignation," wrote Walter Berns, resident constitutional and legal scholar at the American Enterprise Institute in *The Wall Street Journal.* "Federal judges are supposed to be nonpartisan, and they are not supposed to accuse officials in the other branches of the government of arrogance, facile historicism (whatever that means), or plotting wicked schemes to deprive minorities of their rights," Berns chastised.

Surely there must be a middle ground between these two arguments, Columbia Law School Dean Benno C. Schmidt Jr. wrote in the *Los Angeles Times.* "Is the Supreme Court left with such a stark choice" between tying itself "tightly ... to a concrete version of original intent" or claiming "unfettered judicial discretion?" Schmidt wondered. Must the justices demand from the Constitution a certainty that it has rarely provided or abandon the "interpretative connection to an authoritative text that has always been the basis for our ... belief that constitutional law is a body of law and not just a pretentious gaggle of political pronouncements?" he asked.

Another view that both sides of the debate were too inflexible came from Richard Epstein, a young professor at the University of Chicago Law School. Epstein criticized both Meese and Brennan for "the mistaken assumption that strict interpretation mandates judicial restraint." Epstein argued that even justices who espoused the jurisprudence of original intention should not assume that "modern zoning, landmark preservation and rent-control statutes, or collective bargaining and minimum wage laws are beyond constitutional review simply because none was heard of in 1791.... Rightly understood, original intention demands that judges articulate and apply the general constitutional language to novel legislation," he concluded.

"Mr. Meese's version of original intent is a patent fraud on the public," Arthur Schlesinger Jr. wrote early in 1986. "The attorney general uses original intent not as a neutral principle at all but only as a means of getting certain results for the Reagan administration," continued Schlesinger, currently a professor of the humanities at the City University of New York. "If original intention be the only reliable guide for judgment, then one original intention of the framers was plainly to leave the meaning of certain key phrases to be filled out by their descendants according to the needs of later times," Schlesinger declared, referring to phrases such as "due process" and "equal protection."

Addressing the Issues

Moving quickly to implement Meese's call for a jurisprudence of original intent, the Reagan administration in mid-July 1985 asked the Supreme Court to overrule *Roe v. Wade,* its 1973 decision legalizing abortion. President Reagan had long sought to reverse this ruling by amending the Constitution, but those efforts had proved fruitless. During Reagan's first term, Solicitor General Rex E. Lee urged the court to give states and cities more leeway to regulate abortion, but he stopped short of asking it to discard *Roe v. Wade* altogether. The court in 1983 reaffirmed *Roe v. Wade,* 6-3.

Undeterred, Lee's successor, Charles Fried, wasted no time in telling the court it was time to throw out this precedent. "The textual, historical and doctrinal basis of that decision is so far flawed that this court should overrule it and return the law to the condition in which it was before that case was decided," Fried argued in his July friend-of-the-court brief. "There is no explicit textual warrant in the Constitution for a right to an abortion," wrote Fried. "It is true, of course, that words, and certainly the words of general constitutional provisions, do not interpret themselves," he acknowledged. However, "the further afield interpretation travels from its point of departure in the text, the greater the danger that constitutional adjudication will be like a picnic to which the framers bring the words and the judges the meaning."

Roe v. Wade is based upon the view that the personal liberty guaranteed to individuals by the 14th Amendment embraces a right of privacy in matters of marriage, childbearing and family life. That right, the court held in 1973 over the dissenting votes of Byron R. White and William H. Rehnquist, was broad enough to encompass a woman's decision to terminate her pregnancy. That conclusion, Fried argued, had no support in the intent of the men who drafted and approved the 14th Amendment, adopted in the heyday of state laws against abortion. "It is fair to conclude that those who drafted and voted for the 14th Amendment would have been surprised indeed to learn that they had put any part of such subjects beyond the pale of state legislative regulation," he wrote.

Roe v. Wade, the administration continued, sent federal judges off into "a free-ranging, essentially legislative, process of devising regulatory schemes that reflect their notions of morality and social justice. The result has been a set of judicially-crafted rules that has become increasingly more intricate and complex, taking courts further away from what they do best and into the realm of what legislatures do best."

Fried acknowledged that, to overturn this ruling, the court would have to disregard the doctrine of adherence to settled precedent, *stare decisis*, but he said such disregard was more than justified. *Roe v. Wade*, he argued, "stands as a source of trouble in the law not only on its own terms, but also because it invites confusion about the sources of judicial authority and the direction of this court's own future course. *Stare decisis* is a principle of stability. A decision as flawed as we believe *Roe v. Wade* to be becomes a focus of instability, and thus is less aptly sheltered by that doctrine from criticism and abandonment."

The court is not expected to reverse *Roe v. Wade* in 1986, but the administration's position is now clear. For the first time in memory, the executive branch is urging the court to narrow the Constitution's protection for the rights of the individual.

Affirmative Action, Miranda Challenged

Affirmative action — the use of race or gender to benefit rather than disadvantage blacks or women — is another highly visible issue to which the administration applies its original intent approach. The Constitution requires employers to be colorblind, the administration argued in the summer of 1985 in another *amicus* brief. Under the test the administration proposed, an affirmative action plan would only pass muster if it was designed and implemented just to benefit the specific individual victims of race or sex bias.

The guiding principle of equal justice under law, the administration contended, "finds binding legal expression in the equal protection clause of the 14th Amendment: no state shall 'deny to any person within its jurisdiction the equal protection of the laws.' The equal protection clause does not mention any of the characteristics that divide, such as race, religion, or national origin. It sees only 'person[s]' and guarantees to every 'person' the 'equal' protection of the laws."

"Equality before the law, so magnificent in principle, is often a difficult and uncomfortable concept in practice," the government brief conceded. Rejecting the argument that affirmative action is sometimes needed to protect politically powerless minorities, it declared that "there is no evidence that those who framed, proposed and ratified the 14th Amendment had this theory in mind." The court rejected the administration's reasoning in a decision handed down May 19, 1986, even though it invalidated an affirmative action plan at the same time. In *Wygant v. Jackson Board of Education*, the court agreed with the administration, declaring it unconstitutional for the Jackson, Michigan, school board to lay off white teachers in order to preserve the jobs of blacks with less seniority. However, the court made it clear that affirmative action plans giving blacks or women preferential treatment are not inherently unconstitutional. *(1986 CQ Weekly Report, p. 1181)*

To ensure that police respect the constitutional rights of persons suspected of crime, the Warren court expanded the reach of one judge-made rule and devised a second one, both highly controversial because the penalty for police misconduct is exclusion of any evidence thereby obtained. The exclusionary rule and the *Miranda*

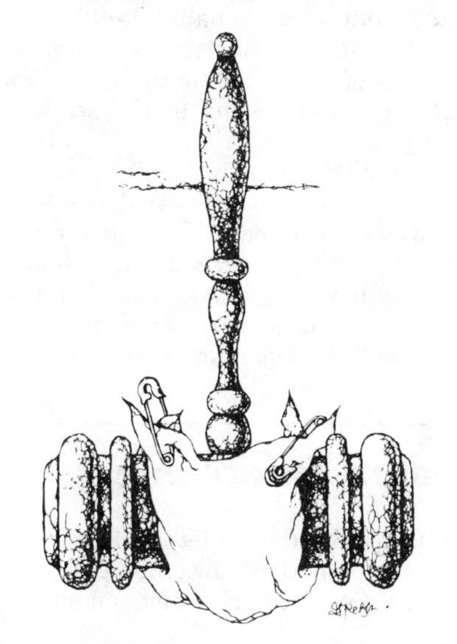

rule are the primary targets of the administration's "original intent" approach in the area of criminal law.

The Fourth Amendment promises Americans security against unreasonable searches, a security which courts generally enforce by requiring police to obtain a warrant before searching a home or office. If a search is conducted without a warrant, or if the warrant turns out to be defective, courts usually exclude any evidence obtained from use in court.

The nation's prosecutors have protested the application of this rule to state courts for more than two decades. Now, with the backing of the Reagan administration, they argue with more success that it is too expensive a way of reminding police to respect the Constitution. Emphasizing that this rule is not found in the language of the Constitution, but only in court decisions, the administration argues that the social costs of excluding evidence far outweigh the benefits.

In 1984 the administration argued successfully for a "good faith exception" to this rule. The court, 6-3, approved use of evidence seized by police in a search authorized by a warrant only later discovered to be flawed. Attorney General Meese, himself once a local prosecutor, is not satisfied. "The exclusionary rule has never helped an innocent person," he declared a year ago. "It only helps the guilty and I think it's a bad rule."

The *Miranda* rule, set out by the court in its 1966 decision in *Miranda v. Arizona*, requires police to advise suspects in custody of their constitutional rights to remain silent when interrogated and to have the aid of an attorney. If police fail to give those warnings or disregard those rights once they are invoked by the suspect, any evidence they obtain as a result is inadmissible against the suspect.

Meese says this rule should be thrown out. "You don't have many suspects who are innocent of a crime," he told *U.S. News & World Report* in October 1985, "That's contradictory. If a suspect is innocent of a crime, then he is not a suspect. The *Miranda* decision was wrong," Meese continued. "We managed very well in this country for 175 years without it. Its practical effect is to prevent the police from talking to the person who knows the most about the crime — namely the perpetrator. As it stands now ... if the police obtain a statement from that person in the course of the initial investigation [without giving him his *Miranda* warnings] the statement may be thrown out at the trial. Therefore, *Miranda* only helps guilty defendants."

Meese's views on *Miranda* drew outraged criticism led by members of the legal community who pointed out the direct conflict between Meese's statements and the basic proposition that in the United States the suspect is presumed innocent until proven guilty. Meese's views have not yet been translated into government legal briefs, but that seems to be only a matter of time. Early in 1986 it was reported that the Justice Department was actively investigating ways to weaken or eliminate the *Miranda* rule.

Narrow Reading of Establishment Clause

The administration has focused its "original intent" argument most sharply on church-state issues. In his July address to the ABA, Meese minced no words in criticizing the court's recent decisions striking down Alabama's moment-of-silence law, programs of public aid to students in non-public schools in Grand Rapids and New York City, and Connecticut's law requiring employers to give employees their Sabbath off. Each of these laws or programs was found to violate the First Amendment ban on state action establishing religion.

The Establishment Clause, Meese said, "was designed to prohibit Congress from establishing a national church. The belief was that the Constitution should not allow Congress to designate a particular faith or sect as politically above the rest. But to have argued, as is popular today, that the amendment demands a strict neutrality between religion and irreligion would have struck the founding generation as bizarre. The purpose was to prohibit religious tyranny, not to undermine religion generally."

Today's court is divided between those who see the Establishment Clause as a wall of separation between church and state,requiring the government to be neutral between religion and irreligion, and those who see it as merely requiring that the government not favor one sect or faith over others. Until recently the court seemed adamant in maintaining the wall of separation. But in 1984 the administration won the majority's endorsement of a new posture of accommodation, rather than separation. In March of that year, the court ruled that the city of Pawtucket, R.I., could include a crèche in its holiday display. Chief Justice Warren E. Burger spoke for five justices when he wrote that the Constitution "affirmatively mandates accommodation, not merely tolerance, of all religions, and forbids hostility toward any."

Hoping to expand the reach of this new approach, the administration in the 1984-85 term urged the court to uphold the moment-of-silence law enacted by Alabama, the New York and Grand Rapids parochiaid programs and Connecticut's Sabbath-off law. In each case the court refused, and indeed seemed to be reinforcing the wall of separation. Some of the strongest language in that vein came from Brennan and Stevens.

In the moment-of-silence case, Stevens declared: "The government must pursue a course of complete neutrality toward religion . . . the individual freedom of conscience protected by the First Amendment embraces the right to select any religious faith or none at all." The First Amendment, Brennan emphasized in the parochiaid cases, was intended to "guard the right of every individual to worship according to the dictates of conscience while requiring the government to maintain a course of neutrality among religions, and between religion and non-religion."

More unexpected than this strong defense of separation was a basic disagreement between the two youngest and most conservative justices over application of original intent in the moment-of-silence case. Not only did O'Connor vote against the Alabama law while Rehnquist supported it, but while Rehnquist found clear guidance for his position in the language of the men who wrote the First Amendment, O'Connor did not.

"Free public education was virtually non-existent in the late eighteenth century," O'Connor wrote. "[I]t is unlikely that the persons who drafted the First Amendment, or the state legislators who ratified it, anticipated the problems of interaction of church and state in the public schools. . . . When the intent of the framers is unclear," she continued, "I believe we must employ both history and reason in our analysis."

Back to the Future

The wellspring of the administration's call for a return to original intent as the standard for constitutional interpretation — and the motivating force behind many of its more specific policy arguments — is the conviction that there is a fundamental imbalance within the federal system. Simply stated, Reagan and Meese believe the federal government has too much power; the states too little.

To redress the balance is vastly more complicated. The president has begun the rebalancing by encouraging Congress and the executive agencies to ease the regulatory burden they impose on state and local governments. But Reagan believes firmly that the federal courts have played a major role in shifting power and responsibility from local and state shoulders to federal ones. As Meese put it with typical bluntness in his ABA speech July 1985: "Nowhere else has the principle of federalism been dealt so politically violent and constitutionally suspect a blow as by the theory of incorporation," which has extended the Bill of Rights to govern state, as well as federal, action.

Original Intent and Modern Enforcement

Every now and then, even Attorney General Edwin Meese's Justice Department finds itself compelled by the needs of modern law enforcement to take a more interpretive view of the Constitution than the framers might have espoused.

Such was the case Dec. 10, 1985, when the government argued to the Supreme Court that aerial searches were exempt from the constitutional requirement of search warrants. Dow Chemical Company, backed by the American Civil Liberties Union (ACLU) challenged as unconstitutional the government's warrantless aerial surveillance of one of its plants in Michigan to monitor Dow's compliance with air pollution regulations.

The government defended this modern-day practice, even though it is virtually impossible to justify it in terms of "original intent." At the time that the Fourth Amendment warrant requirement was drafted and approved, aerial surveillance would have been possible only from tall trees or hot-air balloons, and it is unlikely that the framers gave any thought to that possibility.

Thus the administration found itself in the situation it so often criticizes, forced to surmise how the Founding Fathers would have felt about this undreamed-of type of search. Indeed, it can be convincingly argued that the Founding Fathers, concerned as they were about privacy and property, would have supported Dow's argument and required a warrant for these searches, had they thought about the matter.

Bert Neuborne of the ACLU pointed out the difficulty of stretching a "jurisprudence of original intention" to cover such an issue: "I don't think Meese has thought through the implications of his doctrine of original intent. A strict [application] really cripples modern law enforcement."

If Meese and Reagan can bring about the counterrevolution they wish and convince the Supreme Court that the Bill of Rights does not apply to state action, the constitutional basis for many of the federal court orders affecting state and local officials would vanish. If the First Amendment does not apply to states, then federal judges cannot tell state officials that they must stop prescribing prayers for use in public schools. If the Fourth Amendment does not apply to the states, then federal judges can no longer deny state prosecutors the use of evidence taken in an unreasonable search. If the Fifth and Sixth amendments do not apply to the states, then state and local police no longer have to warn suspects in custody of their Miranda rights.

Today's Supreme Court justices are closely divided over the issue of federal-state power, a division evident in two lines of decisions. Neither has received wide public attention, in part because each concerns little-discussed constitutional provisions.

The 10th Amendment states that all powers that the Constitution does not grant the federal government or deny to the states are reserved to the states and the people. Until 1937 states found this amendment a potent shield against federal intervention and used it to curtail federal power over a number of issues by arguing that because the Constitution did not explicitly grant the federal government power over child labor or farm production, for example, it reserved that matter for the states.

The court packing fight of 1937 was provoked by the court's use of the 10th Amendment to strike down New Deal legislation as interfering in matters that were supposed to be left to the states to regulate. But the court's turnabout in that year and its acceptance of federal power to regulate the economy went hand-in-hand with the apparent demise of the 10th Amendment, which was rarely invoked from 1937 until 1976.

Then, in a major constitutional surprise, the court, 5-4, struck down the extension of federal minimum wage and overtime laws to state and local government employees. It based its ruling in *National League of Cities v. Usery* on the 10th Amendment, raising hopes in state capitals that once again the court would protect state prerogatives from federal power.

That principle proved difficult to implement. In a series of subsequent cases, the court found it tricky to draw any clear line delineating the reach of federal power toward the states. And so, in 1985, the court, 5-4, overruled the *National League of Cities* decision. Justice Harry A. Blackmun, who had voted with the majority in 1976, had changed his mind. No longer, he wrote, did he view the 10th Amendment as an effective limit on federal power to interfere in state affairs. Only the political structure set in place by the Constitution, the fact that states are well-represented in both the House and the Senate, operates to limit that power, he wrote in *Garcia v. San Antonio Metropolitan Transit Authority.*

The court's division over the 10th Amendment is clear: Blackmun, Brennan, Thurgood Marshall, White and Stevens view it as a dead letter. O'Connor, Lewis F. Powell Jr., Rehnquist and Burger are ready to reinvigorate it for use in rebalancing the allocation of power between the states and Washington.

That division shifts slightly — but quite significantly — when the issue is federal judicial power over state affairs. The 11th Amendment, the first added to the Constitution after the Bill of Rights, denies federal courts the power to hear suits "in law or equity" brought by citizens against a state without its consent.

This amendment was added to the Constitution in direct response to the first major Supreme Court decision — *Chisholm v. Georgia,* 1793, permitting federal judges to hear such suits. In the 20th century, however, the court has carved out an exception and now allows federal courts to hear such suits against states when the citizens bringing them charge a violation of their constitutional rights.

But recently the court, 5-4, has limited the power of federal judges to tell state officials what to do. In 1984 the court told federal judges that they could not order state officials to comply with state laws. And in 1985 it used the 11th amendment to shut the doors of the federal courthouse to a citizen who claimed that his state had violated the federal ban on discrimination against the handicapped.

White — who votes against the state on 10th Amendment issues — supports 11th Amendment state claims of immunity from federal judicial interference, forming a majority with Burger, Powell, O'Connor and Rehnquist. In the majority with White on 10th Amendment issues, Brennan, Marshall, Blackmun and Stevens find themselves in the minority on 11th Amendment questions.

Another 11th Amendment case went before the court in the 1985-86 term. In *Papasan v. Mississippi,* local school officials contested a federal court ruling deferring to the 11th Amendment against state officials for discriminating in the distribution of federal funds. However, the firmness of the current alignments within the court on this issue makes any shift unlikely — at least until there is a new justice on the bench.

Balance Could Shift

No matter how many speeches Attorney General Meese gives or how many briefs the solicitor general files, it is unlikely that they will convince the contemporary court to adopt their jurisprudence of original intent unless Ronald Reagan has the chance to name another new justice. The key decisions of the last few terms have been close ones, decided by votes of 5-4 or 6-3. The state powers split illustrates that point. If Brennan, Marshall, Blackmun or Stevens retires and is replaced by a Reagan nominee, the shift toward Meese's point of view could be dramatic.

Major Separation-of-Powers Issues:

Court to Review Pocket Veto, Laws With Legislative Vetoes

The Supreme Court March 3, 1986, took a second helping of separation-of-powers issues, agreeing to decide when the president can pocket veto a bill and when an unconstitutional legislative veto provision dooms the entire statute to which it is attached.

The court acted just a week after it had agreed to rule on the constitutionality of the Gramm-Rudman-Hollings balanced-budget law. A lower court Feb. 5 said key provisions of that law improperly gave executive powers to an officer of the legislative branch. *(1986 CQ Weekly Report p. 513)*

Both the pocket veto case and the new legislative veto controversy will be argued in the Supreme Court term that begins in October 1986. No decision in either is expected before 1987.

Pocket Vetoes: Background

Under Article I of the Constitution, the president has 10 days (excepting Sundays) after Congress sends him a bill to either sign it into law or veto it and return it with his objections. If the president fails to act within 10 days, a bill becomes law without his signature "unless the Congress by their adjournment prevent its return, in which case it shall not be a law." This last phrase describes the pocket veto.

Congress can override a regular presidential veto by a two-thirds majority vote of each chamber. But it has no recourse against a pocket veto.

In 1929, the Supreme Court rejected arguments that a pocket veto could be used only between Congresses, not between sessions or during recesses of a particular Congress.

The court reasoned that when Congress was not in session, it was impossible for the president to return the bill. Thus, circumstances compelled him to use the pocket veto if he did not wish to sign the measure.

Within a decade, however, this decision was undercut by a ruling in *Wright v. United States* (1938) that during a short recess, an official of the House or Senate could receive a veto message and deliver it to the chamber after the recess ended. Thus, the court said, the pocket veto could not be used in those circumstances.

In recent years, the House and Senate have routinely appointed their clerk or secretary to receive messages from the president during a recess.

This practice, underscored by two lower court rulings in the 1970s, has called into further question the validity of the 1929 decision.

In 1973, a federal judge invalidated a pocket veto by President Nixon because it came during a six-day recess; Congress was back in session before expiration of the 10-day period within which the president was to sign or veto the bill. In 1976, a federal appeals court voided a second Nixon pocket veto because both chambers had named agents to receive presidential messages during the recess.

The New Case

The case accepted March 3, *Burke v. Barnes,* involves the administration's appeal of a 1984 ruling by the U.S. Court of Appeals for the District of Columbia. The appeals court ruled that a president may not use the pocket veto during recesses or between the first and second sessions of the same Congress when Congress has appointed someone to receive presidential messages in its absence. He may only pocket veto bills between Congresses.

The ruling came on a case brought in January 1984 by 33 members of the House, led by Michael D. Barnes, D-Md., and joined later by the Senate, the Speaker and the bipartisan leadership of the House. The suit challenged President Reagan's pocket veto of a measure requiring El Salvador to make progress in human rights in order to continue receiving U.S. military aid. The members of Congress argued that Reagan's pocket veto, which came in November 1983 between sessions of the 98th Congress, effectively nullified their votes in favor of the bill, thereby injuring the lawmaking powers of Congress. *(1984 CQ Almanac p. 204)*

Administration attorneys cite the 1929 *Pocket Veto* decision in defending Reagan's veto, arguing that the appointment of an agent to receive messages has no constitutional significance. The U.S. district judge who first heard the *Barnes* case agreed that unless and until the Supreme Court reconsidered its 1929 ruling, presidents could continue to use the pocket veto during recesses and between sessions of a Congress.

That ruling was reversed by a 2-1 ruling of the appeals court.

Times have changed, the majority said. The adjournment practices of Congress envisioned by the drafters of the Constitution "bear no resemblance to the actual adjournment practices of the modern-day Congress."

The long periods between sessions of Congress in its early years, when travel was difficult, required provision of the pocket veto to enable the president to disapprove legislation when there was no sitting Congress to return it to, the panel reasoned. But now that Congress rarely recesses for long and specifically appoints agents to receive vetoed legislation, the only time the president is "prevented" from returning a bill is between Congresses, when the membership is in flux and there actually is no Congress to which legislation could be returned.

In vigorous dissent, Judge Robert H. Bork argued that the courts should refuse to "umpire" such disputes between members of Congress and the president.

By agreeing to hear and resolve such cases, Bork argued, the courts were threatening the basic separation of powers between the three branches of government. "We will become not only a part of the legislative process," he warned, "but perhaps the most important part."

The government's brief urging the court to consider this case leans heavily on Bork's dissenting opinion.

Members of Congress, "like citizens and taxpayers generally, lack standing to challenge the president's action in federal court," the administration argues. Whether a particular bill became a law or not "is a question properly answered only in an action brought by a private person directly affected by the status of the particular bill," the administration says.

Legislative Veto, Deferral Issue

"Severability" is the key issue in the second-generation legislative veto case the court has agreed to hear.

In June 1983, the high court ruled all forms of the legislative veto unconstitutional — a device that permitted one or both houses of Congress to veto executive branch regulations or orders. But that 7-2 ruling in *Immigration and Naturalization Service v. Chadha* left unclear which of the remaining portions of more than 200 laws containing some type of veto provision were still valid. The new case should settle that question.

Sometimes Congress inserts a "severability" clause in a bill specifically stating that other portions of the measure are to remain in effect even if specified sections are invalidated. But often, Congress leaves it to the courts to decide how much of a law survives the loss of a part of it.

The Supreme Court's decision in this case could have far-reaching ramifications for scores of laws that contain now-invalid legislative veto provisions. One of them is the Congressional Budget and Impoundment Control Act of 1974, which among other things authorized the president to defer spending appropriated funds unless the deferral was vetoed by either house of Congress.

On Feb. 20, 1986, a suit was filed by the National League of Cities and several House members, including Bruce A. Morrison, D-Conn.; Mike Lowry, D-Wash.; Charles E. Schumer, D-N.Y.; and Barbara Boxer, D-Calif., challenging the president's deferral authority on the grounds that it was inextricably linked to the legislative veto provision. That case is presently pending before the U.S. District Court in the District of Columbia. *(1986 CQ Weekly Report p. 451)*

The suit is just one of several recent developments pitting key members of Congress against the president in battles over deferral of appropriated funds.

Severability Standard

Since the *Chadha* ruling, Congress has amended some, but not all, of the laws that contained legislative vetoes.

One that it did not change is the Airline Deregulation Act of 1978 (PL 95-504). In *Alaska Airlines v. Brock*, attorneys for the airline criticized an appeals court decision permitting an employee protection plan set up by the law to survive, even though these provisions of the law contained a legislative veto. *(1978 CQ Almanac p. 496)*

The plan set up by that law to protect employees who might lose their jobs in the course of deregulation was to be implemented through regulations issued by the Labor Department. The law made those regulations subject to a legislative veto.

Fourteen airlines sued the secretary of labor early in 1984, claiming the employee protection program was invalidated when the legislative veto provision became unconstitutional. In May 1984, a U.S. District Court judge agreed, finding that the veto was an integral part of this portion of the law, and that Congress would not have enacted the program without it.

In his ruling, Judge Gerhard Gesell set out the standard he used:

"The question is not ... whether Congress would have enacted *some* type of employee protection plan in the absence of a legislative veto provision; rather, the issue is whether Congress would have enacted the *same* statute."

In July 1985, the U.S. Circuit Court of Appeals for the District of Columbia reversed Gesell, upholding the employee protection plan as still valid and setting out a new standard for deciding whether certain portions of a law were severable from other unconstitutional portions.

The new standard presumed the continued viability of a challenged section unless those bringing suit could show that Congress would have enacted no law on the subject in question if it had known the legislative veto portion would be struck down.

"The burden is placed squarely on the party arguing against severability to demonstrate that Congress would not have enacted the provision without the severed portion," the appeals court said.

If that standard is upheld, the airline's attorneys warn, "the courts will be creating laws that Congress would not have created, because the courts will presume that Congress would rather have something than nothing. This approach overlooks the fact that Congress is perfectly capable of filling the vacuum of no legislation with a statute of its own design. . . ." ∎

Senate Subcommittee Approval:

New Tribunal Backed to Ease Supreme Court's Workload

Legislation to create a temporary U.S. court of appeals to ease the Supreme Court's workload was beginning to move in Congress in early 1986.

The bill (S 704), approved by a Senate Judiciary subcommittee Oct. 30, 1985, and marked up by the full committee May 15, 1986, has the support of six justices, led by Chief Justice Warren E. Burger. But it has prompted sharp criticism from federal appeals judges.

Burger has campaigned for years for ways to lighten the Supreme Court's workload, which reached a high of 5,311 cases in the 1981-82 term and has leveled off over the past two terms at about 5,100 cases a year.

But some appeals court judges worry that their authority would be diluted and their own workload problems exacerbated by creation of the new court. The new court's members would be taken from the ranks of the appellate judges.

The judges have allies in three Supreme Court justices, John Paul Stevens, William J. Brennan Jr. and Thurgood Marshall, who say the new court — known as the "inter-circuit tribunal" — is not necessary.

The Senate Judiciary Subcommittee on Courts approved S 704 by a 5-1 vote. Chairman John P. East, R-N.C., cast the only dissenting vote.

East said he doubted the legislation would help reduce the Supreme Court's workload, and expressed concern that it would give new powers to the court, which would name the judges to the inter-circuit panel.

Robert W. Kastenmeier, D-Wis., chairman of the House Judiciary Subcommittee on Courts, Civil Liberties and Administration of Justice, introduced an inter-circuit court bill (HR 4238) in February 1986.

Both the Senate and House subcommittees approved similar legislation in the 98th Congress, but the bills went no further. *(Background, 1983 CQ Almanac p. 311; 1984 CQ Almanac p. 260)*

Court Workload

In 1953, the Supreme Court handled 1,463 cases and issued 65 signed opinions, according to Burger. By contrast, in its 1984-85 term, which ended July 2, the court had 5,006 cases on its docket, accepted 185 cases for argument and issued 139 signed opinions.

The 1985-86 term began Oct. 7, 1985, and by Oct. 31 there already were 2,207 cases on the docket. Most of them — 1,462 — were filed between July 2 and Oct. 31, 1985. The remaining 745 were held over from the previous term.

Court personnel said filings for the term were running about 15 percent ahead of those for the previous term.

As of Nov. 4 the justices had accepted 143 cases for argument.

New Court's Structure

As approved by the Courts Subcommittee, S 704 would establish a nine-member tribunal with four alternates, composed of sitting appeals court judges. The judges would be selected by the Supreme Court. The chief justice would select the presiding judge from the members of the panel.

The so-called inter-circuit tribunal is designed as a judicial experiment and would terminate after five years.

It would have jurisdiction over cases referred to it by the Supreme Court. The high court could refer any case to the tribunal before or after granting or denying *certiorari* — the term used to describe petitions sent to the justices asking them to hear a case. The justices take such cases at their own discretion.

There are other types of cases that the high court must consider on

There have been "only Band-Aids and Bufferin to deal with this growing [caseload] problem.... We have done virtually nothing to deal with that avalanche except work longer hours."

—Chief Justice Warren E. Burger

"The notion of a body whose members are selected by the Supreme Court as special helpers in overseeing their colleagues I find to be a novel and possibly mischievous one."

—Appeals Judge Patricia M. Wald

appeal from the lower courts, even if the justices give them summary treatment. The high court could refer these types of cases to the new court, too.

The new tribunal could deny review in any case stemming from a petition for *certiorari*. However, the high court could direct the panel to decide the case.

Decisions of the new court could be appealed to the Supreme Court. But the rulings would be final and binding on the 12 regional courts of appeals unless the high court modified them or overruled the tribunal.

Amendments Rejected

East offered two amendments to the bill in subcommittee, but both were rejected.

One would have made clear that the new court could handle only cases that would resolve differing rulings on the same point of law among the 12 circuits. The other amendment would have allowed the president to appoint the judges who would serve on the new tribunal.

In a letter to Senate Judiciary Committee Chairman Strom Thurmond, R-S.C., who is also a member of the Courts Subcommittee, Burger said he had serious reservations about "the desirability or propriety of authorizing the executive branch to designate and assign . . . judges who were long since appointed and confirmed."

Burger said senators should remember that the judges were not being appointed to anything but were merely getting new "assignments," and "the internal assignment of judges is not an authority appropriate for the executive branch."

Judges' Concerns

Some appeals court judges disagree, however.

In testimony before East's subcommittee Oct. 9, Judge Patricia M. Wald of the U.S. Court of Appeals for the District of Columbia said that if there is to be a new intermediate appeals court, "it should at least have the legitimacy of presidential nomination and Senate confirmation of its members for that job.

"The notion of a body whose members are selected by the Supreme Court as special helpers in overseeing their colleagues I find to be a novel and possibly mischievous one," she added.

Wald said the selection of 13 special appeals court judges could have "a demoralizing effect" on the operations of the circuits. She noted that the appellate courts' workload grew 600 percent between 1960 and 1983, and said the loss of 13 judges to the new court would mean an even greater workload for the remaining judges.

Judge Harry T. Edwards, another member of the D.C. circuit court of appeals, also said he was worried about morale on the appellate courts.

"Regardless of what method of selection is used, membership on the special panel will disrupt the collegiality of the courts of appeals and create hierarchies among formerly equal judges," he said. "Giving coequal judges the authority to overrule one another's decisions can strain the best of relationships."

Judge Ralph K. Winter Jr. of the 2nd U.S. Circuit Court of Appeals voiced a different concern. He said he feared the Supreme Court would be transformed from one that settled all manner of disputes "to that of philosopher king. . . . It will almost surely accelerate the expansion of judicial power and the trend toward the constitutionalization of every perceived problem," he testified.

Beyond Band-Aids

Despite concerns from the appellate bench, Burger believes the new tribunal is the best method for making the high court's work more manageable. He noted in a May 7 speech that three separate commissions — two private panels and one created by Congress — have endorsed this view.

Burger acknowledged that caseloads in the lower courts have grown, but he said the number of judges has increased substantially to help handle the increased work. Meanwhile, there have been "only Band-Aids and Bufferin to deal with this growing problem in the Supreme Court," he said. "We have done virtually nothing to deal with that avalanche at the top except work longer hours."

Burger said the inter-circuit court proposal is a good one because it creates no new bureaucracy, would only be temporary, involves no new personnel and would require no new appropriations.

Kastenmeier said Nov. 5 he is aware of the concern among appellate judges over the proposed new court.

"One must necessarily conclude that they view it as a challenge to their status, but they generally cloak their arguments in other terms," he said. "My feeling is that although some of their arguments are well made, they are not really controlling here." ▮

High Court Re-Examines Separation of Powers

Patrolling the Lines Between the Branches

Boundary disputes are nothing new at the Supreme Court, but when the boundaries are those separating the powers of Congress, the president and the federal judiciary, the justices sit up and take notice.

The court's attention was thoroughly engaged the morning of April 23, 1986, when it heard arguments challenging the constitutionality of the 1985 Gramm-Rudman-Hollings Deficit Reduction Act (PL 99-177).

On Feb. 7, a key portion of the new law had been declared unconstitutional by a three-judge panel, which found that its delegation of power to the comptroller general violated the separation of powers between Congress and the executive. Lawyers for Congress sought a reversal of that ruling. *(Arguments, 1986 CQ Weekly Report, p. 878; background, 1986 CQ Weekly Report pp. 216, 298)*

Ironically, the lawsuit over the budget-balancing law touched off a new debate likely to wind up in court sooner or later — one centering on the constitutionality of independent agencies such as the Federal Trade Commission. *(1986 CQ Weekly Report, p. 879)*

Blurred Dividing Lines

Every schoolchild in America learns that the U.S. government was built upon a foundation of separated powers: Congress makes the laws, the president executes them and the courts settle disputes over their meaning.

In practice, however, the lines too often are blurred. "It's been clear for 200 years that we don't have a tidy separation-of-powers system. We have every kind of overlapping device that you can think of," says Louis Fisher, a specialist in American government at the Congressional Research Service.

Most power struggles between the branches are resolved through political negotiation and compromise. But when two branches reach an impasse, the matter goes to court.

That has happened with unusual frequency in the last dozen years, and the pace has accelerated during the Reagan era.

Some blame the recent surge of inter-branch disputes primarily on Congress, suggesting that it has resorted to dubious "gimmickry" to evade responsibility for politically painful decisions.

Among those holding this view is Alan B. Morrison, director of the Public Citizen Litigation Group, who is pressing the challenge to the Gramm-Rudman-Hollings law.

"These cases principally arise when people try to monkey around with our basic constitutional patterns," says Morrison, who in 1983

"The hydraulic pressure inherent within each of the separate branches to exceed the outer limits of its power, even to accomplish desirable objectives, must be resisted."

—Chief Justice Warren E. Burger

persuaded the Supreme Court to invalidate the legislative veto, a device permitting either chamber of Congress to nullify executive branch regulations and orders. *(Morrison profile, p. 86; legislative veto ruling, 1983 CQ Almanac p. 565)*

Other observers believe that assertive presidents have provoked many of the contemporary cases. Fisher, for instance, noted that most of the recent disputes arose under Presidents Richard M. Nixon and Ronald Reagan — both aggressive executives — and not under the less combative Gerald R. Ford and Jimmy Carter.

During the Nixon and Reagan administrations, Fisher said, the executive branch adopted "a confrontational attitude" toward Congress, seeking "just to get the last ounce of power at some risk."

The Court as Referee

The Supreme Court is the ultimate referee of clashes between the branches. That was first established in 1803, when the court declared in *Marbury v. Madison* that it had the responsibility — and authority — to review laws passed by Congress to see if they met constitutional standards. *(Major rulings, p. 87)*

This power of judicial review has never been assaulted with any measure of success. The court's decisions have been attacked, its members criticized and its procedures questioned, but its basic power to measure the actions of the other two branches against the Constitution has never been seriously at risk.

From the beginning, the court has recognized the need for restraint in the exercise of this unique power. After *Marbury v. Madison,* more than 50 years passed before the justices again declared an act of Congress unconstitutional. In the 1857 *Dred Scott* case, the court set off an enormous furor when it declared that Congress lacked authority to control the spread of slavery. But the court's power to issue the ruling survived unscathed.

Federal laws have been invalidated more frequently in this century, but it remains a delicate matter for the courts to tell Congress or the president that they have overstepped the bounds of the Constitution.

Fisher quotes a federal judge who told opposing plaintiffs — one a congressional committee and the other the Justice Department — "I can decide this if I have to, but it's a healthier system when each of you can compromise your differences."

The high court clearly agrees. The power of judicial review, wrote Justice Lewis F. Powell Jr. in 1974, does not give the court authority to engage in "some amorphous general supervision of the operations of government."

That power must be exercised in full awareness that "repeated and essentially head-on confrontations between the life-tenured branch [the judiciary] and the representative branches of the government will not, in the long run, be beneficial to either," Powell said. "The public confidence essential to the former . . . may well erode if we do not exercise self-restraint in the utilization of our power to negate the action of the other branches."

More Cases Coming

Despite its uneasiness about separation-of-powers disputes, the court faces a rash of them in 1986 and 1987.

In addition to the Gramm-Rudman case, the justices will define the extent to which the separation of powers shields the president from lower court orders directing him to carry out certain laws.

In *Baldrige v. American Cetacean Society,* argued April 30, 1986, the Reagan administration contended that the courts should not order the president to impose sanctions that Congress required by law against countries that fail to comply with international rules on whaling.

The 1971 Pelly amendment (PL 92-219) to the Fishermen's Protective Act of 1954 and the 1979 Packwood amendment (PL 96-61) to the Magnuson Fishery Conservation and Management Act of 1976 call upon the president to order a reduction of at least 50 percent in the amount of fish offending countries may harvest within 200 miles of U.S. shores.

The administration's argument that it should not be compelled to comply with this mandate poses "a significant threat to the vitality of the separation of powers doctrine and to the future proper functioning of our government," according to House Speaker Thomas P. O'Neill Jr., D-Mass., and the bipartisan House leadership, which filed an advisory brief urging the high court to reject the administration's plea.

"Were the executive empowered to ignore the mandates of legislative enactments requiring executive action, a serious realignment of the delicate balance of our constitutional system would result," the House brief warned.

In the 1986-87 term beginning Oct. 6, 1986, the court will resolve two more separation-of-powers cases.

The first, *Burke v. Barnes,* concerns the circumstances under which a president can "pocket veto" a bill.

In the second, *Alaska Airlines v. Brock,* the court is expected to set a standard for determining how much of any law that includes a legislative veto must be invalidated along with the veto device.

By the time the court sets this "severability" standard, it may be asked to apply it to a key provision of the 1974 Congressional Budget and Impoundment Control Act. Among other things, that law authorized the president to delay spending appropriated funds unless his deferral was vetoed by either chamber of Congress.

Several House members, led by Bruce A. Morrison, D-Conn., have joined outside groups in a lawsuit challenging Reagan's continued use of the deferral power. They insist that authority was inextricably linked to the legislative veto, and must be struck down along with it. *(Pocket Veto, p. 80)*

Reasons for Surge

Why the current surge of separation-of-powers disputes, especially between Congress and the president?

Attorney Morrison considers Congress largely responsible. When confronted with problems that cannot be ignored but are politically risky to address, the first thing Congress does is "to tinker a little bit to see whether it can avoid the pain of having to decide these things," he says.

The Gramm-Rudman-Hollings law, which sets up a mechanism to trigger automatic, across-the-board spending cuts when deficit targets are exceeded, is a classic example, Morrison adds. The legislation relieves Congress of the responsibility of voting for specific cuts, while keeping the choices out of the president's hands.

"It's in times of political stress . . . times when Congress and the president can't work out problems on basic substance," that you see these groupings of lawsuits over the separation of powers, Morrison observes.

Fisher agrees that "there is a pattern of Congress wanting to legislate without passing laws."

He cites, for instance, the decision of Congress in 1967 to end a century and a half of "awkward and embarrassing" episodes related to the need to set members' salaries by handing

Attorney Morrison: Constitutional Gadfly

Alan B. Morrison, the Washington, D.C., attorney fighting to topple the Gramm-Rudman-Hollings deficit-reduction law, relishes his role as a constitutional gadfly.

"I have these rather quaint notions about how the Constitution should be like my third-grade civics book," he says. Congress and the president should not be "monkeying around" with the system of separated powers outlined by the nation's basic document, Morrison insists.

Morrison, 48, is the director of the Public Citizen Litigation Group, the litigating arm of a public interest organization created in 1971 by Ralph Nader. While the ranks of public interest law firms have thinned in the 1980s, Morrison and his group have stayed the course, gaining in expertise and reputation.

And in the 14 years since he took the job, Morrison has had considerable success in persuading courts to endorse his "quaint notions." Under his leadership, the litigation group has won eight of the 15 cases that its attorneys have argued before the Supreme Court.

Nader, who retains a strong interest in the group even though no longer formally linked to it, describes Morrison as "an expanding constitutional pillar."

Morrison's best-known victory came in 1983, when he persuaded the Supreme Court to strike down the legislative veto as unconstitutional. That device, which permitted one or both houses of Congress to block a wide range of executive branch decisions and orders, had been incorporated into more than 200 laws. *(1983 CQ Almanac p. 565)*

Rep. Mike Synar, D-Okla., chose Morrison to press his challenge to the constitutionality of the Gramm-Rudman-Hollings law (PL 99-177). The Supreme Court heard arguments in that case April 23. *(1986 CQ Weekly Report pp. 217, 878)*

Foe of Constitutional Corner-Cutting

A liberal Democrat politically, Morrison is a conservative on constitutional questions, dismissing as "gimmicks" such devices as the legislative veto and the Gramm-Rudman automatic spending-cut trigger.

Morrison says he tends to trust the courts because they "understand the importance of process, of not monkeying around with the constitutional procedures." Congress, he charges, seeks to alter those procedures when members want to avoid hard political choices about problems such as the swollen federal deficit.

Morrison has little sympathy for such dodging. "No one got drafted to be members of the House of Representatives or the Senate," he notes. "In fact, a lot of people pay a lot of money to get elected and they get paid reasonable salaries." (Morrison's own annual income of $43,000 from litigation work and teaching is well below the $75,000 salary that members receive.)

"So the notion that they should have to stand up and be counted hardly offends me at all. If they don't want to stand up and be counted, fine, there's probably a lot of other people who would like the opportunity to do that," Morrison says.

In his work, Morrison finds himself with a varying group of allies. While he and the Reagan administration are on the same side in the Gramm-Rudman case, Morrison's litigation group in a separate case is fighting the administration's efforts to defer spending appropriated funds. *(Deferral case, 1986 CQ Weekly Report pp. 737, 564)*

And Morrison has already targeted another "gimmick" for attack in the future — President Reagan's requirement that all federal agency regulations be approved by the Office of Management and Budget. *(Background, 1985 CQ Weekly Report p. 1809)*

From Wall Street to Washington

A native of Larchmont, N.Y., Morrison graduated from Yale College in 1959, spent four years in the Navy, graduated from Harvard Law School in 1966, and then joined the Wall Street law firm of Cleary, Gottlieb, Steen & Hamilton. After two years, he left to become an assistant U.S. attorney for the Southern District of New York.

But Morrison is by nature an advocate, not a prosecutor. In 1972, he left New York for Washington, D.C., and public interest law.

He is on retainer to no one; his expenses and salary are paid by the parent Public Citizen group, which draws its funds from direct-mail contributions, sales of books and publications, attorneys' fee awards and some foundation grants.

Morrison's disheveled office in an aging building has none of the trappings of the usual Washington law firm. The door stands open, a bicycle is often parked next to his desk, and there is not a three-piece suit in sight.

But the casual air of the collegial 10-attorney "firm" belies the growing reputation of its lawyers as formidable advocates in the courtroom.

And in his own way, Morrison is a thoroughly established member of the Washington legal community. He is even, as a medallion placed prominently on the front of his desk proclaims, a member of the Administrative Conference of the United States, a group that advises the government on matters of administrative practice and procedure. First appointed to that body by President Carter in 1980, Morrison has been twice reappointed during the Reagan era.

He is also at home in the academic community. After returning to Harvard Law School to teach during the 1978-79 school year, he has continued to go back to Cambridge each winter since then to teach a three-week workshop in civil litigation.

Separation of Powers: The Major Decisions

Historically, the Supreme Court has reviewed three types of separation-of-powers disputes: those involving the executive power to appoint and remove government officials, cases testing the relative roles of Congress and the president in the legislative process, and disputes over the scope of judicial power to examine the actions of executive or legislative branch officials.

Following are the court's rulings in the most significant of these cases:

The Removal Power

Myers v. United States (1926). Congress cannot deny the president the power to remove an executive branch official whom he has appointed. The removal power is a corollary of the president's constitutional duty to execute the laws. "The moment that he loses confidence in the intelligence, ability, judgment or loyalty" of an appointee, "he must have the power to remove him without delay."

Humphrey's Executor v. United States (1935). Congress *can* limit the president's power to remove members of independent regulatory commissions.

Buckley v. Valeo (1976). Congress may not appoint members of the Federal Election Commission, which exercises executive powers in enforcing federal election laws. Only the president may make such appointments.

Legislative Power

Panama Refining Co. v. Ryan (1935). Congress impermissibly delegated legislative power to the president when it authorized him to bar from interstate commerce oil produced in violation of state regulations. Such a broad delegation, contained in a major New Deal statute, "left the matter to the president without standard or rule, to be dealt with as he pleased."

Youngstown Sheet and Tube Co. v. Sawyer (1952). President Harry S Truman improperly attempted to make law when he took over the nation's steel mills in order to prevent a strike during the Korean conflict. The Constitution limits a president's participation in the legislative process "to the recommending of laws he thinks wise and the vetoing of laws he thinks bad."

Train v. City of New York (1975). President Richard M. Nixon exceeded his authority when he impounded $9 billion that Congress in 1972 expressly appropriated for federal water pollution control programs.

Immigration and Naturalization Service v. Chadha (1983). The legislative veto, a device permitting one or both houses of Congress to nullify executive branch orders and regulations, was an improper attempt by Congress to participate in the executive's administration of the laws and to circumvent the Constitution's "explicit and unambiguous" procedure for passing laws, which requires the approval of both houses and the president's signature.

Judicial Authority and Independence

Marbury v. Madison (1803). The Supreme Court is responsible for policing the boundaries separating the powers of the various branches of the federal government. "It is emphatically the province and duty of the judicial department to say what the law is."

United States v. Nixon (1974). Although a president has some executive privilege to shield certain information from disclosure, he does not enjoy absolute immunity from judicial demands for evidence for a criminal trial — in this case, White House tape recordings sought for the Watergate conspiracy trial.

Nixon v. Fitzgerald (1982). The president, by virtue of his office, is immune from civil damage suits brought against him by individuals who allege that they have suffered injury to their guaranteed rights because of some official action of the president.

United States v. Brewster (1972). The "speech or debate" clause of the Constitution protects members of Congress from prosecution for their legislative actions *per se*, but not from prosecution for crimes that might be related to their legislative roles — such as taking a bribe to cast a certain vote. The "shield" of legislative immunity "does not extend beyond what is necessary to preserve the integrity of the legislative process."

United States v. Will (1980) and *Northern Pipeline Construction Co. v. Marathon Pipe Line Co., United States v. Marathon Pipe Line Co.* (1982). Congress may not encroach upon such guarantees of judicial independence as a salary not diminished during a judge's tenure and life tenure during good behavior.

the matter over to a quadrennial commission. That was a clear example of Congress "unloading a responsibility that was theirs under the Constitution," Fisher says.

Congress has been searching for new mechanisms for a long time, notes Senate Legal Counsel Michael Davidson. When Congress created the first independent regulatory commission in 1887 — and again when it removed the post of comptroller general from the executive branch in 1921 — many of these same separation-of-powers concerns were discussed.

"Some fairly ingenious devices can survive until the point of abuse," comments Fisher. "We can live with anomalies of an informal non-statutory nature," he continues, but when those informal arrangements are overused or written into law, it becomes more difficult to overlook them.

Davidson points to the legislative veto as an example. First inserted into government reorganization acts in the 1930s, the device was used sparingly until the 1970s. After that time, Congress began adding it to more and more laws.

"What happened with the legislative veto was that Congress began to take a method and apply it almost universally, and that created a perception that Congress was no longer being discreet about a particular arrangement but was fundamentally reshaping" the way in which laws are administered, Davidson says.

Morrison recalls his amazement when the House in 1976 came within two votes of passing a bill making all agency regulations subject to the legislative veto. "Congress can't run the things it's supposed to do. It certainly shouldn't be doing the things it can't do," he says.

Like the legislative veto, the other two pending issues — the status of the comptroller general and the pocket veto — have been simmering for years.

"The disagreement between the two branches about the constitutionality of them has been clear for any number of years — with respect to the comptroller general, right from the very beginning," says Davidson, noting it had been an issue when Congress set up the office as independent of the executive in the Budget and Accounting Act of 1921.

"So no one was taken by surprise that the Department of Justice has a very clear view about the role of the comptroller general and particularly about the congressional removal power. It's finally gotten a case in which to make that point."

Davidson was referring not only to the budget-law case, but also to *Ameron v. Army Corps of Engineers,* which tests the constitutionality of provisions of the 1984 Competition in Contracting Act (PL 98-369) that authorized the comptroller general to suspend the awarding of federal contracts until protests by losing bidders are adjudicated. The 3rd U.S. Circuit Court of Appeals ruled March 27, 1986, that these provisions were constitutional, producing no actual conflict among the separated powers.

But the Gramm-Rudman fight, Fisher says, arose "not just because of the inadequacy of the internal congressional process, but also because of a breakdown in the relationship between Congress and the president over the budget."

The Congressional Budget and Impoundment Control Act of 1974 (PL 93-344) grew in large measure out of Congress' anger at Nixon's repeated impoundment of appropriated funds.

While that law put a halt to the accretion of presidential budgeting power that had been under way for decades, it created new strains for Congress.

"Congress stated that it could make a budget. And that could take the president off the hook," Fisher notes. "President Reagan has been able to say, 'OK, you make the budget and you figure it out.' And Congress can't do that. It can't receive a budget that's $200 billion in deficit and correct it."

The Last Battle Era: The 1920s

There was another time when the lines were drawn on many of the same issues, Davidson notes, pointing to the 1920s as "the really litigious time" for separation-of-powers isues. In the middle of that decade, a senator appeared before the court to argue the congressional side of a dispute over the power to remove an executive branch official. But the president won that case, *Myers v. United States.*

Then came the first *Pocket Veto* case, in which the chairman of the House Judiciary Committee presented the position of the legislative branch to the court. Again, the president's view prevailed when the court ruled in 1929 that the president could use the pocket veto any time that Congress was not in session.

It was perhaps not a coincidence that the president was so successful in these two cases; the chief justice at the time, William Howard Taft, had himself been president before assuming the nation's highest judicial post.

There was another appointments dispute during this time, a case in which the Senate had first confirmed the president's nominee as chairman of the Federal Power Commission, and then voted to reconsider the nomination, and on reconsideration, rejected it. The Senate took the matter to court to test the right of the nominee to remain in office, retaining a lawyer to argue its case before the court. Once again, the Senate lost. (*United States v. Smith,* 1932)

Moving to a Harder Line

More recently, the court in the 1970s took a flexible view of the separation of powers, invoking the doctrine only when necessary to protect the effective functioning of each branch. Its decisions were generally narrow in scope, carefully confined to the particular situation involved.

Typical is the 1974 Watergate tapes decision. The justices acknowledged that President Nixon, like any president, had an executive privilege to maintain confidentiality in presidential conversations. But the court held that in this particular set of circumstances, that privilege was outweighed by the special prosecutor's need to obtain Nixon's White House tapes for use as evidence in the Watergate conspiracy trial.

In 1975, the court struck down Nixon's impoundment of water pollution-control funds, but its decision was based on the language and circumstances of the particular law authorizing the funds at issue; it did not deal in broad fashion with the president's claim of an inherent power to refuse to spend appropriated funds.

When the court in 1976 held that Congress could not appoint members of the Federal Election Commission and then authorize the FEC to enforce campaign finance laws, it recognized that some agencies do exercise both executive and judicial functions.

All three of these decisions were unanimous.

By 1983, however, the court had moved to a harder line. The decision in the legislative veto case, says Fisher, reflected "a highly formalistic model of separated powers," whose boundaries must be vigilantly policed.

"The hydraulic pressure inherent within each of the separate branches to exceed the outer limits of its power, even to accomplish desirable objectives, must be resisted," declared Chief Justice Warren E. Burger for the majority in that veto case.

The harder line has produced divided decisions. Of the three separation-of-powers rulings in 1982 and 1983, one came by a vote of 5-4, one by 6-3 and one by 7-2.

Justice Byron R. White is the court's most consistent critic of a rigid line. "The history of the separation of powers doctrine is also a history of accommodation and practicality," he wrote in dissenting from the legislative veto ruling.

"I regret the destructive scope of the court's ruling. It reflects a profoundly different conception of the Constitution than that held by the courts which sanctioned the modern administrative state," White said.

The legislative veto ruling may have sparked some of the more recent litigation on separation-of-powers issues, according to Davidson.

Because the court made clear that decades of use had not legitimized the legislative veto, it tacitly encouraged the Reagan administration to reassert some of its longstanding constitutional objections to other aspects of administrative government, he says.

"It may have encouraged them to seize upon cases that allowed them to raise positions which the [Justice] department had felt for some period of time" but had not previously litigated, Davidson says. ▮

Biographies of Supreme Court Justices

The following are biographical sketches of each of the justices who currently serve on the Supreme Court.

Warren Earl Burger

When President Nixon announced on May 21, 1969, that Warren E. Burger was his choice as Chief Justice of the United States, most observers were caught by surprise. For despite the white-haired nominee's years of service on the Court of Appeals for the District of Columbia Circuit, Burger was little-known outside the legal community. But Burger was a natural choice for the president. During Burger's years as an appeals court judge, he had consistently argued that judges should read the Constitution narrowly — a point Nixon emphasized during his campaign. That conservative bent predictably became the hallmark of the court under the leadership of the new chief justice.

Burger was born Septemer 17, 1907, in St. Paul, Minn., the fourth of seven children of Swiss and German parents.

Financially unable to attend college full-time, Burger spent the six years following his 1925 graduation from high school attending college and law school evening classes — two years at the University of Minnesota and the remainder at St. Paul College of Law, now Mitchell College of Law. To support himself, Burger worked during the day selling life insurance.

After graduating with honors from law school in 1931, Burger joined one of the oldest law firms in Minnesota, Boyesen, Otis and Faricy. Involved in local civic work, Burger also became active in state Republican politics. In 1938, he was one of a group of men who worked successfully for the election of Governor Harold E. Stassen. It was during Stassen's unsuccessful bid for the Republican presidential nomination 10 years later that Burger first met a man who was to figure largely in his future — Herbert Brownell, campaign manager for the GOP nominee Gov. Thomas E. Dewey, R-N.Y., and later attorney general in the Eisenhower administration. It was Brownell who would bring Burger to Washington in 1953 to be assistant attorney general in charge of the claims division (now the civil division).

Burger's stint as assistant attorney general from 1953-56 was not without controversy. His decision to defend the government's actions in a case involving the dismissal of John F. Peters, a part-time federal employee, on grounds of disloyalty — after Solicitor General Simon E. Sobeloff had bowed out on grounds of conscience — won Burger the enmity of many liberals.

But Burger's overall record as assistant attorney general apparently won Eisenhower's approval, for in 1955 he was appointed to the U.S. Court of Appeals for the District of Columbia Circuit. As an appeals court judge, Burger developed a reputation as a conservative, especially in criminal justice cases.

Off the bench, Burger became increasingly outspoken in his support of major administrative reform of the judicial system — a cause he continued to advocate effectively as chief justice. Due in large part to Burger's efforts, the American Bar Association and other legal groups established the Institute of Court Management to train court executive officers, bring new management techniques to courts, and relieve judges of paperwork. Also during his first year as chief justice, Congress approved a number of measures to streamline and modernize the operations of the federal judiciary.

Burger has a deep interest in art and is himself an accomplished sculptor, interests which make it particularly appropriate that he, as chief justice, is chairman of the board of the National Gallery of Art. He is also an antiques buff, a connoisseur of fine wines, and, as chief justice, serves as chancellor of the Smithsonian Institution.

Burger has been married to Elvera Stromberg since 1933. They have a son and a daughter.

Born Sept. 17, 1907, St. Paul, Minn.; University of Minnesota 1925-27; St. Paul College of Law LL.B (1931) *magna cum laude;* married 1933; one son, one daughter; practiced law 1931-53; member of faculty Mitchell College of Law (formerly St. Paul College of Law) 1931-48; U.S. assistant attorney general 1953-56; judge, U.S. Court of Appeals for the District of Columbia Circuit 1956-69; nominated as chief justice of the United States by President Nixon May 21, 1969; confirmed June 9, 1969.

William Joseph Brennan Jr.

As a member of the activist Warren court, William J. Brennan Jr. became known as an articulate judicial scholar, who framed some of the court's key decisions. On the more conservative Burger court, however, Brennan has been largely confined to writing dissents. But while he has been relegated to a minority voice on the court, Brennan has continued to rise in the esteem of legal scholars, some of whom characterize him as the court's most eminent jurist.

Brennan was born April 25, 1906, in Newark, N.J., the second of eight children of Irish parents who immigrated to the United States in 1890. Brennan displayed impressive academic abilities early in his life. He was an outstanding student in high school, an honors student at the University of Pennsylvania's Wharton School of Finance and graduated in the top 10 percent of his Harvard Law School class in 1931.

Following law school, Brennan returned to Newark, where he joined the law firm of Pitney, Hardin and Skinner. After several years of general practice and the passage of the Wagner Labor Relations Act in 1937, he began to specialize in labor law. With the outbreak of World War II, Brennan entered the Army, serving as a manpower trouble-shooter on the staff of Under Secretary of War Robert B. Patterson.

At the conclusion of the war, Brennan returned to his old law firm. But as his practice swelled, Brennan, a dedicated family man, began to resent the demands which it placed on his time. "My practice was bidding to kill me," he once recalled.

A desire to temper the pace of his work was one of the reasons which prompted Brennan to accept an appointment to the newly-created New Jersey Superior Court. Brennan had been a leader in the movement to establish the court as part of a larger program of judicial reform. Thus it was not surprising when Republican Governor Alfred E. Driscoll named Brennan, a registered, but inactive Democrat, to the Superior Court bench in 1949.

During his tenure on the Superior Court, Brennan's use of pretrial procedures to speed up the disposition of cases brought him to the attention of New Jersey Supreme Court Justice Arthur T. Vanderbilt. It was reportedly at Vanderbilt's suggestion that Brennan was moved first in 1950 to the appellate division of the Superior Court and then in 1952 to the state Supreme Court. Late in 1956, President Eisenhower gave Brennan a recess appointment to the United States Supreme Court, sending his nomination to Congress early in 1957 when the new Congress convened.

Brennan is a football fan and a walker. Aside from these diversions, he is committed to his family and the law. Brennan was married in 1928 to Marjorie Leonard and has three children. After his wife's death in 1982, he married Mary Fowler in March 1983.

Born April 25, 1906, in Newark, N.J.; University of Pennsylvania B.S. (1928); Harvard Law School LL.B (1931); married 1928; two sons, one daughter; practiced law Newark 1931-49; N.J. Superior Court judge 1949; appellate division 1951-52; associate justice N.J. Supreme Court 1952-56; received recess appointment as associate justice, U.S. Supreme Court, from President Eisenhower Oct. 16, 1956; nominated as associate justice by President Eisenhower Jan. 14, 1957; confirmed March 19, 1957.

Byron Raymond White

Byron R. White is noted for his quick and precise legal mind, and his peppery and incisive questioning during oral argument.

White was born June 8, 1917, in Fort Collins, Colo., but grew up in Wellington, a small town in a sugar beet growing area of the state. Ranking first in his high school class, White won a scholarship to the University of Colorado, which he entered in 1934.

At the university White earned his reputation as an outstanding scholar-athlete. He was first in his class, a member of Phi Beta Kappa and the winner of three varsity letters in football, four in basketball and three in baseball. By the end of his college career in 1938 he had been dubbed "Whizzer" White for his outstanding performance as a football player, a performance which earned him not only a national reputation but also a one-year contract with the Pittsburgh Pirates (now the Steelers). White had already accepted a coveted Rhodes Scholarship for study at Oxford, but decided to postpone his year in England.

Despite his success as a pro football player, at the end of the football season, White sailed for England to attend Oxford. When the European war broke out in September 1939, White returned to the United States and entered Yale Law School. But during 1940 and 1941, he alternated law study with playing football for the Detroit Lions.

After the United States entered the war, White served in the Navy in the South Pacific. There he renewed an old acquaintance with John F. Kennedy, whom he had met in England and who later would nominate White to the Supreme Court. After the war, White returned to Yale, earning his law degree *magna cum laude* in 1946. Following graduation, White served as law clerk to U.S. Chief Justice Fred M. Vinson. In 1947, he returned to his native Colorado, where for the next 14 years he practiced law with the Denver firm of Lewis, Grant and Davis.

White renewed his contact with Kennedy during the 1960 presidential campaign, leading the nationwide volunteer group, Citizens for Kennedy. After the election, Kennedy named White to the post of deputy attorney general, a position he held until his Supreme Court appointment in 1962.

White has been married since 1946 to Marion Stearns. They have one son and one daughter.

Born June 8, 1917, in Fort Collins, Colo.; University of Colorado B.A. (1938); Phi Beta Kappa; Rhodes scholar, Oxford University; Yale Law School LL.B *magna cum laude* (1946); married 1946; one son, one daughter; law clerk to Chief Justice Fred M. Vinson, U.S. Supreme Court 1946-47; practiced law, Denver, 1947-60; U.S. deputy attorney general 1961-62; nominated as associate justice, U.S. Supreme Court, by President Kennedy March 30, 1962; confirmed April 11, 1962.

Thurgood Marshall

Unlike some jurists who undergo striking philosophical changes once elevated to the Supreme Court, Thurgood Marshall has deviated little from his earlier convictions. For more than a quarter of a century, Marshall exemplified, through his work with the National Association for the Advancement of Colored People (NAACP), that part of the civil rights movement which sought change through legal processes. Once on the court, Marshall has continued to champion the rights of minorities. And as a member of the court's minority liberal wing, Marshall has persisted in his defense of individual rights.

Marshall was born July 2, 1908, in Baltimore, Md., the son of a primary school teacher and a club steward. In 1926, he left Baltimore to attend all-black Lincoln University in Chester, Pa., where he developed a reputation as an outstanding debater. After graduating *cum laude* in 1930, Marshall decided to study law, and in 1931 he entered Howard University in Washington, D.C.

During his law school years, Marshall began to develop an interest in civil rights. After graduating first in his law school class in 1933, Marshall commenced a long and historic involvement with the NAACP.

In 1940 Marshall became the head of the newly formed NAACP Legal Defense and Educational Fund, a position he held for more than 20 years.

Over the next two and one-half decades, Marshall coordinated the fund's attack on segregation in voting, housing, public accommodations and education. But the culmination of his career as a civil rights attorney came in 1954 as chief counsel in a series of cases grouped under the title *Brown v. Board of Education.* In that historic case, which Marshall argued before the court, civil rights advocates convinced the court to declare that segregation in public schools was unconstitutional.

In 1961, Marshall was appointed by President Kennedy to the U.S. Court of Appeals for the 2nd Circuit, but because of heated opposition from Southern Democratic senators, he was not confirmed until a year later.

Four years after he was named to the circuit court, Marshall was chosen by President Johnson to be the nation's first black solicitor general. During his years as the government's chief advocate before the Supreme Court, Marshall scored impressive victories in the areas of civil and constitutional rights. He won Supreme Court approval of the 1965 Voting Rights Act, voluntarily informed the court that the government had used electronic eavesdropping devices in two cases, and joined in a suit that successfully overturned a California constitutional amendment that prohibited open housing legislation.

On June 13, 1967, Marshall became the first black appointed to be a justice of the Supreme Court, chosen by President Johnson.

Marshall was married in 1955 to Cecelia A. Suyat. He has two sons by his first wife who died in 1955.

Born July 2, 1908, in Baltimore, Md.; Lincoln University B.A. (1930); Howard University LL.B (1933); practiced law 1933-37; assistant special counsel NAACP 1936-38; special counsel 1938-50; married 1955; two sons; director-counsel, NAACP Legal Defense and Educational Fund 1940-61; judge, U.S. Court of Appeals for the 2nd Circuit 1961-65; U.S. Solicitor General 1965-67; nominated as associate justice, U.S. Supreme Court, by President Johnson June 13, 1967; confirmed Aug. 30, 1967.

Harry Andrew Blackmun

During his first years on the court Harry A. Blackmun was frequently described as one of the "Minnesota Twins" along with the court's other Minnesota native, Chief Justice Warren E. Burger. Blackmun and Burger are lifelong friends who initially voted together on important court decisions.

However, Blackmun, who originally impressed observers as a modest, even meek, addition to the court's conservative bloc, has authored some of the court's most controversial decisions, among them its 1973 ruling upholding a woman's right to an abortion. And he has broken frequently enough with his conservative colleagues to earn a reputation as an independent, if still fundamentally conservative, justice.

Blackmun was born in Nashville, Ill., on November 12, 1908, but spent most of his early years in Minneapolis-St. Paul, where his father was an official of the Twin Cities Savings and Loan Co. It was in grade school that Blackmun began his lifelong friendship with Burger.

"A whiz at math," according to his mother, Blackmun went East after high school to attend Harvard College on a scholarship. At Harvard, Blackmun majored in mathematics and toyed briefly with the idea of becoming a physician.

But Blackmun chose the law instead. After graduating from Harvard in 1929, Phi Beta Kappa, Blackmun entered Harvard Law School, from which he graduated in 1932. During his law school years, Blackmun supported himself with a variety of odd jobs, including tutoring in math and driving the launch for the college crew team.

Following law school, Blackmun returned to St. Paul, where he served for a year-and-a-half as a law clerk to United States Circuit Court Judge John B. Sanborn, whom Blackmun succeeded 20 years later. He left the clerkship at the end of 1933 and joined the Minneapolis law firm of Dorsey, Colman, Barker, Scott and Barber. At the same time he taught for a year at William Mitchell College of Law in St. Paul, Chief Justice Burger's alma mater. In addition to his practice he also taught for two years during the 1940s at the University of Minnesota Law School.

In 1950 he accepted a post as "house counsel" for the world-famous Mayo Clinic in Rochester, Minn.

Among his colleagues at the clinic, Blackmun quickly developed a reputation as a serious man, totally engrossed in his profession.

The reputation followed him to the bench of the U.S. Court of Appeals for the 8th Circuit, to which Blackmun was appointed by Eisenhower in 1959. As a judge, he was known for his scholarly and thorough opinions.

Blackmun's total devotion to the law leaves little time for outside activities. He is an avid reader, delving primarily into judicial tomes. Over the years, he has also been active in Methodist church affairs. Before a knee gave out, Blackmun was a proficient squash and tennis player. It was on the tennis court that Blackmun met his future wife, Dorothy E. Clark. They were married in 1941 and have three daughters.

Born Nov. 12, 1908 in Nashville, Ill.; Harvard College B.A. (1929); Phi Beta Kappa; Harvard Law School LL.B. (1932); clerk, John Sanborn, U.S. Court of Appeals for the 8th Circuit, St. Paul 1932-33; practiced law, Minneapolis, 1934-50; married 1941; three daughters; resident counsel, Mayo Clinic, Rochester, Minn. 1950-59; judge, U.S. Court of Appeals for the 8th Circuit 1959-70; nominated as associate justice U.S. Supreme Court, by President Nixon April 14, 1970; confirmed May 12, 1970.

Lewis Franklin Powell Jr.

At the time of his nomination to the Supreme Court in 1971, former American Bar Association President Lewis F. Powell Jr. was hailed for his professional excellence and for the moderation of his political views. Those views had been fashioned by a lifetime of private law practice in Richmond, Virginia, years of active participation in the American Bar Association, and deep involvement in the sensitive question of desegregating Virginia's public schools.

Following his appointment to the Supreme Court, Powell continued to build a reputation as a moderate. And, according to observers, Powell quickly rose to a position of influence among the other eight justices disproportionate to his low seniority on the court.

Powell was born September 19, 1907, in Suffolk, Va., but he spent most of his life in Richmond. He attended college and law school at Washington and Lee University in Lexington, Va., earning his B.S. in 1929 and law degree in 1931. From Lexington, Powell journeyed north to Cambridge, Mass., where he attended Harvard Law School, earning a master's degree in 1932.

Following his year at Harvard, Powell returned to Virginia, where he joined one of the state's oldest and most prestigious law firms, later called Hunton, Williams, Gay, Powell and Gibson. Powell rose to become a senior partner, continuing his association with the firm until his nomination to the Supreme Court.

Over the years, Powell's practice made him no stranger to blue chip board rooms. Among the companies Hunton, Williams represented during Powell's years with the firm were the Baltimore & Ohio Railroad Co., the Prudential Insurance Co. and the Virginia Electric and Power Co. Powell himself did no work for these corporations.

Powell's reputation as a moderate stemmed from his work as president from 1952-61 of the Richmond school board, and later as a member of the state board of education. According to civil rights advocates in Richmond, Powell, in the face of intense pressure to "massively" resist desegregation, consistently advocated keeping the city schools open.

A one-year stint, from 1964-65, as the president of the American Bar Association (ABA) provided Powell with a national platform from which to express his views on a range of subjects. The exposure enhanced his reputation as a moderate. On the liberal side, Powell spoke out against inadequate legal services for the poor and worked to create the legal services program of the Office of Economic Opportunity. A more conservative tone characterized his pronouncements against "excessive tolerance" by parents and his stern denunciations of civil disobedience and other forms of civil demonstrations. And, as a member in 1966 of President Johnson's Crime Commission, Powell participated in a minority statement criticizing Supreme Court rulings upholding the right of criminal suspects to remain silent. Powell was the only Democrat among President Nixon's Supreme Court appointees.

A first-rate tennis player, Powell is also an avid sports fan. Powell has been married since 1936 to Josephine Rucker. They have three daughters and a son.

Born Sept. 19, 1907, Suffolk, Va.; Washington and Lee University B.S. (1929); Phi Beta Kappa; LL.B (1931); Harvard Law School LL.M (1932); practiced law in Richmond, 1932-71; married 1936; three daughters, one son; president, American Bar Association 1964-65; president, American College of Trial Lawyers 1968-69; nominated associate justice, U.S. Supreme Court, by President Nixon Oct. 21, 1971; confirmed Dec. 6, 1971.

William Hubbs Rehnquist

With his modish sideburns and youthful mien, William H. Rehnquist in the mid-1970s looked as if he should be the court's most liberal member. However, in Rehnquist's case, appearances were deceiving, for the court's youngest justice was also its most conservative.

Born in Milwaukee, Wisconsin, October 1, 1924, Rehnquist went west to college. At Stanford University, where he received both his undergraduate and law degrees, classmates recalled him as a brilliant student whose already well-entrenched conservative views set him apart from his more liberal classmates.

After graduating from law school in 1952, Rehnquist traveled east to Washington, D.C., to serve as a law clerk to Supreme Court Justice Robert H. Jackson. There in 1952, he wrote a memorandum that later would come back to haunt him during his Senate confirmation hearings. In the memorandum, Rehnquist favored separate but equal schools for blacks and whites. Asked about those views by the Senate Judiciary Committee in 1971, Rehnquist repudiated them, declaring that they were Justice Jackson's not his own.

Following his clerkship, Rehnquist decided to begin law practice in the Southwest. In 1953, Rehnquist moved to Phoenix, Ariz., and immediately became immersed in state Republican politics. From his earliest days in the state, he was associated with the party's most conservative wing. A 1957 speech denouncing the liberality of the Warren court typified his views at the time.

During the 1964 presidential campaign, Rehnquist campaigned ardently for Barry Goldwater. It was during the campaign that Rehnquist met and worked with Richard G. Kleindienst, who later as President Nixon's deputy attorney general, would appoint Rehnquist to head the Justice Department's Office of Legal Counsel as an assistant attorney general.

Rehnquist quickly became one of the administration's chief spokesmen on Capitol Hill, commenting on issues ranging from wiretapping to the rights of the accused. It was Rehnquist's job to review the legality of all presidential executive orders and other constitutional law questions in the executive branch. He frequently testified before congressional committees in support of the administration's policies — most of which matched his own conservative philosophy. So tightly reasoned and articulate was his testimony backing government surveillance of American citizens and tighter curbs on obscene materials, that even some liberal members of Congress applauded his ability.

In 1971, the once-obscure Phoenix lawyer was nominated by President Nixon to the Supreme Court.

Rehnquist has been married since 1953 to Natalie Cornell. They have two daughters and a son.

Born Oct. 1, 1924, Milwaukee, Wis.; Stanford University B.A. (1948); Phi Beta Kappa; LL.B (1952); Harvard University M.A. (1949); law clerk to Justice Robert H. Jackson, U.S. Supreme Court 1952-53; married 1953; two daughters, one son; practiced law 1953-69; assistant U.S. attorney general, office of legal counsel 1969-71; nominated as associate justice, U.S. Supreme Court, by President Nixon Oct. 21, 1971; confirmed Dec. 10, 1971.

John Paul Stevens

When President Ford nominated federal appeals court Judge John Paul Stevens to the Supreme Court seat vacated by veteran liberal William O. Douglas in 1975, court-watchers and other observers struggled to pin an ideological label on the new nominee. The consensus which emerged was that Stevens was neither a doctrinaire liberal nor conservative, but a judicial "centrist," whose well-crafted, scholarly opinions made him a "judge's judge." His subsequent opinions bear out this description.

A soft-spoken, mild-mannered man who occasionally sports a bow tie under his judicial robes, Stevens had a long record of excellence in scholarship. A member of a prominent Chicago family, Stevens graduated Phi Beta Kappa from the University of Chicago in 1941. After a wartime stint in the Navy, during which he earned the Bronze Star, he returned to Chicago to enter Northwestern University Law School, from which he graduated *magna cum laude* in 1947. From there, Stevens left for Washington, where he served as a law clerk to Supreme Court Justice Wiley Rutledge. He returned to Chicago to join the prominent law firm of Poppenhusen, Johnston, Thompson and Raymond, which specialized in antitrust law. Stevens developed a reputation as a pre-eminent antitrust lawyer, and after three years with Poppenhusen, he left in 1952 to form his own firm, Rothschild, Stevens, Barry and Myers. He remained there, engaging in private practice and teaching part-time at Northwestern and the University of Chicago law schools, until his appointment by President Nixon in 1970 to the U.S. Court of Appeals for the 7th Circuit.

Stevens developed a reputation as a political moderate during his undergraduate days at the University of Chicago, then an overwhelmingly liberal campus. But although he is a registered Republican, he has never been active in partisan politics. Nevertheless, Stevens did serve as Republican counsel in 1951 to the House Judiciary Committee's Subcommittee on the Study of Monopoly Power. He also served from 1953 to 1955, during the Eisenhower administration, as a member of the Attorney General's National Committee to Study the Antitrust Laws.

An enthusiastic pilot, Stevens flies his own small plane. According to friends, he is also a creditable bridge player and golfer. Stevens underwent open heart surgery several years ago, from which he is said to have recovered fully. However, the operation did force him to give up the game of squash. In 1942, Stevens married Elizabeth Jane Sheeren. They have four children. They were divorced in 1979. Stevens subsequently married Maryan Mulholland Simon, a longtime neighbor in Chicago.

Born April 20, 1920, Chicago, Ill.; University of Chicago B.A. (1941); Phi Beta Kappa; Northwestern University School of Law J.D. (1947); *magna cum laude;* married 1942; three daughters, one son; divorced 1979; married Maryan Mulholland Simon 1980; law clerk to Justice Wiley Rutledge, U.S. Supreme Court 1947-48; practiced law Chicago, 1949-70; judge, U.S. Court of Appeals for the 7th Circuit 1970-75; nominated as associate justice, U.S. Supreme Court, by President Ford Nov. 28, 1975; confirmed Dec. 17, 1975.

Sandra Day O'Connor

Pioneering came naturally to Sandra Day O'Connor. Her grandfather left Kansas in 1880 to take up ranching in the desert land that would eventually become the state of Arizona. O'Connor, born in El Paso where her mother's parents lived, was raised on the Lazy B Ranch, the 162,000-acre spread that her grandfather had founded in southeastern Arizona near Duncan. She spent her school years in El Paso, living with her grandmother and attending the schools there. She graduated from high school at age 16 and then entered Stanford University.

Six years later, in 1952, Sandra Day had won degrees, with great distinction, both from the university, in economics, and from Stanford Law School. There she met John J. O'Connor III, her future husband, and was also a classmate of William H. Rehnquist, a future colleague on the Supreme Court. During her law school years, Sandra Day was an editor of the Stanford Law Review and a member of Order of the Coif, both reflecting her academic leadership.

But despite her outstanding law school record, she found it difficult to locate a job as an attorney in 1952 when relatively few women were practicing law. She applied, among others, to the firm in which William French Smith — attorney general in the Reagan administration — was a partner, only to be offered a job as a secretary.

After a short stint as deputy county attorney for San Mateo County (Calif.) while her new husband completed law school at Stanford, the O'Connors moved with the U.S. Army to Frankfurt, Germany. There Sandra O'Connor worked as a civilian attorney for the Army, while John O'Connor served his tour of duty.

In 1957, they returned to Phoenix to live. In the next

eight years, their three sons were born and O'Connor's life was a mix of mothering, homemaking, volunteer work and some "miscellaneous legal tasks" on the side.

In 1965, O'Connor resumed her legal career full time, taking a job as an assistant attorney general for Arizona. After four years in that post, she was appointed to fill a vacancy in the state Senate, where she served on the judiciary committee. In 1970, she was elected to the Senate, and two years later was chosen its majority leader; the first woman in the nation to hold such a post.

O'Connor was active in Republican Party politics and was co-chairman of the Arizona Committee to Re-Elect the President in 1972.

In 1974, she was elected to the Superior Court for Maricopa County where she served for five years. Then in 1979, Gov. Bruce Babbitt — acting, some said, to remove a potential rival for the governorship — appointed O'Connor to the Arizona Court of Appeals. It was from that seat that President Reagan chose her as his first nominee to the Supreme Court, describing her as "a person for all seasons."

She was confirmed unanimously Sept. 21, 1981, by the Senate as the first woman associate justice of the U.S. Supreme Court.

Born March 26, 1930 in El Paso, Texas; Stanford University, B.A. (1950); *magna cum laude*; Stanford University Law School, LL.B. (1952); with high honors; deputy county attorney, San Mateo, Calif., 1952-53; assistant attorney general, Arizona, 1965-69; Arizona state senator, 1969-1975, Senate majority leader, 1972-75; judge, Maricopa County Superior Court, 1974-79; judge, Arizona Court of Appeals, 1979-81; married John J. O'Connor III, Dec. 20, 1952; three sons; nominated associate justice U.S. Supreme Court, by President Ronald Reagan Aug. 19, 1981, to replace Potter Stewart, who retired; confirmed by the U.S. Senate Sept. 21, 1981, by a vote of 99-0.

Reference Guide to the Supreme Court

Biographical Directory of the Federal Judiciary — Biographical data on judges of the Supreme Court, Court of Appeals, District Courts, Court of Claims; statistical data on religious and political persuasions. Detroit, Michigan, Gale Research Corp., 1983.

Black's Law Dictionary edited by Henry C. Black — Definitions of terms and phrases of American and English jurisprudence. St. Paul, Minnesota, West Publishing Co., 1979.

Congressional Quarterly's Guide to the U.S. Supreme Court — A 1,000 page volume documenting the development and working of the court. Includes summaries of major decisions and biographies of all justices. Washington, D.C., Congressional Quarterly Inc., 1979.

The Constitution of the United States of America: Analysis and Interpretation — Discussion of each phrase of the Constitution and annotations of cases decided by the Supreme Court. Washington, D.C., Government Printing Office, 1979.

Court and Constitution in the Twentieth Century by William F. Swindler — Two-volume history of the court from 1889 through 1968. Indianapolis, Bobbs-Merrill, 1969.

Justices and Presidents: A Political History of Appointments to the Supreme Court by Henry J. Abraham — History of appointments to the Supreme Court from George Washington through Lyndon Johnson. New York, Oxford University Press, 1974.

The Justices of the United States Supreme Court: Their Lives and Major Opinions, edited by Leon Friedman and Fred Israel — Five volumes on the lives and major opinions of the Supreme Court justices from 1789 through 1971. New York, R. R. Bowker.

Landmark Briefs and Arguments of the Supreme Court of the United States: Constitutional Law, edited by Philip B. Kurland and Gerhard Casper — Includes briefs, transcripts of oral arguments and decisions of the Supreme Court on major constitutional law cases from 1793 through 1973. Washington, D.C., University Publications of America Inc., 1975.

Lawyer's Edition of the United States Supreme Court — Weekly report of court opinions, summary of arguments, digest of court decisions; bound volumes issued annually. Rochester, N.Y., Lawyer's Cooperative Publishing Co.

Significant Decisions of the Supreme Court by Bruce E. Fein — Annual review of all major opinions and analyses since 1969. Washington, D.C., American Enterprise Institute for Public Policy Research.

The Supreme Court by Lawrence Baum — Analysis of the Supreme Court's policy-making role. Washington, D.C., CQ Press, 1985.

The Supreme Court in United States History by Charles Warren — Two volume history covers the period 1789 through 1918. Boston, Little, Brown and Co., 1922.

A Different Justice by Elder Witt — Examination of President Reagan's influence on the Supreme Court. Washington, D.C., Congressional Quarterly Inc., 1985.

Supreme Court Practice by Robert L. Stern and Eugene Gressman. Washington, D.C., Bureau of National Affairs, 1978.

Supreme Court Reporter — Bimonthly coverage of Supreme Court decisions and proceedings; bound cumulative reports issued annually. St. Paul, Minnesota, West Publishing Co.

The United States Law Week — Digest and analysis of current developments, opinions and rulings of the Supreme Court. Washington, D.C., Bureau of National Affairs.

The United States Reports — Official record of Supreme Court decisions and proceedings; issued daily in "slip opinions"; cumulative volumes issued annually. Washington, D.C., Government Printing Office.

CONGRESS

Congress Has Broad Authority To Regulate Fiscal Affairs, Commerce

The authors of the Constitution recognized that the new government needed an executive to carry out the laws and a judiciary to resolve conflicts in them. But Congress would be the heart of the new republic. The House of Representatives was the only part of the federal government originally elected by the people; consequently, Congress was the branch of government expected to respond directly to their needs.

It was thus to the national legislature that the framers entrusted most of the power necessary to govern the new nation. To Congress the Constitution granted "all legislative Powers." These included the power to tax, regulate commerce, declare war, approve treaties and raise and maintain armies.

The framers also gave Congress some authority over the other two branches. Congress was granted the power to establish whatever federal judicial system below the Supreme Court seemed desirable and to impeach and convict the president, federal judges and other federal officers for treason, bribery or other high crimes and misdemeanors. Each chamber has authority to seat and discipline its own members.

The exercise of these powers is subject to some limitation. The Constitution specifically prevents Congress from singling out individuals for punishment and from imposing a direct tax that is unapportioned or an indirect tax that is not uniform. The most significant constitutional limitations may be those added by the First Amendment, prohibiting Congress from interfering with the free exercise of speech, the press, assembly, or religion, and the Fifth Amendment, prohibiting the taking of life, liberty or property without due process of law.

Fiscal Powers

Perhaps the most important of the constitutional prerogatives granted to Congress are the powers to tax and to spend. Congress may use its power to tax both to raise revenue to run the country and as a regulatory device. The power to spend allows Congress to determine policy on almost every matter that affects daily life in the United States.

Taxation

Taxes on the income and profits of individuals and corporations have become the federal government's basic sources of revenue since the 16th Amendment permitting a general income tax was ratified in 1913. In addition, Congress has imposed an excess profits tax on corporations during wartime, levied a variety of excise taxes, authorized estate and gift taxes and imposed payroll taxes to underpin the old-age insurance and unemployment compensation systems.

Tax legislation must, under a constitutional provision, originate in the House of Representatives. Tax and tariff bills are handled there by the Ways and Means Committee. After the House acts, such bills go to the Senate where they are referred to the Finance Committee. Because that committee and the full Senate may amend the House version of a tax bill, the Senate plays an influential role in the consideration and adoption of tax legislation. In a departure from tradition and constitutional dictates, the Senate initiated a major tax bill in 1982. It was enacted, although some House members challenged the constitutionality of the legislation.

In the post-World War II era, initiatives on raising, lowering, or enacting new taxes generally have been taken by the executive branch; it has prepared the initial recommendations and Congress has acted on them. But there is no requirement that the executive initiate tax changes. Congress itself generated a major tax reform bill in 1969 and a wide-ranging tax revision bill in 1976.

Appropriations

Revenue raised through taxation is not available in the Treasury to be disbursed by the executive branch to meet governmental needs simply as agency officials see fit. The Constitution gives to Congress the sole authority to determine how monies collected shall be spent and requires a regular statement of expenditures.

This appropriations procedure works in two steps after the president presents his annual budget requests to Congress. First, the various congressional committees consider the parts of the request that fall under their jurisdictions and report out bills authorizing expenditures and setting a ceiling on the amount of funds that can be spent for the programs. After the authorization becomes law, Congress actually provides (appropriates) the money to fund the programs. The amount of money appropriated often is less than the maximum amount specified in the authorization for the program.

Although the Constitution does not require it, appropriations traditionally originate in the House. Appropriations initially are considered by the relevant subcommittee of the House Appropriations Committee where the bulk of basic spending decisions are made, although both the full committee and the House may amend a bill before it is passed and sent to the Senate. What the Senate does in effect is to review the House action and hear appeals from agencies seeking changes in the allotments accorded them by the House.

Budget Control

Congress, having long treated its taxing and spending powers separately, in 1974 enacted the Congressional Budget and Impoundment Control Act (PL 93-344) to provide a method of setting overall fiscal policy for the federal government, and in some respects constrain congressional committees from acting against the goals espoused in the budget.

The budget law set up House and Senate Budget committees to write annual budgets and keep track of Congress' performance in adhering to them, and it created a Congressional Budget Office to provide technical information about the economy and the budget that previously was available only from the president's budget agency, the Office of Management and Budget.

In December 1985, the perceived failure of the 1974 law to prevent steadily increasing, multibillion-dollar deficits led Congress to make radical changes in budget procedures that presumably would force a balanced budget by October 1990. The new law, known as Gramm-Rudman-Hollings (PL 99-177) for its Senate sponsors, set maximum annual allowable deficits for the years 1986-91, and mandated automatic, across-the-board spending cuts if Congress failed to meet those goals.

Aside from a legal challenge to a key element of the process making the automatic cuts, the law was seen by many observers as a significant political step for a Congress previously unwilling to address huge deficits.

In theory under the new law, the president submits a budget request on the first Monday after Jan. 3 of each year. Congress then acts on the request, completing action on its budget resolution by April 15. The budget is not signed into law by the president, however. Through procedural rules that are somewhat different for each chamber, it is supposed to bind future congressional action increasing or cutting taxes, making appropriations (giving agencies money to spend), and authorizing new programs, or reauthorizing expiring ones.

A process created by the 1974 law, and used with varying success since 1980, envisions enactment as law of a so-called reconciliation bill that combines budget-cutting measures from all committees into one bill to help meet the spending targets in the budget. Under the timetable in Gramm-Rudman, reconciliation bills are to be enacted by June 15, and the House is to complete action on appropriations by June 30.

In any year that by Oct. 1 Congress and the president fail to devise a budget that meets the deficit target for the upcoming fiscal year, and then to achieve the budget's goals through regular legislative means, federal spending — with some key exceptions, including Social Security and interest payments on the federal debt — is to be cut automatically by a uniform percentage to achieve the target for that year.

The key steps in the budget process did not change under the new law, except that deadlines for congressional action — which typically had not been met — were made even earlier. The most important changes included the mandated spending cuts and new procedural roadblocks to congressional action on bills that would breach tax, spending and deficit limits. Those roadblocks were not impossible to bypass, however, and it was unclear if Congress would strictly adhere to the law's requirements. There had been procedural constraints under the 1974 law designed to keep spending from exceeding revenues, but Congress had almost uniformly failed to meet its budget goals in the years before Gramm-Rudman's enactment.

Advocates of the bill hoped the threat of automatic cuts would force the president, Congress and the public to spend less on government or to agree to pay higher taxes. Since enacting the 1974 budget law, Congress mostly shied away from making the tough decisions required to reverse the climb of federal spending; in fiscal 1985 the federal deficit reached a record $212 billion.

It was this situation that motivated Congress and the president to take the historic step of binding themselves to five years of forced deficit reduction. Gramm-Rudman-Hollings made many members of Congress uneasy; and they often said in private that it was neither wise nor workable. Nevertheless, it won strong, bipartisan support in both chambers because of members' fears of the economic and political consequences of continued deficit spending. Sponsor Warren B. Rudman, R-N.H., called it "a bad idea whose time has come."

Commerce Powers

Nearly as important as the powers to tax and spend is the power to regulate interstate and foreign commerce. Congress' exercise of its virtually exclusive authority in these areas has produced extensive government regulation not only of the actual transport of goods but also of their manufacture, sale and, in many, cases their purity and safety.

The Constitution gave Congress a broad and positive grant of power to regulate interstate and foreign commerce but left interpretation of the extent of the power to precedent and judicial determination. Although the Supreme Court initially gave Congress almost complete control over interstate commerce, the legislative branch seldom exercised its power. But with the passage of the Interstate Commerce Act of 1887, Congress moved decisively into the area of domestic regulation. The act, prompted by the individual states' inability to curb increasing abuses by railroads, ultimately was broadened to include regulation of trucking companies, bus lines, freight forwarders, water carriers, oil pipelines, transportation brokers and express agencies. The act, which established the Interstate Commerce Commission as the first regulatory agency, also led to creation of several other agencies that regulate various aspects of commercial transactions in the United States, as well as entire industries, such as communications and energy.

In 1890 Congress moved into federal regulation of commercial enterprise with enactment of the Sherman Antitrust Act "to protect commerce against unlawful restraints and monopolies." With the turn of the century, Congress began to regulate interstate commerce to protect the health and morals of the general populace. To this end, Congress banned interstate shipment of such items as lottery tickets, impure food and drugs and prostitutes.

Although the Supreme Court sanctioned most of these new uses of the interstate commerce power, it balked occasionally at certain regulations, such as the congressional attempt in 1916 to outlaw child labor by barring the shipment of goods made by children. It was this narrower view of the commerce power that prevailed when the Supreme Court reviewed and declared unconstitutional many of the early New Deal economic recovery programs. The confrontation resulted in the court's recognition of Congress' authority to regulate virtually all aspects of business and manufacture affecting interstate commerce.

Only once since 1937 has the court found an exercise of the commerce clause to be unconstitutional. In that same period it has sanctioned broadened uses of the commerce power. In the Civil Rights Act of 1964, Congress found justification in the commerce clause and the "equal protection" clause of the 14th Amendment for a ban on racial discrimination in most public accommodations. Congress used the commerce clause in 1968 as the basis for legislation making it a federal crime to travel in interstate commerce for the purpose of inciting or participating in a riot. The commerce clause is also the basis for the far-reaching federal clean air and water laws.

Foreign Policy Powers

While the president generally takes the initiative in foreign relations, Congress possesses several constitutionally granted powers that are indispensable to the success of the president's policies. These include the powers to raise taxes (to finance wars), create and maintain an armed force, regulate foreign commerce and ratify treaties. Except for votes on the Vietnam War in the 1970s, and Lebanon and Central America in the 1980s, Congress in the 20th century has chosen to use its powers to support the president in these matters rather than to challenge him.

While the Constitution gives Congress the power to declare war and "provide for the common Defence," both the initiation and conduct of war have come to be almost entirely directed by the president. In November 1973 Congress sought to restore some of its control over war efforts when it enacted, over President Nixon's veto, the War Powers Resolution (PL 93-148). In addition to certain reporting requirements, the measure set a 60-day limit on any presidential commitment of U.S. troops abroad without specific congressional authorization, unless troops were sent to respond to an "attack upon the United States, its territories or possessions or its armed forces." Unauthorized commitments could be terminated prior to the 60-day deadline through congressional passage of a concurrent resolution — a measure that does not require the president's signature to take effect.

Although Congress had never used that "legislative veto" authority to force a president to withdraw troops, the threat of a veto may have forced chief executives to consult more closely with Congress in taking military actions abroad. The Supreme Court's June 1983 ruling that legislative vetoes were unconstitutional dealt a blow to congressional influence over such commitments by nullifying that provision of the War Powers Resolution. In the wake of that ruling Congress wrestled with ways to develop an alternative method of influencing decisions. After the April 14, 1986, bombing of Libya, Congress again addressed the question of presidential prerogative. This time the debate centered on if and when the president should consult Congress in cases involving a U.S. response to terrorism.

Another area in which the Supreme Court's ruling could have a potentially far-reaching impact is congressional control of arms sales. In 1976 Congress enacted the Arms Export Control Act (PL 94-329), substantially expanding its power to veto arms sales to foreign countries through adoption of a concurrent resolution. Again, although most arms sales have raised little controversy, Congress has repeatedly challenged the president's judgment on specific sales to countries, particularly those in the volatile Middle East. As with the War Powers Resolution, Congress never has actually vetoed a proposed arms sale, but the possibility forced Presidents Jimmy Carter and Ronald Reagan to make compromises.

In spite of the Supreme Court's legislative veto ruling, congressional power over some other aspects of foreign policy has increased substantially. Legislative authority over the massive post-World War II foreign aid and military assistance programs is an example. The programs have required specific congressional authorizations and repeated congressional appropriations. Frequently Congress has disagreed with the president over the amounts and allocations for these programs, making its views known either through directives in the authorizing legislation, or by changing funding requests in appropriations bills.

The Constitition gives the president authority to make treaties with other countries if two-thirds of the Senate concur. For years this power served as a cornerstone of American foreign policy. Treaties forged peace agreements with other nations, supported U.S. territorial expansion, established national boundaries, protected U.S. commerce and regulated government affairs with Indian tribes.

Except for rejection of the Versailles Treaty after World War I, Senate action on treaties has not been a major factor in foreign policy. Although the Senate has killed several treaties by inaction, it had by the end of 1985 rejected only 20 treaties since 1789. However, the lengthy debates on the Panama Canal and U.S.-Soviet strategic arms limitation talks (SALT II) treaties in 1978 and 1979, respectively, were seen as Senate moves to expand its power in the foreign policy field.

In recent years the Senate's role has been eroded somewhat by the use of executive agreements instead of treaties with foreign countries; such agreements do not require Senate approval.

Confirmations of Nominations

Under the Constitution the Senate must approve all presidential nominations of federal officers. Most nominations involve promotions of military officers and Senate action is only a formality. But each year several hundred major nominations are subjected to varying degrees of Senate scrutiny. These include nominations to Cabinet and sub-Cabinet positions, independent boards and regulatory agencies, major diplomatic and military posts and the federal judiciary.

The Senate role in Supreme Court appointments has proved particularly important. It may not be able to dictate Supreme Court nominees, but historically the Senate has not been afraid to reject them. Slightly more than one-fifth of all Supreme Court nominations have failed to win Senate confirmation.

Appointments to lower federal courts are another matter. Traditionally the president has used this power — particularly those at the district court level — to please members of both chambers. Generally the president names as district court judge the person recommended by the House member of Congress from that district. These lower court appointments thus provide the president with his important patronage power — the opportunity to win the good will of a member of Congress or a vote on a crucial issue.

The Senate carefully considers nominations of Cabinet officers, but such officers usually are confirmed with little difficulty on the theory that the president should have great leeway in choosing the members of his official "family." There have been exceptions though. President Reagan first nominated Edwin Meese to be attorney general in January 1984. After 13 months — longer than any other Cabinet nominee in recent history — he was confirmed.

Presidential appointments to independent boards and commissions present a somewhat different situation. These agencies are created by Congress and are not subordinate to the executive branch. Congress expects these agencies to implement congressional goals and therefore it plays a large role in the selection process. Contests over these nominations have been frequent, although few nominees actually have been rejected.

Impeachment

Impeachment of federal officers is perhaps the most awesome, though the least used, power of Congress. The Constitution specifies that the House shall impeach (indict) federal officials that it believes guilty of treason, bribery or high crimes and misdemeanors. The charges are drawn up in an impeachment resolution, usually reported by the House Judiciary Committee. If the House adopts the resolution, the Senate holds a trial, with House members acting as prosecutors. If a president is impeached the chief justice presides at the Senate trial. Conviction requires two-thirds approval of the senators present. Punishment is limited to removal from office and disqualification for further federal office. There is no appeal.

The two most famous cases of impeachment resulted in acquittal after sensational trials. They involved President Andrew Johnson, accused of violating the Tenure of Office Act, and Supreme Court Justice Samuel Chase, accused of partisan conduct on the bench. Since 1789 only 13 federal officials have been impeached by the House. Of the 12 cases that went to Senate trial, two were dismissed before trial after the person impeached left office, six resulted in acquittal and four ended in conviction. President Nixon's resignation on Aug. 9, 1974, foreclosed House action on impeachment charges approved by the Judiciary Committee.

Constitutional Amendments

Congress shares with the states the power to propose amendments to the Constitution. Amendments may be offered by two-thirds of both chambers of Congress or by a convention called by Congress at the request of the legislatures of two-thirds of the states. Amendments must be ratified by the legislatures or conventions of three-fourths of the states. Congress has always specified ratification by the state legislatures, except for the 21st Amendment.

Although these constitutional provisions anticipated a substantial role for the states, Congress has dominated the amendment process. Not once have the states been successful in calling for a convention to propose an amendment to the Constitution. The states fell one short in 1969 when 33 of them called for a convention to write an amendment overturning the Supreme Court's "one person, one vote" decisions. As of 1985 the states were two short of the two-thirds required to call a constitutional convention to draft an amendment requiring a balanced federal budget.

Restrained use of the amendment procedure has enabled the Constitution to remain the fundamental law of the land even though the United States has been transformed beyond recognition since the Constitution was drafted. The states have ratified only 26 amendments. Included among those are the ten amendments comprising the Bill of Rights, extension of the right to vote to blacks and women and the guarantees of equal protection and due process of the law against them.

Altogether, Congress has submitted to the states only 33 amendments. The states failed to ratify seven of these, including a proposal to give the District of Columbia voting representation in Congress. The proposed amendment, approved by Congress in 1978, failed to win ratification by its 1985 deadline.

The Equal Rights Amendment, approved in 1972 by Congress, failed to win ratification by the extended deadline of June 30, 1982. Despite a massive lobby effort, only 35 states had approved the proposal, three short of the necessary 38. The congressionally approved extension and efforts by five states to rescind their ratification raised constitutional questions about the amendment procedure.

Election of the President

Congress under the Constitution has two key responsibilities relating to the election of the president and vice president. First it must receive and in joint session count the electoral votes certified by the states. Second, if no candidate has a majority of the electoral vote, the House must elect the president and the Senate the vice president.

In modern times the formal counting of electoral votes has been largely a ceremonial function. The House actually has chosen the president only twice, in 1801 and 1825. In the course of the nation's history, however, a number of campaigns deliberately have been designed to throw elections into the House. Apprehension over this has nurtured many electoral reform efforts. The most recent attempt came in 1979 when the Senate rejected a proposed constitutional amendment that would have abolished the electoral college system and replaced it with direct popular election of the president.

The 20th and 25th Amendments authorize Congress to settle problems arising from the death of a president-elect or candidate or the disability of a president. The 25th Amendment, ratified in 1967 to cover what its authors assumed would be rare occurrences, was applied twice in 12 months and gave rise to executive leadership unique in the nation's history. The amendment provides that whenever the office of vice president becomes vacant, the president shall appoint a replacement, subject to confirmation by Congress.

Gerald R. Ford was the first vice president to take office under the amendment. He was sworn in Dec. 6, 1973, to replace Spiro T. Agnew, who had resigned after pleading no contest to a charge of federal income tax evasion. Little more than a year later, Nelson A. Rockefeller was sworn in Dec. 19, 1974, to succeed Ford. Ford had become president upon the Aug. 8, 1974, resignation of President Nixon. Thus neither of the nation's two chief officials in 1975 and 1976 was elected by the people.

Congressional Ethics

The Constitution empowers each chamber of Congress to seat, unseat and punish its own members. The House and Senate have the power to determine whether a member fulfills the constitutional requirements for service, to settle contested elections and to censure members for misconduct. Some of these powers come into conflict with the right of voters to decide who will represent them. As a result Congress has been cautious in using its authority. While it has acted often to determine the winner in contested elections, it has rejected the clear choice of the voters, for lack of the requisite qualification, in fewer than 20 cases since 1789.

Censure Proceedings. Congress has shown like restraint in expelling or punishing members for disorderly or improper conduct. Expulsions have numbered 15 in the Senate and four in the House, including the expulsion of Rep. Michael "Ozzie" Myers, D-Pa., in the fall of 1980. Seven senators, 22 representatives and one territorial delegate have been formally censured by their colleagues. In 1979-80 the House censured Charles C. Diggs Jr., a Michigan Democrat who resigned in June 1980, and Charles H. Wilson, D-Calif., both for financial misconduct. In July 1983 Reps. Daniel B. Crane, R-Ill., and Gerry E. Studds, D-Mass., were censured for sexual misconduct with teen-age congressional pages.

One historical reason for the comparatively few instances of congressional punishment of its members had been the difficulty in determining what constitutes conflict of interest and misuse of power. But an increasing incidence of scandals in the 1960s led to creation of ethics committees in both houses to oversee members' conduct.

By the mid-1970s Congress' reputation suffered as a number of current and former members were accused of criminal or unethical behavior. In 1976 Rep. Wayne L. Hays, D-Ohio, was forced to resign under threat of a House probe into charges that he kept a mistress on the public payroll. The same year the House voted to reprimand Robert L. F. Sikes, D-Fla., for financial misconduct.

Shortly after Congress convened in 1977, special committees in both the House and Senate began drawing up new codes of ethics adopted by both chambers in March. The new rules were codified into law and extended to top officials in the executive and legislative branches in 1978.

Still more scandal was unveiled in 1980 through a government undercover investigation of political corruption — known as "Abscam" — in which law enforcement agents, posing as businessmen or wealthy Arabs, attempted to induce some members of Congress and other elected officials to use their influence, for pay, for such things as helping Arabs obtain U.S. residency, get federal grants and arrange real estate transactions.

The expulsion of Ozzie Myers, which resulted from his Abscam conviction, was something of a milestone for a House that had long been the butt of derisive jokes about lax punishment of wayward members. The other congressmen involved in the scandal escaped expulsion. Two of the convicted House members resigned: John W. Jenrette Jr., D-S.C., on Dec. 19, 1980, and Raymond F. Lederer, D-Pa., on May 5, 1981. Three others were defeated for re-election: Richard Kelly, R-Fla., John M. Murphy, D-N.Y., and Frank Thompson Jr., D-N.J.

The lone senator convicted in the Abscam scandal, Harrison A. Williams Jr., D-N.J., resigned on March 11, 1982, hours before the Senate was expected to vote on his expulsion.

In the wake of the Abscam convictions, both the House and Senate ethics committees considered revising their codes of conduct.

Power of Investigation. The power of Congress to undertake investigations — perhaps its most controversial of legislative branch power — is not specified in the Constitution. It is based instead on tradition and the belief that investigations are indispensable to the legislative process. Yet, the Supreme Court never has questioned the right of Congress to conduct investigations.

No period of American history has been without congressional investigation. The first was held in 1792, to investigate the massacre of U.S. soldiers in Indian territory. Since then, congressional probes have gathered information on the need for possible future legislation, tested the effectiveness of past legislative action, questioned executive branch actions and laid the groundwork for impeachment proceedings. Investigations have elevated comparatively minor political figures to national fame, broken the careers of important public men and women and captured the attention of millions of newspaper readers and television viewers.

Members' Pay

A very ticklish power held by Congress is that of setting members' salaries. Although Congress traditionally has tried to bury its own salary increases in general pay raises for federal workers, increases nevertheless have led to public criticism.

In December 1982, in a break with nearly two centuries of tradition, Congress decided to pay House members more than senators, while the latter could earn unlimited amounts in outside income, including honoraria.

Effective Dec. 18, 1982, House members' salaries were raised to $69,800. Salaries for senators remained at $60,662.50, but they were allowed to earn as much as they chose in outside honoraria. Outside earnings for representatives continued to be limited by the House rules to 30 percent of members' salaries. A limit on outside earned income for senators equal to 15 percent of their congressional salaries, or about $9,100, would have gone into effect Jan. 1, 1983, if the Senate had not acted to change its own rules.

The Senate voted to raise members' salaries to the House level of $69,800 in June 1983. But amid public criticism of senators' outside income, they agreed to place a cap on Senate honoraria effective Jan. 1, 1984, that was equal to the House limit.

In 1985 the annual 3.5 percent pay increase came on top of a 4 percent raise that federal white-collar employees and Congress received in 1984. The 1985 raise boosted the salaries of senators and representatives from $72,600 to $75,100.

Four Seeking House Democratic Whip Position

Nobody likes to be No. 3. But leaders have to start somewhere, and the majority whip's office is the first real step on the ladder to the House speakership.

That is why four candidates began jockeying early for position in a race to succeed the current whip, Thomas S. Foley of Washington, when House Democrats choose new leaders at the end of 1986.

The Democratic Caucus vote for a whip in December will be the first time the job will be filled by election. Previously the whip was appointed by the Speaker and majority leader. The change was designed to give rank-and-file members more say in shaping their party's hierarchy.

"The next whip will be even more powerful because he will be elected by the party rather than appointed by its leaders. It's much more of a guarantee that you're looking at a Speaker 15 or 20 years down the line," said Joe Moakley of Massachusetts, a Democratic deputy whip.

The jostling for whip — the person who traditionally rounds up votes for the leadership but has become a party spokesman as well — casts region against region, old blood against new blood, liberals against moderates and conservatives. But above all, the race for majority whip is a contest that will be decided on personal popularity.

At this point, four men are actively in the race: Bill Alexander of Arkansas, Tony Coelho of California, W. G. "Bill" Hefner of North Carolina and Charles B. Rangel of New York.

Other Contests

The whip contest is just one of a series of leadership changes that will result from the retirement of Speaker Thomas P. O'Neill Jr., D-Mass., at the end of the 99th Congress.

It is widely assumed that Majority Leader Jim Wright, D-Texas, has the votes to succeed O'Neill as Speaker, and that Foley is almost certainly going to become majority leader.

Job Seen as Doorway To Leadership

There has been talk that a challenge to Wright or Foley could be mounted by Ways and Means Chairman Dan Rostenkowski, D-Ill., or Energy and Commerce Chairman John D. Dingell, D-Mich., but neither is given a strong chance.

Besides the contest to fill Foley's position as whip, there may be a race for the chairmanship of the Democratic Caucus. Richard A. Gephardt of Missouri may leave that post to concentrate on running for the presidency in 1988. If he does, David E. Bonior of Michigan, Mary Rose Oakar of Ohio and Mike Synar of Oklahoma may seek the job.

There also may be a vacancy for chairman of the Democratic Congressional Campaign Committee (DCCC), which raises money for Democratic House candidates, since Coelho, the current chairman, is running for whip. Should Coelho become majority whip, a replacement would have to be elected.

An active race for the DCCC chairman's job has not developed, but two leading names mentioned are Steny H. Hoyer of Maryland and Vic Fazio of California — both close friends of Coelho.

Coelho Leading

In the view of the four candidates, Coelho is the front-runner in the whip's race.

Most assessments put Rangel in second place, followed by Hefner. Alexander is viewed as coming in last.

In spite of these impressions, members are quick to say that no one can safely claim victory yet.

"There are too many candidates out there for someone to believe he can lock it now," Rangel said.

"One bad turn, one bad move can change the picture. There are a lot of opportunities, but also a lot of pitfalls," said a Democratic leadership aide.

Another reason why it is difficult to project a winner is that candidates tend to inflate the number of commitments they have received. There are 253 Democrats in the House now; the number voting in the December 1986 caucus will depend on how many Democrats are elected the month before.

But adding up the candidates' assertions shows that far more than 253 votes had been promised as early as a year before the election.

History's lessons also make the candidates cautious about handicapping any race decided by secret ballot. Several pointed to last year's contest for Senate majority leader, when James A. McClure, R-Idaho, claimed the most commitments beforehand but came in last on the secret ballot. *(1984 CQ Almanac p. 3)*

Others recall the 1976 contest for House majority leader, when long-shot Jim Wright upset Phillip Burton of California, Richard Bolling of Missouri and the incumbent whip, John J. McFall of California. *(1977 CQ Almanac p. 5)*

With so many candidates, the closed-door election is likely to take several ballots. Under the rules, if no member wins a clear majority on the first ballot, the bottom man drops out. The low-man-out procedure continues until someone has a majority.

Republicans in both chambers and Senate Democrats have elected their whips for years, but House Democrats have resisted the change. Twice in the 1970s the Democratic Caucus considered making the whip's job elective, but members rejected the proposal both times.

Proponents finally succeeded in January 1985, when Democrats voted 133-36 for the change. To protect Foley, it was decided that the new system would not take effect until the next time the job became vacant — presumably when O'Neill retired. *(1985 CQ Weekly Report p. 176)*

Opponents of the change wanted the Speaker and majority leader to continue appointing the whip to make sure he disseminated leadership views. But reformers said all Democrats should have a vote because the whip almost always moves up to become majority leader and then Speaker.

"To the extent that the whip is a steppingstone to other leadership jobs, people felt they should have a say," Sabo said.

O'Neill was whip before becoming majority leader and Speaker, although Wright was not. But Wright was a rare case; his 1977 upset victory marked the only time in more than 50 years that the whip did not move up to the majority leader's post.

Majority Whip Thomas S. Foley (center), along with Speaker Thomas P. O'Neill Jr. (right) and Majority Leader Jim Wright, presides at weekly meetings of House Democratic whips (below). Wright and Foley are expected to move up the leadership ladder when O'Neill retires, setting off a race for the whip's position.

Campaign Promises

In making leadership choices, members look at geography, ideology, seniority and personality. Committee loyalty is also a factor, as is friendship.

"You might vote for somebody you met when you came here five years ago, someone you have dinner with, with your wives," Fazio said.

Although it is difficult to determine the degree to which personal favors influence a member, they are a factor.

Coelho, as DCCC chairman, has the most to offer because he controls the money doled out to Democratic House candidates.

Rangel can use his position as a member of the Ways and Means Committee to do some favors on tax bills, and then collect the chits.

Alexander and Hefner serve on the Appropriations Committee, another center of power in the House.

Because the whip's job is one of the most influential in Congress, there is interest — and some participation — by outside lobbyists.

Some members frown on this type of external interference, but Alexander maintains that members "are subject to communication on anything. There is definitely a lobbying factor in this race."

In Alexander's case, grass-roots members of the National Association of Development Organizations, a group of rural economic development officials, have made calls to Democratic members to promote his candidacy.

In campaigning for the whip's job, the four candidates have engaged in discussions about the future shape of the House Democratic leadership. Out of these talks, most of them have pledged to try to make the legislative schedule more predictable.

Nearly all of them also promise to give rank-and-file Democrats a louder voice in party policy-making, letting ideas work their way from the bottom up, rather than from the top down to members.

None of the contestants directly criticizes Foley, who is well-liked by his colleagues, but all say they would make changes in the whip's office.

"They didn't make the job elective just so they could do business as usual," said an aide to one contender.

The following summarizes each candidate's reasons for running for whip and what he wants to do with the job, as well as how his prospects for winning look:

Coelho

Coelho says more than 100 Democrats have promised to vote for him on the first ballot. Even though he claims more commitments than the other candidates, he and his 40-member steering committee "are trying to pick up three people a week," he said.

As chairman of the DCCC since 1981, Coelho has been in a position to win friends among Democrats by funneling money and technical help to

TONY COELHO

Age 43 ... Represents California's 15th District ... Elected in 1978 ... Chairman of Democratic Congressional Campaign Committee ... At-large whip ... Chairs Agriculture Subcommittee on Livestock, Dairy and Poultry ... Member of House Administration, Interior and Insular Affairs committees

their campaigns. He also may gain support from members newly elected in 1986 who received DCCC assistance.

"It's a lot more difficult for people to say no to him because he has such direct control over their lives," said a leadership assistant.

But Coelho said the job also brings its problems: "I've made enemies telling people I can't give them money or help."

Coelho's strongest base is the California delegation, which has 26 Democrats besides himself, and younger members elected with his help. But he also claims backers from all regions and age groups, citing Energy and Commerce Chairman Dingell of Michigan and conservative Democratic leader Charles W. Stenholm of Texas as examples of the diversity of his support.

Coming from California could work against Coelho if Wright and Foley win the top two jobs. Members who want regional balance in the leadership could opt for someone like Rangel, from the Northeast.

Yet, as one House observer noted, "if anyone can transcend the regional thing, it's someone who was campaign chairman, because he is sensitive to the problems of different regions."

Although Coelho has won praise for revitalizing the DCCC, his detractors suggest he is too partisan and ambitious. But a supporter said, "That's his job right now. He's supposed to be political."

Coelho, 43, was elected to Congress in 1978, and served on Capitol Hill for 13 years before that as a congressional aide.

Currently one of 32 at-large whips, he says he wants the top job because "I'm an organizer and the whip operation gives me the ability to organize the Democrats."

Coelho also said he wants to "provide new life to the whip's office ... and provide a political sense I think it needs."

One change Coelho promotes is to make the whip organization more membership-oriented.

"We need to make sure the members know what the leadership needs and wants, but also that the leadership knows what the membership needs and wants," he said.

Coelho said the whip also needs to be more sensitive to family needs when scheduling legislation and work periods. "An awful lot of members have children," says Coelho, who has two, "and family situations need to be considered."

CHARLES B. RANGEL

55 years old ... Represents New York's 16th District ... Elected in 1970 ... Deputy whip ... Chairman, Ways and Means Subcommittee on Select Revenue Measures ... Chairman, Select Committee on Narcotics Abuse and Control

Rangel

While Coelho stresses his ties to the House's younger generation, Rangel has not tried to hide his connections to the established powers. He volunteers that O'Neill "is a long and dear friend" and implies that he would have the Speaker's support if O'Neill got involved in the race.

O'Neill, according to an aide, plans to stay neutral.

Opponents of Rangel, who is 55 years old and was elected to Congress in 1970, say the new whip should be a more junior member to bring a fresher perspective to leadership meetings. But his supporters disagree, pointing to his popularity throughout the House. And Rangel emphasizes the value of his 10 years of experience in the whip's organization, most recently as one of seven deputy whips.

"My ability to work with Jim Wright and the rest of them is proven because I've been doing it for the last 10 years," he said. "I'm not here to redo the entire system. It's not my idea to just throw experience out the window."

Rangel, who describes himself as a "legislator's legislator," said he is seeking the job because "it's an excellent opportunity to have hands-on impact on legislation that's going to be considered by the whole Congress. And it also gives me a chance to service members."

A large chunk of Rangel's support comes from the 18 other Democrats in the New York delegation and his 19 fellow members of the Congressional Black Caucus. He also lists Southern backers, such as Charlie Rose of North Carolina and Robin Tallon of South Carolina. He will not say, however, precisely how many commitments he holds.

Rangel is more liberal than Coelho and tends to draw support from like-minded members. While he says he is not running a campaign based strictly on representing Northeastern liberals, "I do stress that there is nobody east of the Mississippi" in the leadership if Wright and Foley win.

Some members speculate that Rangel could be hurt by the fact that another prominent black member, William H. Gray III, D-Pa., was elected this year as chairman of the Budget Committee. But Rangel dismisses the potential influence of racial discrimination.

"For the few members who feel

Today's Whip: Not Just Keeping Pack in Line

Once upon a time a "whip" was a "whipper-in," a man assigned to keep the hounds from leaving the pack in a fox hunt.

The word moved into the political lexicon in 18th-century England. In the British Parliament, with its strong party discipline, the whip's major concern was ensuring good attendance when a vote was at hand. But in the 20th century U.S. House of Representatives, the job has expanded far beyond that.

No longer is the whip's job simply to see that members stick with the party line. Today's whip runs a large intelligence-gathering network, and given the growing independence of House members, that network conveys members' wishes to the leadership as often as vice versa.

"The dictatorial power of the House leadership isn't there anymore," said Joe Moakley, Mass., a Democratic deputy whip. "You're dealing with members who are more sophisticated, and you need to convince them through logic, debate and facts that this is what they should do — not because it's do-or-die for the party."

The four-way contest to succeed Thomas S. Foley, D-Wash., as House majority whip in the 100th Congress features much talk of giving the Democratic membership at large a louder voice in party strategy decisions. But Foley dismisses such demands as campaign rhetoric; he contends the whip's office already sweeps in a broad range of viewpoints.

The regular forum for this give-and-take is the whip meeting each Thursday morning, usually attended by more than 50 Democrats. "The whip meetings are the single most lively expression of views and attitudes of the Democrats," said Foley. "It is a chance to sound off and say what you think the party ought to do. Members are not bashful," he added.

"Those are very electric meetings," a leadership assistant agreed. "There's a lot of debate and a lot of strategy decided, and it's one regular place to confront the leadership. Very often there are screaming matches. It's not a tea party."

Growing Organization

The whip's organization has ballooned since the first majority whip was appointed in 1897. A few deputies were added in 1909, and now the majority whip heads a four-tier system that includes a chief deputy whip, seven deputy whips, 32 at-large whips and 23 assistant whips. There also are three task force chairmen at the deputy whip level.

Foley this year increased the number of deputy whips from four to seven and at-large whips from 21 to 32. The assistant whips are elected by region; the others are appointed by top leaders.

In the 1970s, special task forces were added to the organization to smooth the way for passage of complicated bills. The idea was to get younger members more involved in the legislative process. The ad hoc groups caught on so well that they are deployed in about 75 percent of the whip activities.

The whip's organization comes into play on about 20 bills a year, usually on such major topics as the budget, the debt limit, the MX missile and aid to Nicaraguan rebels. Whips also get involved when a committee chairman seeks extra help.

In the case, for example, of President Reagan's request for aid to "contras" battling the Nicaraguan government — which the Democratic leadership opposed — the first step in the whip process was for the 23 assistant whips to poll members in their zones about how they planned to vote.

"Will you oppose aid to the contras?" was the question posed, and it was worded so the leadership position was implicit. " 'Yes' is always the answer we want" in any whip check, according to a Foley aide.

After tallying the number for or against the bill, a task force contacts members who are undecided or not strongly committed one way or the other. The task force usually includes several assistant whips and others with an interest in the legislation.

"That group talks about strategy and problems with the bill, and then talks to people to find out why they are undecided," Foley's aide said. "By talking to people and learning their problems, we may offer an amendment that will help bring everyone together to have a more unified Democratic Party."

Once a closely contested bill is ready for the floor, the whips help check attendance and work the floor during the debate, trying to sway members to the leadership's side.

The whip's office also offers an information service for members. Besides publicizing the daily floor schedule, the whip distributes memos summarizing a bill's provisions and possible amendments. The whip also gives members "recess packets" and "speech cards" to help them discuss legislation with constituents.

color is a handicap, Bill Gray shatters that perception," he said.

Like Coelho, Rangel said the whip needs to do a better job in scheduling floor activity to give members more time with their families.

Rangel also said it was important that the whip seek ideas from junior members, rather than simply conveying the leadership's position on legislation.

"The whip's office shouldn't be whipping on a one-way street," Rangel said.

Hefner

Hailing from North Carolina, Hefner bills himself as the candidate of the Democratic moderates and conservatives.

"I think we need somebody, not necessarily from our part of the world, but from our moderate-conservative philosophy, to meet with the leadership and let them know in good strong terms what we're thinking about," he said.

"We don't really have people with their ear to the ground," Hefner said. "I'm not being critical of the leadership. But an awful lot of people have no say-so. The whip can be an office that really can bring people together and meld us into a real consensus."

Although he would not name his backers, Hefner said he has more than 60 promises of support. "And we haven't even started our TV ads yet," he joked.

To dispel rumors that he had dropped out of the race for health reasons following a heart attack last June, Hefner recently sent Democrats a "Dear Colleague" letter reminding them he still wants the job.

Hefner, who is 55 and was elected to Congress in 1974, has served as a regional whip and on the Steering and Policy Committee, but currently holds no leadership title.

W. G. "BILL" HEFNER

55 years old . . . Represents 8th District of North Carolina . . . Elected in 1974 . . . Chairman of Appropriations Subcommittee on Military Construction . . . Member of Budget Committee

Alexander

Of the six candidates, Alexander now holds the highest job in the whip organization. Since 1981, he has served as Foley's chief deputy whip, an appointment made by Wright. Elected to the House in 1968, Alexander has served longer than any of the other contestants.

Despite those credentials, Alexander is given poor prospects for winning. He is not as personally popular as the other contenders, and he lacks the strong regional base that Coelho and Rangel have. In addition, he represents a traditional Southern district and must vie against Hefner for moderate and conservative support.

Alexander would not say how many commitments he has at this point. But he acknowledges he suffered a setback in 1985 when he obtained a military jet to take a congressional delegation to Brazil, and then turned out to be the only member on board. The trip was estimated to cost the Air Force more than $50,000, and Alexander was sharply criticized by his colleagues for abusing congressional privileges.

BILL ALEXANDER

51 years old . . . Represents 1st District of Arkansas . . . Elected in 1968 . . . House Democrats' chief deputy whip . . . Member of Appropriations Committee

"It slowed my momentum for a month to six weeks," Alexander said. "I met the wrath of the press who judged the trip to be a useless junket. For a while it gave fuel to my opposition."

In his campaign, Alexander, 51, talks about using the whip's office "to make the Democratic Party more competitive with the Republicans." One way, he said, would be for House Democrats to use television more effectively to promote their ideas.

Other things he would like to do as whip, Alexander said, include improving coordination between House Democrats and state parties on reapportionment, and using computer technology to keep members better apprised of daily floor activities. He also suggested a more predictable House schedule. ▮

Foley: Rising to Top by Accident and Design

As House Majority Whip Thomas S. Foley tells it, his first campaign for Congress was a model of cordiality. No mud was slung; indeed, the candidates sometimes exchanged compliments in that 1964 campaign. After winning the election, Foley held a reception for the man he beat, 11-term incumbent Republican Walt Horan.

It was an appropriate initiation for Foley, whose temperament and tactics have led him throughout his career to shun confrontation and seek consensus.

The Washington Democrat's skill at brokering compromises, both across party lines and among House Democrats, has earned him wide respect. It also has helped spare him a contest as he seeks to climb another step up the leadership ladder.

After five years as Democratic whip, Foley is running without apparent challenge for the job of majority leader in the 100th Congress. The current majority leader, Jim Wright, D-Texas, is widely expected to succeed House Speaker Thomas P. O'Neill Jr., when the Massachusetts Democrat retires after this year. *(20th-century majority leaders, p. 106)*

House Democrats will choose their new leaders in December, after the 1986 congressional elections. As of now, Wright and Foley seem assured of victory.

A Paradoxical Choice

In one sense, Foley's ascent to the No. 2 leadership job is predictable: It is the obvious step up from the post he now holds. But in other ways, Foley is an implausible candidate to have risen to the top levels of the Democratic Party leadership.

He is an urbane, intellectual Democrat representing the state of Washington's conservative, largely rural 5th District — not an ideal match that one would expect to survive 11 elections.

Foley shows little taste for aggressive politicking for advancement and seems uncomfortable with the self-promotion of campaigning.

Although he has had a hand in crafting many major pieces of legislation, his name is rarely found on a law. While he does not shun publicity, neither does he seek it.

"Tom's influence is a subtler kind of influence," says Philip R. Sharp, D-Ind. "It's not always front-page influence, not always high visibility. That's one of the things that generates a broader base of trust for Tom."

As whip, Foley has functioned largely behind the scenes, corralling votes for the leadership and keeping his finger on the pulse of House Democrats.

Among Foley's tools are a broad knowledge of the workings of the House, a prodigious memory and a gift for explaining complex issues.

"He knows so much about both sides of a question he can argue both sides ferociously," says Pat Williams, D-Mont.

Although Foley's thoughtful, evenhanded style is generally regarded as his greatest strength, he is sometimes criticized for being too cautious. "Tom Foley has too many hands," as one quip has it. "He's always saying on the one hand and on the other hand."

Foley's conciliatory, pragmatic approach can frustrate members looking for a party leader to yell "Charge!" He would rather help the troops pick their way through enemy lines than seek to overpower the opposition.

Foley is aware of criticism that he is not partisan enough, but he is unperturbed. "The best partisanship is not necessarily the most obvious or most strident," he said.

"I'm not going to be a 19th-century opposition-basher," he added. "I don't think that's my style and I don't think it's effective. It doesn't attract people who weren't already knee-jerk supporters. The task is to convince people who are subject to being influenced or persuaded."

A Wright-Foley Team

As majority leader, Foley would be the Democrats' point man in floor debate, and would join the Speaker in setting the legislative schedule and serving as a party spokesman.

Leadership sources say Wright and Foley work well together, despite differences in style. Foley's cool temperament and non-confrontational manner contrast sharply with Wright's often feisty, combative partisanship.

House Majority Whip Thomas S. Foley, right, meets with Dan Glickman of Kansas at one of the weekly gatherings of the whip's organization.

House Majority Leaders 1899-1986

Sereno E. Payne, R-N.Y.
1899-1911

Oscar W. Underwood, D-Ala.
1911-15

Claude Kitchin, D-N.C.
1915-19

Franklin W. Mondell, R-Wyo.
1919-23

Nicholas Longworth, R-Ohio
1923-25*

John Q. Tilson, R-Conn.
1925-31

Henry T. Rainey, D-Ill.
1931-33*

Joseph W. Byrns, D-Tenn.
1933-35*

William B. Bankhead, D-Ala.
1936*

Sam Rayburn, D-Texas
1937-40*

John W. McCormack, D-Mass.
1940-47, 1949-53, 1955-62*

Charles A. Halleck, R-Ind.
1947-49, 1953-55

Carl Albert, D-Okla.
1962-71*

Hale Boggs, D-La.
1971-73

Thomas P. O'Neill Jr., D-Mass.
1973-77*

Jim Wright, D-Texas
1977-

Above are the House majority leaders of the 20th century and the years they served as leader. Asterisks (*) indicate leaders who subsequently became Speaker of the House.

"Wright will shoot from the hip, he'll give the rousing speech," says one Democrat. "Foley's is the more thoughtful, careful approach."

Wright as Speaker would likely be the leading public spokesman for House Democrats. But some members say that Foley would be as good, if not better, at presenting the Democratic Party's case to the public.

"Foley has not been tagged as someone who carries with him the party of the past," says Leon E. Panetta, D-Calif. "He bridges the gap between Wright and his supporters and the younger members in the party who are looking for some change of direction."

However, some liberals worry that while a Wright-Foley leadership team may improve the party's media image, there would be no strong voice at the top for their wing of the party. "There is no strong liberal in there to make up for the loss of Tip," says one Democrat. "Foley's a good spokesman, but what do they have to say?"

Liberal interest groups have given higher ratings to both Wright and Foley in recent years. Foley's rating from Americans for Democratic Action rose from 55 percent "correct" in 1981, when he became whip, to 80 percent in 1984. In 1985, his rating dipped to 75.

Eclectic Tastes

If some liberals would like Foley to move left, his opponents back home say he is too liberal for his district, which cast 60 percent of its votes for Ronald Reagan in 1984.

Indeed, Foley's continuing electoral success seems improbable for several reasons. Although he is one of the House's leading experts on farm programs, he lacks the folksy style one might expect of a member who represents a largely rural district.

He is as comfortable quoting Shakespeare as commodity prices. He knows a smattering of Japanese, and uses it on nearly annual trips to Japan.

Although he has no major source of income outside his congressional salary and speaking fees, Foley has expensive tastes in contemporary art, modern furniture and high-tech stereo equipment that might seem out of place among his wheat-farming constituents.

"In the past, I've suggested that he loosen up and go hunting, fishing, or pose [for photographs] with a cow, but he's always a three-piece-suit kind of guy out here, too," says William F. Mullen, a professor at Washington State University at Pullman who has been a county campaign coordinator for Foley in the last several elections.

While Foley often holds town meetings with voters when he visits the district, he does not revel in campaign glad-handing. "He doesn't like to ask people to vote for him," says Mullen. "He prefers talking issues."

Rising by Accident and Design

Foley's rise through the House Democratic ranks came about through a combination of low-key determination and fortuitous circumstances.

A lawyer, Foley came to the Capitol in 1961 as counsel to Sen. Henry M. Jackson, D-Wash., then chairman of the Interior Committee. It was Jackson who encouraged Foley to run for Congress two years later.

Foley dragged his heels for months and did not file as a candidate until the last possible date in the summer of 1964. Like many other Democrats that year, he was helped to victory by President Johnson's landslide triumph over Barry Goldwater.

Foley describes his early years in Congress as a series of "accidental advances," fueled by such factors as the retirement of more senior members of committees to which he was assigned.

Foley chaired the liberal Democratic Study Group (DSG) in 1974, at a time when the DSG was spearheading a drive to open up committee proceedings and weaken the seniority system. Foley was active in the campaign for such changes, but he was clearly a reformer — not a radical.

He backed a change in House rules that allowed secret-ballot elections of committee chairmen, but he opposed a 1975 move to oust the aging chairman of the Agriculture Committee, W. R. Poage, D-Texas. Poage was defeated nonetheless, and Foley — as the next most senior Democrat on the panel — was chosen chairman.

"[Foley] was thrust into the chairmanship over the political body of a guy he respected and worked with," recalls Morris K. Udall, D-Ariz. "It was a real test for Tom, and he handled it in a classy kind of way."

Foley recognized from the first that Poage's ouster and his own elevation signaled lasting changes in the seniority system. He said at the time:

"People think of me as chairman as if we were back in the days when chairmen ruled as well as reigned. It isn't that way anymore. The newcomers may pay a certain amount of respect to the leadership, but they're not going to defer to my judgment."

Foley says his first deliberate step onto the leadership ladder was his election as chairman of the Democratic Caucus in late 1976 — the year that O'Neill became Speaker and Wright won an upset victory in the race for majority leader.

In that stormy majority leader's contest, Foley supported the leadership bid of Wright's rival, Phillip Burton, a California liberal who was viewed with distrust by O'Neill.

Nonetheless, Foley soon won the trust and respect of the two more senior Democrats. When Indiana Democrat John Brademas, the majority whip, was defeated in his 1980 re-election bid, O'Neill and Wright named Foley to the post. Dan Rostenkowski, D-Ill., then chief deputy whip, was in line for it, but he chose instead to take the chairmanship of the Ways and Means Committee — which had been opened by the defeat of Al Ullman, D-Ore.

In a logical extension of some of the democratizing reforms Foley helped put in place in the 1970s, House Democrats last year decided to make the whip an elective post, beginning with Foley's successor.

Performance as Whip

As majority whip, Foley, more than his predecessor, has practiced what one member called the "politics of inclusion." He has expanded participation in the whip's organization, thus increasing the number of people with a stake in leadership decision-making. Last year, he increased the number of deputy and at-large whips.

Foley also has made heavy use of task forces to ease passage of important, complex bills and to get junior members involved in the process.

Whip meetings are not always harmonious. When key elements of the party are unhappy about a leadership decision, the dissent is clear at the weekly whip gatherings, usually attended by more than 50 Democrats.

For example, at one whip's meeting, Foley was the sounding board for bitter complaints from urban liberals about leadership plans to bring up legislation (HR 4188) to ease the effects of the Gramm-Rudman-Hollings budget-cutting law on milk price supports. Liberals maintained that the dairy industry should not be protected from the across-the-board cuts that faced all other programs.

O'Neill claimed he was "blindsided" by the Agriculture Committee's decision to report the bill, despite the fact that Foley is vice chairman of the committee. Foley, who supported the bill, was taken by surprise by the depth of opposition from urban members, aides said. After the volatile whip's meeting, the leadership pulled the dairy bill from the schedule.

Close Calls Back Home

Foley remains demure about the majority leader's race. He has canvassed all House Democrats, but refuses to report the results. "I'm continuing to talk to people," he says, "and am very, very encouraged by the results."

A decade ago, Foley learned the hard way the perils of overconfidence in a campaign. In 1976, he stopped campaigning a month before the election after his GOP opponent died in a plane crash. But the Republicans came up with another candidate, and through vigorous last-minute campaigning held Foley to 58 percent of the vote.

The message seemed to be that Foley was vulnerable, and he faced serious challenges in the next two elections: He garnered only 48 percent of the vote in a three-way contest in 1978 and 52 percent in 1980.

Since then, Foley seems to have surmounted his political problems at home. In 1984, he was re-elected with 70 percent of the vote. Although Republicans have charged Foley is out of touch with his district and more interested in national issues, his constituents apparently appreciate the value of having a representative in the upper ranks of the House leadership.

Still, some members are wary of electing as party leaders members who might — like Brademas — be dumped by the voters in part because they are linked with party positions that are unpopular in their districts. One member critical of Foley's cautious style attributes it in part to insecurity about his conservative district.

"It is a definite disadvantage for us to have as a majority leader someone who has to look over his or her shoulder at his or her constituency," this liberal Democrat said. "You like to have your leaders fearless."

But Foley says the days of very close elections are probably behind him now. And he dismisses any interpretation of his caution as being linked to concerns about political vulnerability at home.

"To the extent that I'm cautious, I want to be cautious and I don't propose to change that," he said. "I have a mental habit of wanting to think through a policy or position."

"I'm not going to be a 19th-century opposition-basher. I don't think that's my style and I don't think it's effective."

—Rep. Thomas S. Foley

Crossing Lines on Agriculture

Foley's non-confrontational approach allows him to cross party lines to forge compromises. "He is trusted [by many Republicans] because he seems in his present role to be less political, until he needs to be, than the others" in the Democratic leadership, says Sid Morrison, R-Wash.

Foley has worked most openly and consistently on a bipartisan basis in the Agriculture Committee, where farm-state interests tend to divide more along regional than party lines.

Although Foley had to give up the Agriculture chairmanship when he became whip in 1981, he has continued to play a major role in shaping farm legislation. He still chairs the Subcommittee on Wheat, Soybeans and Feed

Grains — the panel of most interest to his many wheat-growing constituents.

His bipartisan approach had put Foley at odds with some Democrats on the Agriculture Committee during the panel's consideration of the 1985 farm bill. The dissenters wanted to stake out a clearly Democratic farm policy. "The farm bloc is politically the most volatile bloc in 1986 and 1988," says Dan Glickman, D-Kan. "We needed more counterpoint to the president."

Foley backed a price-support proposal that drew the strongest opposition from fellow Democrats rather than from Republicans. The plan, which lowered price supports while maintaining high income subsidies for farmers, was in part a reflection of the interests of Foley's district. Price supports in effect set a floor on prices, and many of Foley's export-dependent farmers favored lowering supports to make their crops more competitive on world markets.

Foley initially objected to alternatives pushed by Berkley Bedell of Iowa and other committee Democrats. They wanted to allow wheat and feed grain farmers to decide in a referendum whether to accept sharp government production controls in exchange for higher price supports.

However, Foley surprised his adversaries and cast a crucial committee vote to include a version of the referendum in the bill sent to the floor. He swallowed his misgivings, an aide said, to ensure broader support from committee Democrats and to head off a potential mutiny on the floor.

The bill that finally passed the House, however, reflected Foley's original preferences. While he gave referendum supporters their chance on the floor and voted against a GOP amendment to strike the provision, he offered only a mild defense of the concept. The referendum was killed when the House approved the GOP amendment.

Gramm-Rudman Role

Foley's role in negotiations over the Gramm-Rudman-Hollings law exemplified his consensus-building *modus operandi.*

He was never a prime mover or enthusiast for the legislation. Rather, he helped House Democrats decide how to make the best of what many saw as a bad deal. He played a key role in reshaping the legislation along lines more acceptable to his colleagues — and more painful for Reagan and the Republicans.

Background

Foley: named Agriculture Committee chairman, 1975 CQ Almanac p. 32; elected Democratic Caucus chairman, 1977 Almanac p. 9; appointed majority whip, 1981 Almanac p. 5.

Other background: Jim Wright and the speakership, 1984 CQ Weekly Report p. 775; whip's post made elective, 1985 Weekly Report p. 176; whip's race, 1985 Weekly Report p. 2498; 1985 farm bill, 1985 Weekly Report pp. 1828, 2055, 2673; Gramm-Rudman-Hollings law, 1985 Weekly Report p. 2604; milk price support bill, 1986 Weekly Report p. 523.

The budget-balancing bill originated in the Senate as an amendment to "must" legislation raising the ceiling on the national debt. While the measure was still in the Senate, Foley was asked by O'Neill to chair a task force of House Democrats to monitor the legislation and begin developing a response. That task force brought together Democrats from as far apart on the political spectrum as liberal Henry A. Waxman of California and conservative Marvin Leath of Texas.

House leaders first had to decide whether to try to defeat the bill, pass it unchanged or seek improvements.

Foley was the prime proponent of the strategy ultimately followed by the Democrats: Send the bill to conference with the Senate, thus buying time to analyze the measure and come up with alternatives and changes to improve it.

Initially he was at odds with many House Democrats — both opponents and proponents of the budget-balancing measure — who wanted an immediate House vote on the Senate-passed bill. Several senior committee chairmen wanted to meet the issue head-on and try to kill the bill. But Foley told them that was not a realistic option, citing whip counts indicating that Democrats did not have enough votes to defeat the bill.

"It would have been disastrous to rush out and have an up-or-down vote on the issue," says Foley.

"Foley, more than anyone else, understood there was no gain to be made by pretending it could be stopped," said one leadership aide.

However, some Democrats still believe the leadership conceded too much to supporters of Gramm-Rudman-Hollings by basing their strategy on the assumption that passage of the bill was inevitable. "I think we should have had a bold stroke early, and undercut the need for Gramm-Rudman," says Williams. "It was a mistake to amend Gramm-Rudman to make it better."

But Waxman says he was persuaded by Foley's assessment. "He turned to us and said, 'We're going to get Gramm-Rudman. What kind of Gramm-Rudman is it going to be?' " said Waxman. "It was a clear statement of political reality and a convincing reason for us to work together."

House leaders, including Foley, point with pride to the display of party unity House Democrats ultimately showed on the issue. After the first round of conference negotiations over the Senate measure broke down, the House passed an alternative version of its own with only two dissenting Democratic votes.

The House alternative protected certain poverty programs against automatic cuts and made an important change in the timing of the mandated deficit reductions. It ensured that the first round of cuts would be felt before the 1986 elections, when the Republicans must defend 22 Senate seats.

Political Fallout

It remains to be seen whether House Democrats' role in shaping the Gramm-Rudman-Hollings law will, in the end, be a political asset or a liability. Foley's view is that incumbents of both parties will share the praise — or blame — for Congress' performance on the budget in 1986.

Given his pivotal role in the Democrats' strategy for handling the new budget law, Foley's standing among his colleagues could be affected by the political fallout from the measure between the law's passage and the time Democrats choose their next majority leader.

But, Foley's success in brokering a unified House Democratic position seems to have raised his stock even among those most antagonistic to the budget-balancing measure.

"Foley showed he could lead in a moment of crisis and pull together diverse elements of the party," says Waxman. "But members are going to be looking not only at how leadership candidates performed in the past, but by what happens to the Democratic Party this year." ∎

Senate Sidesteps Decision on PAC Spending

Thorny Issue Put Off Pending Hearings

The Senate Dec. 3, 1985, avoided a definitive vote on legislation to curb the role of political action committees (PACs), effectively agreeing instead to postpone the issue until sometime in 1986.

The much-anticipated showdown on the PAC proposal by David L. Boren, D-Okla., dissipated when supporters and critics joined together in calling for hearings by the Senate Rules Committee in early 1986 on Boren's plan and other campaign finance measures.

That paved the way for an overwhelming 7-84 vote against tabling (killing) the PAC proposal, which was offered as an amendment to a bill (S 655) dealing with low-level radioactive waste. Under a previous agreement, the bill was then pulled from further consideration. *(1985 CQ Weekly Report, p. 2584)*

Although the Senate did not reject Boren's amendment, Boren failed to pin down Majority Leader Robert Dole, R-Kan., on when his PAC plan would return to the Senate floor.

Dole said it might be wise to appoint a commission to study campaign finance changes — a suggestion that, if followed, might further delay congressional action on the subject.

The Senate's disposition of the PAC issue largely reflected a lack of desire on the part of many members to declare themselves one way or the other on the touchy political issue of "special interest" campaign contributions.

Nonetheless, Boren said he was "elated" by the Senate's vote. "This is an issue that is not going to go away," he declared. "We're much more likely to get back to it with a positive vote than with a negative vote."

The Senate turned to other legislation after the tabling motion was rejected, and neither S 655 nor the PAC amendment was brought up again in 1985.

The Boren Amendment

Under Boren's proposal, House candidates could accept a maximum of $100,000 in PAC contributions, with another $25,000 permitted if they faced opposition in both primary and general elections. A Senate candidate could collect $175,000 to $750,000 depending on the size of the state. *(1985 CQ Weekly Report p. 2445)*

In addition, the plan would lower the ceiling on individual PAC contributions from $5,000 to $3,000 per election while increasing maximum individual gifts from $1,000 to $1,500.

Another provision would require television and radio broadcasters to provide free response time to candidates opposed by groups operating "independent expenditure" campaigns.

Too Much Influence?

During Senate debate Dec. 2 and 3, Boren and his allies charged that PAC money in politics has led to excessive special-interest influence over Congress.

"We cannot expect members of Congress to act in the national interest when their election campaigns are being financed more and more by special interests," said Boren.

During the 1983-84 election cycle, PACs contributed a record $105.3 million to House and Senate candidates, with 72 percent of the total funneled to incumbents, according to a Dec. 1 report by the Federal Election Commission. *(Earlier story, 1985 CQ Weekly Report p. 1115)*

Opponents of Boren's package claimed it would boost the role of political "fat cats" by increasing individual contributions and would favor wealthy and well-organized PACs that could shower candidates with donations early in the campaign season before running up against overall PAC ceilings.

Some foes also disputed the no-

"I don't worry about being bought, because I'm not for sale. The truth is I am proud of the PACs and the people who support me."

—Sen. Phil Gramm, R-Texas

"This is a phony vote. This is a non-entity."

—Fred Wertheimer, president, Common Cause

tion that PACs are a threat to the legislative process.

"I don't worry about being bought, because I'm not for sale," said Phil Gramm, R-Texas, one of the seven senators who voted to table Boren's amendment. "The truth is I am proud of the PACs and the people who support me," Gramm said.

The freshman senator said he did not understand why an individual who gives $1,000 is not considered a special interest while 100 individuals who give $10 apiece to a PAC, which then gives $1,000 to a candidate, are considered a special interest.

During his 1984 Senate campaign, Gramm received $1.3 million in PAC gifts. That amounted to about 14 percent of the $9.8 million he raised from all sources, including individuals.

Tactics and Votes

The decision to stave off conclusive Senate action on the PAC-limiting amendment came after both sides said they were uncertain how the votes were lining up.

Ninety minutes before the vote, Boren told a reporter he would be pleased if he got 40 votes for his position. That view was shared by lobbyists for Common Cause, the anti-PAC group that led the lobbying campaign for the amendment.

Boren later said there was a narrow majority for his proposal.

John Heinz, R-Pa., who led the debate against the amendment, thought he might have mustered a majority on his side, but there were enough undecided senators to put the outcome in doubt, according to Dwight Howes, a Heinz aide.

With the vote a tossup, Boren's opponents found themselves in a difficult position — against his PAC proposal but unenthusiastic about being on the losing side in a close roll call and being accused of caving in to special interest groups.

Minutes before the vote began, Dole suggested at the GOP senators' weekly luncheon that his colleagues oppose a tabling amendment because that would postpone any further consideration of the issue.

Heinz, Dole and others "came to realize it wouldn't be a good idea tactically to only give people an option of voting against campaign reform," said Howes. "The way this [the vote on the Boren amendment] was structured, you were either for it or against it."

Heinz went ahead with his tabling motion, but said he would vote against it and urged others to do the same.

"This put people on record in favor of campaign reform but also in favor of having the Senate continue to examine this problem and have the flexibility of studying other alternatives," said Howes.

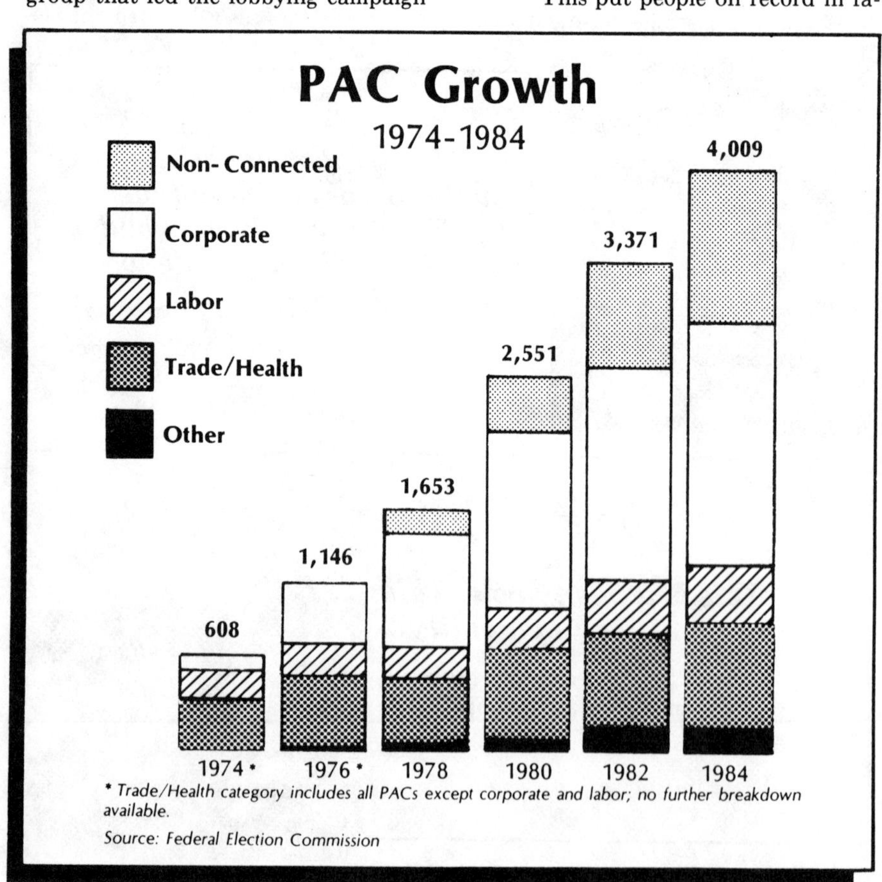

* Trade/Health category includes all PACs except corporate and labor; no further breakdown available.

Source: Federal Election Commission

Something for Everyone

The approach taken by the Senate essentially allowed almost everyone to come away from the debate able to claim a victory.

Boren did just that, seizing on the vote as evidence of the Senate's desire to act on campaign finance reform. Heinz and other critics succeeded in temporarily derailing the anti-PAC measure without appearing to be against campaign reform — and they did so without forcing any colleagues into a potentially embarrassing vote.

That left only frustrated officials of Common Cause, who have been waiting impatiently for congressional action on PACs.

Common Cause already had indicated plans for a major anti-PAC lobbying campaign in 1986, using the Senate vote as a centerpiece of that effort. The campaign might still go forward, but the way the Senate dealt with the Boren amendment made the vote much less significant.

"This is a phony vote. This is a non-entity," grumbled Common Cause President Fred Wertheimer.

Boren acknowledged that the outcome fell short of the "vote of conscience" he had sought on the controversial PAC issue. "There were some votes of conscience, and there were some votes of people looking over their shoulders at the people at home," he said.

If the Senate does return to campaign finance issues, it will have much more than Boren's PAC proposal on its plate. For example, Charles McC. Mathias Jr., R-Md., a longtime advocate of public financing of congressional campaigns, is expected to push such a proposal. Mathias is chairman of the Rules Committee, which has jurisdiction over campaign finance legislation.

Heinz, meanwhile, introduced his own campaign bill Dec. 3. His legislation (S 1891) would leave PAC and individual contribution limits intact but would raise significantly the amount of money that can be supplied to candidates from political party committees.

Heinz is chairman of the National Republican Senatorial Committee, which raises money for GOP Senate candidates. ■

PAC Money: Source of Evil or Scapegoat?

In the Congress of the 1980s, a debate about campaign finance is a debate about corruption — nothing more and nothing less.

A few weeks ago, when the Senate discussed a proposal to limit contributions from political action committees, members from both parties took turns identifying PACs and their campaign gifts as the root of modern congressional evil.

"PAC money is destroying the electoral process," said Republican Barry Goldwater of Arizona. Democrat Gary Hart of Colorado said PACs represented the "toxic waste of American politics."

There is no question that something is wrong in campaign finance. American voters ought not to feel that public office is for sale to the highest bidder, and in the current climate, many of them do. Restricting the flow of PAC money may be a reasonable way of dealing with that problem.

But it is also reasonable, as senators compete with each other to tell PAC horror stories, to wonder whether there isn't a little bit of scapegoating going on.

The last decade of congressional history has written a record of disturbing policy failures. Throughout most of the 1970s, Congress argued endlessly about how to reduce energy imports, but no action was taken and the country imported more oil — and more inflation — with each passing year.

Since 1980, there has been a bipartisan consensus that the federal deficit is out of control, and yet the deficit has grown to $200 billion. In 1985, Congress conceded its inability to solve the problem and passed legislation putting budget cuts on automatic pilot.

Given the seriousness of all this — and the rhetoric about PAC money destroying the political system — it seems fair to ask what role political action committees have played in creating our recurrent legislative paralysis.

A moment's reflection supplies the answer: hardly any role at all.

Is it PAC influence that makes members unwilling to raise taxes, or trim entitlement programs, or pull the plug on federal subsidies to their states? Of course not.

It would be silly to insist that PAC money never turns the outcome of a House or Senate vote. But when it comes to crucial policy decisions — and policy failures — the source of the corruption is somewhere else.

Congress fails to solve problems because members routinely sell out to a set of interests more respectable and yet more dangerous than the PACs. They sell out to the pressures of public opinion in the places they represent.

It may seem unfair to talk of members "selling out" to the voters. They are elected, after all, to give ordinary people a voice in public policy.

But the conflict between the demands of leading people and the temptations of pandering to them has been a fact of legislative life as long as Western democracies have existed. It has been more than 200 years since Edmund Burke told his constituents that a member of Parliament owed them "not his industry only, but his judgment."

In Congress, the pendulum swings back and forth. At some moments in history, members have been crippled by slavish devotion to the prejudices of those who elected them. At other times, the desire to lead and make decisions has won out.

One has to look back only to the 1950s to find a Congress whose dominant figures felt free to make policy as they wished. Senators such as Harry F. Byrd of Virginia and congressmen such as Clarence Cannon of Missouri did what they thought was right, and depended on constituents to accept it.

Much of what they thought was right does not look very good in retrospect. The Congress of the 1950s condoned legal segregation in the South and ignored legitimate demands for some federal role in areas ranging from education to health care. Those legislators carried autonomy to a fault.

Now we have the opposite problem. Members of Congress win election through the ceaseless monitoring and cultivation of voter desire. They keep that process up once they are sworn in. It is no accident that the overwhelming majority of staff people in any congressional office work on constituent service, not legislative research.

The Congress of the 1950s failed for lack of responsiveness. The current Congress fails for an excess of responsiveness. At no point in recent times has there been so wide a gap between what members are willing to propose in private — whether it is a tax increase on one side or a reduction in Social Security benefits on the other — and what they are willing to endorse in public.

Given the way congressional careers have evolved since the 1950s, perhaps a hyper-responsive Congress is inevitable. Those who decide to run often give up many months of their time and too much of their own money for a job whose year-round responsibilities all but require them to sever any ties to private life or jobs back home. It is no surprise that people who go through a process like that emerge desperate to stay in office, and timid about saying or doing anything that might turn a fickle electorate against them.

This — not the prevalence of PAC money — is what has rendered Congress so weak in dealing with hard national problems. Corruption is the right word for it. To thunder against the evils of the PAC system is to magnify a small problem — and to ignore a huge one.

Farm Bill Offers Limited 'Win' for All Sides

President Reagan signed a $169.2 billion farm and nutrition measure the week of Dec. 23, 1985, defusing a political powder keg that threatened to explode under Congress throughout 1985.

Administration officials said the president signed the five-year bill (HR 2100 — H Rept 99-447) Dec. 23, despite his reservations about many of its key tenets, and despite the estimated $52 billion three-year price tag for the price- and income-support sections of the bill. He had threatened to veto any bill over $50 billion.

The president also signed separate legislation to reorganize and rescue the Farm Credit System. *(1985 CQ Weekly Report p. 2685)*

Reagan's ultimate blessing for HR 2100, announced Dec. 19 by then secretary of agriculture John R. Block, brought the tense standoff between the White House and Congress to a classic "win-win" conclusion: The results pleased few in Congress or the administration, but, more important politically, they angered fewer. This was especially important given the upcoming election year.

"It didn't leave here as a partisan document," said Senate Majority Leader Robert Dole, R-Kan., moments after House and Senate negotiators Dec. 14 unanimously approved the compromise package.

The administration, which had fought since the previous February to cut the tether that binds farmers and the federal government, won a bill that immediately lowered basic price supports. The bill also promises to reduce by half the annual federal outlays for agriculture within five years.

An election-conscious Congress, swayed by powerful sentiment for struggling "family farmers," won a bill that subsidizes farmers' incomes at the current record levels of 1985 for at least three additional years — and two congressional elections.

Both chambers approved the measure on Dec. 18. The

Political Storm Eases —At Least for Now

conference report was adopted by the House on a 325-96 vote; Senate action came hours later on a 55-38 vote.

Divisive Pattern Scrapped

The wide margin of approval in the House, coupled with the emergence of a bipartisan alliance voting for the bill in the Senate, represented a sharp break from the divisive pattern set in both chambers early last summer that continued through the final conference negotiations the weekend of Dec. 14.

For the Senate, where the GOP majority could hang in the balance with 22 seats up for re-election in 1986, the bill provided farm-state Republicans with a measure of distance from the administration's Draconian image back home.

In the House, Democrats won assurance that farm policy will continue on the path of protective federal intervention begun 50 years ago in President Franklin D. Roosevelt's New Deal.

However, that course could alter significantly over the five-year life of the bill, depending on how the administration chooses to use its broad new discretionary powers to set price-support rates for major crops, and on the ultimate success of a number of experimental policies spelled out for key commodity programs.

But neither the Democratic nor Republican parties will have much opportunity in the three years following the bill's passage to take widescale, partisan advantage of the farm bill itself. The president's approval, following previous veto threats, should extinguish most of the partisan feuding that characterized much of the debate during 1985.

"It would be a political disaster for Republicans in the Farm Belt if the president vetoed this bill," said Rep. Edward R. Madigan, R-Ill.

"The best politics for the Democratic Party," said Rep. Thomas S. Foley, D-Wash., "is trying to do the best job we can on the legislation. I've

The omnibus farm bill — all 13 pounds of it — got a lift from three senators shortly before the Senate cleared the bill Dec. 18. From left: Edward Zorinsky, D-Neb.; Agriculture Committee Chairman Jesse Helms, R-N.C.; and Majority Leader Robert Dole, R-Kan.

not been one who's trying to play [political] games with the farm bill."

Removing partisan politics from the farm bill, these leaders said, gives the U.S. farmer a little more room to survive the worst economic depression in agriculture since the 1930s.

"The program is compassionate," agreed Block. "It may give some farmers in trouble a chance to recover.

"But at the same time, agriculture will be moving in the direction we want it to be moving . . . toward a market-based economy," he said.

For the most part, members of Congress expressed the same notion with a slightly different twist.

"The truth is," summed up one Democratic conferee, "we got the money, and the secretary got a little bit of principle."

Cost Breakdown

HR 2100 contains a variety of farm programs expected to cost $100.6 billion over five years, according to Agriculture Department estimates released Dec. 17.

Food assistance programs, such as food stamps, will cost another $68.6 billion.

One-third of the farm programs' cost will come from the Farmers Home Administration and other agriculture credit agencies ($10.2 billion over five years), and agricultural export, research and conservation programs ($21 billion).

As usual, however, the bulk of the cost will stem from the price- and income-support programs for major crops, such as wheat, corn, cotton, rice and soybeans. The price tag will total $69.4 billion over five years.

The department's expected yearly cost breakdown is $16.6 billion in fiscal 1986, $15.7 billion in 1987, $16.5 billion in 1988, $12.9 billion in 1989 and $7.7 billion in 1990.

Support programs in the expired four-year farm bill (PL 97-98) cost $54.7 billion over the life of that measure, including $16.8 billion in fiscal 1985. Before 1981, price- and income-support programs averaged less than $3 billion a year.

Grappling for Benefits

While partisan politics became an overriding component of farm policy debate in 1985, budget reduction also was a pervasive theme throughout the year, particularly for the key commodity groups that were forced to grapple for dwindling federal benefits.

Both House and Senate Agriculture committees spent months trying to whittle the programs to a size that would take care of the special commodity interests of each member and still cut costs enough to ward off a congressional revolt against farm programs by urban members.

The administration, often allying itself with urban Democrats, fired several unsuccessful broadsides at some of the more treasured farm benefits, such as high price supports for dairy, sugar, honey and peanuts, and unlimited income subsidies.

But the Democratic House leadership made the package reported by the Agriculture Committee a leadership issue, arguing that every piece of the farm mosaic must remain intact to put added pressure on Reagan and the Republican Party.

The farm coalition held fast and won all but one key vote: an alternative plan to let farmers themselves vote on strict production controls for their crops. As it turned out, that was the one issue on which the House leadership itself was divided, and it was summarily defeated on the floor, 174-251, before the bill was approved Oct. 8, 282-141.

Senate GOP Defections

Partisan emotions were much more intense — and chaotic — in the Senate, particularly after farm-state Republicans on the Agriculture Committee helped to report a Democrat-drafted bill.

The Republicans nearly lost control on the Senate floor as well, when 12 GOP senators quickly defected and voted with farm-state Democrats against an administration-backed plan to cut the cost of the bill by lowering income subsidies.

Those income subsidies, or deficiency payments, cover the difference between actual market prices and higher "target" prices set in farm law. Although Democrats generally accepted the administration's plan to begin reducing price supports that put a floor on crop prices, they made deficiency payments a symbolic point of departure.

Whether to freeze current target prices for the life of the bill, or begin reducing them in 1987, was the question that dominated the Senate debate.

That immediately put Dole — up for re-election in 1986 — on the defensive, both as majority leader responsible to the Republican Party and as a senior member of the Agriculture Committee with allegiance to his Kansas farm constituency.

Dole cast his damage-control mission simply: Stake out the middle ground and fashion a bill that could pass Congress before the end of the year, and still avoid a presidential veto. Throughout the Senate committee and floor debates, and well into the 10-day conference with the House, it was never certain he could accomplish such an agenda.

The bill emerged from the Senate Nov. 23 as an effective one-year freeze on target prices but with other "sweeteners" for nearly every commodity group, reflecting the compromises Dole made with key Democrats to win enough votes for his middle-of-the-road approach.

Dole-Foley Handiwork

Foley had assumed a similar role as pragmatic mediator in the House. As majority whip and chairman of the Agriculture Subcommittee on Wheat, Soybeans and Feed Grains, he was the chief architect of the central section of the House bill, which effectively set a five-year freeze on target prices for all major commodities.

Although Foley was unable to attend early House-Senate conference sessions because of a conflict with conferences on the Gramm-Rudman-Hollings deficit-reduction bill, the final farm bill reflects his handiwork as well as Dole's.

When the two finally met face-to-face Dec. 11, they hammered out a compromise package within hours. The key section on target prices — providing for a two-year freeze and only a 2 percent reduction in the third year — was ratified quickly by the full conference the next day.

"I think we balanced it very well," Foley said. "This is an extraordinary bill, considering what we're facing in the budget. It's only a modification in [current] farm policy . . . [but] there is only so much that government policy can do. An agriculture bill can't turn around world economic decisions."

The White House had drawn its line at capping the three-year cost at $50 billion, on reducing target prices, on eliminating a House provision to assess dairy producers, and on giving the president wide discretion to increase sugar imports from debt-ridden Caribbean nations.

Instead, it got a $52 billion three-year bill, a target-price freeze, an assessment on milk producers and a directive to cut sugar imports.

Any further attempt to make political points in agriculture policy must focus on agricultural banks and issues beyond those contained in HR 2100.

Nevertheless, Congress assured itself of further partisan battles over basic farm policy by setting a political time bomb: Instead of a traditional four-year reauthorization, the conference agreed to make HR 2100 a five-year bill.

The next farm bill debate is scheduled for the election year of 1990.

Wheat, Feed Grains

As in the past, the core of the 1985 farm bill debate dealt with price- and income-supports for wheat, corn and other feed grains, mainly because those commodities consume most of the federal outlays for farm programs. They also have taken the brunt of depressed economic conditions that plague the Midwestern breadbasket.

That also is why Dole and Foley, who represent wheat-growing regions, played such key roles in shaping the direction of the entire bill.

The package they crafted is a careful compromise between the administration's goals of reducing the artificial floor the government puts on wheat and corn prices, and giving struggling farmers some cash security if prices continue to plummet below the costs of production.

The bill will reduce sharply the rates the government sets for price-support crop loans, which are given to farmers at harvest at a per-bushel rate, with the crops held as collateral. Farmers who cannot get a price for their crops at least equal to the loan rate can forfeit the crop to the government and keep the principal. In practice, the loan rates set a floor on domestic prices.

In the past, Congress arbitrarily set loan rates on a rising scale, keeping an eye on inflation, with the result that current rates are generally higher than prices on most world markets. That has led farmers to forfeit much of their crops to the government.

Under HR 2100, the basic wheat loan rate, at $3.30 a bushel in 1985, will have dropped 10 percent to $3 in 1986, and another 5 percent a year through 1990. Corn rates will have dropped in similar fashion, from $2.55 a bushel to $2.40 in 1986.

Southern lawmakers held key power positions and won major concessions for their cotton farmers.

Also, the agriculture secretary will have the power to reduce the rate another 20 percent a year, which could bring the 1986 rate for wheat down to $2.40 a bushel.

That will be much closer to the prevailing market price, giving agriculture officials hope that foreign nations will have much more difficulty underselling U.S. grain on overseas markets. Nearly half of domestic grains currently are grown for export.

Cutting the loan rates, however, only serves to widen the gap between market prices and target prices, which means the government will have to pay more in income subsidies.

The Foley-Dole compromise, which freezes 1985 target prices for wheat at $4.38 a bushel (and for corn at $3.03 a bushel) for two years, allows the rates to drop a total of 10 percent over the remaining three years of the bill, in annual increments of 2 percent, 3 percent and 5 percent.

Allowing no major cuts until the fourth year created another problem, however. Lawmakers were afraid the agriculture secretary might not use his full authority to lower loan rates beyond the basic rate — or might not be allowed to by White House budget officials. To force the administration's hand, the bill required the secretary to lower loan rates by at least 10 percent in 1986.

Some Democrats maintained that a two- to three-year freeze would lower farmers' incomes, mainly because the bill also allows the secretary to impose harsher production controls on farmers participating in the federal program, giving them lower potential crop yields on which to earn benefits.

The Democrats' continuing doubts, and promises of a filibuster in the Senate, threatened to scuttle the Foley-Dole agreement as soon as it was introduced.

But recognizing the politically symbolic importance of a target price freeze in itself, Foley insisted that conferees vote on that section and then go back to the bargaining table to work out the details of the acreage-reduction issue.

By the time the conference wrapped up the other provisions of the bill and returned to the topic of acreage reduction on Saturday afternoon, Dec. 14, weary members had lost most of their partisan mettle. What had been a political debate on income subsides suddenly turned to a pragmatic discussion of how to make ends meet. A deal was pounded out with relative ease.

Cotton, Rice

Although cotton and rice farmers are a smaller group than other commodity interests, legislators representing Southern states where cotton and rice are grown played a proportionately larger role in the debate than any other special interest.

As a result, the cotton and rice programs contain some of the most radical — and possibly expensive — provisions in the entire package.

Southern senators, in particular, held swing votes in committee and on the floor, forcing Dole to acquiesce in their pet projects in order to win over their votes for his wheat package.

Sens. Thad Cochran, R-Miss., and David Pryor, D-Ark., along with Rep. Jerry Huckaby, D-La., parlayed their senior positions on the respective Agriculture panels into a powerful alliance in conference for a new kind of price-support mechanism for cotton and rice farmers, called a "marketing loan."

The plan calls for the government to issue crop loans to farmers at low rates, much like wheat and feed grain programs, but with a key difference:

Rather than allow farmers to default on their loans if prices do not rise above the loan rate, the agriculture secretary must allow rice farmers, and has the option to allow cotton farmers, the opportunity to pay back the loan only at the rate he can get at market.

The farmer-borrower who sells his crop at a lower rate would keep the remaining principal.

As a further benefit for rice farmers, whose crops were earning only half of the current loan rate of $8 per hundred pounds, the marketing loan took effect immediately for the already-harvested 1985 crop.

"We're going back to the marketplace, and it's clear to me we're going to increase sales," Huckaby said. "I think the wheat and corn people are going to want to go to this approach before long."

Dairy

House Democrats won their biggest victory over the administration when Senate conferees finally gave in on a new program to reduce milk surpluses by requiring the government to buy up entire herds of dairy cows.

The administration, despite losing floor votes in both the House and Senate, continued to fight in the conference for an immediate cut in the dairy price-support rate. (The government buys milk solids, such as cheese, butter and nonfat dry milk, from dairy processors at a current rate of $11.60 per hundred pounds.)

But after a week of private negotiations by dairy-state conferees, a compromise package on milk price supports finally emerged Dec. 14.

The bill requires the agriculture secretary to offer bids to dairy producers to send to slaughter or sell for export their entire dairy herds, calves and bulls included. The farmers must agree to stay out of the dairy business for three to five years.

Tony Coelho, D-Calif., chairman of the House dairy subcommittee, said the 18-month program should remove 800,000 of the nation's 11 million dairy cows from milk production, reducing current government surpluses of 16.5 million pounds down to less than five million pounds.

Agriculture Secretary Block steadfastly resisted efforts to assess dairy producers for the herd buyout scheme. Reagan had often referred to the assessment as a "milk tax."

Rudy Boschwitz, R-Minn., who was leading the conference negotiations for the Senate, said the president and those around him were more "dug in" on dairy provisions than any other commodity. "It's simpler to understand," he said.

The Senate bill contained a straightforward one-year freeze on dairy price supports, with a 50-cent cut in 1987. The House bill contained a hike in the support rate, the whole-herd buyout plan, plus a revival of a diversion plan to pay producers to cut back on their production. The buyout and diversion plans, to be paid for by farmer assessments, were inserted at the insistence of the dairy industry.

"We decided to put as much as possible in the House bill, knowing we could give up some things and still not give away the guts of the program," Coelho said.

Coelho gave up on the diversion plan when Dole agreed to the buyout "experiment," financed by 40-cent-per-hundred-pound assessments in 1986 and a 25-cent assessment in 1987. In return, Coelho agreed to a graduated cut in the price-support rates in 1987 — 25-cents per hundred pounds on Jan. 1 and another 25 cents on Oct. 1 — if surpluses are not reduced below five billion pounds a year.

On the dairy talks, "he [Majority Leader Robert Dole] became a kingpin. We didn't reach a deal until Dole walked in the door."

—Rep. Tony Coelho, D-Calif.

The assessments and price cuts combined will put the effective price support at $11.20 in 1986 and $11.10 through 1987.

Coelho said Dole held the key vote among the five Republican and four Democratic Senate conferees. "He became a kingpin," Coelho said. "We didn't reach a deal until Dole walked in the door."

Sugar

Part of Dole's deal with Southern Democrats and farm-state Republicans involved the sugar program, which supports cane growers in the Gulf States and Hawaii and sugar beet growers in Midwestern states, such as North and South Dakota.

Much to the chagrin of the State Department, Dole agreed to a provision on the Senate floor that effectively forces the White House to reduce the flow of imported sugar. The administration has been trying to increase the flow of sugar from debt-ridden Caribbean nations that need hard U.S. currency to pay off massive U.S. bank debts.

After the House rebuffed Senate efforts to drop the sugar provision, Dole agreed to a compromise that would delay the effect of the plan until later in the year.

"Dole honored his commitment," said Huckaby, chairman of the House sugar subcommittee.

The only remaining dispute involved a turf battle among House conferees from the Agriculture and Ways and Means committees. Huckaby said House conferees finally worked out compromise wording that carefully skirts the issue of tariffs, which are the sole province of Ways and Means.

Conservation

Conferees had no trouble reaching agreement on the conservation section, which included two new programs that could be the most popular in the entire bill.

A tough "sodbuster" provision will deny any federal farm benefits to farmers who till highly erodible soil. A similar "swampbuster" program will give like protection to much of the nation's wetlands.

To further encourage farmers to take fragile land out of crop production, the bill also establishes a "conservation reserve" of at least 40 million acres. Over the next five years, the agriculture secretary must offer bids to farmers to place farm land in the reserve for 10 to 15 years, and must help pay for the expense of planting grass, trees or other covering.

The House had passed sodbuster legislation in each of the past two years, but the reluctant Senate would never go along. *(1984 CQ Almanac, p. 364)*

In 1985 the Senate, with the administration's blessing and added pressure from environmental groups, passed even more restrictive conservation provisions than the House.

"Everybody was really for it last year, too," said Ed Jones, D-Tenn., chairman of the House Agriculture Conservation Subcommittee. "But the administration told me they wanted to wait until 1985. They were hoping it would make their [entire] farm bill popular enough to pass it." ∎

Chernobyl Has Many Side Effects:

Disaster Raises New Questions About Fate of Nuclear Energy

While no immediate U.S. health threats are expected from the Soviet Union's Chernobyl nuclear power plant accident, political fallout from the disaster could have a profound effect on the future of nuclear energy in this country.

Even congressional supporters of nuclear power said its future as a viable energy source was at stake.

The disaster may also have an effect on foreign policy. The House May 1, 1986, passed a resolution (H Res 440) criticizing the Soviet Union for not paying more attention to safety and for not sharing information with other countries. A similar resolution (S Res 390) was proposed in the Senate.

The accident is believed to have taken place on April 25 at a nuclear power station in Pripyat, about 15 miles northeast of Chernobyl. The plant is about 70 miles from Kiev, a city with a population of 2.5 million, and about 250 miles from the Polish border. *(Map, p. 117)*

The outside world learned of the accident only when radiation monitors in Sweden and Finland began picking up windblown debris and gases. Although the Russians eventually admitted that an accident had occurred, substantial facts were slow in coming throughout the first week following the incident.

Members got much of their information from U.S. intelligence agencies, which held closed-door briefings featuring dramatic spy satellite photos of the Chernobyl plant's No. 4 unit with its roof and some walls blown away.

Members of a House Energy subcommittee were also briefed by Vitaly Churkin, second secretary of the Soviet Embassy. While not unprecedented, it is extremely rare for foreign officials to appear before congressional committees.

Churkin, however, hewed closely to the official line and did not add much to what was known. But he admitted that the "accident, obviously, is not all over with."

Resolutions

The House May 1 passed H Res 440 deploring the Soviet Union's failure to notify the rest of the world and calling on that country to allow international press coverage of the situation.

The resolution, introduced by Mary Rose Oakar, D-Ohio, was passed by voice vote.

"This terrible accident," Oakar said, "is an international problem and it has profound human dimensions.... This is the time to break down the barrier of communication so we can soberly address this enormous catastrophe."

> ***"Nuclear fission is a menace to humanity. Its safety cannot be guaranteed here or in Russia."***
>
> **—Rep. Ted Weiss, D-N.Y.**

The measure, whisked to the floor after approval by the Foreign Affairs Committee earlier in the day, also called on the Russians to allow inspection of the site by the International Atomic Energy Agency (IAEA). It expressed sympathy to victims of the disaster and called on the Soviets to allow people of Ukrainian birth living in the United States to communicate with relatives in the Ukraine, the region where the accident occurred.

About 1 percent of the population of Oakar's Cleveland district is of Ukrainian ancestry, and there are higher concentrations of other East European ethnic groups.

A House resolution (H Res 439) introduced April 29 by Robert S. Walker, R-Pa., along with some 140 cosponsors, contained similar provisions. He supported the final version of Oakar's resolution, which was amended to combine provisions of both.

A number of other resolutions prompted by the Soviet disaster were introduced the same week. H Res 438, by John Edward Porter, R-Ill., called for multilateral negotiations to strengthen safety standards for the world's nuclear power plants.

The Senate resolution, S Res 390, was introduced by William V. Roth Jr., R-Del., and cosponsored by Mitch McConnell, R-Ky. It called on the IAEA to assess whether the Soviet nuclear program threatened international health, called on any nation experiencing such an accident to notify other nations immediately, and called on the president to raise the issue of Soviet nuclear safety at the next U.S.-Soviet summit.

In calling for a re-examination of nuclear safety standards, Roth said he did not agree with either anti-Soviet hard-liners who view the accident as proof of the Soviet Union's barbarity toward its own people, or with anti-nuclear activists who see it as evidence that nuclear power should be abandoned.

Anti-Soviet Feeling

While many members of Congress expressed sympathy for victims of the Chernobyl accident, the Soviet government came in for much criticism.

"In my judgment," George W. Gekas, R-Pa., told the House during one-minute speeches April 29, "the Soviet Union has committed an international crime in not reporting that tragedy ... to the world, so that the Scandinavian countries and Western Europe ... could adequately prepare for it." Gekas' district includes the Three Mile Island nuclear power plant, where a 1979 accident occurred.

Sen. Alfonse M. D'Amato, R-N.Y., charged the Soviets with attempting a "cover-up" of the accident. "If the radioactive cloud had not been detected by officials in Sweden, the Soviet Union would have remained silent," D'Amato said. "Apparently their hope was that nobody would ever know."

Sen. John W. Warner, R-Va., who met with Soviet leader Mikhail S. Gorbachev in 1985, said Gorbachev had failed to practice the new candor he had called for. "He has missed that golden opportunity to establish credibility for himself and his new government," Warner said.

Some members said the lack of Soviet candor could have an impact on U.S.-Soviet arms control negotiations. Kenneth L. Adelman, director of the U.S. Arms Control and Disarmament Agency, appearing before the Senate Armed Services Committee April 29 to discuss verification methods, said the Russian claims of no more than two deaths were "frankly preposterous."

Minority Leader Robert C. Byrd, D-W.Va., said on the Senate floor the Chernobyl accident was "still small compared to the devastation of even a limited exchange of nuclear weapons," and urged the Soviets to "recommit themselves" to arms control.

Nuclear Energy's Future

The Chernobyl accident immediately became part of the debate over the future of nuclear energy in the United States.

A coalition of 18 consumer, environmental and scientific groups declared April 29 that nuclear power plants were becoming uneconomical as well as unsafe and should be phased out quickly. Spokesmen for the Atomic Industrial Forum, however, said the accident was no reason to junk the 15 percent of U.S. generating capacity that is nuclear-fueled.

Within Congress, members supportive of nuclear power stressed that an accident like that at Chernobyl is unlikely to happen here. They noted that the Soviet graphite reactor was of a type rare in this country, and that it lacked a real "containment" structure, standard on U.S. power reactors. U.S. reactors were far safer, they argued, because they are sited, designed, licensed and operated in the harsh glare of publicity with safety in mind.

But Ted Weiss, D-N.Y., argued against assurances that such an accident could not happen here. Pointing to the Three Mile Island accident, he declared: "Nuclear fission is a menace to humanity. Its safety cannot be guaranteed here or in Russia."

Five reactors in the United States lack containment structures capable of confining the steam, gas and debris from a serious accident. All are run by the Energy Department for production of nuclear weapon materials and other purposes. One in Hanford, Wash., uses graphite to control the nuclear chain reaction, as did the Soviet reactor.

Sen. Mark O. Hatfield, R-Ore., called April 30 for an investigation of the Hanford reactor by the General Accounting Office (GAO). "If GAO determines that the reactor is a safety risk, it should be shut down," he said. Rep. Ron Wyden, D-Ore., arranged for the House Energy Subcommittee on Oversight and Investigations to broaden an ongoing investigation to include the Hanford facility.

Alan K. Simpson, R-Wyo., who chairs the Senate Environment Subcommittee on Nuclear Regulation, said it would be difficult for members to work their way through issues surrounding the future of nuclear power in the midst of such "high drama."

"We're really looking at our own fears," he said.

Even as the intense graphite fire still raged at the Soviet plant, one House committee was debating the damage such an accident could wreak on the United States. Another was debating whether and how to make reactor licenses easier for utilities to get.

Price-Anderson

The House Interior Committee April 30 met to mark up a reauthorization (HR 3653) of the basic nuclear insurance law, the Price-Anderson Act (PL 85-256). It limits the damages companies operating nuclear plants must pay if they have an accident.

Committee Republicans went to the markup session poised to push through an amendment lowering the damage ceiling from $8.2 billion to $2.5 billion, but instead agreed with Democrats that in view of the situation it would be better to adjourn for two weeks.

Ranking Republican Don Young, Alaska, one of those wanting to lower the liability limit, said: "I am very concerned at the hysterical attitude of many members of this Congress over the events that supposedly have happened in Russia."

But John F. Seiberling, D-Ohio, who opposed lowering the limit, said: "I don't see how, in light of the events in the Soviet Union of the last three

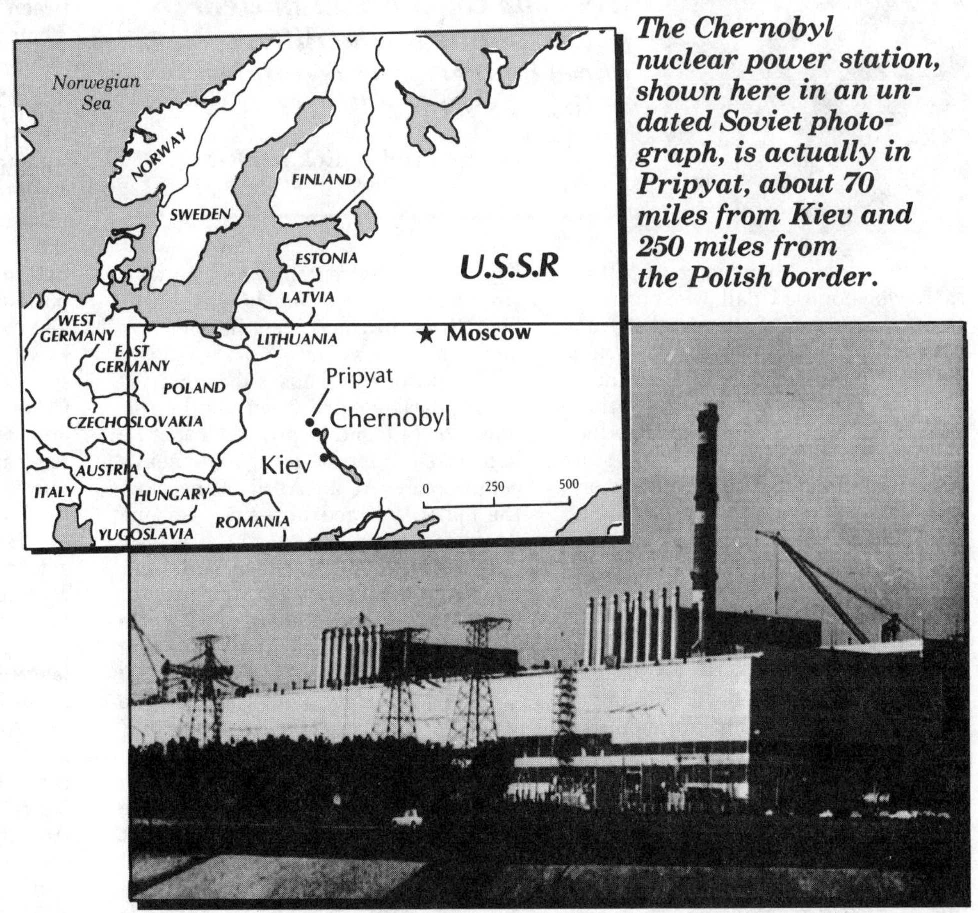

The Chernobyl nuclear power station, shown here in an undated Soviet photograph, is actually in Pripyat, about 70 miles from Kiev and 250 miles from the Polish border.

days, the members can face their constituents and tell them that they've voted to reduce coverage from $8 billion to $2 billion in the event of a similar accident."

Members debated the liability limit and the Chernobyl incident for an hour before Austin J. Murphy, D-Pa., moved to adjourn. No one objected.

It was unclear immediately which side gained more from the decision to adjourn, partly because it was unclear which side had the votes. Democrats standing with Chairman Morris K. Udall, D-Ariz., had succeeded in raising the limit from $2.5 billion to $8.2 billion by a margin of only 21-20 the week before. Ron Marlenee, R-Mont., who offered the amendment to reverse that decision, said he had the votes. Some Democrats on Udall's side believed Marlenee did. If that is true, then adjournment saved Udall's camp from defeat.

"The Soviet plant involved in this accident is as different from our commercial nuclear power plants as the differences between our countries' political systems."

—Rep. Fred J. Eckert, R-N.Y.

But it was Murphy, representing those who oppose Udall, who moved to adjourn. His camp gained relief from the political discomfort of taking such a stand in the shadow of Chernobyl. Murphy complained of the "atmosphere" in which the markup was being held, saying it was "not fair . . . to be determining the future of our energy sources under the suspicions of what's been happening in the Soviet Union."

Licensing Reform

That same day three bills dealing with nuclear power (HR 1029, HR 1447, HR 2488) were being considered by the House Energy Subcommittee on Energy Conservation and Power. The bills, being advanced by the electric utility industry, the Energy Department and the Nuclear Regulatory Commission (NRC), would overhaul the process for licensing commercial nuclear power reactors.

The electric industry has long complained about the slowness and uncertainty of that process. Industry critics, while not entirely satisfied with the process either, say the multiyear series of hearings and reviews is needed to ensure public safety.

That debate has gone on for years and has become increasingly theoretical since 1978, the last time a utility ordered a new nuclear power plant. More recently, proposals have emerged that backers claim will satisfy industry's desire for certainty and the critics' desire for safety. Typically, they include standardizing plant designs, one-step licensing, early approval of reactor sites and limits on the ability of the public to second-guess licensing decisions.

Subcommittee Chairman Edward J. Markey, D-Mass., is an outspoken critic of nuclear power. Pro-nuclear members from both parties command a decisive majority on Markey's panel, but as chairman he controls scheduling. So far, he has scheduled three hearings, but has not set any markup sessions.

A majority of his subcommittee wrote Markey April 24 urging him to move the bill, and he answered that he had asked interest groups to seek a compromise. At an April 30 hearing, the majority urged him again and he demurred again.

"I just want to make sure that people understand what they're doing," Markey said. "There are a whole range of issues here that members need to comprehend."

Nuclear safety groups, such as the Union of Concerned Scientists, support none of the bills.

Michael E. Faden, a representative of the group, told the Senate Energy Committee April 22 that streamlining the licensing process will not produce a demand for more nuclear power plants. "Only a dramatic change in electricity economics and a sustained period of trouble-free operation that instills greater public confidence can accomplish that result," he said.

Safety groups prefer bills like S 2291, introduced by Sen. Joseph R. Biden Jr., D-Del., which would set up an independent nuclear safety board. They also lean toward proposals that would give NRC an independent inspector general as a watchdog on its integrity.

Markey and nuclear safety groups say the licensing reform proposals threaten to cut the public out of the NRC licensing process — and that NRC has ignored massive safety defects in plants about to be licensed until citizen groups have forced it to recognize them.

Markey called the Russian accident "a glaring example of the dangers of nuclear power if public pressure for safety is stifled."

Fred J. Eckert, R-N.Y., drew a different conclusion. "It is crucial to remember," he said, "that the Soviet plant involved in this accident is as different from our commercial nuclear power plants as the differences between our countries' political systems. Their reactor was nurtured in a closed society which places little emphasis on safety and certainly stifles all public participation."

"I would hope," said ranking subcommittee Republican Carlos J. Moorhead, Calif., "that we not let hysteria replace common sense." He said the licensing reform legislation was not an effort to restrict public participation in any way and called on Markey to move the bill before Memorial Day.

On the Senate side, James A. McClure, R-Idaho, chairman of the Energy and Natural Resources Committee, said he still intended to mark up nuclear licensing reform legislation this year.

But McClure's committee has gotten into a dispute with the Environment and Public Works Committee, which also claims jurisdiction on the matter. That conflict could lengthen the time needed to complete a bill in the Senate.

And one senior Democratic aide on the House Energy Committee said it would be difficult to enact a licensing reform bill in 1986, given the controversy surrounding the subject, the shortness of the election-year session, and the uncertain voting margin it could command. ∎

Finance Panel OKs Radical Tax Overhaul Bill

In a turnabout of such swiftness and scope that it astounded the very men who brought it off, the Senate Finance Committee May 7, 1986, unanimously approved a tax bill that couples severe curtailment of legal tax avoidance with large reductions in tax rates.

The proposed changes in the individual income tax are the most fundamental since 1943, when tax withholding and a steeply progressive tax rate structure first became law.

While the changes in corporate taxation are less basic, they are major and are expected to have diverse effects on different types of businesses.

The legislation, which was designed neither to increase nor reduce overall government tax receipts, will cut individual income taxes (and a few minor taxes) by an estimated $105 billion to $110 billion and hike the total tax load on corporations by the same amount.

The measure is nonetheless expected to benefit from considerable business support, as well as meet with fierce opposition.

The heads of many corporations, large and small, have taken the position that the best thing that could happen to the economy and to their businesses would be lower tax rates and the creation of a "level playing field," without special tax provisions that favor investment in some industries over others.

Other corporate chiefs have taken an opposite view; they fear dire economic consequences if various tax incentives disappear.

The key political question may be whether the extraordinary bipartisan coalition that pushed the bill through the Finance Committee will hold together and pick up other supporters for a bipartisan approach.

Committee Chairman Bob Packwood, R-Ore., predicted that the coalition will hold and that the bill the Senate finally passes will closely resemble the one his committee wrote. He concedes, "We'll lose some," while declining to specify which.

Politically, the pressures on senators to back amendments restoring tax breaks appear likely to be matched in intensity only by pressure on members of both political parties to make sure they will be able to claim the credit if tax reform finally turns out to be a popular issue with the public.

But it is not clear yet whether the dramatic contents of the Finance Committee's bill will, finally, generate a groundswell of public demand for tax reform that has failed to materialize in the past.

House Speaker Thomas P. O'Neill Jr., D-Mass., plainly expected such a turnaround in public opinion all along and tried to make sure it helped the Democrats politically.

At the end of the highly partisan House debate on the tax bill in December 1985, he claimed credit for his party and said, "Only the Republican Senate can stop tax reform now."

Whether O'Neill's strategy will work when President Reagan has so plainly made tax reform a top priority of his second term is a good question.

Changes for Individuals

Among the major provisions of the Finance Committee bill that directly affect individuals are these:

- The present individual tax rate structure of 14 brackets, ranging from 11 to 50 percent, would be reduced to two brackets, 15 and 27 percent, with 80 percent of all taxpayers taxed solely at the 15 percent rate. The rate cuts would take effect July 1, 1987.
- More than six million of the working poor, all those with incomes at or slightly above the officially defined poverty level, would be removed from the tax rolls.
- Capital gains would be taxed at the same rates as ordinary income.
- A long list of deductions and exemptions, some used by middle-income families and others almost entirely by the well-to-do, would be abolished.

Among them are the following:

Interest on consumer purchases and loans, which would no longer be permitted as deductions on individual tax returns. There would be a transitional period of three years when they would be partly al-

> ***"It was like a poker game. Everyone anted up to make the pot worthwhile."***
>
> **—Sen. Bob Packwood, R-Ore., Finance Committee chairman**

Evolution of Proposals to Overhaul the Tax Code

The chart below compares the provisions of existing income tax law, the tax overhaul proposal announced May 28, 1985, by President Reagan and the version passed by the House Dec. 17, 1985 (HR 3838), with the version ordered reported to the Senate floor on the morning of May 7, 1986, by the Senate Finance Committee.

	Current Law	Reagan Plan	House Bill	Senate Finance Bill
Individual tax rates	11-50 percent (14 brackets)	15, 25 and 35 percent	15, 25, 35 and 38 percent	15 and 27 percent (lower rate would be phased out for high-income taxpayers)
Personal exemption	$1,080	$2,000	$2,000 for non-itemizers; $1,500 for itemizers	$2,000 for low- and middle-income taxpayers (exemption would be phased out for high-income taxpayers)
Corporate tax rates	15-40 percent on first $100,000 of income; 46 percent thereafter	33 percent; lower rates for income below $75,000	15-30 percent up to $75,000; 36 percent above $75,000	33 percent; same as House bill for income below $75,000
Interest payments	Deductions for home mortgage and non-business interest	Unlimited deduction for primary residences; additional interest deductions capped at $5,000	Unlimited deduction for mortgages on first and second residences; additional deduction of $10,000 ($20,000 for joint returns) plus the value of a taxpayer's investment income	Unlimited deduction for mortgages on first and second residences; no consumer interest deduction; interest paid on borrowing to produce investment income would be deductible equal to the value of the investment earnings
Health benefits	Employer-paid health premiums not taxed; medical expenses deductible if more than 5 percent of adjusted gross income	First $10 a month in employer-paid premiums for individuals ($25 for families) taxed as income; retain existing law for medical deductions	Retain existing law on taxation of health benefits and medical deductions	Retain existing law on taxation of health benefits; medical expenses would be deductible to the extent they exceed 10 percent of adjusted gross income
Charitable donations	Deductible	Full deductions for itemizers; none for non-itemizers	No change for itemizers; non-itemizers could deduct amount above $100	Full deductions for itemizers; none for non-itemizers
State and local taxes	Deductible	Deduction eliminated	No change from existing law	Deductions for state and local sales taxes would be repealed; income, real estate and personal property taxes would be deductible
Depreciation	Recovery periods of 3-19 years with accelerated write-off	More generous write-off over 4-28 years; value adjusted for inflation	Recovery periods of 3-30 years; partially indexed for inflation	Retain current system of rapid write-offs, permitting larger write-offs for most property over longer periods
Capital gains	60 percent exclusion; top effective rate of 20 percent	Top effective rate of 17.5 percent, but assets eligible would be limited	42 percent exclusion; top effective rate of 22 percent	Special exclusion repealed; taxed as regular income
Investment tax credit	6-10 percent	Repealed	Repealed	Repealed
Oil and gas	Allow percentage depletion, and expensing of intangible drilling costs	Repeal oil depletion allowance for all but small wells; keep "intangible" drilling breaks, but subject to minimum tax	Repeal percentage depletion allowance for all but small wells; allow expensing of intangible drilling costs for non-producing wells; 26-month write-off for producing wells	No change from existing law
Business expenses	Deductible	Deduction for entertainment repealed; limit on meals	Deduction of 80 percent of business meals and 80 percent of entertainment costs	Similar to House for meals and entertainment; most miscellaneous deductions eliminated

SOURCES: Treasury Department, HR 3838, Senate Finance Committee

lowed.

The $2,000 annual tax-exempt investment in Individual Retirement Accounts (IRAs), which would be restricted to those who are not covered by any pension plan except Social Security. The amounts already in IRAs would remain untaxed until the money is withdrawn and the interest on both previous and future investments would be non-taxable.

New restrictions would also be imposed on so-called 401(k) retirement plans and no taxpayer with a 401(k) would be permitted to make tax-exempt contributions to an IRA.

The use of tax shelter investments would be effectively barred, except for certain investments in exploration for oil. These shelters create paper losses that are used to offset taxable income from other sources.

Despite the limitations and terminations of these and other tax breaks, most individuals are expected to wind up paying lower taxes, and the average cut would be about 6 percent. *(Table, this page)*

Change in Tax Liability by Income Class

(As Computed for 1988)

Percentage Change in Income Tax Liability

Taxable Income	Administration Proposal	House Bill	Senate Committee Bill [1]
Less than $10,000	−67.1%	−74.7%	−62.2%
$10,000-$20,000	−16.3	−22.8	−18.0
$20,000-$30,000	−8.1	−9.7	−8.0
$30,000-$40,000	−6.3	−9.3	−5.0
$40,000-$50,000	−6.1	−7.9	−6.5
$50,000-$75,000	−6.3	−7.8	−3.7
$75,000-$100,000	−9.9	−6.0	−3.2
$100,000-$200,000	−10.1	−7.5	−3.6
$200,000 and above	−13.6	−6.0	−4.7
TOTAL	−9.8	−9.1	−6.2

NOTE: These figures do not take into account certain proposals affecting individuals. Thus, the total tax reductions under the administration proposal, the House bill and the Senate committee bill could be slightly different from what is indicated in this table. Also, the chart does not account for fully phasing in the Senate committee provision curtailing the deduction for tax shelter losses; thus the percentage change for taxpayers with income above $200,000 will be somewhat less.

[1] Figures are preliminary.

SOURCE: Joint Committee on Taxation

The abolition of most tax shelters was estimated to bring in $48.5 billion in revenue over five years. That is the major chunk of tax revenue that enabled the committee to vote for a bigger individual rate cut than envisioned by either Reagan or the House in its tax overhaul bill (HR 3838), while at the same time adding less than the House did to the taxes paid by corporations.

Reagan had proposed a three-bracket structure, with rates of 15, 25 and 35 percent, and the House added a fourth rate of 38 percent. *(Evolution of tax bill, p. 120; House-passed tax bill, 1985 CQ Weekly Report p. 2705)*

Key Changes for Corporations

The major changes in corporate taxation include the following:

- A reduction in the top corporate tax rate from 46 to 33 percent.
- Repeal of the 10 percent investment tax credit, retroactive to Jan. 1, 1986 — the only major retroactive provision anywhere in the bill. Loss of the tax credit would be somewhat offset by more generous deductions for depreciation.
- A tightening of the corporate minimum tax, which its authors hope will absolutely prevent corporations with large real economic profits from entirely escaping the income tax.
- Current tax breaks for the oil and gas industry, and other mining and natural resources businesses, would be maintained without major changes.

The Finance Committee bill would also leave excise taxes unchanged. However, several committee members publicly expressed their expectation that increases in excises will be needed later this year to meet the deficit-reduction targets required by the Gramm-Rudman-Hollings anti-deficit act (PL 99-177).

Both the Senate-passed fiscal 1987 budget resolution (S Con Res 120) and the companion resolution adopted May 8 by the House Budget Committee envision $10.7 billion in new revenues for fiscal 1987. *(House and Senate action, 1986 CQ Weekly Report p. 955; p. 1061)*

The Finance Committee bill contains at least one group of provisions that would have little effect on tax revenues but that are of widespread importance: those dealing with qualified pension plans.

The bill would increase the number of persons who must be covered under such plans, shorten the time periods for vesting and limit the extent to which employers may offset the benefits paid retired workers by the amount of their income from Social Security.

The chief beneficiaries of these changes are expected to be women, who tend to remain in jobs for shorter periods of time than men, and blue-collar and other less highly paid employees.

Miracle Cure

The coalition that brought the bill to completion in the Finance Committee and the speed with which it was done were as extraordinary as the contents of the legislation itself.

The bill, which had been abandoned as all but dead less than two weeks earlier, was before the committee in a newly invigorated and radically different form for just two long days. Only 28 hours elapsed from the time the committee took its first formal votes on amendments to the time it voted final approval. *(Most recent action, 1986 CQ Weekly Report p. 962; markup suspended, p. 840)*

The successful strategy for reviving the bill was devised by Packwood and what he described as a "core group of Democrats and Republicans, liberals and conservatives, rural and urban" senators.

The six other members were Democrats Bill Bradley of New Jersey, Daniel Patrick Moynihan of New York and George J. Mitchell of Maine,

Political Donation Credit Dropped

The Senate Finance Committee, like the House Ways and Means Committee before it, has rebuffed proponents of tax credits for political contributions.

The panel, in approving a radical overhaul of the federal tax code, voted to do away with the current 50 percent credit on contributions up to $100 ($200 for joint returns) to candidates, political parties and political action committees (PACs). *(Story, p. 119)*

Although Ways and Means eliminated the provision in its version of a major tax overhaul bill (HR 3838), a new, larger, and at the same time more limited credit was included in the final House-passed bill. A successful floor amendment, similar to one defeated in the House committee, allowed a 100 percent credit for donations up to $100 to congressional candidates in a taxpayer's home state. Prospects for a similar move in the Senate are unclear. *(House bill, 1985 CQ Weekly Report p. 2711)*

Proponents of the tax credit argue that it encourages small contributors and dilutes the influence of PACs. But even longtime PAC critics, such as Common Cause, the self-styled citizens' lobby, have voiced concern that the credit can also increase the influence of PACs, which take contributions their supporters have made directly to a candidate and transmit them in a "bundle" that carries the message of the sponsoring PAC.

Rep. Matthew F. McHugh, D-N.Y., sponsor of the House amendment, placated those critics by specifying that credits could not be taken for contributions funneled through a PAC.

But members who endorse retaining the credit must also fight the perception that they are retaining a tax break from which they benefit directly, while at the same time eliminating numerous business and individual tax breaks.

The Senate committee bill and the House bill both leave intact the current $1 checkoff through which taxpayers can designate contributions from the Treasury to the Presidential Election Campaign Fund. President Reagan had proposed eliminating the checkoff.

and Republicans John H. Chafee of Rhode Island, John C. Danforth of Missouri and Malcolm Wallop of Wyoming.

They met privately every day with staff and sometimes also with Deputy Treasury Secretary Richard G. Darman, beginning April 18, the day Packwood temporarily halted committee consideration of the bill, because it was becoming so loaded down with revenue-losing provisions. Some of those provisions had been sponsored by Packwood.

The key, these senators decided, was for them, themselves, to stop trying to preserve or expand tax benefits enjoyed by their own constituents and supporters in exchange for the prospect of a major reduction in tax rates and simplification of the tax law.

"It was like a poker game. Everyone anted up to make the pot worthwhile," Packwood said.

The reform package publicly unveiled by Packwood May 2 resulted from the private deliberations of these seven senators plus, probably, at least two others: Senate Majority Leader Robert Dole, R-Kan., and Dave Durenberger, R-Minn.

During its consideration by the full Finance Committee May 5 and 6 and until 12:19 a.m. May 7, dozens of amendments were added.

Most were small in their revenue impact. More importantly, under an agreement Packwood successfully pressed on the committee early in its deliberations (over the objections of former Chairman Russell B. Long, D-La., and a few others) all amendments were required to be revenue-neutral.

That is, if a provision cost the government revenue, it had to be counterbalanced by another provision as part of the same amendment, that raised an equal amount of revenue. One big package of more than three dozen amendments, $14 billion-plus worth of revenue-losers and an equal dollar value in gainers, was hammered out in a five-hour, closed-door meeting late May 6.

Battle Over Oil Shelters

It was this session that later produced the final public dispute in the committee's remarkable two days of work. It was almost the only one that was argued in public with any obvious anger. That was the decision essentially to exempt oil investments from the crackdown on tax shelters.

The advocates of this change said the investors in these shelters were taking real economic risks, and thus entitled to deduct their losses, whereas opponents claimed the decision to continue deductibility of losses from oil shelter investments rested on nothing except the political power of the oil industry in the Finance Committee.

Bradley, one of the earliest advocates of a low-rate, few-preferences tax law, made two attempts to undo the oil shelter provision — first all of it and then part of it — but lost both times. He vowed to resume the fight on the Senate floor.

However, critical comments from senators were strikingly few, while supporters vied to praise the bill.

Danforth summed up the prevailing view with a rhetorical question:

"The most basic issue is: Do we want to have a tax system that pays for tax shelters with high tax rates?" The clearly indicated answer was no.

When it was all over, and the unexpected 20-0 vote to report the bill had been recorded, Packwood said that some people who had come by to shake his hand after the session had told him that approval of such a bill was "a miracle."

"If you don't believe in miracles, you're just not a realist," he said.

Bob Packwood: A Tax Reform 'Convert'

For a year, Bob Packwood, R-Ore., espoused a revised tax code with fewer breaks and a top rate halved to 25 percent. Even so, good fortune more than design explains how that idea became the basis for what could be the capstone of his 18-year Senate career.

Packwood, the chairman of the Senate Finance Committee, engineered a 20-0 vote May 7, 1986, for the most radical overhaul of the code in 43 years. It was, said longtime reform proponent Bill Bradley, D-N.J., "the story of a powerful political idea." *(Story, p.119)*

But it was an idea Packwood seemed to have forgotten in the year before he endorsed it. Instead, he had led his committee — misled, many say — through tax writing the more traditional way: by trading breaks for special interests. Only when that failed, and the panel's draft threatened to swell the deficit, did Packwood turn to the idea of drastically lowering rates by curtailing tax breaks. He was, in his words, a "convert."

Packwood's earlier suggestion of a simpler tax code with lower rates had long been overshadowed by a 1984 comment: "I kind of like the present tax code." He insisted that remark was misinterpreted. But the perception remained that Packwood was an unwilling reformer, and nothing he said or did after assuming the Finance chairmanship in 1985 dispelled that view.

Even before President Reagan sent Congress his own tax-overhaul plan a year ago, Packwood publicly warned that his support would turn on one issue. "If taxation of employee benefits is in the bill," he said, "that in and of itself will make the entire bill unacceptable to me and I will work hard to defeat it regardless of what else it contains."

Then, when Finance began tax hearings last summer, Packwood told the Oregon news media that tax breaks for the state's timber industry would remain or there would be no tax bill. The next day in Washington, Packwood backed away from the statement a bit.

Nevertheless, the industry was fully protected when he released a draft bill March 13. Also included were tax breaks from "wish lists" of other Finance members. *(1986 CQ Weekly Report p. 591)*

The revenue-draining provisions mounted rapidly when the committee sat down to mark up a bill. The result was a spate of embarrassing publicity about what seemed an orgy of special-interest trading. "It even turned off the people who were doing pretty well in the trades," Bradley said.

Finally, on Friday, April 18, Packwood pulled the bill from the table. At lunch with Bill Diefenderfer, his committee staff chief, he returned to the concept of a 25 percent top rate. "We looked at each other and said, 'Why not?' " Packwood recalled.

Desperation apparently was not the only motivation. Long before, Packwood said, in talks with business friends he had asked, "How low would the top rate have to be before you wouldn't care if you lost deductions? The answer kept coming back, 'Around 25 percent.' "

Also, Packwood said a review of the witness lists from the tax hearings was "a turning point" leading to his conversion: "I thought, is there any group in America not on these lists? ... They all have a [tax] preference and they can't conceive how they can act without that preference."

Packwood said he decided the groups, from ballet companies to builders, should have a chance to try.

On April 24, he presented the committee with a plan that abolished all deductions and capped individual rates at 25 percent. But a day later, he called a press conference to disassociate himself from its specifics and to introduce as the proposal's author an unknown bureaucrat, David H. Brockway, chief of staff of the Joint Committee on Taxation.

Meanwhile, some members were enticed by the low rates. A bipartisan group of six senators met privately with Packwood each morning before the committee's closed-door sessions. From that core coalition, Packwood built unanimous support for a plan with few deductions and top rates of 27 percent for individuals and 33 percent for corporations.

Crucial to breaking the impasse, observers say, was Packwood's professed willingness to bargain his own interests. In the end, he gave up a break for home builders, whose industry is vital to Oregon's timber firms.

In the aftermath of the committee's action, some members implied that the initial round of indulging special interests was part of a grand strategy. But all sources interviewed agreed Packwood had no such plan.

"Packwood put out his first package and thought members would sign off because he had taken care of individuals' interests," a Republican aide said. "But he either didn't listen to them, or he misinterpreted. If he had given them 20 percent, they wanted more. There was a strong feeling that he had taken too much for himself at the outset."

In retrospect, Packwood's unpredictable course on tax revision was no surprise. He is a political maverick, supporting abortion rights, civil-rights issues and certain labor causes that his party and president reject. His outspokenness — most notably a 1982 condemnation of Reagan for alienating blacks, Jews, women and laborers — cost him the chairmanship of the National Republican Senatorial Committee a year later.

After the tax victory, many still withheld praise of his overall leadership, but praised him as "a miracle worker." And, as Packwood said, "If you don't believe in miracles, you're not a realist."

APPENDIX

Glossary of Congressional Terms

Act—The term for legislation once it has passed both houses of Congress and has been signed by the president or passed over his veto, thus becoming law. *(See below.)* Also used in parliamentary terminology for a bill that has been passed by one house and engrossed. *(See Engrossed Bill.)*

Adjournment Sine Die—Adjournment without definitely fixing a day for reconvening; literally "adjournment without a day." Usually used to connote the final adjournment of a session of Congress. A session can continue until noon, Jan. 3, of the following year, when, under the 20th Amendment to the Constitution, it automatically terminates. Both houses must agree to a concurrent resolution for either house to adjourn for more than three days.

Adjournment to a Day Certain—Adjournment under a motion or resolution that fixes the next time of meeting. Under the Constitution, neither house can adjourn for more than three days without the concurrence of the other. A session of Congress is not ended by adjournment to a day certain.

Amendment—A proposal of a member of Congress to alter the language, provisions or stipulations in a bill or in another amendment. An amendment usually is printed, debated and voted upon in the same manner as a bill.

Amendment in the Nature of a Substitute—Usually an amendment that seeks to replace the entire text of a bill. Passage of this type of amendment strikes out everything after the enacting clause and inserts a new version of the bill. An amendment in the nature of a substitute also can refer to an amendment that replaces a large portion of the text of a bill.

Appeal—A member's challenge of a ruling or decision made by the presiding officer of the chamber. In the Senate, the senator appeals to members of the chamber to override the decision. If carried by a majority vote, the appeal nullifies the chair's ruling. In the House, the decision of the Speaker traditionally has been final; seldom are there appeals to the members to reverse the Speaker's stand. To appeal a ruling is considered an attack on the Speaker.

Appropriations Bill—A bill that gives legal authority to spend or obligate money from the Treasury. The Constitution disallows money to be drawn from the Treasury "but in Consequence of Appropriations made by Law."

By congressional custom, an appropriations bill originates in the House, and it is not supposed to be considered by the full House or Senate until a related measure authorizing the funding is enacted; appropriations bills need not provide the full amount permissible under the authorization measures. Under the 1985 Gramm-Rudman-Hollings law, the House is supposed to pass by June 30 the last regular appropriations bill for the fiscal year starting the following Oct. 1. *(See also Authorization, Budget Process.)*

In addition to general appropriations bills, there are two specialized types. *(See Continuing Resolution, Supplemental Appropriations Bill.)*

Authorization—Basic, substantive legislation that establishes or continues the legal operation of a federal program or agency, either indefinitely or for a specific period of time, or which sanctions a particular type of obligation or expenditure. An authorization normally is a prerequisite for an appropriation or other kind of budget authority. Under the rules of both houses, the appropriation for a program or agency may not be considered until its authorization has been considered. An authorization also may limit the amount of budget authority to be provided or may authorize the appropriation of "such sums as may be necessary." *(See also Backdoor Spending.)*

Backdoor Spending—Budget authority provided in legislation outside the normal appropriations process. The most common forms of backdoor spending are borrowing authority, contract authority and entitlements. *(See below.)*

In some cases, such as interest on the public debt, a permanent appropriation is provided that becomes available without further action by Congress.

Bills—Most legislative proposals before Congress are in the form of bills and are designated by HR in the House of Representatives or S in the Senate, according to the house in which they originate, and by a number assigned in the order in which they are introduced during the two-year period of a congressional term. "Public bills" deal with general questions and become public laws if approved by Congress and signed by the president. "Private bills" deal with individual matters such as claims against the government, immigration and naturalization cases, land titles, etc., and become private laws if approved and signed. *(See also Concurrent Resolution, Joint Resolution, Resolution.)*

Bills Introduced—In both the House and Senate, any number of members may join in introducing a single bill or resolution. The first member listed is the sponsor of the bill, and all members' names following his are the bill's cosponsors.

Many bills are committee bills and are introduced under the name of the chairman of the committee or subcommittee. All appropriations bills fall into this category. A committee frequently holds hearings on a number of related bills and may agree to one of them or to an entirely new bill. *(See also Report, Clean Bill, By Request.)*

Bills Referred—When introduced, a bill is referred to the committee or committees that have jurisdiction over the subject with which the bill is concerned. Under the standing rules of the House and Senate, bills are referred by the Speaker in the House and by the presiding officer in the Senate. In practice, the House and Senate parliamentarians act for these officials and refer the vast majority of bills.

Borrowing Authority—Statutory authority that permits a federal agency to incur obligations and make payments for specified purposes with borrowed money.

Budget—The document sent to Congress by the president early each year estimating government revenue and expenditures for the ensuing fiscal year.

Budget Authority—Authority to enter into obligations that will result in immediate or future outlays involving federal funds. The basic forms of budget authority are appropriations, contract authority and borrowing authority. Budget authority may be classified by (1) the period of availability (one-year, multiple-year or without a time limitation), (2) the timing of congressional action (current or permanent), or (3) the manner of determining the amount available (definite or indefinite).

Budget Process—Congress in 1985 strengthened its 11-year-old budget process with the goal of balancing the federal budget by October 1990. The law, known as Gramm-Rudman-Hollings for its congressional sponsors, established annual maximum deficit targets and mandated across-the-board automatic cuts if the deficit goals were not achieved through regular budget and appropriations actions.

The 1985 law also established an accelerated timetable for presidential submission of budgets and for congressional approval of budget resolutions and reconciliation bills, two mechanisms created by the Congressional Budget and Impoundment Control Act of 1974. Budget resolutions, due by April 15 annually, set guidelines for congressional action on spending and tax measures; they are adopted by the House and Senate but are not signed by the president and do not have the force of law. Reconciliation bills, due by June 15, actually make changes in existing law to meet budget resolution goals. *(See Budget Reconciliation)*

The Supreme Court was expected to rule in mid-1986 on a constitutional challenge to the automatic budget-cutting procedure established by Gramm-Rudman-Hollings. Under that procedure, the Congressional Budget Office (CBO) and the Office of Management and Budget (OMB) must separately calculate likely deficits for an upcoming fiscal year and the across-the-board cuts that would be needed to meet the deficit target fixed by the statute. The General Accounting Office (GAO) would review, and could revise, the CBO-OMB numbers. GAO then would submit the final figures to the president, who must issue a "sequester" order making the cuts. Should this procedure be invalidated by the courts, the law provided that the cuts would take effect only if approved by both houses of Congress and the president.

Budget Reconciliation—The 1974 budget act provides for a "reconciliation" procedure for bringing existing tax and spending laws into conformity with the congressional budget resolutions. Under the procedure, Congress instructs designated legislative committees to approve measures adjusting revenues and expenditures by a certain amount. The committees have a deadline by which they must report the legislation, but they have the discretion of deciding what changes are to be made. The recommendations of the various committees are consolidated without change by the Budget committees into an omnibus reconciliation bill, which then must be considered and approved by both houses of Congress.

By Request—A phrase used when a senator or representative introduces a bill at the request of an executive agency or private organization but does not necessarily endorse the legislation.

Calendar—An agenda or list of business awaiting possible action by each chamber. The House uses five legislative calendars. *(See Consent, Discharge, House, Private and Union Calendar.)*

In the Senate, all legislative matters reported from committee go on one calendar. They are listed there in the order in which committees report them or the Senate places them on the calendar, but may be called up out of order by the majority leader, either by obtaining unanimous consent of the Senate or by a motion to call up a bill. The Senate also uses one non-legislative calendar; this is used for treaties and nominations. *(See Executive Calendar.)*

Calendar Wednesday—In the House, committees, on Wednesdays, may be called in the order in which they appear in Rule X of the House, for the purpose of bringing up any of their bills from either the House or the Union Calendar, except bills that are privileged. General debate is limited to two hours. Bills called up from the Union Calendar are considered in Committee of the Whole. Calendar Wednesday is not observed during the last two weeks of a session and may be dispensed with at other times by a two-thirds vote. This procedure is rarely used and routinely is dispensed with by unanimous consent.

Call of the Calendar—Senate bills that are not brought up for debate by a motion, unanimous consent or a unanimous consent agreement are brought before the Senate for action when the calendar listing them is "called." Bills must be called in the order listed. Measures considered by this method usually are non-controversial, and debate is limited to a total of five minutes for each senator on the bill and any amendments proposed to it.

Chamber—The meeting place for the membership of either the House or the Senate; also the membership of the House or Senate meeting as such.

Clean Bill—Frequently after a committee has finished a major revision of a bill, one of the committee members, usually the chairman, will assemble the changes and what is left of the original bill into a new measure and introduce it as a "clean bill." The revised measure, which is given a new number, then is referred back to the committee, which reports it to the floor for consideration. This often is a timesaver, as committee-recommended changes in a clean bill do not have to be considered and voted on by the chamber. Reporting a clean bill also protects committee amendments that might be subject to points of order concerning germaneness.

Clerk of the House—Chief administrative officer of the House of Representatives, with duties corresponding to those of the secretary of the Senate. *(See also Secretary of the Senate.)*

Cloture—The process by which a filibuster can be ended in the Senate other than by unanimous consent. A motion for cloture can apply to any measure before the Senate, including a proposal to change the chamber's rules. A cloture motion requires the signatures of 16 senators to be introduced, and to end a filibuster the cloture motion must obtain the votes of three-fifths of the entire Senate membership (60 if there are no vacancies), except that to end a filibuster against a proposal to amend the standing rules of the Senate a two-thirds vote of senators present and voting is required. The cloture request is put to a roll-call vote one hour after the Senate meets on the second day following introduction of the motion. If approved, cloture limits each senator to one hour of debate. The bill or amendment in question comes to a final vote after 100 hours of consideration (including debate time and the time it takes to conduct roll calls, quorum calls and other procedural motions). *(See Filibuster.)*

Committee—A division of the House or Senate that prepares legislation for action by the parent chamber or makes investigations as directed by the parent chamber. There are several types of committees. *(See Standing and Select or Special Committees.)* Most standing committees are divided into subcommittees, which study legislation, hold hearings and report bills, with or without amendments, to the full committee. Only the full committee can report legislation for action by the House or Senate.

Committee of the Whole—The working title of what is formally "The Committee of the Whole House (of Representatives) on the State of the Union." The membership is comprised of all House members sitting as a committee. Any 100 members who are present on the floor of the chamber to consider legislation comprise a quorum of the committee. Any legislation, however, must first have passed through the regular legislative or Appropriations committee and have been placed on the calendar.

Technically, the Committee of the Whole considers only bills directly or indirectly appropriating money, authorizing appropriations or involving taxes or charges on the public. Because the Committee of the Whole need number only 100 representatives, a quorum is more readily attained, and legislative business is expedited. Before 1971, members' positions were not individually recorded on votes taken in Committee of the Whole. *(See Teller Vote.)*

When the full House resolves itself into the Committee of the Whole, it supplants the Speaker with a "chairman." A measure is debated and amendments may be proposed, with votes on amendments as needed. *(See Five-Minute Rule.)* When the committee completes its work on the measure, it dissolves itself by "rising." The Speaker returns, and the chairman of the Committee of the Whole reports to the House that the committee's work has been completed. At this time members may demand a roll-call vote on any amendment *adopted* in the Committee of the Whole. The final vote is on passage of the legislation.

Committee Veto—A requirement added to a few statutes directing that certain policy directives by an executive department or agency be reviewed by certain congressional committees before they are implemented. Under common practice, the government department or agency and the committees involved are expected to reach a consensus before the directives are carried out. *(See also Legislative Veto.)*

Concurrent Resolution—A concurrent resolution, designated H Con Res or S Con Res, must be adopted by both houses, but it is not sent to the president for his signature and therefore does not have the force of law. A concurrent resolution, for example, is used to fix the time for adjournment of a Congress. It also is used as the vehicle for expressing the sense of Congress on various foreign policy and domestic issues, and it serves as the vehicle for coordinated decisions on the federal budget under the 1974 Congressional Budget and Impoundment Control Act. *(See also Bills, Joint Resolution, Resolution.)*

Conference—A meeting between the representatives of the House and the Senate to reconcile differences between the two houses on provisions of a bill passed by both chambers. Members of the conference committee are appointed by the Speaker and the presiding officer of the Senate and are called "managers" for their respective chambers. A majority of the managers for each house must reach agreement on the provisions of the bill (often a compromise between the versions of the two chambers) before it can be considered by either chamber in the form of a "conference report." When the conference report goes to the floor, it cannot be amended, and, if it is not approved by both chambers, the bill may go back to conference under certain situations, or a new conference must be convened. Many rules and informal practices govern the conduct of conference committees.

Bills that are passed by both houses with only minor differences need not be sent to conference. Either chamber may "concur" in the other's amendments, completing action on the legislation. Sometimes leaders of the committees of jurisdiction work out an informal compromise instead of having a formal conference. *(See Custody of the Papers.)*

Confirmations—*(See Nominations.)*

Congressional Record—The daily, printed account of proceedings in both the House and Senate chambers, showing substantially verbatim debate, statements and a record of floor action. Highlights of legislative and committee action are embodied in a Daily Digest section of the Record, and members are entitled to have their extraneous remarks printed in an appendix known as "Extension of Remarks." Members may edit and revise remarks made on the floor during debate, and quotations from debate reported by the press are not always found in the Record.

The Record provides a way to distinguish remarks spoken on the floor of the House and Senate from undelivered speeches. In the Senate, all speeches, articles and other matter that members insert in the Record without actually reading them on the floor are set off by large black dots, or bullets. However, a loophole allows a member to avoid the bulleting if he delivers any portion of the speech in person. In the House, undelivered speeches and other material are printed in a distinctive typeface.

Congressional Terms of Office—Normally begin on Jan. 3 of the year following a general election and are two years for representatives and six years for senators. Representatives elected in special elections are sworn in for the remainder of a term. A person may be appointed to fill a Senate vacancy and serve until a successor is elected; the successor serves until the end of the term applying to the vacant seat.

Consent Calendar—Members of the House may place on this calendar most bills on the Union or House Calendar that are considered to be non-controversial. Bills on the Consent Calendar normally are called on the first and third Mondays of each month. On the first occasion that a bill is called in this manner, consideration may be blocked by the objection of any member. The second time, if there are three objections, the bill is stricken from the Consent Calendar. If fewer than three members object, the bill is given immediate consideration.

A bill on the Consent Calendar may be postponed in

another way. A member may ask that the measure be passed over "without prejudice." In that case, no objection is recorded against the bill, and its status on the Consent Calendar remains unchanged. A bill stricken from the Consent Calendar remains on the Union or House Calendar.

Cosponsor—*(See Bills Introduced.)*

Continuing Resolution—A joint resolution drafted by Congress "continuing appropriations" for specific ongoing activities of a government department or departments when a fiscal year begins and Congress has not yet enacted all of the regular appropriations bills for that year. The continuing resolution usually specifies a maximum rate at which the agency may incur obligations. This usually is based on the rate for the previous year, the president's budget request or an appropriation bill for that year passed by either or both houses of Congress, but not cleared.

Contract Authority—Budget authority contained in an authorization bill that permits the federal government to enter into contracts or other obligations for future payments from funds not yet appropriated by Congress. The assumption is that funds will be available for payment in a subsequent appropriation act.

Controllable Budget Items—In federal budgeting this refers to programs for which the budget authority or outlays during a fiscal year can be controlled without changing existing, substantive law. The concept "relatively uncontrollable under current law" includes outlays for open-ended programs and fixed costs such as interest on the public debt, Social Security benefits, veterans' benefits and outlays to liquidate prior-year obligations.

Correcting Recorded Votes—Rules prohibit members from changing their votes after the result has been announced. But, occasionally hours, days or months after a vote has been taken, a member may announce that he was "incorrectly recorded." In the Senate, a request to change one's vote almost always receives unanimous consent. In the House, members are prohibited from changing their votes if tallied by the electronic voting system installed in 1973. If taken by roll call, it is permissible if consent is granted.

Current Services Estimates—Estimated budget authority and outlays for federal programs and operations for the forthcoming fiscal year based on continuation of existing levels of service without policy changes. These estimates of budget authority and outlays, accompanied by the underlying economic and policy assumptions upon which they are based, are transmitted by the president to Congress when the budget is submitted.

Custody of the Papers—To reconcile differences between the House and Senate versions of a bill, a conference may be arranged. The chamber with "custody of the papers" — the engrossed bill, engrossed amendments, messages of transmittal — is the only body empowered to request the conference. By custom, the chamber that asks for a conference is the last to act on the conference report once agreement has been reached on the bill by the conferees. Custody of the papers sometimes is manipulated to ensure that a particular chamber acts either first or last on the conference report.

Deferral—Executive branch action to defer, or delay, the spending of appropriated money. The 1974 Congressional Budget and Impoundment Control Act requires a special message from the president to Congress reporting a proposed deferral of spending. Deferrals may not extend beyond the end of the fiscal year in which the message is transmitted. A federal district court in 1986 struck down the president's authority to defer spending for policy reasons; the Justice Department planned to appeal. *(See also Rescission Bill.)*

Dilatory Motion—A motion made for the purpose of killing time and preventing action on a bill or amendment. House rules outlaw dilatory motions, but enforcement is largely within the discretion of the Speaker or chairman of the Committee of the Whole. The Senate does not have a rule banning dilatory motions, except under cloture.

Discharge a Committee—Occasionally, attempts are made to relieve a committee from jurisdiction over a measure before it. This is attempted more often in the House than in the Senate, and the procedure rarely is successful.

In the House, if a committee does not report a bill within 30 days after the measure is referred to it, any member may file a discharge motion. Once offered, the motion is treated as a petition needing the signatures of 218 members (a majority of the House). After the required signatures have been obtained, there is a delay of seven days. Thereafter, on the second and fourth Mondays of each month, except during the last six days of a session, any member who has signed the petition must be recognized, if he so desires, to move that the committee be discharged. Debate on the motion to discharge is limited to 20 minutes, and, if the motion is carried, consideration of the bill becomes a matter of high privilege.

If a resolution to consider a bill is held up in the Rules Committee for more than seven legislative days, any member may enter a motion to discharge the committee. The motion is handled like any other discharge petition in the House.

Occasionally, to expedite non-controversial legislative business, a committee is discharged by unanimous consent of the House, and a petition is not required. *(Senate procedure, see Discharge Resolution.)*

Discharge Calendar—The House calendar to which motions to discharge committees are referred when they have the required number of signatures (218) and are awaiting floor action.

Discharge Petition—*(See Discharge a Committee.)*

Discharge Resolution—In the Senate, a special motion that any senator may introduce to relieve a committee from consideration of a bill before it. The resolution can be called up for Senate approval or disapproval in the same manner as any other Senate business. *(House procedure, see Discharge a Committee.)*

Division of a Question for Voting—A practice that is more common in the Senate but also used in the House, a member may demand a division of an amendment or a motion for purposes of voting. Where an amendment or motion can be divided, the indiyidual parts are voted on separately when a member demands a division. This procedure occurs most often during the consideration of conference reports.

Division Vote—*(See Standing Vote.)*

Enacting Clause—Key phrase in bills beginning, "Be it enacted by the Senate and House of Representatives. . . ." A successful motion to strike it from legislation kills the measure.

Engrossed Bill—The final copy of a bill as passed by one chamber, with the text as amended by floor action and certified by the clerk of the House or the secretary of the Senate.

Enrolled Bill—The final copy of a bill that has been passed in identical form by both chambers. It is certified by an officer of the house of origin (clerk of the House or secretary of the Senate) and then sent on for the signatures of the House Speaker, the Senate president pro tempore and the president of the United States. An enrolled bill is printed on parchment.

Entitlement Program—A federal program that guarantees a certain level of benefits to persons or other entities who meet requirements set by law, such as Social Security or unemployment benefits. It thus leaves no discretion with Congress on how much money to appropriate.

Executive Calendar—This is a non-legislative calendar in the Senate on which presidential documents such as treaties and nominations are listed.

Executive Document—A document, usually a treaty, sent to the Senate by the president for consideration or approval. Executive documents are identified for each session of Congress as Executive A, 97th Congress, 1st Session; Executive B, etc. They are referred to committee in the same manner as other measures. Unlike legislative documents, however, treaties do not die at the end of a Congress but remain "live" proposals until acted on by the Senate or withdrawn by the president.

Executive Session—A meeting of a Senate or House committee (or occasionally of either chamber) that only its members may attend. Witnesses regularly appear at committee meetings in executive session — for example, Defense Department officials during presentations of classified defense information. Other members of Congress may be invited, but the public and press are not allowed to attend.

Expenditures—The actual spending of money as distinguished from the appropriation of funds. Expenditures are made by the disbursing officers of the administration; appropriations are made only by Congress. The two are rarely identical in any fiscal year. In addition to some current budget authority, expenditures may represent budget authority made available one, two or more years earlier.

Filibuster—A time-delaying tactic associated with the Senate and used by a minority in an effort to prevent a vote on a bill or amendment that probably would pass if voted upon directly. The most common method is to take advantage of the Senate's rules permitting unlimited debate, but other forms of parliamentary maneuvering may be used. The stricter rules used by the House make filibusters more difficult, but delaying tactics are employed occasionally through various procedural devices allowed by House rules. *(Senate filibusters, see Cloture.)*

Fiscal Year—Financial operations of the government are carried out in a 12-month fiscal year, beginning on Oct. 1 and ending on Sept. 30. The fiscal year carries the date of the calendar year in which it ends. (From fiscal year 1844 to fiscal year 1976, the fiscal year began July 1 and ended the following June 30.)

Five-Minute Rule—A debate-limiting rule of the House that is invoked when the House sits as the Committee of the Whole. Under the rule, a member offering an amendment is allowed to speak five minutes in its favor, and an opponent of the amendment is allowed to speak five minutes in opposition. Debate is then closed. In practice, amendments regularly are debated more than 10 minutes, with members gaining the floor by offering pro forma amendments or obtaining unanimous consent to speak longer than five minutes. *(See Strike Out the Last Word.)*

Floor Manager—A member who has the task of steering legislation through floor debate and the amendment process to a final vote in the House or the Senate. Floor managers are usually chairmen or ranking members of the committee that reported the bill. Managers are responsible for apportioning the debate time granted supporters of the bill. The ranking minority member of the committee normally apportions time for the minority party's participation in the debate.

Frank—A member's facsimile signature, which is used on envelopes in lieu of stamps, for the member's official outgoing mail. The "franking privilege" is the right to send mail postage-free.

Germane—Pertaining to the subject matter of the measure at hand. All House amendments must be germane to the bill being considered. The Senate requires that amendments be germane when they are proposed to general appropriation bills, bills being considered once cloture has been adopted, or, frequently, when proceeding under a unanimous consent agreement placing a time limit on consideration of a bill. The 1974 budget act also requires that amendments to concurrent budget resolutions be germane. In the House, floor debate must be germane, and the first three hours of debate each day in the Senate must be germane to the pending business.

Grandfather Clause—A provision exempting persons or other entities already engaged in an activity from rules or legislation affecting that activity. Grandfather clauses sometimes are added to legislation in order to avoid antagonizing groups with established interests in the activities affected.

Grants-in-Aid—Payments by the federal government to states, local governments or individuals in support of specified programs, services or activities.

Guaranteed Loans—Loans to third parties for which the federal government in the event of default guarantees, in whole or in part, the repayment of principal or interest to a lender or holder of a security.

Hearings—Committee sessions for taking testimony from witnesses. At hearings on legislation, witnesses usually include specialists, government officials and spokesmen for persons or entities affected by the bill or bills under study. Hearings related to special investigations bring forth a variety of witnesses. Committees sometimes use their subpoena power to summon reluctant witnesses. The public and press may attend open hearings, but are barred from closed, or "executive," hearings. The vast majority of hearings are open to the public. *(See Executive Session.)*

Hold-Harmless Clause—A provision added to legislation to ensure that recipients of federal funds do not receive less in a future year than they did in the current year if a new formula for allocating funds authorized in the legislation would result in a reduction to the recipients. This clause has been used most frequently to soften the impact of sudden reductions in federal grants.

Hopper—Box on House clerk's desk where members deposit bills and resolutions to introduce them. *(See also Bills Introduced.)*

Hour Rule—A provision in the rules of the House that permits one hour of debate time for each member on amendments debated in the House of Representatives sitting as the House. Therefore, the House normally amends bills while sitting as the Committee of the Whole, where the five-minute rule on amendments operates. *(See Committee of the Whole, Five-Minute Rule.)*

House—The House of Representatives, as distinct from the Senate, although each body is a "house" of Congress.

House as in Committee of the Whole—A procedure that can be used to expedite consideration of certain measures such as continuing resolutions and, when there is debate, private bills. The procedure only can be invoked with the unanimous consent of the House or a rule from the Rules Committee and has procedural elements of both the House sitting as the House of Representatives, such as the Speaker presiding and the previous question motion being in order, and the House sitting as the Committee of the Whole, such as the five-minute rule pertaining.

House Calendar—A listing for action by the House of public bills that do not directly or indirectly appropriate money or raise revenue.

Immunity—The constitutional privilege of members of Congress to make verbal statements on the floor and in committee for which they cannot be sued or arrested for slander or libel. Also, freedom from arrest while traveling to or from sessions of Congress or on official business. Members in this status may be arrested only for treason, felonies or a breach of the peace, as defined by congressional manuals.

Impoundments —Any action taken by the executive branch that delays or precludes the obligation or expenditure of budget authority previously approved by Congress. *(See also Deferral, Rescission Bill.)*

Joint Committee—A committee composed of a specified number of members of both the House and Senate. A joint committee may be investigative or research-oriented, an example of the latter being the Joint Economic Committee. Others have housekeeping duties such as the joint committees on Printing and on the Library of Congress.

Joint Resolution—A joint resolution, designated H J Res or S J Res, requires the approval of both houses and the signature of the president, just as a bill does, and has the force of law if approved. There is no practical difference between a bill and a joint resolution. A joint resolution generally is used to deal with a limited matter such as a single appropriation.

Joint resolutions also are used to propose amendments to the Constitution in Congress. They do not require a presidential signature, but become a part of the Constitution when three-fourths of the states have ratified them.

Journal—The official record of the proceedings of the House and Senate. The *Journal* records the actions taken in each chamber, but, unlike the *Congressional Record*, it does not include the substantially verbatim report of speeches, debates, etc.

Law—An act of Congress that has been signed by the president or passed over his veto by Congress. Public bills, when signed, become public laws, and are cited by the letters PL and a hyphenated number. The two digits before the number correspond to the Congress, and the one or more digits after the hyphen refer to the numerical sequence in which the bills were signed by the president during that Congress. Private bills, when signed, become private laws. *(See also Slip Laws, Statutes at Large, U.S. Code.)*

Legislative Day—The "day" extending from the time either house meets after an adjournment until the time it next adjourns. Because the House normally adjourns from day to day, legislative days and calendar days usually coincide. But in the Senate, a legislative day may, and frequently does, extend over several calendar days. *(See Recess.)*

Legislative Veto—A procedure, no longer allowed, permitting either the House or Senate, or both chambers, to review proposed executive branch regulations or actions and to block or modify those with which they disagreed.

The specifics of the procedure varied, but Congress generally provided for a legislative veto by including in a bill a provision that administrative rules or action taken to implement the law were to go into effect at the end of a designated period of time unless blocked by either or both houses of Congress. Another version of the veto provided for congressional reconsideration and rejection of regulations already in effect.

The Supreme Court June 23, 1983, struck down the legislative veto as an unconstitutional violation of the lawmaking procedure provided in the Constitution.

Lobby—A group seeking to influence the passage or defeat of legislation. Originally the term referred to persons frequenting the lobbies or corridors of legislative chambers in order to speak to lawmakers.

The definition of a lobby and the activity of lobbying is a matter of differing interpretation. By some definitions, lobbying is limited to direct attempts to influence lawmakers through personal interviews and persuasion. Under other definitions, lobbying includes attempts at indirect, or "grass-roots," influence, such as persuading members of a group to write or visit their district's representative and state's senators or attempting to create a climate of opinion favorable to a desired legislative goal.

The right to attempt to influence legislation is based on the First Amendment to the Constitution, which says Congress shall make no law abridging the right of the people "to petition the government for a redress of grievances."

Majority Leader—The majority leader is elected by his party colleagues. In the Senate, in consultation with the minority leader and his colleagues, the majority leader directs the legislative schedule for the chamber. He also is his party's spokesman and chief strategist. In the House, the majority leader is second to the Speaker in the majority party's leadership and serves as his party's legislative strategist.

Majority Whip—In effect, the assistant majority leader, in either the House or Senate. His job is to help marshal majority forces in support of party strategy and legislation.

Manual—The official handbook in each house prescribing in detail its organization, procedures and operations.

Marking Up a Bill—Going through the contents of a piece of legislation in committee or subcommittee, considering its provisions in large and small portions, acting on amendments to provisions and proposed revisions to the language, inserting new sections and phraseology, etc. If the bill is extensively amended, the committee's version may be introduced as a separate bill, with a new number, before being considered by the full House or Senate. *(See Clean Bill.)*

Minority Leader—Floor leader for the minority party in each chamber. *(See also Majority Leader.)*

Minority Whip—Performs duties of whip for the minority party. *(See also Majority Whip.)*

Morning Hour—The time set aside at the beginning of each legislative day for the consideration of regular, routine business. The "hour" is of indefinite duration in the House, where it is rarely used.

In the Senate it is the first two hours of a session following an adjournment, as distinguished from a recess. The morning hour can be terminated earlier if the morning business has been completed.

Business includes such matters as messages from the president, communications from the heads of departments, messages from the House, the presentation of petitions, reports of standing and select committees and the introduction of bills and resolutions.

During the first hour of the morning hour in the Senate, no motion to proceed to the consideration of any bill on the calendar is in order except by unanimous consent. During the second hour, motions can be made but must be decided without debate. Senate committees may meet while the Senate conducts morning hour.

Motion—In the House or Senate chamber, a request by a member to institute any one of a wide array of parliamentary actions. He "moves" for a certain procedure, the consideration of a measure, etc. The precedence of motions, and whether they are debatable, is set forth in the House and Senate manuals. *(See some specific motions above and below.)*

Nominations—Presidential appointments to office subject to Senate confirmation. Although most nominations win quick Senate approval, some are controversial and become the topic of hearings and debate. Sometimes senators object to appointees for patronage reasons — for example, when a nomination to a local federal job is made without consulting the senators of the state concerned. In some situations a senator may object that the nominee is "personally obnoxious" to him. Usually other senators join in blocking such appointments out of courtesy to their colleagues. *(See Senatorial Courtesy.)*

One-Minute Speeches—Addresses by House members at the beginning of a legislative day. The speeches may cover any subject but are limited to one minute's duration.

Override a Veto—If the president disapproves a bill and sends it back to Congress with his objections, Congress may try to override his veto and enact the bill into law. Neither house is required to attempt to override a veto. The override of a veto requires a recorded vote with a two-thirds majority in each chamber. The question put to each house is: "Shall the bill pass, the objections of the president to the contrary notwithstanding?" *(See also Pocket Veto, Veto.)*

Oversight Committee—A congressional committee, or designated subcommittee of a committee, that is charged with general oversight of one or more federal agencies' programs and activities. Usually, the oversight panel for a particular agency also is the authorizing committee for that agency's programs and operations.

Pair—An voluntary arrangement between two lawmakers, usually on opposite sides of an issue. If passage of the measure requires a two-thirds majority vote, a pair would require two members favoring the action to one opposed to it. Pairs can take one of three forms — specific, general and live. The names of lawmakers pairing on a given vote and their stands, if known, are published in the *Congressional Record.*

The specific pair applies to one or more votes on the same subject. On special pairs, lawmakers usually specify how they would have voted.

A general pair in the Senate, now rarely used, applies to all votes on which the members pairing are on opposite sides. It usually does not specify the positions of the senators pairing. In a general pair in the House, no agreement is involved. A representative expecting to be absent may notify the House clerk he wishes to make a "general" pair. His name then is paired arbitrarily with that of another member desiring a pair, and the list is published in the *Congressional Record.* He may or may not be paired with a member taking the opposite position. General pairs in the House give no indication of how a member would have voted.

A live pair involves two members, one present for the vote, the other absent. The member present casts his vote and then withdraws it and votes "present." He then announces that he has a live pair with a colleague, identifying how each would have voted on the question. A live pair subtracts the vote of the member in attendance from the final vote tabulation.

Petition—A request or plea sent to one or both chambers from an organization or private citizens' group asking support of particular legislation or favorable consideration of a matter not yet receiving congressional attention. Petitions are referred to appropriate committees.

Pocket Veto—The act of the president in withholding his approval of a bill after Congress has adjourned. When Congress is in session, a bill becomes law without the president's signature if he does not act upon it within 10 days, excluding Sundays, from the time he gets it. But if Congress adjourns sine die within that 10-day period, the bill will die even if the president does not formally veto it.

The Supreme Court in 1986 agreed to decide whether the president can pocket veto a bill during recesses and between sessions of the same Congress or only between Congresses, as a lower court had ruled. *(See also Veto.)*

Point of Order—An objection raised by a member that the chamber is departing from rules governing its conduct of business. The objector cites the rule violated, the chair sustaining his objection if correctly made. Order is restored by the chair's suspending proceedings of the chamber until it conforms to the prescribed "order of business."

President of the Senate—Under the Constitution, the vice president of the United States presides over the Senate. In his absence, the president pro tempore, or a senator designated by the president pro tempore, presides over the chamber.

President Pro Tempore—The chief officer of the Senate in the absence of the vice president; literally, but loosely, the president for a time. The president pro tempore is elected by his fellow senators, and the recent practice has been to elect the senator of the majority party with the longest period of continuous service.

Previous Question—A motion for the previous question, when carried, has the effect of cutting off all debate, preventing the offering of further amendments, and forcing a vote on the pending matter. In the House, the previous question is not permitted in the Committee of the Whole. The motion for the previous question is a debate-limiting device and is not in order in the Senate.

Printed Amendment—A House rule guarantees five minutes of floor debate in support and five minutes in opposition, and no other debate time, on amendments printed in the *Congressional Record* at least one day prior to the amendment's consideration in the Committee of the Whole.

In the Senate, while amendments may be submitted for printing, they have no parliamentary standing or status. An amendment submitted for printing in the Senate, however, may be called up by any senator.

Private Calendar—In the House, private bills dealing with individual matters such as claims against the government, immigration, land titles, etc., are put on this calendar. The private calendar must be called on the first Tuesday of each month, and the Speaker may call it on the third Tuesday of each month as well.

When a private bill is before the chamber, two members may block its consideration, which recommits the bill to committee. Backers of a recommitted private bill have recourse. The measure can be put into an "omnibus claims bill" — several private bills rolled into one. As with any bill, no part of an omnibus claims bill may be deleted without a vote. When the private bill goes back to the House floor in this form, it can be deleted from the omnibus bill only by majority vote.

Privilege—Privilege relates to the rights of members of Congress and to the relative priority of the motions and actions they may make in their respective chambers. The two are distinct. "Privileged questions" deal with legislative business. "Questions of privilege" concern legislators themselves.

Privileged Questions—The order in which bills, motions and other legislative measures are considered by Congress is governed by strict priorities. A motion to table, for instance, is more privileged than a motion to recommit. Thus, a motion to recommit can be superseded by a motion to table, and a vote would be forced on the latter motion only. A motion to adjourn, however, takes precedence over a tabling motion and thus is considered of the "highest privilege." *(See also Questions of Privilege.)*

Pro Forma Amendment—*(See Strike Out the Last Word.)*

Public Laws—*(See Law.)*

Questions of Privilege—These are matters affecting members of Congress individually or collectively. Matters affecting the rights, safety, dignity and integrity of proceedings of the House or Senate as a whole are questions of privilege in both chambers.

Questions involving individual members are called questions of "personal privilege." A member rising to ask a question of personal privilege is given precedence over almost all other proceedings. An annotation in the House rules points out that the privilege rests primarily on the Constitution, which gives him a conditional immunity from arrest and an unconditional freedom to speak in the House. *(See also Privileged Questions.)*

Quorum—The number of members whose presence is necessary for the transaction of business. In the Senate and House, it is a majority of the membership. A quorum is 100 in the Committee of the Whole House. If a point of order is made that a quorum is not present, the only business that is in order is either a motion to adjourn or a motion to direct the sergeant-at-arms to request the attendance of absentees.

Readings of Bills—Traditional parliamentary procedure required bills to be read three times before they were passed. This custom is of little modern significance. Normally a bill is considered to have its first reading when it is introduced and printed, by title, in the *Congressional Record*. In the House, its second reading comes when floor consideration begins. (This is the most likely point at which there is an actual reading of the bill, if there is any.) The second reading in the Senate is supposed to occur on the legislative day after the measure is introduced, but before it is referred to committee. The third reading (again, usually by title) takes place when floor action has been completed on amendments.

Recess—Distinguished from adjournment *(see above)* in that a recess does not end a legislative day and therefore does not interrupt unfinished business. The rules in each house set forth certain matters to be taken up and disposed of at the beginning of each legislative day. The House usually adjourns from day to day. The Senate often recesses, thus meeting on the same legislative day for several calendar days or even weeks at a time.

Recognition—The power of recognition of a member is lodged in the Speaker of the House and the presiding officer of the Senate. The presiding officer names the member who will speak first when two or more members simultaneously request recognition.

Recommit to Committee—A motion, made on the floor after a bill has been debated, to return it to the committee that reported it. If approved, recommittal usually is considered a death blow to the bill. In the House, a motion to recommit can be made only by a member opposed to the bill, and, in recognizing a member to make the motion, the Speaker gives preference to members of the minority party over majority party members.

A motion to recommit may include instructions to the committee to report the bill again with specific amendments or by a certain date. Or, the instructions may direct that a particular study be made, with no definite deadline given for further action.

If the recommittal motion includes instructions to "report the bill back forthwith" and the motion is adopted, floor action on the bill continues; the committee does not actually reconsider the legislation.

Reconciliation—*(See Budget Reconciliation.)*

Reconsider a Vote—A motion to reconsider the vote by which an action was taken has, until it is disposed of, the effect of putting the action in abeyance. In the Senate, the motion can be made only by a member who voted on the prevailing side of the original question or by a member who did not vote at all. In the House, it can be made only by a member on the prevailing side.

A common practice in the Senate after close votes on an issue is a motion to reconsider, followed by a motion to table the motion to reconsider. On this motion to table, senators vote as they voted on the original question, which allows the motion to table to prevail, assuming there are no switches. The matter then is finally closed and further motions to reconsider are not entertained. In the House, as a routine precaution, a motion to reconsider usually is made every time a measure is passed. Such a motion almost always is tabled immediately, thus shutting off the possibility of future reconsideration, except by unanimous consent.

Motions to reconsider must be entered in the Senate within the next two days of actual session after the original vote has been taken. In the House they must be entered either on the same day or on the next succeeding day the House is in session.

Recorded Vote—A vote upon which each member's stand is individually made known. In the Senate, this is accomplished through a roll call of the entire membership, to which each senator on the floor must answer "yea," "nay" or, if he does not wish to vote, "present." Since January 1973, the House has used an electronic voting system for recorded votes, including yea-and-nay votes formerly taken by roll calls.

When not required by the Constitution, a recorded vote can be obtained on questions in the House on the demand of one-fifth (44 members) of a quorum or one-fourth (25) of a quorum in the Committee of the Whole. *(See Yeas and Nays.)*

Report—Both a verb and a noun as a congressional term. A committee that has been examining a bill referred to it by the parent chamber "reports" its findings and recommendations to the chamber when it completes consideration and returns the measure. The process is called "reporting" a bill.

A "report" is the document setting forth the committee's explanation of its action. Senate and House reports are numbered separately and are designated S Rept or H Rept. When a committee report is not unanimous, the dissenting committee members may file a statement of their views, called minority views and referred to as a minority report. Members in disagreement with some provisions of a bill may file additional or supplementary views. Sometimes a bill is reported without a committee recommendation.

Adverse reports occasionally are submitted by legislative committees. However, when a committee is opposed to a bill, it usually fails to report the bill at all. Some laws require that committee reports — favorable or adverse — be made.

Rescission Bill—A bill rescinding or canceling budget authority previously made available by Congress. The president may request a rescission to reduce spending or because the budget authority no longer is needed. Under the 1974 budget act, however, unless Congress approves a rescission bill within 45 days of continuous session after receipt of the proposal, the funds must be made available for obligation. *(See also Deferral.)*

Resolution—A "simple" resolution, designated H Res or S Res, deals with matters entirely within the prerogatives of one house or the other. It requires neither passage by the other chamber nor approval by the president, and it does not have the force of law. Most resolutions deal with the rules or procedures of one house. They also are used to express the sentiments of a single house such as condolences to the family of a deceased member or to comment on foreign policy or executive business. A simple resolution is the vehicle for a "rule" from the House Rules Committee. *(See also Concurrent and Joint Resolutions, Rules.)*

Rider—An amendment, usually not germane, that its sponsor hopes to get through more easily by including it in other legislation. Riders become law if the bills embodying them are enacted. Amendments providing legislative directives in appropriations bills are outstanding examples of riders, though technically legislation is banned from appropriations bills.

The House, unlike the Senate, has a strict germaneness rule; thus, riders usually are Senate devices to get legislation enacted quickly or to bypass lengthy House consideration and, possibly, opposition.

Rules—The term has two specific congressional meanings. A rule may be a standing order governing the conduct of House or Senate business and listed among the permanent rules of either chamber. The rules deal with duties of officers, the order of business, admission to the floor, parliamentary procedures on handling amendments and voting, jurisdictions of committees, etc.

In the House, a rule also may be a resolution reported by its Rules Committee to govern the handling of a particular bill on the floor. The committee may report a "rule," also called a "special order," in the form of a simple resolution. If the resolution is adopted by the House, the temporary rule becomes as valid as any standing rule and lapses only after action has been completed on the measure to which it pertains. A rule sets the time limit on general debate. It also may waive points of order against provisions of the bill in question such as non-germane language or against certain amendments intended to be proposed to the bill from the floor. It may even forbid all amendments or all amendments except those proposed by the legislative committee that handled the bill. In this instance, it is known as a "closed" or "gag" rule as opposed to an "open" rule, which puts no limitation on floor amendments, thus leaving the bill completely open to alteration by the adoption of germane amendments.

Secretary of the Senate—Chief administrative officer of the Senate, responsible for overseeing the duties of Senate employees, educating Senate pages, administering oaths, handling the registration of lobbyists, and handling other tasks necessary for the continuing operation of the Senate. *(See also Clerk of the House.)*

Select or Special Committee—A committee set up for a special purpose and, usually, for a limited time by resolution of either the House or Senate. Most special committees are investigative and lack legislative authority — legislation is not referred to them and they cannot report bills to their parent chamber. *(See also Standing Committees.)*

Senatorial Courtesy—Sometimes referred to as "the courtesy of the Senate," it is a general practice — with no written rule — applied to consideration of executive nominations. Generally, it means that nominations from a state are not to be confirmed unless they have been approved by the senators of the president's party of that state, with other senators following their colleagues' lead in the attitude they take toward consideration of such nominations. *(See Nominations.)*

Sequester Order. *(See Budget Process.)*

Sine Die—*(See Adjournment Sine Die.)*

Slip Laws—The first official publication of a bill that has been enacted and signed into law. Each is published separately in unbound single-sheet or pamphlet form. *(See also Law, Statutes at Large, U.S. Code.)*

Speaker—The presiding officer of the House of Representatives, selected by the caucus of the party to which he belongs and formally elected by the whole House.

Special Session—A session of Congress after it has adjourned sine die, completing its regular session. Special sessions are convened by the president.

Spending Authority—The 1974 budget act defines spending authority as borrowing authority, contract authority and entitlement authority *(see above)*, for which budget authority is not provided in advance by appropriation acts.

Sponsor—*(See Bills Introduced.)*

Standing Committees—Committees permanently established by House and Senate rules. The standing committees of the House were last reorganized by the committee reorganization of 1974. The last major realignment of Senate committees was in the committee system reorganization of 1977. The standing committees are legislative committees — legislation may be referred to them and they may report bills and resolutions to their parent chambers. *(See also Select or Special Committees.)*

Standing Vote—A non-recorded vote used in both the House and Senate. (A standing vote also is called a division vote.) Members in favor of a proposal stand and are counted by the presiding officer. Then members opposed stand and are counted. There is no record of how individual members voted.

Statutes at Large—A chronological arrangement of the laws enacted in each session of Congress. Though indexed, the laws are not arranged by subject matter, and there is not an indication of how they changed previously enacted laws. *(See also Law, Slip Laws, U.S. Code.)*

Strike From the Record—Remarks made on the House floor may offend some member, who moves that the offending words be "taken down" for the Speaker's cognizance, and then expunged from the debate as published in the *Congressional Record.*

Strike Out the Last Word—A motion whereby a House member is entitled to speak for five minutes on an amendment then being debated by the chamber. A member gains recognition from the chair by moving to "strike out the last word" of the amendment or section of the bill under consideration. The motion is pro forma, requires no vote and does not change the amendment being debated.

How a Bill Becomes Law

Note: Parliamentary terms used below are defined in the Glossary.

Introduction of Bills

A House member (including the resident commissioner of Puerto Rico and non-voting delegates of the District of Columbia, Guam, the Virgin Islands, and American Samoa) may introduce any one of several types of bills and resolutions by handing it to the clerk of the House or placing it in a box called the hopper. A senator first gains recognition of the presiding officer to announce the introduction of a bill. If objection is offered by any senator the introduction of the bill is postponed until the following day.

As the next step in either the House or Senate, the bill is numbered, referred to the appropriate committee, labeled with the sponsor's name, and sent to the Government Printing Office so that copies can be made for subsequent study and action. Senate bills may be jointly sponsored and carry several senators' names. Until 1978, the House limited the number of members who could co-sponsor any one bill; the ceiling was eliminated at the beginning of the 96th Congress. A bill written in the Executive Branch and proposed as an administration measure usually is introduced by the chairman of the congressional committee which has jurisdiction.

Bills—Prefixed with "HR" in the House, "S" in the Senate, followed by a number. Used as the form for most legislation, whether general or special, public or private.

Joint Resolutions—Designated H J Res or S J Res. Subject to the same procedure as bills, with the exception of a joint resolution proposing an amendment to the Constitution. The latter must be approved by two-thirds of both houses and is thereupon sent directly to the administrator of general services for submission to the states for ratification rather than being presented to the president for his approval.

Concurrent Resolutions—Designated H Con Res or S Con Res. Used for matters affecting the operations of both houses. These resolutions do not become law.

Resolutions—Designated H Res or S Res. Used for a matter concerning the operation of either house alone and adopted only by the chamber in which it originates.

Committee Action

A bill is referred to the appropriate committee by a House parliamentarian on the Speaker's order, or by the Senate president. Sponsors may indicate their preferences for referral, although custom and chamber rule generally govern. An exception is the referral of private bills, which are sent to whatever group is designated by their sponsors. Bills are technically considered "read for the first time" when referred to House committees.

When a bill reaches a committee it is placed upon the group's calendar. At that time it comes under the sharpest congressional focus. Its chances for passage are quickly determined — and the great majority of bills fall by the legislative roadside. Failure of a committee to act on a bill is equivalent to killing it; the measure can be withdrawn from the group's purview only by a discharge petition signed by a majority of the House membership on House bills, or by adoption of a special resolution in the Senate. Discharge attempts rarely succeed.

The first committee action taken on a bill usually is a request for comment on it by interested agencies of the government. The committee chairman may assign the bill to a subcommittee for study and hearings, or it may be considered by the full committee. Hearings may be public, closed (executive session), or both. A subcommittee, after considering a bill, reports to the full committee its recommendations for action and any proposed amendments.

The full committee then votes on its recommendation to the House or Senate. This procedure is called "ordering a bill reported." Occasionally a committee may order a bill reported unfavorably; most of the time a report, submitted by the chairman of the committee to the House or Senate, calls for favorable action on the measure since the committee can effectively "kill" a bill by simply failing to take any action.

When a committee sends a bill to the chamber floor, it explains its reasons in a written statement, called a report, which accompanies the bill. Often committee members opposing a measure issue dissenting minority statements which are included in the report.

Usually, the committee "marks up" or proposes amendments to the bill. If they are substantial and the measure is complicated, the committee may order a "clean bill" introduced, which will embody the proposed amendments. The original bill then is put aside and the "clean bill," with a new number, is reported to the floor.

The chamber must approve, alter, or reject the committee amendments before the bill itself can be put to a vote.

Floor Action

After a bill is reported back to the house where it originated, it is placed on the calendar.

There are five legislative calendars in the House, issued in one cumulative calendar titled *Calendars of the United States House of Representatives and History of Legislation.* The House calendars are:

The Union Calendar to which are referred bills raising revenues, general appropriation bills and any measures directly or indirectly appropriating money or property. It is the Calendar of the Committee of the Whole House on the State of the Union.

The House Calendar to which are referred bills of a public character not raising revenue or appropriating money or property.

The Consent Calendar to which are referred bills of a non-controversial nature that are passed without debate when the Consent Calendar is called on the first and third Mondays of each month.

The Private Calendar to which are referred bills for relief in the nature of claims against the United States or private immigration bills that are passed without debate when the Private Calendar is called the first and third Tuesdays of each month.

The Discharge Calendar to which are referred motions to discharge committees when the necessary signatures are signed to a discharge petition.

There is only one legislative calendar in the Senate and one "executive calendar" for treaties and nominations

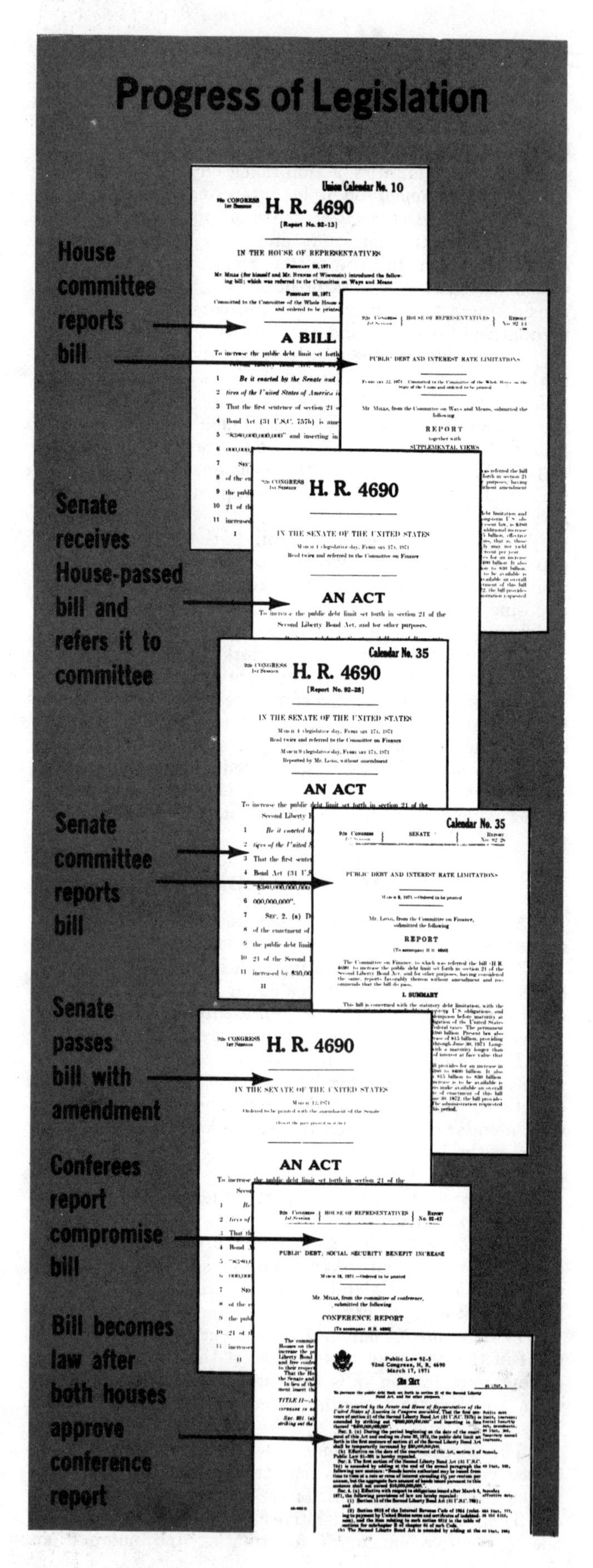

submitted to the Senate When the Senate Calendar is called, each senator is limited to five minutes debate on each bill.

DEBATE. A bill is brought to debate by varying procedures. If a routine measure, it may await the call of the calendar. If it is urgent or important, it can be taken up in the Senate either by unanimous consent or by a majority vote. The policy committee of the majority party in the Senate schedules the bills that it wants taken up for debate.

In the House, precedence is granted if a special rule is obtained from the Rules Committee. A request for a special rule is usually made by the chairman of the committee that favorably reported the bill, supported by the bill's sponsor and other committee members. The request, considered by the Rules Committee in the same fashion that other committees consider legislative measures, is in the form of a resolution providing for immediate consideration of the bill. The Rules Committee reports the resolution to the House where it is debated and voted upon in the same fashion as regular bills. If the Rules Committee should fail to report a rule requested by a committee, there are several ways to bring the bill to the House floor — under suspension of the rules, on Calendar Wednesday or by a discharge motion.

The resolutions providing special rules are important because they specify how long the bill may be debated and whether it may be amended from the floor. If floor amendments are banned, the bill is considered under a "closed rule," which permits only members of the committee that first reported the measure to the House to alter its language, subject to chamber acceptance.

When a bill is debated under an "open rule," amendments may be offered from the floor. Committee amendments are always taken up first, but may be changed, as may all amendments up to the second degree, i.e., an amendment to an amendment to an amendment is not in order.

Duration of debate in the House depends on whether the bill is under discussion by the House proper or before the House when it is sitting as the Committee of the Whole House on the State of the Union. In the former, the amount of time for debate is determined either by special rule or is allocated with an hour for each member if the measure is under consideration without a rule. In the Committee of the Whole the amount of time agreed on for general debate is equally divided between proponents and opponents. At the end of general discussion, the bill is read section by section for amendment. Debate on an amendment is limited to five minutes for each side.

Senate debate is usually unlimited. It can be halted only by unanimous consent by "cloture," which requires a three-fifths majority of the entire Senate except for proposed changes in the Senate rules. The latter requires a two-thirds vote.

The House sits as the Committee of the Whole when it considers any tax measure or bill dealing with public appropriations. It can also resolve itself into the Committee of the Whole if a member moves to do so and the motion is carried. The Speaker appoints a member to serve as the chairman. The rules of the House permit the Committee of the Whole to meet with any 100 members on the floor, and to amend and act on bills with a quorum of the 100, within the time limitations mentioned previously. When the Committee of the Whole has acted, it "rises," the Speaker returns as the presiding officer of the House and the member appointed chairman of the Committee of the Whole reports the action of the committee and its recommendations (amendments adopted).

VOTES. Voting on bills may occur repeatedly before they are finally approved or rejected. The House votes on the rule for the bill and on various amendments to the bill. Voting on amendments often is a more illuminating test of a bill's support than is the final tally. Sometimes members approve final passage of bills after vigorously supporting amendments which, if adopted, would have scuttled the legislation.

The Senate has three different methods of voting: an untabulated voice vote, a standing vote (called a division) and a recorded roll call to which members answer "yea" or "nay" when their names are called. The House also employs voice and standing votes, but since January 1973 yeas and nays have been recorded by an electronic voting device, eliminating the need for time-consuming roll calls.

Another method of voting, used in the House only, is the teller vote. Traditionally, members filed up the center aisle past counters; only vote totals were announced. Since 1971, one-fifth of a quorum can demand that the votes of individual members be recorded, thereby forcing them to take a public position on amendments to key bills. Electronic voting now is commonly used for this purpose.

After amendments to a bill have been voted upon, a vote may be taken on a motion to recommit the bill to committee. If carried, this vote removes the bill from the chamber's calendar. If the motion is unsuccessful, the bill then is "read for the third time." An actual reading usually is dispensed with. Until 1965, an opponent of a bill could delay this move by objecting and asking for a full reading of an engrossed (certified in final form) copy of the bill. After the "third reading," the vote on final passage is taken.

The final vote may be followed by a motion to reconsider, and this motion itself may be followed by a move to lay the motion on the table. Usually, those voting for the bill's passage vote for the tabling motion, thus safeguarding the final passage action. With that, the bill has been formally passed by the chamber. While a motion to reconsider a Senate vote is pending on a bill, the measure cannot be sent to the House.

Action in Second House

After a bill is passed it is sent to the other chamber. This body may then take one of several steps. It may pass the bill as is — accepting the other chamber's language. It may send the bill to committee for scrutiny or alteration, or reject the entire bill, advising the other house of its actions. Or it may simply ignore the bill submitted while it continues work on its own version of the proposed legislation. Frequently, one chamber may approve a version of a bill that is greatly at variance with the version already passed by the other house, and then substitute its amendments for the language of the other, retaining only the latter's bill designation.

A provision of the Legislative Reorganization Act of 1970 permits a separate House vote on any non-germane amendment added by the Senate to a House-passed bill and requires a majority vote to retain the amendment. Previously the House was forced to act on the bill as a whole; the only way to defeat the non-germane amendment was to reject the entire bill.

Often the second chamber makes only minor changes.

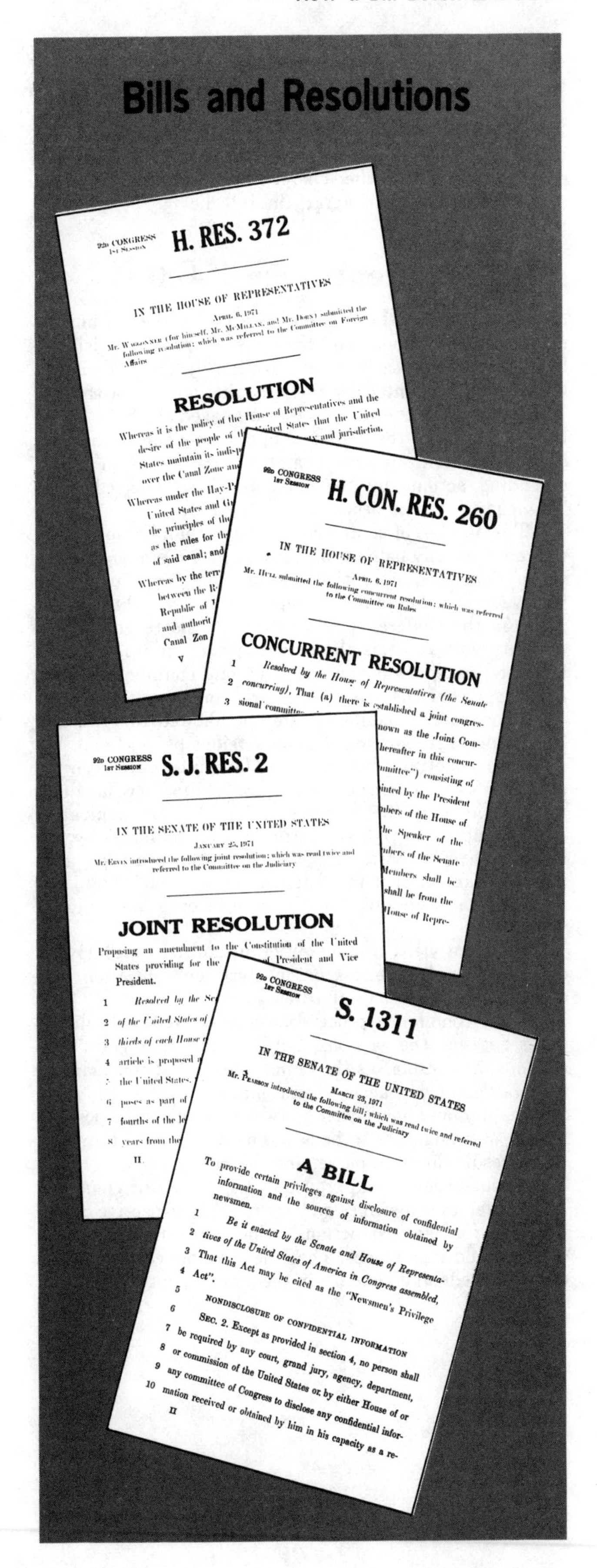

If these are readily agreed to by the other house, the bill then is routed to the White House for signing. However, if the opposite chamber basically alters the bill submitted to it, the measure usually is "sent to conference." The chamber that has possession of the "papers" (engrossed bill, engrossed amendments, messages of transmittal) requests a conference and the other chamber must agree to it. If the second house does not agree, the bill dies.

Conference, Final Action

CONFERENCE. A conference undertakes to harmonize conflicting House and Senate versions of a legislative bill. The conference is usually staffed by senior members (conferees), appointed by the presiding officers of the two houses, from the committees that managed the bills. Under this arrangement the conferees of one house have the duty of trying to maintain their chamber's position in the face of amending actions by the conferees (also referred to as "managers") of the other house.

The number of conferees from each chamber may vary, the range usually being from three to nine members in each group, depending upon the length or complexity of the bill involved. There may be five representatives and three senators on the conference committee, or the reverse. But a majority vote controls the action of each group so that a larger representation does not give one chamber a voting advantage over the other chamber's conferees.

Theoretically, conferees are not allowed to write new legislation in reconciling the two versions before them, but this curb sometimes is bypassed. Many bills have been put into acceptable compromise form only after new language was provided by the conferees. The 1970 Reorganization Act attempted to tighten restrictions on conferees by forbidding them to introduce any language on a topic that neither chamber sent to conference or to modify any topic beyond the scope of the different House and Senate versions.

Frequently the ironing out of difficulties takes days or even weeks. Conferences on involved appropriation bills sometimes are particularly drawn out.

As a conference proceeds, conferees reconcile differences between the versions, but generally they grant concessions only insofar as they remain sure that the chamber they represent will accept the compromises. Occasionally, uncertainty over how either house will react, or the positive refusal of a chamber to back down on a disputed amendment, results in an impasse, and the bills die in conference even though each was approved by its sponsoring chamber.

Conferees sometimes go back to their respective chambers for further instructions, when they report certain portions in disagreement. Then the chamber concerned can either "recede and concur" in the amendment of the other house, or "insist on its amendment."

When the conferees have reached agreement, they prepare a conference report embodying their recommendations (compromises). The reports, in document form, must be submitted to each house.

The conference report must be approved by each house. Consequently, approval of the report is approval of the compromise bill. In the order of voting on conference reports, the chamber which asked for a conference yields to the other chamber the opportunity to vote first.

FINAL STEPS. After a bill has been passed by both the House and Senate in identical form, all of the original papers are sent to the enrolling clerk of the chamber in which the bill originated. He then prepares an enrolled bill which is printed on parchment paper. When this bill has been certified as correct by the secretary of the Senate or the clerk of the House, depending on which chamber originated the bill, it is signed first (no matter whether it originated in the Senate or House) by the Speaker of the House and then by the president of the Senate. It is next sent to the White House to await action.

If the president approves the bill he signs it, dates it and usually writes the word "approved" on the document. If he does not sign it within 10 days (Sundays excepted) and Congress is in session, the bill becomes law without his signature.

However, should Congress adjourn before the 10 days expire, and the president has failed to sign the measure, it does not become law. This procedure is called the pocket veto.

A president vetoes a bill by refusing to sign it and before the 10-day period expires, returning it to Congress with a message stating his reasons. The message is sent to the chamber which originated the bill. If no action is taken there on the message, the bill dies. Congress, however, can attempt to override the president's veto and enact the bill, "the objections of the president to the contrary notwithstanding." Overriding of a veto requires a two-thirds vote of those present, who must number a quorum and vote by roll call.

Debate can precede this vote, with motions permitted to lay the message on the table, postpone action on it, or refer it to committee. If the president's veto is overridden by a two-thirds vote in both houses, the bill becomes law. Otherwise it is dead.

When bills are passed finally and signed, or passed over a veto, they are given law numbers in numerical order as they become law. There are two series of numbers, one for public and one for private laws, starting at the number "1" for each two-year term of Congress. They are then identified by law number and by Congress — i.e., Private Law 21, 97th Congress; Public Law 250, 97th Congress (or PL 97-250).

How a Bill Becomes Law

This graphic shows the most typical way in which proposed legislation is enacted into law. There are more complicated, as well as simpler, routes, and most bills never become law. The process is illustrated with two hypothetical bills, House bill No. 1 (HR 1) and Senate bill No. 2 (S 2). Bills must be passed by both houses in identical form before they can be sent to the president. The path of HR 1 is traced by a solid line, that of S 2 by a broken line. In practice most bills begins as similar proposals in both houses.

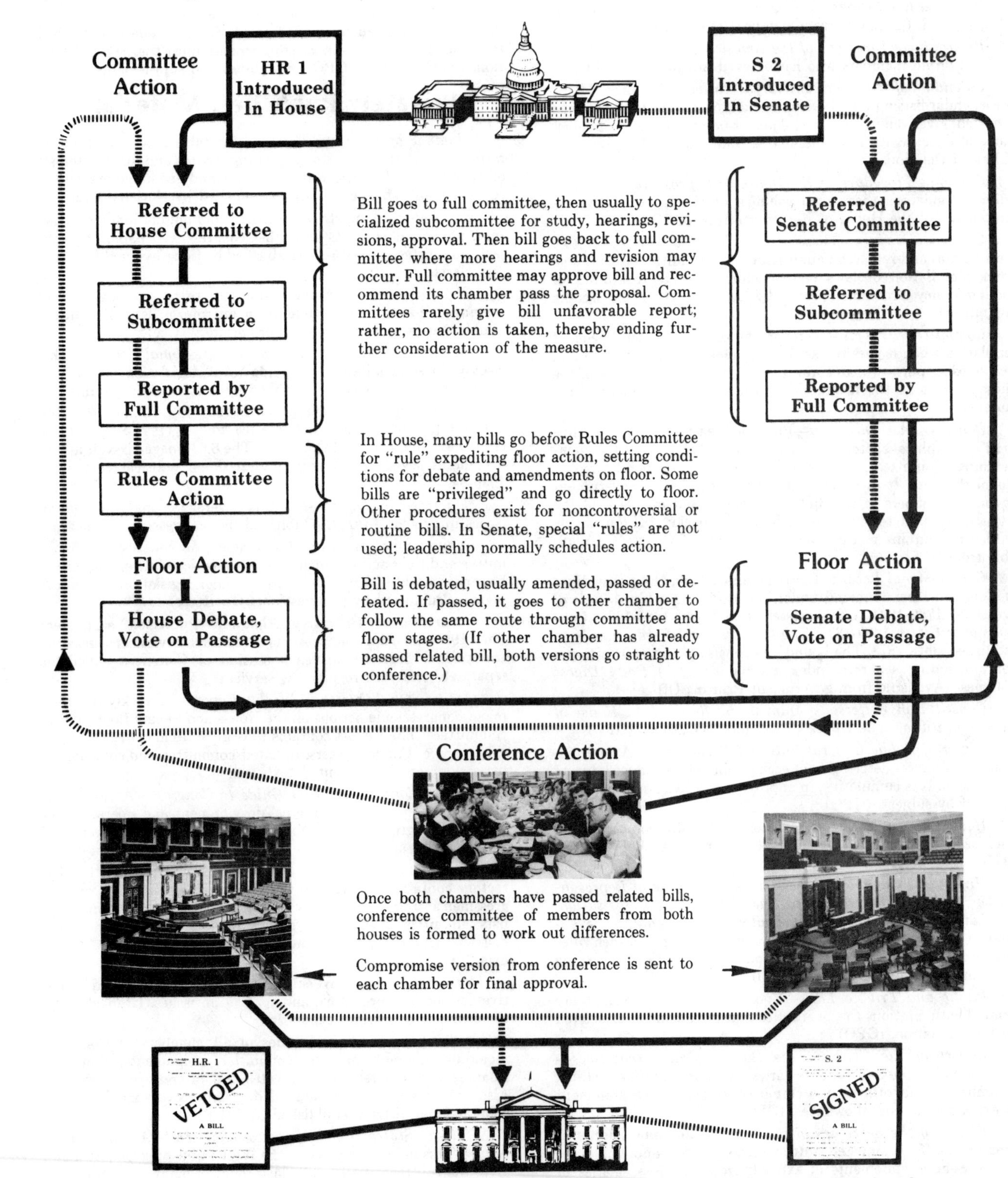

Compromise bill approved by both houses is sent to the president, who can sign it into law or veto it and return it to Congress. Congress may override veto by a two-thirds majority vote in both houses; bill then becomes law without president's signature.

REFERENCE GUIDE TO CONGRESS AND LEGISLATION

Current Government Documents

Bills and Resolutions—All legislation is printed daily after it is introduced. (Available from members of Congress)

Biographical Directory of the American Congress 1774-1971 — Data on all members who have served in Congress. (GPO)

Calendars of the House of Representatives—Published daily, the calendar lists all bills — Senate and House — which have been reported: gives report numbers, dates of passage in each chamber, dates of enactments, etc. Cumulative. Indexed on Mondays only. (Clerk of the House)

Cannon's Procedure in the House of Representatives—This volume condenses the eleven volumes of Hinds' and Cannon's Precedents of the House of Representatives. (GPO)

Committee Prints—These documents are usually committee staff studies and research papers issued by committees; they range from compilation of laws on particular subjects to studies of foreign policy problems. (Generally available from the issuing committee)

Committee Reports—A report accompanies each piece of legislation when it goes to the floor. It generally analyzes the bill, describes its purposes, and states the views of the members of the committee as to the desirability of enactment. (Available from committees)

Congressional Directory—Published each year, it contains brief biographical sketches of each member, lists committee memberships, committee assignments by member, maps of all congressional districts. It also lists major executives of all government agencies, members of the diplomatic corps, and members of the press accredited to the press galleries. A pocket edition of the Directory contains pictures of each member of Congress. (Available from GPO).

Congressional Record (Bound)—Since 1789, the proceedings of Congress have appeared under four different titles: *Annals of Congress*, 1789-1824; *The Register of Debates*, 1824-1837; *Congressional Globe*, 1833-1873; *The Congressional Record* has been published since 1873. The bound sets consist of 15 to 20 parts per year, including separate index and (since 1947) *Daily Digest* volumes. (Available from government Printing Office)

Constitution, Jefferson's Manual and Rules of the House of Representatives—The House's rules and regulations. (GPO)

Digest of Public General Bills and Resolutions—A compilation giving a brief description of each public bill introduced during the session. It is cumulative, in approximately five issues per year. Indexed by subject. (GPO)

Hearings—Copies of all testimony taken by committees in open session are printed by the GPO and made available by the issuing committee.

Hinds' and Cannon's Precedents of the House of Representatives Including References to Provisions of the Constitution, the Laws and Decisions of the United States Senate—Eleven-volume set contains the constitutional provisions, established rules and procedures, with explanation and documentation, governing the House of Representatives. (GPO)

Public and Private Laws—Copies of all laws enacted are printed with citations to the statutes that are amended or deleted by the legislation. (GPO)

Report of the Clerk of the House of Representatives—Semiannual report includes salaries of representatives, staffs, committee staffs, officers and employees of the House; statement of expenditures and allowances. (GPO)

Report of the Secretary of the Senate—Contains salaries of senators, staffs, committee staff members, officers and employees of the Senate; statements of expenditures and gross salaries of senators; issued semiannually. (GPO)

Senate Manual—The Manual contains "standing rules, orders, laws and regulations . . ." of the Senate. (GPO)

United States Code—The 50 titles of the code include all the general and permanent laws of the U.S. The Code is published every six years, with annual supplements until the next publication. (Available from GPO, 14 volumes and supplements)

Privately Published Materials

Almanac of American Politics—Contains biographies, group ratings, committee assignments, voting records and lobby interests of members, and political, demographic and economic makeup of congressmen's state or district. (Published by National Journal)

CIS Index—A monthly, quarterly, and annual index to hearings, reports, documents and other congressional papers by subject, committee and witness. (Published by Congressional Information Service)

CIS Microfiche Library—Complete texts of congressional hearings, reports and documents in microform; issued monthly. (Published by Congressional Information Service)

Commerce Clearing House Congressional Index—This weekly, loose-leaf index is a guide to all legislation by subject, author and bill number. (Published by C.C.H., Chicago, Ill.)

Congress and the Nation, Vol. I (1945-46), *Vol. II* (1965-68), *Vol. III* (1969-72), *Vol. IV* (1973-76) *Vol. V* (1977-80), *Vol. VI* (1981-84), Congressional Quarterly. The 6,600-page-six-volume set documents legislative actions and national political campaigns 1945-84.

Congressional Digest—Monthly coverage of major legislative issues in pro-con format. (Published by Congressional Digest)

Congressional Monitor—Daily report on congressional committee and floor actions, including advance schedule of committee hearings, weekly listing of status of major legislation and documents. (Published by Congressional Quarterly)

Congressional Quarterly Almanac—Published each year since 1945, the Almanac presents a thorough review of legislative and political activity for each session of Congress. (Available separately and with regular CQ service)

Congressional Quarterly Weekly Report—A weekly report of major congressional actions on the House and Senate floors and in committees. The Report contains roll-call votes and weekly political coverage. Carries rosters, updated committee and subcommittee assignments, presidential texts, etc.

Congressional Quarterly's Guide to Congress—A 1,000-page volume documenting the origins, development and operations of the U.S. Congress. Explains how Congress works, its powers and the pressures upon it.

Congressional Staff Directory—Published annually, the Directory contains biographical sketches of many members of congressmen's staffs; lists employees of members and committees; lists all cities of 1,500 or more population by congressional districts. (Available from Congressional Staff Directory, Alexandria, Va.)

National Journal—Weekly report of congressional and executive actions and programs, and reports on issues. (Published by Government Research Corporation)

Politics in America—Profiles of all members of Congress, including biographical data, committee assignments, campaign finances, election returns, key votes and interest group ratings. Also provides maps and detailed descriptions of each state and congressional district. (Published by CQ Press)

United States Code Congressional and Administrative News—This monthly service of the West Publishing Co., St. Paul, gives the full text of all public laws, and, in many cases, includes committee reports on the legislation.

CONSTITUTION OF THE UNITED STATES

We the People of the United States, in Order to form a more perfect Union, establish Justice, insure domestic Tranquility, provide for the common defence, promote the general Welfare, and secure the Blessings of Liberty to ourselves and our Posterity, do ordain and establish this Constitution for the United States of America.

ARTICLE I

Section 1. All legislative Powers herein granted shall be vested in a Congress of the United States, which shall consist of a Senate and House of Representatives.

Section 2. The House of Representatives shall be composed of Members chosen every second Year by the People of the several States, and the Electors in each State shall have the Qualifications requisite for Electors of the most numerous Branch of the State Legislature.

No Person shall be a Representative who shall not have attained to the age of twenty five Years, and been seven Years a Citizen of the United States, and who shall not, when elected, be an Inhabitant of that State in which he shall be chosen.

[Representatives and direct Taxes shall be apportioned among the several States which may be included within this Union, according to their respective Numbers, which shall be determined by adding to the whole Number of free Persons, including those bound to Service for a Term of Years, and excluding Indians not taxed, three fifths of all other Persons.][1] The actual Enumeration shall be made within three Years after the first Meeting of the Congress of the United States, and within every subsequent Term of ten Years, in such Manner as they shall by Law direct. The Number of Representatives shall not exceed one for every thirty Thousand, but each State shall have at Least one Representative; and until such enumeration shall be made, the State of New Hampshire shall be entitled to chuse three, Massachusetts eight, Rhode-Island and Providence Plantations one, Connecticut five, New-York six, New Jersey four, Pennsylvania eight, Delaware one, Maryland six, Virginia ten, North Carolina five, South Carolina five, and Georgia three.

When vacancies happen in the Representation from any State, the Executive Authority thereof shall issue Writs of Election to fill such Vacancies.

The House of Representatives shall chuse their Speaker and other Officers; and shall have the sole Power of Impeachment.

Section 3. The Senate of the United States shall be composed of two Senators from each State, [chosen by the Legislature thereof,][2] for six Years; and each Senator shall have one Vote.

Immediately after they shall be assembled in Consequence of the first Election, they shall be divided as equally as may be into three Classes. The Seats of the Senators of the first Class shall be vacated at the Expiration of the second Year, of the second Class at the Expiration of the fourth Year, and of the third Class at the Expiration of the sixth Year, so that one third may be chosen every second Year; [and if Vacancies happen by Resignation, or otherwise, during the Recess of the Legislature of any State, the Executive thereof may make temporary Appointments until the next Meeting of the Legislature, which shall then fill such Vacancies.][3]

No Person shall be a Senator who shall not have attained to the Age of thirty Years, and been nine Years a Citizen of the United States, and who shall not, when elected, be an Inhabitant of that State for which he shall be chosen.

The Vice President of the United States shall be President of the Senate, but shall have no Vote, unless they be equally divided.

The Senate shall chuse their other Officers, and also a President pro tempore, in the Absence of the Vice President, or when he shall exercise the Office of President of the United States.

The Senate shall have the sole Power to try all Impeachments. When sitting for that Purpose, they shall be on Oath or Affirmation. When the President of the United States is tried the Chief Justice shall preside: And no Person shall be convicted without the Concurrence of two thirds of the Members present.

Judgment in Cases of Impeachment shall not extend further than to removal from Office, and disqualification to hold and enjoy any Office of honor, Trust or Profit under the United States: but the Party convicted shall nevertheless be liable and subject to Indictment, Trial, Judgment and Punishment, according to Law.

Section 4. The Times, Places and Manner of holding Elections for Senators and Representatives, shall be prescribed in each State by the Legislature thereof; but the Congress may at any time by Law make or alter such Regulations, except as to the Places of chusing Senators.

The Congress shall assemble at least once in every Year, and such Meeting shall [be on the first Monday in December],[4] unless they shall by Law appoint a different Day.

Section 5. Each House shall be the Judge of the Elections, Returns and Qualifications of its own Members, and a Majority of each shall constitute a Quorum to do Business; but a smaller Number may adjourn from day to day, and may be authorized to compel the Attendance of absent Members, in such Manner, and under such Penalties as each House may provide.

Each House may determine the Rules of its Proceedings, punish its Members for disorderly Behaviour, and, with the Concurrence of two thirds, expel a Member.

Each House shall keep a Journal of its Proceedings, and from time to time publish the same, excepting such Parts as may in their Judgment require Secrecy; and the Yeas and Nays of the Members of either House on any question shall, at the Desire of one fifth of those Present, be entered on the Journal.

Neither House, during the Session of Congress, shall, without the Consent of the other, adjourn for more than three days, nor to any other Place than that in which the two Houses shall be sitting.

Section 6. The Senators and Representatives shall receive a Compensation for their Services, to be ascertained by Law, and paid out of the Treasury of the United States. They shall in all Cases, except Treason, Felony and Breach of the Peace, be privileged from Arrest during their Attendance at the Session of their respective Houses, and in going to and returning from the same; and for any Speech or Debate in either House, they shall not be questioned in any other Place.

No Senator or Representative shall, during the Time for which he was elected, be appointed to any civil Office under the Authority of the United States, which shall have been created, or the Emoluments whereof shall have been encreased during such time; and no Person holding any Office under the United States, shall be a Member of either House during his Continuance in Office.

Section 7. All Bills for raising Revenue shall originate in the House of Representatives; but the Senate may propose or concur with amendments as on other Bills.

Every Bill which shall have passed the House of Representatives and the Senate, shall, before it become a Law, be presented to the President of the United States; If he approve he shall sign it, but if not he shall return it, with his Objections to that House in which it shall have originated, who shall enter the Objections at large on their Journal, and proceed to reconsider it. If after such Reconsideration two thirds of that House shall agree to pass the Bill, it shall be sent, together with the Objections, to the other House, by which it shall likewise be reconsidered, and if approved by two thirds of that House, it shall become a Law. But in all such Cases the Votes of both Houses shall be determined by yeas and Nays, and the Names of the Persons voting for and against the Bill shall be entered on the Journal of each House respectively. If any Bill shall not be returned by the President within ten Days (Sunday excepted) after it shall have been presented to him, the Same shall be a Law, in like Manner as if he had signed it, unless the Congress by their Adjournment prevent its Return, in which Case it shall not be a Law.

Every Order, Resolution, or Vote to which the Concurrence of the Senate and House of Representatives may be necessary (except on a question of Adjournment) shall be presented to the President of the United States; and before the Same shall take Effect, shall be approved by him, or being disapproved by him, shall be repassed by two thirds of the Senate and House of Representatives, according to the Rules and Limitations prescribed in the Case of a Bill.

Section 8. The Congress shall have Power To lay and collect Taxes, Duties, Imposts and Excises, to pay the Debts and provide for the common Defence and general Welfare of the United States; but all Duties, Imposts and Excises shall be uniform throughout the United States;

To borrow Money on the credit of the United States;

To regulate Commerce with foreign Nations, and among the several States, and with the Indian Tribes;

To establish an uniform Rule of Naturalization, and uniform Laws on the subject of Bankruptcies throughout the United States;

To coin Money, regulate the Value thereof, and of foreign Coin, and fix the Standard of Weights and Measures;

To provide for the Punishment of counterfeiting the Securities and current Coin of the United States;

To establish Post Offices and post Roads;

To promote the Progress of Science and useful Arts, by securing for limited Times to Authors and Inventors the exclusive Right to their respective Writings and Discoveries;

To constitute Tribunals inferior to the supreme Court;

To define and punish Piracies and Felonies committed on the high Seas, and Offences against the Law of Nations;

To declare War, grant Letters of Marque and Reprisal, and make Rules concerning Captures on Land and Water;

To raise and support Armies, but no Appropriation of Money to that Use shall be for a longer Term than two Years;

To provide and maintain a Navy;

To make Rules for the Government and Regulation of the land and naval Forces;

To provide for calling forth the Militia to execute the Laws of the Union, suppress Insurrections and repel Invasions;

To provide for organizing, arming, and disciplining, the Militia, and for governing such Part of them as may be employed in the Service of the United States, reserving to the States respectively, the Appointment of the Officers, and the Authority of training the Militia according to the discipline prescribed by Congress;

To exercise exclusive Legislation in all Cases whatsoever, over such District (not exceeding ten Miles square) as may, by Cession of Particular States, and the Acceptance of Congress, become the Seat of the Government of the United States, and to exercise like Authority over all Places purchased by the Consent of the Legislature of the State in which the Same shall be, for the Erection of Forts, Magazines, Arsenals, dock-Yards, and other needful Buildings; — And

To make all Laws which shall be necessary and proper for carrying into Execution the foregoing Powers, and all other Powers vested by this Constitution in the Government of the United States, or in any Department or Officer thereof.

Section 9. The Migration or Importation of such Persons as any of the States now existing shall think proper to admit, shall not be prohibited by the Congress prior to the Year one thousand eight hundred and eight, but a Tax or duty may be imposed on such Importation, not exceeding ten dollars for each Person.

The Privilege of the Writ of Habeas Corpus shall not be suspended, unless when in Cases of Rebellion or Invasion the public Safety may require it.

No Bill of Attainder or ex post facto Law shall be passed.

No capitation, or other direct, Tax shall be laid, unless in Proportion to the Census of Enumeration herein before directed to be taken.[5]

No Tax or Duty shall be laid on Articles exported from any State.

No Preference shall be given by any Regulation of Commerce or Revenue to the Ports of one State over those of another; nor shall Vessels bound to, or from, one State, be obliged to enter, clear or pay Duties in another.

No Money shall be drawn from the Treasury, but in Consequence of Appropriations made by Law; and a regular Statement and Account of the Receipts and Expenditures of all public Money shall be published from time to time.

No Title of Nobility shall be granted by the United States: And no Person holding any Office of Profit or Trust under them, shall, without the Consent of the Congress, accept of any present, Emolument, Office, or Title, of any kind whatever, from any King, Prince or foreign State.

Section 10. No State shall enter into any Treaty, Alliance, or Confederation; grant Letters of Marque and Reprisal; coin Money; emit Bills of Credit; make any Thing but gold and silver Coin a Tender in Payment of Debts; pass any Bill of Attainder, ex post facto Law, or Law impairing the Obligation of Contracts, or grant any Title of Nobility.

No State shall, without the Consent of the Congress, lay any Imposts or Duties on Imports or Exports, except what may be absolutely necessary for executing it's inspection Laws: and the net Produce of all Duties and Imposts, laid by any State on Imports or Exports, shall be for the Use of the Treasury of the United States; and all such Laws shall be subject to the Revision and Controul of the Congress.

No State shall, without the Consent of Congress, lay any Duty of Tonnage, keep Troops, or Ships of War in time of Peace, enter into any Agreement or Compact with another State, or with a foreign Power, or engage in War, unless actually invaded, or in such imminent Danger as will not admit of delay.

ARTICLE II

Section 1. The executive Power shall be vested in a President of the United States of America. He shall hold his Office during the Term of four Years, and, together with the Vice President, chosen for the same Term, be elected, as follows.

Each State shall appoint, in such Manner as the Legislature thereof may direct, a Number of Electors, equal to the whole Number of Senators and Representatives to which the State may be entitled in the Congress: but no Senator or Representative, or Person holding an Office of Trust or Profit under the United States, shall be appointed an Elector.

[The Electors shall meet in their respective States, and vote by Ballot for two Persons, of whom one at least shall not be an Inhabitant of the same State with themselves. And they shall make a List of all the Persons voted for, and of the Number of Votes for each; which List they shall sign and certify, and transmit sealed to the Seat of the Government of the United States, directed to the President of the Senate. The President of the Senate shall, in the Presence of the Senate and House of Representatives, open all the Certificates, and the Votes shall then be counted. The Person having the greatest Number of Votes shall be the President, if such Number be a Majority of the whole Number of Electors appointed; and if there be more than one who have such Majority, and have an equal Number of Votes, then the House of Representatives shall immediately chuse by Ballot one of them for President; and if no Person have a Majority, then from the five highest on the list the said House shall in like Manner chuse the President. But in chusing the President, the Votes shall be taken by States, the Representation from each State having one Vote; a quorum for this Purpose shall consist of a Member or Members from two thirds of the States, and a Majority of all the States shall be necessary to a Choice. In every Case, after the Choice of the President, the Person having the greatest Number of Votes of the Electors shall be the Vice President. But if there should remain two or more who have equal Votes, the Senate shall chuse from them by Ballot the Vice President.][6]

The Congress may determine the Time of chusing the Electors, and the Day on which they shall give their Votes; which Day shall be the same throughout the United States.

No Person except a natural born Citizen, or a Citizen of the United States, at the time of the Adoption of this Constitution, shall be eligible to the Office of President; neither shall any Person be eligible to that Office who shall not have attained to the Age of thirty five Years, and been fourteen Years a Resident within the United States.

In Case of the Removal of the President from Office, or of his Death, Resignation, or Inability to discharge the Powers and Duties of the said Office,[7] the Same shall devolve on the Vice President, and the Congress may by Law provide for the Case of Removal, Death, Resignation or Inability, both of the President and Vice President, declaring what Officer shall then act as President, and such Officer shall act accordingly, until the Disability be removed, or a President shall be elected.

The President shall, at stated Times, receive for his Services, a Compensation, which shall neither be encreased nor diminished during the Period for which he shall have been elected, and he shall not receive within that Period any other Emolument from the United States, or any of them.

Before he enter on the Execution of his Office, he shall take the following Oath or Affirmation: — "I do solemnly swear (or affirm) that I will faithfully execute the Office of President of the United States, and will to the best of my Ability, preserve, protect and defend the Constitution of the United States."

Section 2. The President shall be Commander in Chief of the Army and Navy of the United States, and of the Militia of the several States, when called into the actual Service of the United States; he may require the Opinion, in writing, of the principal Officer in each of the executive Departments, upon any Subject relating to the Duties of their respective Offices, and he shall have Power to grant Reprieves and Pardons for Offenses against the United States, except in Cases of Impeachment.

He shall have Power, by and with the Advice and Consent of the Senate, to make Treaties, provided two thirds of the Senators present concur; and he shall nominate, and by and with the Advice and Consent of the Senate, shall appoint Ambassadors, other public Ministers and Consuls, Judges of the supreme Court, and all other Officers of the United States, whose Appointments are not herein otherwise provided for, and which shall be established by Law: but the Congress may by Law vest the Appointment of such inferior Officers, as they think proper, in the President alone, in the Courts of Law, or in the Heads of Departments.

The President shall have Power to fill up all Vacancies that may happen during the Recess of the Senate, by granting Commissions which shall expire at the End of their next Session.

Section 3. He shall from time to time give to the Congress Information of the State of the Union, and recommend to their Consideration such Measures as he shall judge necessary and expedient; he may, on extraordinary Occasions, convene both Houses, or either of them, and in Case of Disagreement between them, with Respect to the Time of Adjournment, he may adjourn them to such Time as he shall think proper; he shall receive Ambassadors and other public Ministers; he shall take Care that the Laws be faithfully executed, and shall Commission all the Officers of the United States.

Section 4. The President, Vice President and all Civil Officers of the United States, shall be removed from office on Impeachment for, and Conviction of, Treason, Bribery, or other high Crimes and Misdemeanors.

ARTICLE III

Section 1. The judicial Power of the United States, shall be vested in one supreme Court, and in such inferior Courts as the Congress may from time to time ordain and establish. The Judges, both of the supreme and inferior Courts, shall hold their Offices during good Behaviour, and shall, at stated Times, receive for their Services, a Compensation, which shall not be diminished during their Continuance in Office.

Section 2. The judicial Power shall extend to all Cases, in Law and Equity, arising under this Constitution, the Laws of the United States, and Treaties made, or which shall be made, under their Authority; — to all Cases affecting Ambassadors, other public Ministers and Consuls; — to all Cases of admiralty and maritime Jurisdiction; — to Controversies to which the United States shall be a Party; — to Controversies between two or more States; — between a State and Citizens of another State;[8] — between Citizens of different States; — between Citizens of the same State claiming Lands under Grants of different States, and between a State, or the Citizens thereof, and foreign States, Citizens or Subjects.[8]

In all Cases affecting Ambassadors, other public Ministers and Consuls, and those in which a State shall be Party, the supreme Court shall have original Jurisdiction. In all the other Cases before mentioned, the supreme Court shall have appellate Jurisdiction, both as to Law and Fact, with such Exceptions, and under such Regulations as the Congress shall make.

The Trial of all Crimes, except in cases of Impeachment, shall be by Jury; and such Trial shall be held in the State where the said Crimes shall have been committed; but when not committed within any State, the Trial shall be at such Place or Places as the Congress may by Law have directed.

Section 3. Treason against the United States, shall consist only in levying War against them, or in adhering to their Enemies, giving them Aid and Comfort. No Person shall be convicted of Treason unless on the Testimony of two Witnesses to the same overt Act, or on Confession in open Court.

The Congress shall have Power to declare the Punishment of Treason, but no Attainder of Treason shall work Corruption of Blood, or Forfeiture except during the Life of the Person attainted.

ARTICLE IV

Section 1. Full Faith and Credit shall be given in each State to the public Acts, Records, and judicial Proceedings of every other State. And the Congress may by general Laws prescribe the Manner in which such Acts, Records and Proceedings shall be proved, and the Effect thereof.

Section 2. The Citizens of each State shall be entitled to all Privileges and Immunities of Citizens in the several States.

A Person charged in any State with Treason, Felony, or other Crime, who shall flee from Justice, and be found in another State, shall on Demand of the executive Authority of the State from which he fled, be delivered up, to be removed to the State having Jurisdiction of the Crime.

[No Person held to Service or Labour in one State, under the Laws thereof, escaping into another, shall, in Consequence of any Law or Regulation therein, be discharged from such Service or Labour, but shall be delivered up on Claim of the Party to whom such Service or Labour may be due.][9]

Section 3. New States may be admitted by the Congress into this Union; but no new State shall be formed or erected within the Jurisdiction of any other State; nor any State be formed by the Junction of two or more States, or Parts of States, without the Consent of the Legislatures of the States concerned as well as of the Congress.

The Congress shall have Power to dispose of and make all needful Rules and Regulations respecting the Territory or other Property belonging to the United States; and nothing in this Constitution shall be so construed as to Prejudice any Claims of the United States, or of any particular State.

Section 4. The United States shall guarantee to every State in this Union a Republican Form of Government, and shall protect each of them against Invasion; and on Application of the Legislature, or of the Executive (when the Legislature cannot be convened) against domestic Violence.

ARTICLE V

The Congress, whenever two thirds of both Houses shall deem it necessary, shall propose Amendments to this Constitution, or, on the Application of the Legislatures of two thirds of the several States, shall call a Convention for proposing Amendments, which, in either Case, shall be valid to all Intents and Purposes, as Part of this Constitution, when ratified by the Legislatures of three fourths of the several States, or by Conventions in three fourths thereof, as the one or the other Mode of Ratification may be proposed by the Congress; Provided [that no Amendment which may be made prior to the Year One thousand eight hundred and eight shall in any Manner affect the first and fourth Clauses in the Ninth Section of the first Article; and][10] that no State, without its Consent, shall be deprived of its equal Suffrage in the Senate.

ARTICLE VI

All Debts contracted and Engagements entered into, before the Adoption of this Constitution, shall be as valid against the United States under this Constitution, as under the Confederation.

This Constitution, and the Laws of the United States which shall be made in Pursuance thereof; and all Treaties made, or which shall be made, under the Authority of the United States, shall be the supreme Law of the Land; and the Judges in every State shall be bound thereby, any Thing in the Constitution or Laws of any State to the Contrary notwithstanding.

The Senators and Representatives before mentioned, and the Members of the several State Legislatures, and all executive and judicial Officers, both of the United States and of the several States, shall be bound by Oath or Affirmation, to support this Constitution; but no religious Test shall ever be required as a Qualification to any Office or public Trust under the United States.

ARTICLE VII

The Ratification of the Conventions of nine States, shall be sufficient for the Establishment of this Constitution between the States so ratifying the Same. Done in Convention by the Unanimous Consent of the States present the Seventeenth Day of September in the Year of our Lord one thousand seven hundred and Eighty seven and of the Independence of the United States of America the Twelfth. In witness whereof We have hereunto subscribed our Names, George Washington, President and deputy from Virginia.

New Hampshire: John Langdon, Nicholas Gilman.

Massachusetts: Nathaniel Gorham, Rufus King.

Connecticut: William Samuel Johnson, Roger Sherman.

New York: Alexander Hamilton

New Jersey: William Livingston, David Brearley, William Paterson, Jonathan Dayton.

Pennsylvania: Benjamin Franklin, Thomas Mifflin, Robert Morris, George Clymer, Thomas FitzSimons, Jared Ingersoll, James Wilson, Gouverneur Morris.

Delaware: George Read, Gunning Bedford Jr., John Dickinson, Richard Bassett, Jacob Broom.

Maryland: James McHenry, Daniel of St. Thomas Jenifer, Daniel Carroll.

Virginia: John Blair, James Madison Jr.

North Carolina: William Blount, Richard Dobbs Spaight, Hugh Williamson.

South Carolina: John Rutledge, Charles Cotesworth Pinckney, Charles Pinckney, Pierce Butler.

Georgia: William Few, Abraham Baldwin.

[The language of the original Constitution, not including the Amendments, was adopted by a convention of the states on Sept. 17, 1787, and was subsequently ratified by the states on the following dates: Delaware, Dec. 7, 1787; Pennsylvania, Dec. 12, 1787; New Jersey, Dec. 18, 1787; Georgia, Jan. 2, 1788; Connecticut, Jan. 9, 1788; Massachusetts, Feb. 6, 1788; Maryland, April 28, 1788; South Carolina, May 23, 1788; New Hampshire, June 21, 1788.

Ratification was completed on June 21, 1788.

The Constitution subsequently was ratified by Virginia, June 25, 1788; New York, July 26, 1788; North Carolina, Nov. 21, 1789; Rhode Island, May 29, 1790; and Vermont, Jan. 10, 1791.]

AMENDMENTS

Amendment I

(First ten amendments ratified Dec. 15, 1791.)

Congress shall make no law respecting an establishment of religion, or prohibiting the free exercise thereof; or abridging the freedom of speech, or of the press; or the right of the people peaceably to assemble, and to petition the Government for a redress of grievances.

Amendment II

A well regulated Militia, being necessary to the security of a free State, the right of the people to keep and bear Arms, shall not be infringed.

Amendment III

No Soldier shall, in time of peace be quartered in any house, without the consent of the Owner, nor in time of war, but in a manner to be prescribed by law.

Amendment IV

The right of the people to be secure in their persons, houses, papers, and effects, against unreasonable searches and seizures, shall not be violated, and no Warrants shall issue, but upon probable cause, supported by Oath or affirmation, and particularly describing the place to be searched, and the persons or things to be seized.

Amendment V

No person shall be held to answer for a capital, or otherwise infamous crime, unless on a presentment or indictment of a Grand Jury, except in cases arising in the land or naval forces, or in the Militia, when in actual service in time of War or public danger; nor shall any person be subject for the same offence to be twice put in jeopardy of life or limb; nor shall be compelled in any criminal case to be a witness against himself, nor be deprived of life, liberty, or property, without due process of law; nor shall private property be taken for public use, without just compensation.

Amendment VI

In all criminal prosecutions, the accused shall enjoy the right to a speedy and public trial, by an impartial jury of the State and district wherein the crime shall have been committed, which district shall have been previously ascertained by law, and to be informed of the nature and cause of the accusation; to be confronted with the witnesses against him; to have compulsory process for obtaining witnesses in his favor, and to have the Assistance of Counsel for his defence.

Amendment VII

In Suits at common law, where the value in controversy shall exceed twenty dollars, the right of trial by jury shall be preserved, and no fact tried by a jury, shall be otherwise re-examined in any Court of the United States, than according to the rules of the common law.

Amendment VIII

Excessive bail shall not be required, nor excessive fines imposed, nor cruel and unusual punishments inflicted.

Amendment IX

The enumeration in the Constitution, of certain rights, shall not be construed to deny or disparage others retained by the people.

Amendment X

The powers not delegated to the United States by the Constitution, nor prohibited by it to the States, are reserved to the States respectively, or to the people.

Amendment XI *(Ratified Feb. 7, 1795)*

The Judicial power of the United States shall not be construed to extend to any suit in law or equity, commenced or prosecuted against one of the United States by Citizens of another State, or by Citizens or Subjects of any Foreign State.

Amendment XII *(Ratified June 15, 1804)*

The Electors shall meet in their respective states and vote by ballot for President and Vice-President, one of whom, at least, shall not be an inhabitant of the same state with themselves; they shall name in their ballots the person voted for as President, and in distinct ballots the person voted for as Vice-President, and they shall make distinct lists of all persons voted for as President, and of all persons voted for as Vice-President, and of the number of votes for each, which lists they shall sign and certify, and transmit sealed to the seat of the government of the United States, directed to the President of the Senate; — The President of the Senate shall, in the presence of the Senate and House of Representatives, open all the certificates and the votes shall then be counted; — The person having the greatest number of votes for President, shall be the President, if such number be a majority of the whole number of Electors appointed; and if no person have such majority, then from the persons having the highest numbers not exceeding three on the list of those voted for as President, the House of Representatives shall choose immediately, by ballot, the President. But in choosing the President, the votes shall be taken by states, the representation from each state having one vote; a quorum for this purpose shall consist of a member or members from two-thirds of the states, and a majority of all the states shall be necessary to a choice. [And if the House of Representatives shall not choose a President whenever the right of choice shall devolve upon them, before the fourth day of March next following, then the Vice-President shall act as President, as in the case of the death or other constitutional disability of the President —][11] The person having the greatest number of votes as Vice-President, shall be the Vice-President, if such number be a majority of the whole number of Electors appointed, and if no person have a majority, then from the two highest numbers on the list, the Senate shall choose the Vice-President; a quorum for the purpose shall consist of two-thirds of the whole number of Senators, and a majority of the whole number shall be necessary to a choice. But no person constitutionally ineligible to the office of President shall be eligible to that of Vice-President of the United States.

Amendment XIII *(Ratified Dec. 6, 1865)*

Section 1. Neither slavery nor involuntary servitude, except as a punishment for crime whereof the party shall have been duly convicted, shall exist within the United States, or any place subject to their jurisdiction.

Section 2. Congress shall have power to enforce this article by appropriate legislation.

Amendment XIV *(Ratified July 9, 1868)*

Section 1. All persons born or naturalized in the United States and subject to the jurisdiction thereof, are citizens of the United States and of the State wherein they reside. No State shall make or enforce any law which shall abridge the privileges or immunities of citizens of the United States; nor shall any State deprive any person of life, liberty, or property, without due process of law; nor deny to any person within its jurisdiction the equal protection of the laws.

Section 2. Representatives shall be apportioned among the several States according to their respective numbers, counting the whole number of persons in each State, excluding Indians not taxed. But when the right to vote at any election for the choice of electors for President and Vice President of the United States, Representatives in Congress, the Executive and Judicial officers of a State, or the members of the Legislature thereof, is denied to any of the male inhabitants of such State, being twenty-one years of age,[12] and citizens of the United States, or in any way abridged, except for participation in rebellion, or other crime, the basis of representation therein shall be reduced in the proportion which the number of such male citizens shall bear to the whole number of male citizens twenty-one years of age in such State.

Section 3. No person shall be a Senator or Representative in Congress, or elector of President and Vice President, or hold any office, civil or military, under the United States, or under any State, who, having previously taken an oath, as a member of Congress, or as an officer of the United States, or as a member of any State legislature, or as an executive or judicial officer of any State, to support the Constitution of the United States, shall have engaged in insurrection or rebellion against the same, or given aid or comfort to the enemies thereof. But Congress may by a vote of two-thirds of each House, remove such disability.

Section 4. The validity of the public debt of the United States, authorized by law, including debts incurred for payment of pensions and bounties for services in suppressing insurrection or rebellion, shall not be questioned. But neither the United States nor any State shall assume or pay any debt or obligation incurred in aid of insurrection or rebellion against the United States, or any claim for the loss or emancipation of any slave; but all such debts, obligations and claims shall be held illegal and void.

Section 5. The Congress shall have power to enforce, by appropriate legislation, the provisions of this article.

Amendment XV *(Ratified Feb. 3, 1870)*

Section 1. The right of citizens of the United States to vote shall not be denied or abridged by the United States or by any State on account of race, color, or previous condition of servitude.

Section 2. The Congress shall have power to enforce this article by appropriate legislation.

Amendment XVI *(Ratified Feb. 3, 1913)*

The Congress shall have power to lay and collect taxes on incomes, from whatever source derived, without apportionment among the several States, and without regard to any census or enumeration.

Amendment XVII *(Ratified April 8, 1913)*

The Senate of the United States shall be composed of two Senators from each State, elected by the people thereof, for six years; and each Senator shall have one vote. The electors in each State shall have the qualifications requisite for electors of the most numerous branch of the State legislatures.

When vacancies happen in the representation of any State in the Senate, the executive authority of such State shall issue writs of election to fill such vacancies: *Provided,* That the legislature of any State may empower the executive thereof to make temporary appointments until the people fill the vacancies by election as the legislature may direct.

This amendment shall not be so construed as to affect the election or term of any Senator chosen before it becomes valid as part of the Constitution.

Amendment XVIII *(Ratified Jan. 16, 1919)*

Section 1. After one year from the ratification of this article the manufacture, sale, or transportation of intoxicating liquors within, the importation thereof into, or the exportation thereof from the United States and all territory subject to the jurisdiction thereof for beverage purposes is hereby prohibited.

Section 2. The Congress and the several States shall have concurrent power to enforce this article by appropriate legislation.

Section 3. This article shall be inoperative unless it shall have been ratified as an amendment to the Constitution by the legislatures of the several States, as provided in the Constitution, within seven years from the date of the submission hereof to the States by the Congress.][13]

Amendment XIX *(Ratified Aug. 18, 1920)*

The right of citizens of the United States to vote shall not be denied or abridged by the United States or by any State on account of sex.

Congress shall have power to enforce this article by appropriate legislation.

Amendment XX *(Ratified Jan. 23, 1933)*

Section 1. The terms of the President and Vice President shall end at noon on the 20th day of January, and the terms of Senators and Representatives at noon on the 3d day of January, of the years in which such terms would have ended if this article had not been ratified; and the terms of their successors shall then begin.

Section 2. The Congress shall assemble at least once in every year, and such meeting shall begin at noon on the 3d day of January, unless they shall by law appoint a different day.

Section 3.[14] If, at the time fixed for the beginning of the term of the President, the President elect shall have died, the Vice President elect shall become President. If a President shall not have been chosen before the time fixed for the beginning of his term, or if the President elect shall have failed to qualify, then the Vice President elect shall act as President until a President shall have qualified; and the Congress may by law provide for the case wherein neither a President elect nor a Vice President elect shall have qualified, declaring who shall then act as President, or the manner in which one who is to act shall be selected, and such person shall act accordingly until a President or Vice President shall have qualified.

Section 4. The Congress may by law provide for the case of the death of any of the persons from whom the House of Representatives may choose a President whenever the right of choice shall have devolved upon them, and for the case of the death of any of the persons from whom the Senate may choose a Vice President whenever the right of choice shall have devolved upon them.

Section 5. Sections 1 and 2 shall take effect on the 15th day of October following the ratification of this article.

Section 6. This article shall be inoperative unless it shall have been ratified as an amendment to the Constitution by the legislatures of three-fourths of the several States within seven years from the date of its submission.

Amendment XXI *(Ratified Dec. 5, 1933)*

Section 1. The eighteenth article of amendment to the Constitution of the United States is hereby repealed.

Section 2. The transportation or importation into any State, Territory or possession of the United States for delivery or use therein of intoxicating liquors, in violation of the laws thereof, is hereby prohibited.

Section 3. This article shall be inoperative unless it shall have been ratified as an amendment to the Constitution by conventions in the several States, as provided in the Constitution, within seven years from the date of the submission hereof to the States by the Congress.

Amendment XXII *(Ratified Feb. 27, 1951)*

Section 1. No person shall be elected to the office of the President more than twice, and no person who has held the office of President, or acted as President, for more than two years of a term to which some other person was elected President shall be elected to the office of the President more than once. But this Article shall not apply to any person holding the office of President when this Article was proposed by the Congress, and shall not prevent any person who may be holding the office of President, or acting as President, during the term within which this Article become operative from holding the office of President or acting as President during the remainder of such term.

Section 2. This Article shall be inoperative unless it shall have been ratified as an amendment to the Constitution by the legislatures of three-fourths of the several States within seven years from the date of its submission to the States by the Congress.

Amendment XXIII *(Ratified March 29, 1961)*

Section 1. The District constituting the seat of Government of the United States shall appoint in such manner as the Congress may direct:

A number of electors of President and Vice President equal to the whole number of Senators and Representatives in Congress to which the District would be entitled if it were a State, but in no event more than the least populous State; they shall be in addition to those appointed by the States, but they shall be considered, for the purposes of the election of President and Vice President, to be electors appointed by a State; and they shall meet in the District and perform such duties as provided by the twelfth article of amendment.

Section 2. The Congress shall have power to enforce this article by appropriate legislation.

Amendment XXIV *(Ratified Jan. 23, 1964)*

Section 1. The right of citizens of the United States to vote in any primary or other election for President or

Vice President, for electors for President or Vice President, or for Senator or Representative in Congress, shall not be denied or abridged by the United States or any State by reason of failure to pay any poll tax or other tax.

Section 2. The Congress shall have power to enforce this article by appropriate legislation.

Amendment XXV *(Ratified Feb. 10, 1967)*

Section 1. In case of the removal of the President from office or of his death or resignation, the Vice President shall become President.

Section 2. Whenever there is a vacancy in the office of the Vice President, the President shall nominate a Vice President who shall take office upon confirmation by a majority vote of both Houses of Congress.

Section 3. Whenever the President transmits to the President pro tempore of the Senate and the Speaker of the House of Representatives his written declaration that he is unable to discharge the powers and duties of his office, and until he transmits to them a written declaration to the contrary, such powers and duties shall be discharged by the Vice President as Acting President.

Section 4. Whenever the Vice President and a majority of either the principal officers of the executive departments or of such other body as Congress may by law provide, transmit to the President pro tempore of the Senate and the Speaker of the House of Representatives their written declaration that the President is unable to discharge the powers and duties of his office, the Vice President shall immediately assume the powers and duties of the office as Acting President.

Thereafter, when the President transmits to the President pro tempore of the Senate and the Speaker of the House of Representatives his written declaration that no inability exists, he shall resume the powers and duties of his office unless the Vice President and a majority of either the principal officers of the executive department or of such other body as Congress may by law provide, transmit within four days to the President pro tempore of the Senate and the Speaker of the House of Representatives their written declaration that the President is unable to discharge the powers and duties of his office. Thereupon Congress shall decide the issue, assembling within forty-eight hours for that purpose if not in session. If the Congress, within twenty-one days after receipt of the latter written declaration, or, if Congress is not in session, within twenty-one days after Congress is required to assemble, determines by two-thirds vote of both houses that the President is unable to discharge the powers and duties of his office, the Vice President shall continue to discharge the same as Acting President; otherwise, the President shall resume the powers and duties of his office.

Amendment XXVI *(Ratified July 1, 1971)*

Section 1. The right of citizens of the United States, who are eighteen years of age or older, to vote shall not be denied or abridged by the United States or by any State on account of age.

Section 2. The Congress shall have power to enforce this article by appropriate legislation.

Footnotes

1. The part in brackets was changed by section 2 of the Fourteenth Amendment.
2. The part in brackets was changed by section 1 of the Seventeenth Amendment.
3. The part in brackets was changed by the second paragraph of the Seventeenth Amendment.
4. The part in brackets was changed by section 2 of the Twentieth Amendment.
5. The Sixteenth Amendment gave Congress the power to tax incomes.
6. The material in brackets has been superseded by the Twelfth Amendment.
7. This provision has been affected by the Twenty-fifth Amendment.
8. These clauses were affected by the Eleventh Amendment.
9. This paragraph has been superseded by the Thirteenth Amendment.
10. Obsolete.
11. The part in brackets has been superseded by section 3 of the Twentieth Amendment.
12. See the Twenty-sixth Amendment.
13. This Amendment was repealed by section 1 of the Twenty-first Amendment.
14. See the Twenty-fifth Amendment.

Source: U.S. Congress, House, Committee on the Judiciary, *The Constitution of the United States of America, As Amended Through July 1971*, H. Doc. 93-215, 93rd Cong., 2nd sess., 1974.

INDEX